TETRIS

BOX BROWN

TETRIS

The Games People Play

First Second
New York

ALEXEY PAJITNOV,
COMPUTER SCIENTIST AT
MOSCOW ACADEMY OF SCIENCE
CREATOR OF TETRIS

VLADIMIR POKHILKO,
COMPUTER SCIENTIST AT
MOSCOW ACADEMY OF SCIENCE
FRIEND OF THE CREATOR OF TETRIS

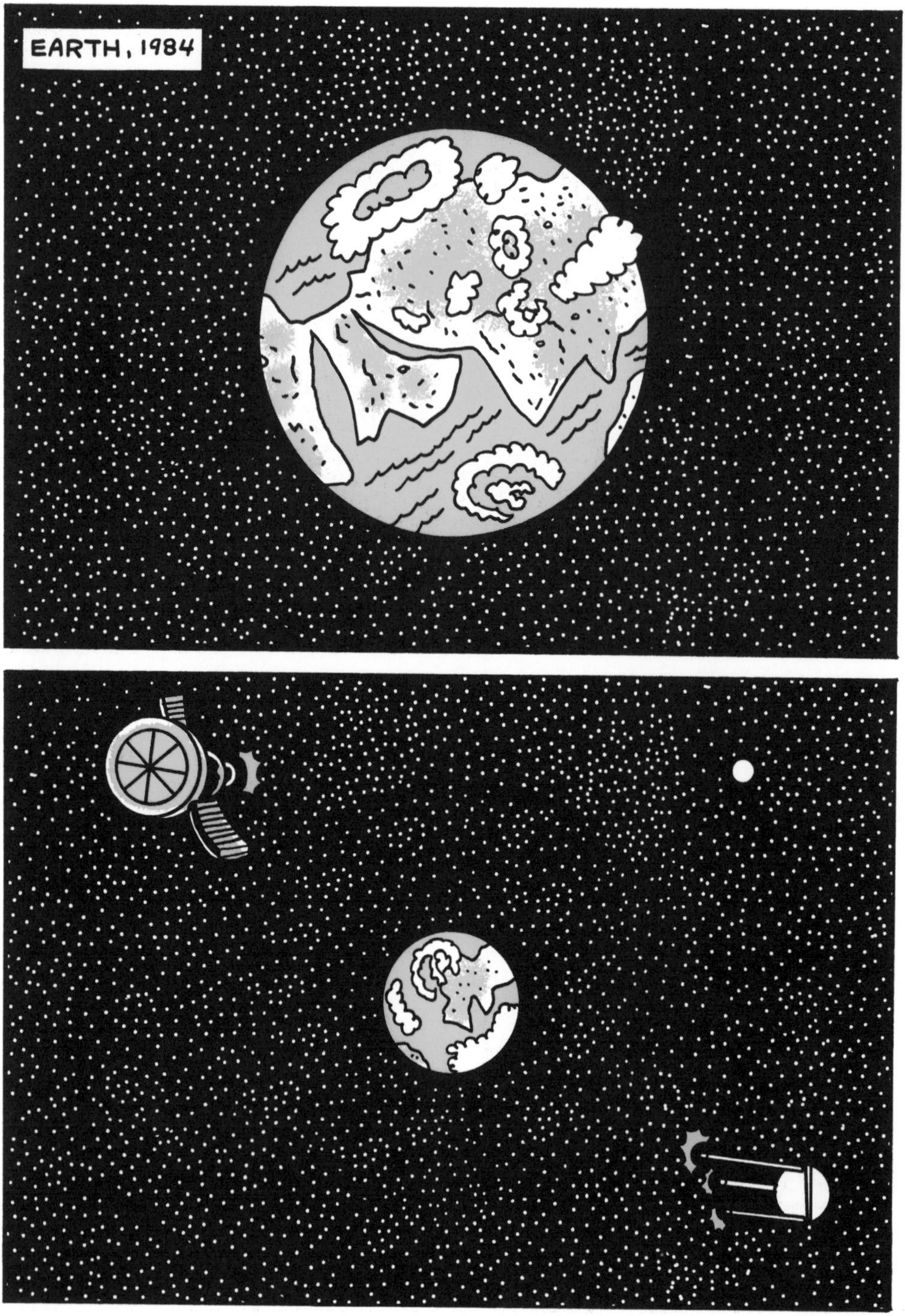
EARTH, 1984

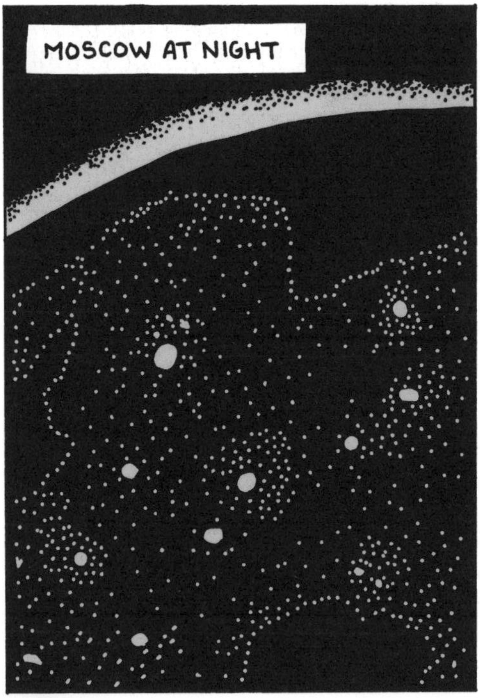
MOSCOW AT NIGHT

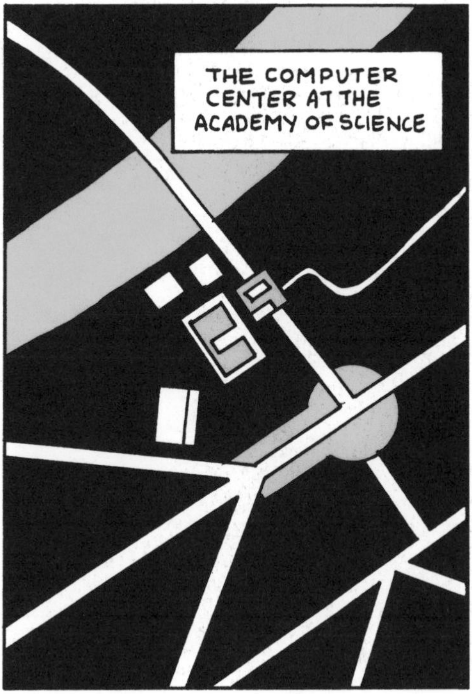
THE COMPUTER CENTER AT THE ACADEMY OF SCIENCE

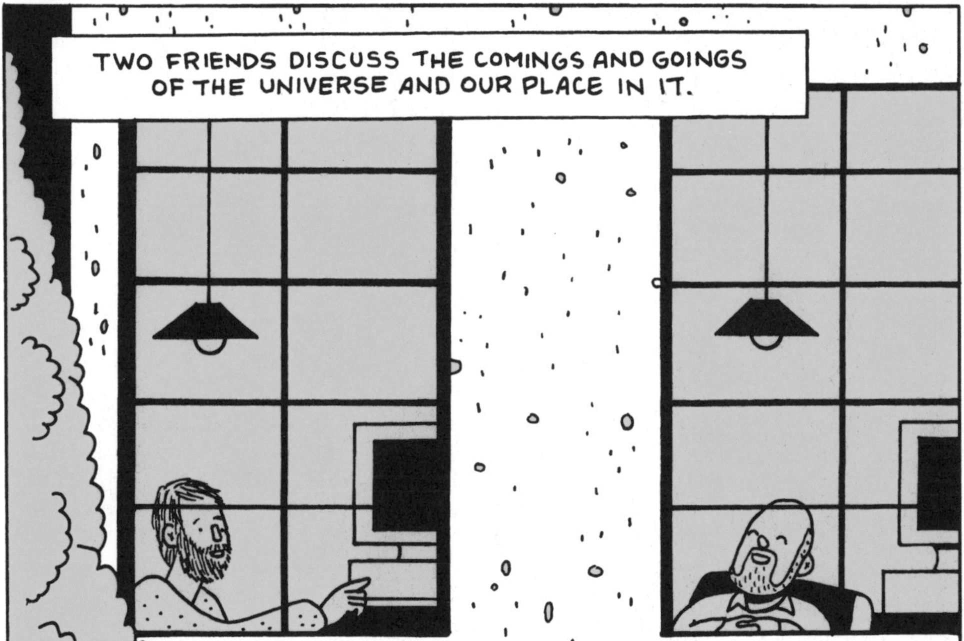
TWO FRIENDS DISCUSS THE COMINGS AND GOINGS OF THE UNIVERSE AND OUR PLACE IN IT.

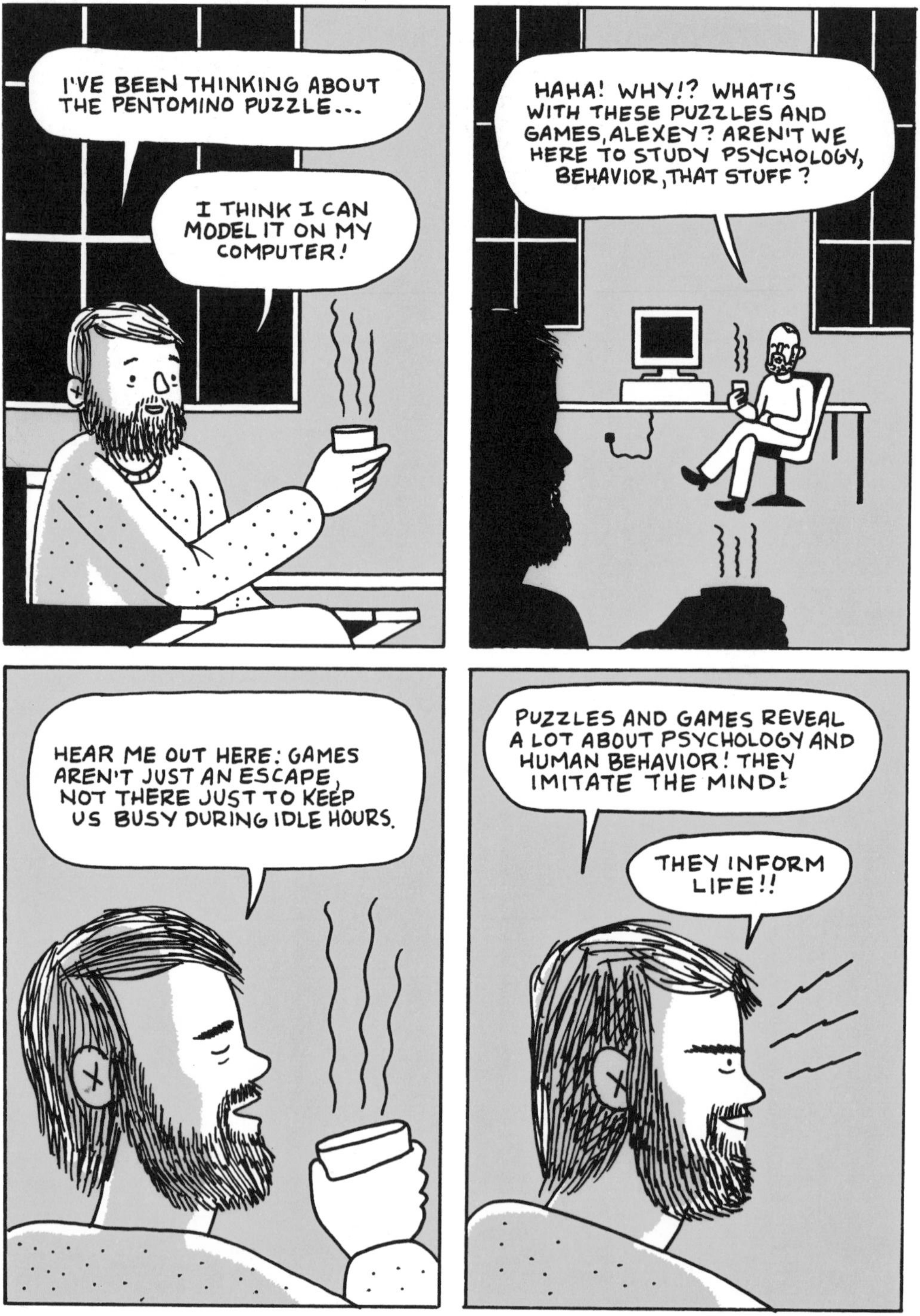
I'VE BEEN THINKING ABOUT THE PENTOMINO PUZZLE...
I THINK I CAN MODEL IT ON MY COMPUTER!
HAHA! WHY!? WHAT'S WITH THESE PUZZLES AND GAMES, ALEXEY? AREN'T WE HERE TO STUDY PSYCHOLOGY, BEHAVIOR, THAT STUFF?
HEAR ME OUT HERE: GAMES AREN'T JUST AN ESCAPE, NOT THERE JUST TO KEEP US BUSY DURING IDLE HOURS.
PUZZLES AND GAMES REVEAL A LOT ABOUT PSYCHOLOGY AND HUMAN BEHAVIOR! THEY IMITATE THE MIND!
THEY INFORM LIFE!!

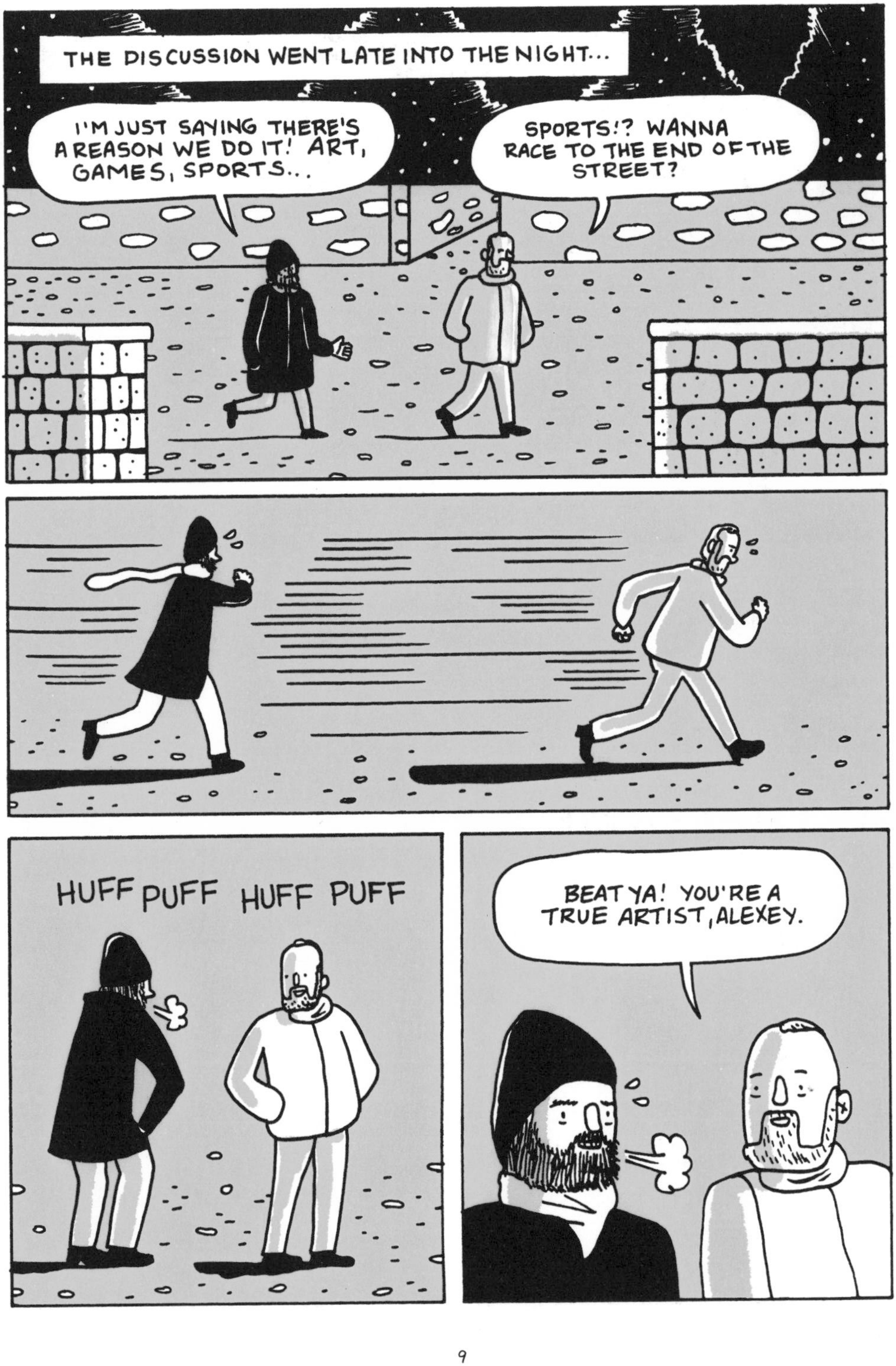
THE DISCUSSION WENT LATE INTO THE NIGHT...
I'M JUST SAYING THERE'S A REASON WE DO IT! ART, GAMES, SPORTS...
SPORTS!? WANNA RACE TO THE END OF THE STREET?
HUFF PUFF HUFF PUFF
BEAT YA! YOU'RE A TRUE ARTIST, ALEXEY.

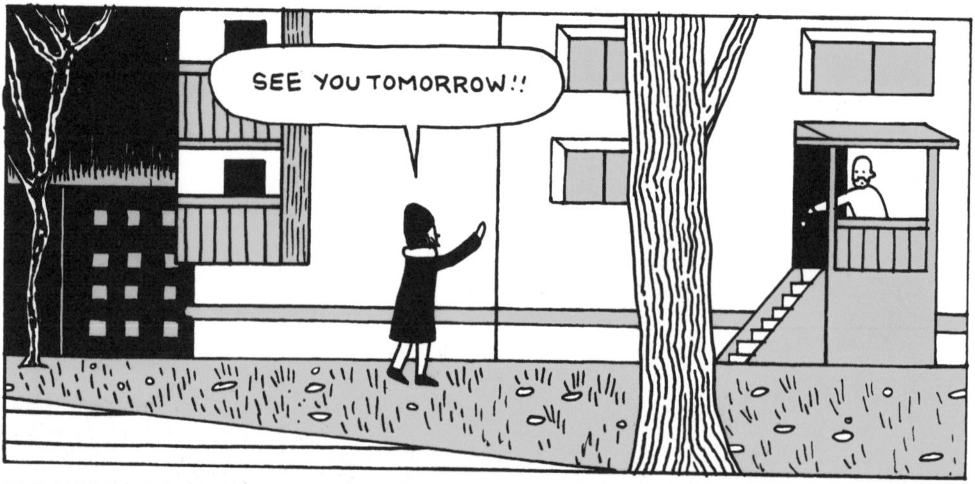
SEE YOU TOMORROW!!

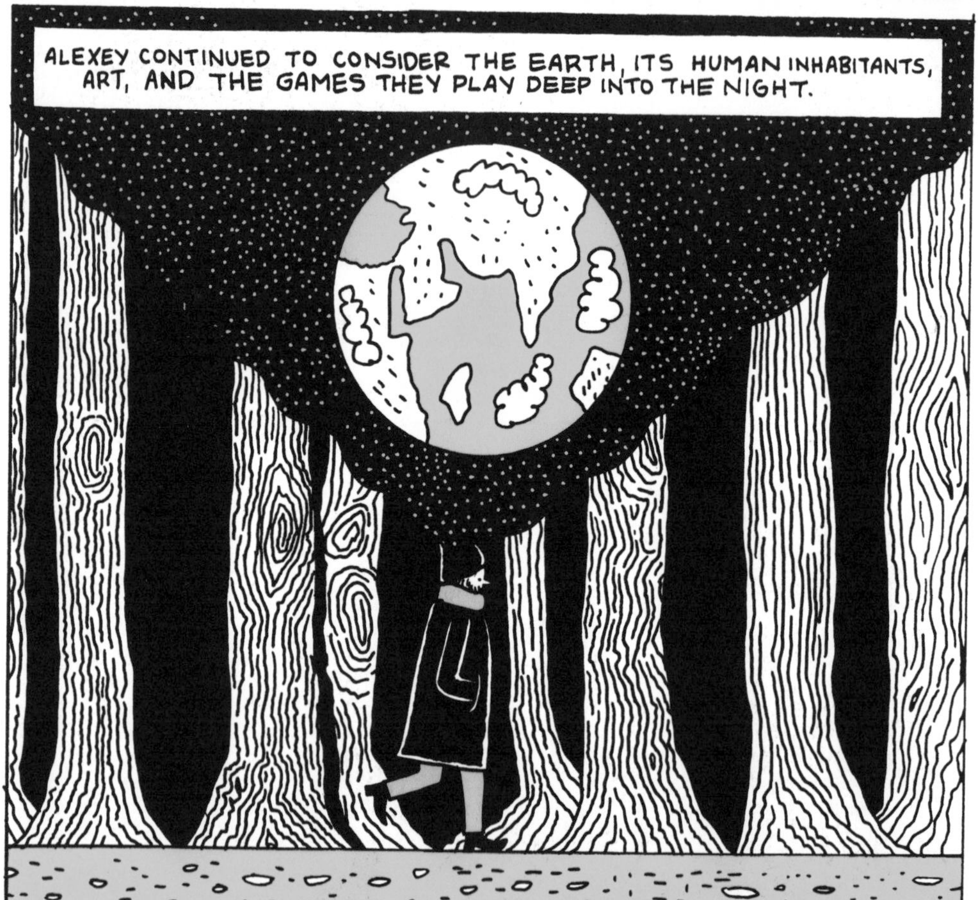
ALEXEY CONTINUED TO CONSIDER THE EARTH, ITS HUMAN INHABITANTS, ART, AND THE GAMES THEY PLAY DEEP INTO THE NIGHT.

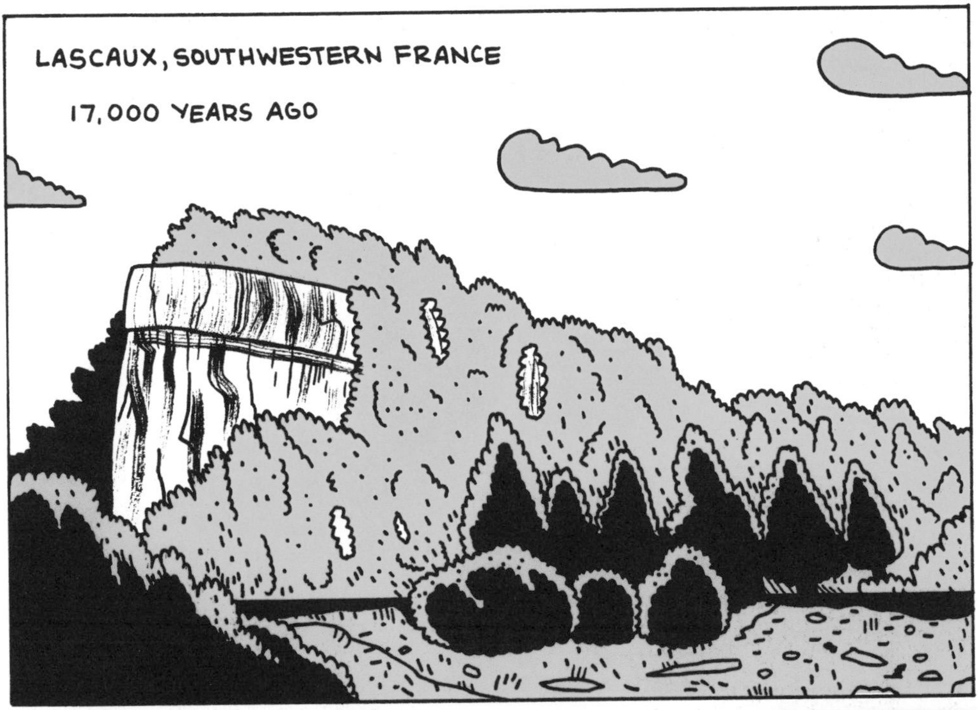
LASCAUX, SOUTHWESTERN FRANCE
17,000 YEARS AGO

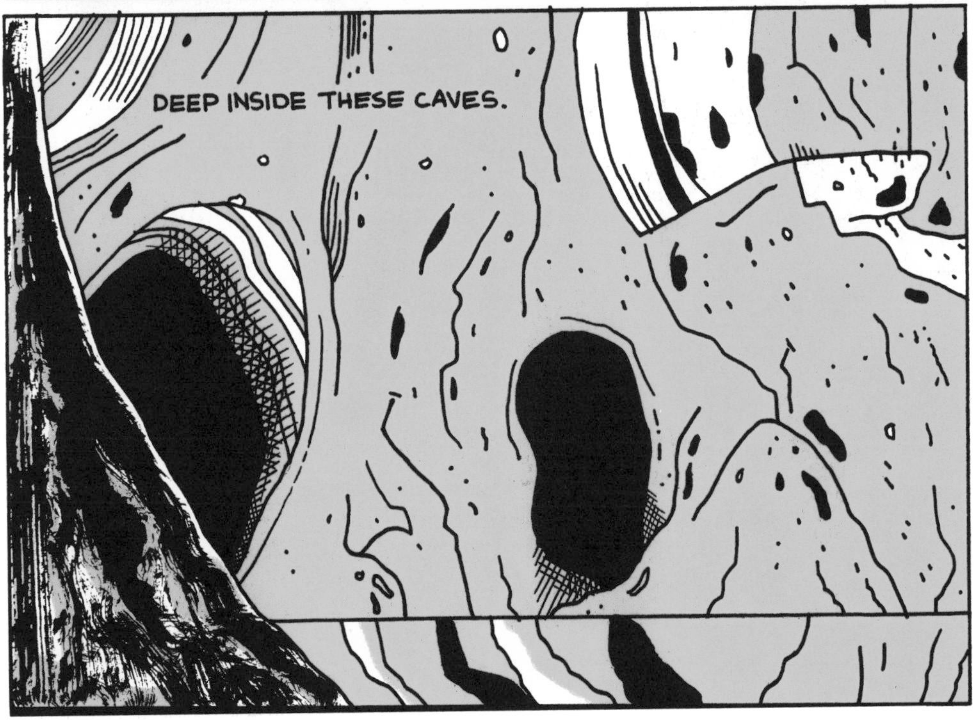
DEEP INSIDE THESE CAVES.

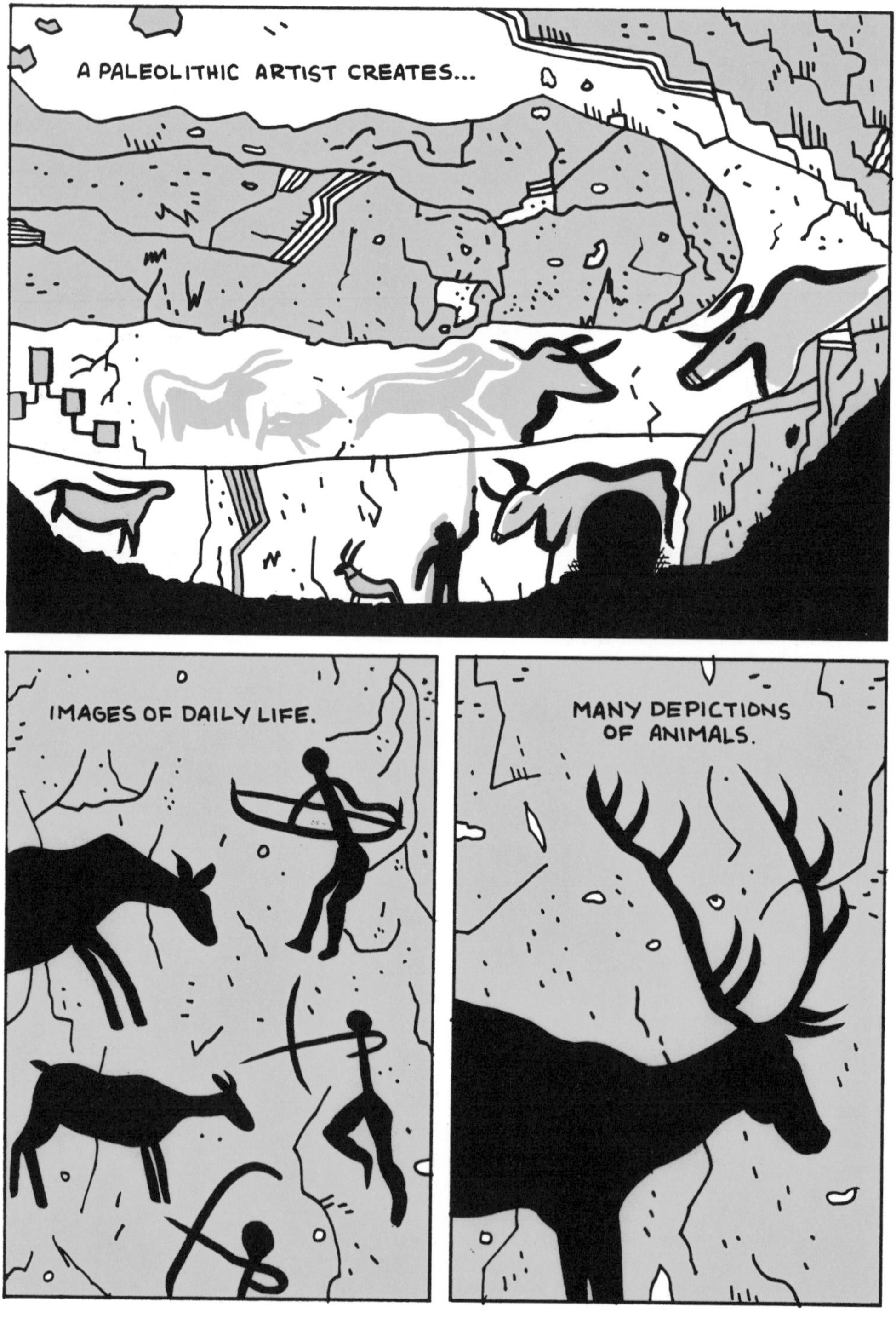
A PALEOLITHIC ARTIST CREATES...
IMAGES OF DAILY LIFE.
MANY DEPICTIONS OF ANIMALS.

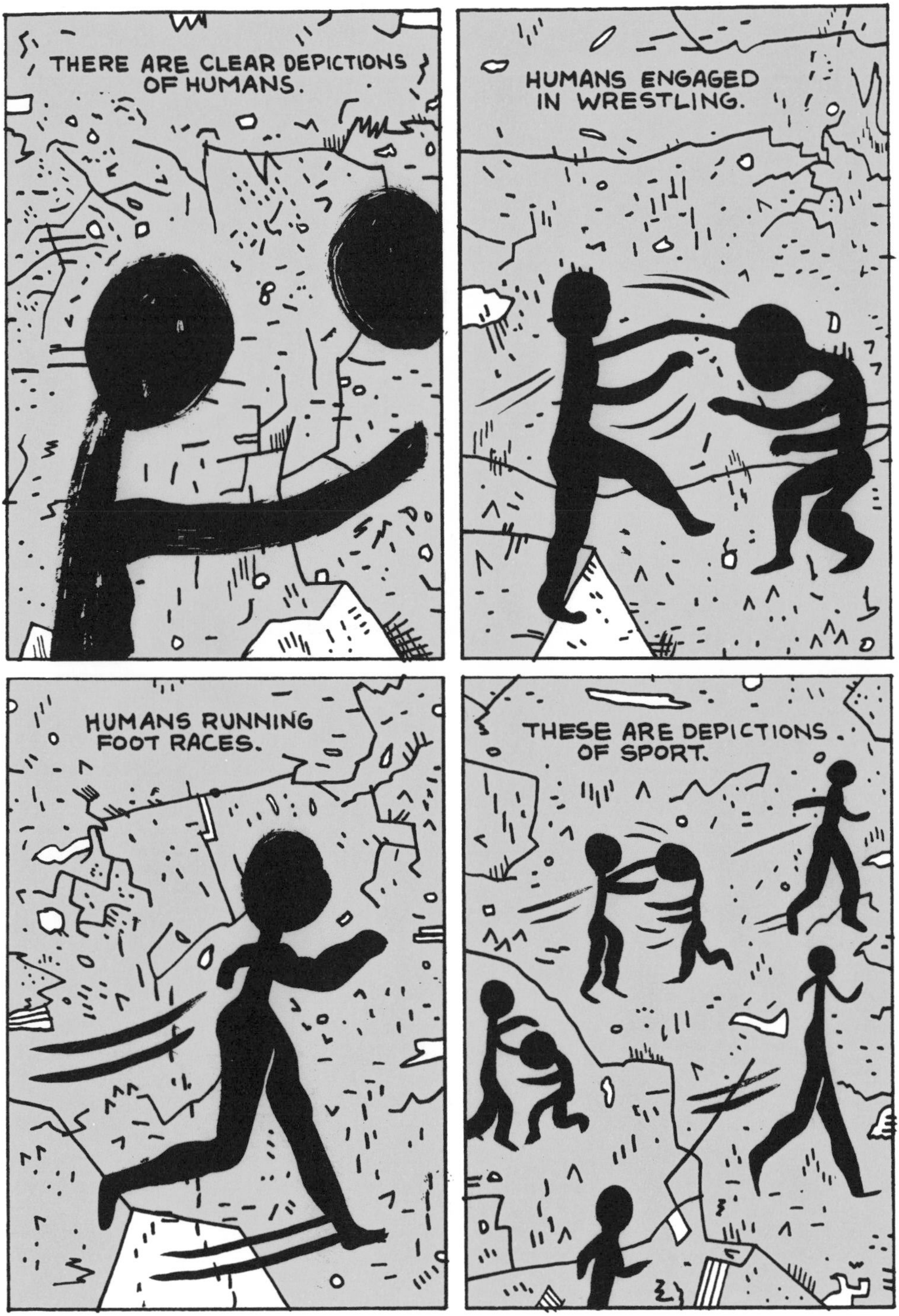
THERE ARE CLEAR DEPICTIONS OF HUMANS.
HUMANS ENGAGED IN WRESTLING.
HUMANS RUNNING FOOT RACES.
THESE ARE DEPICTIONS OF SPORT.

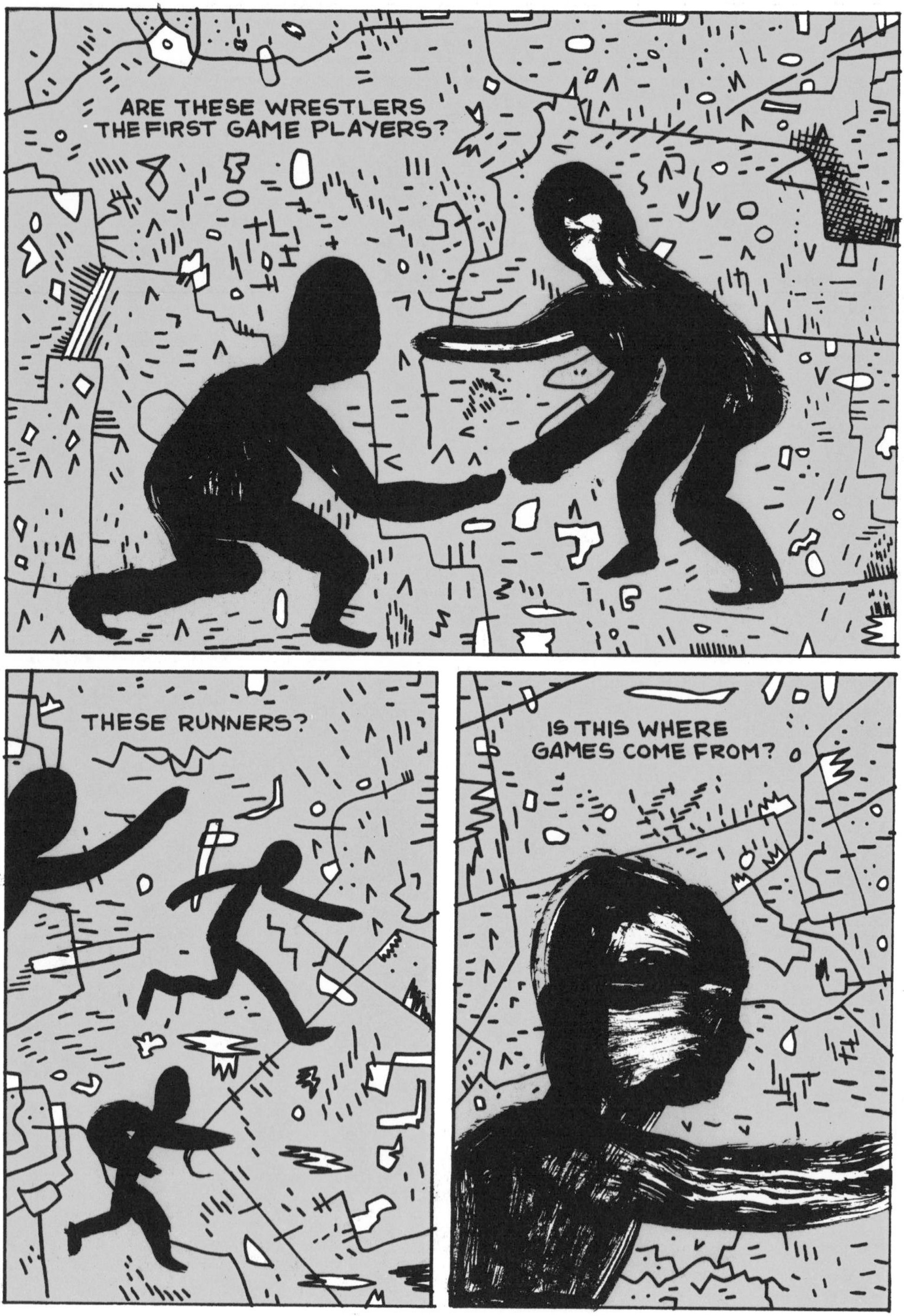
ARE THESE WRESTLERS THE FIRST GAME PLAYERS?
THESE RUNNERS?
IS THIS WHERE GAMES COME FROM?

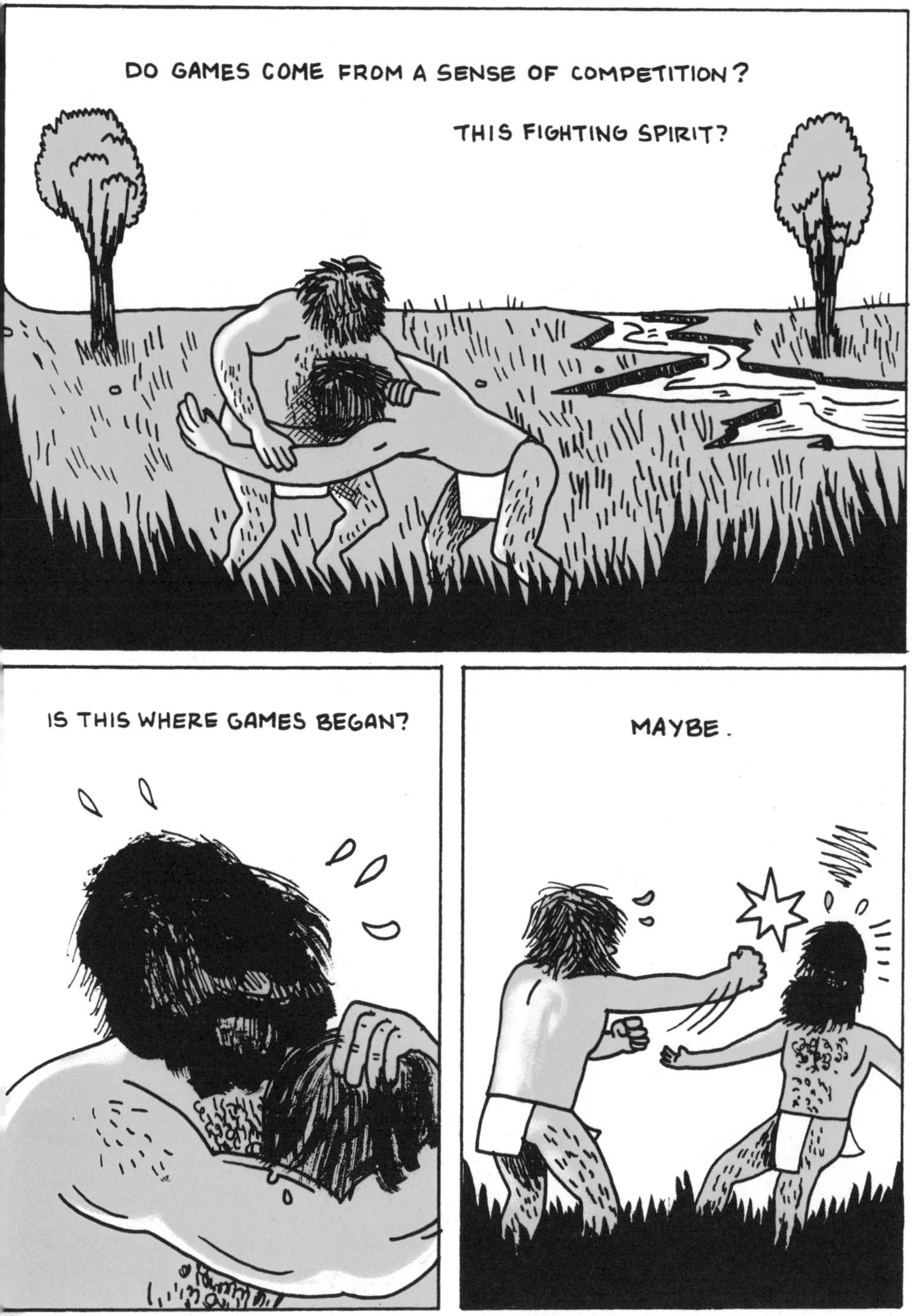
DO GAMES COME FROM A SENSE OF COMPETITION?
THIS FIGHTING SPIRIT?
IS THIS WHERE GAMES BEGAN?
MAYBE.

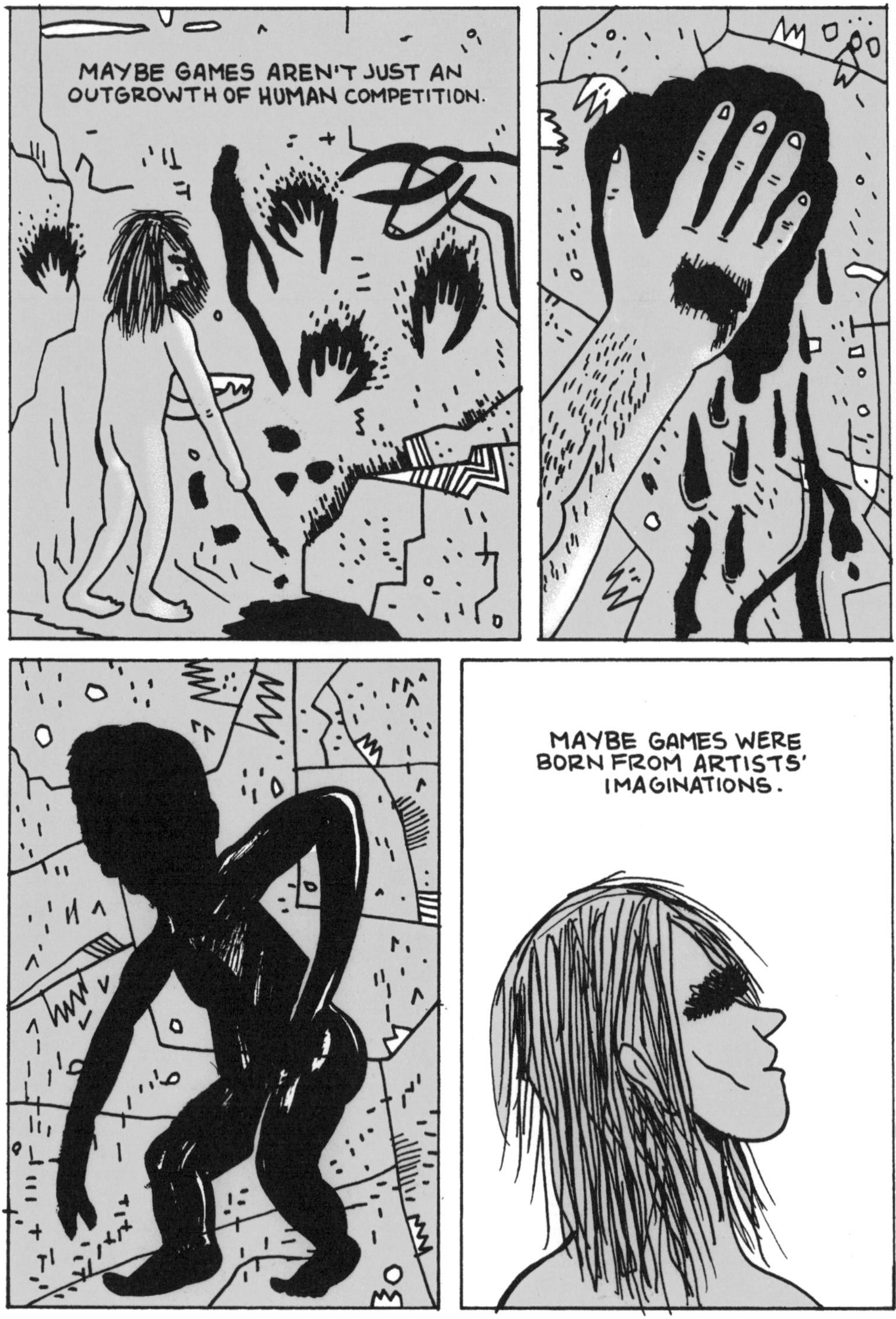

MAYBE GAMES AREN'T JUST AN OUTGROWTH OF HUMAN COMPETITION.
MAYBE GAMES WERE BORN FROM ARTISTS' IMAGINATIONS.

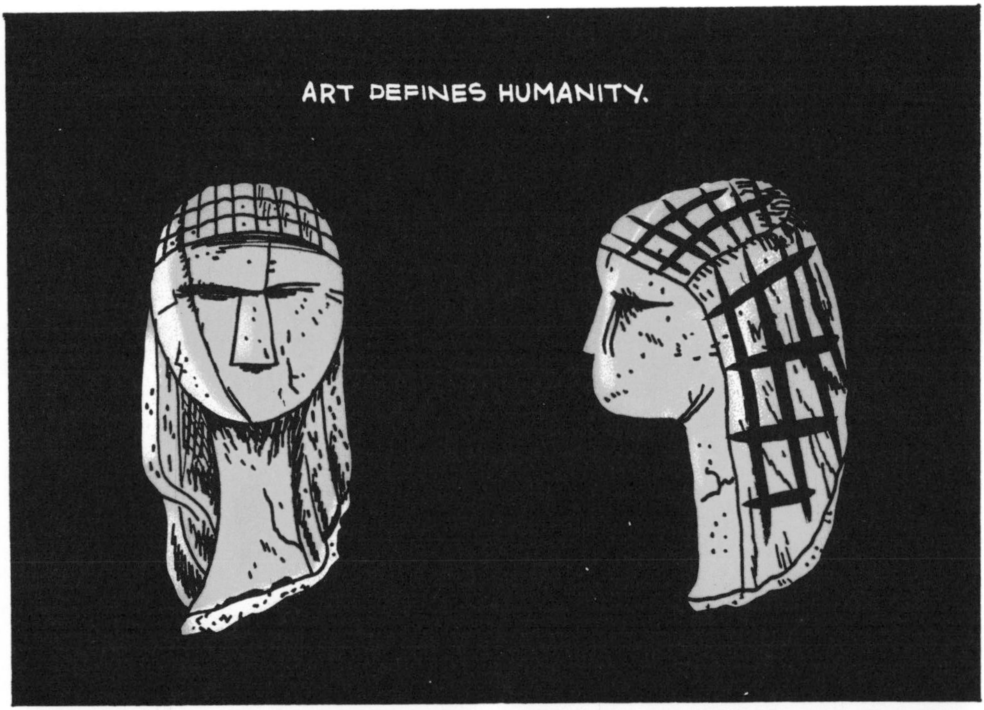
ART DEFINES HUMANITY.

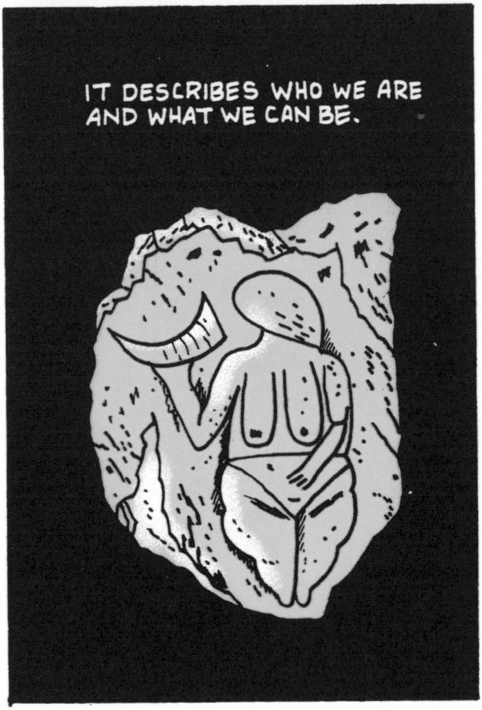
IT DESCRIBES WHO WE ARE AND WHAT WE CAN BE.

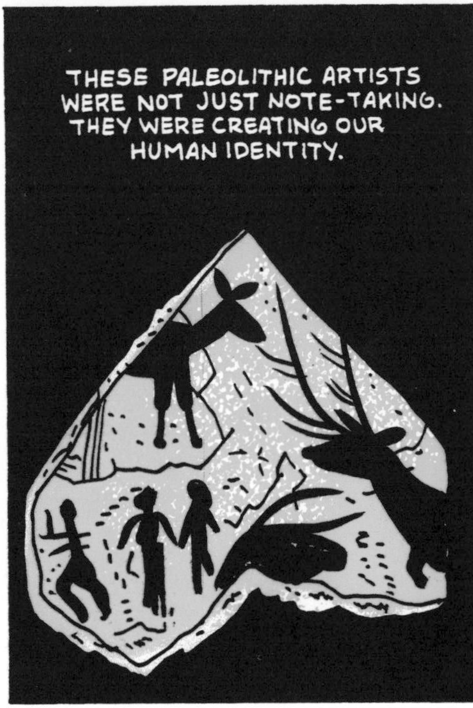
THESE PALEOLITHIC ARTISTS WERE NOT JUST NOTE-TAKING. THEY WERE CREATING OUR HUMAN IDENTITY.

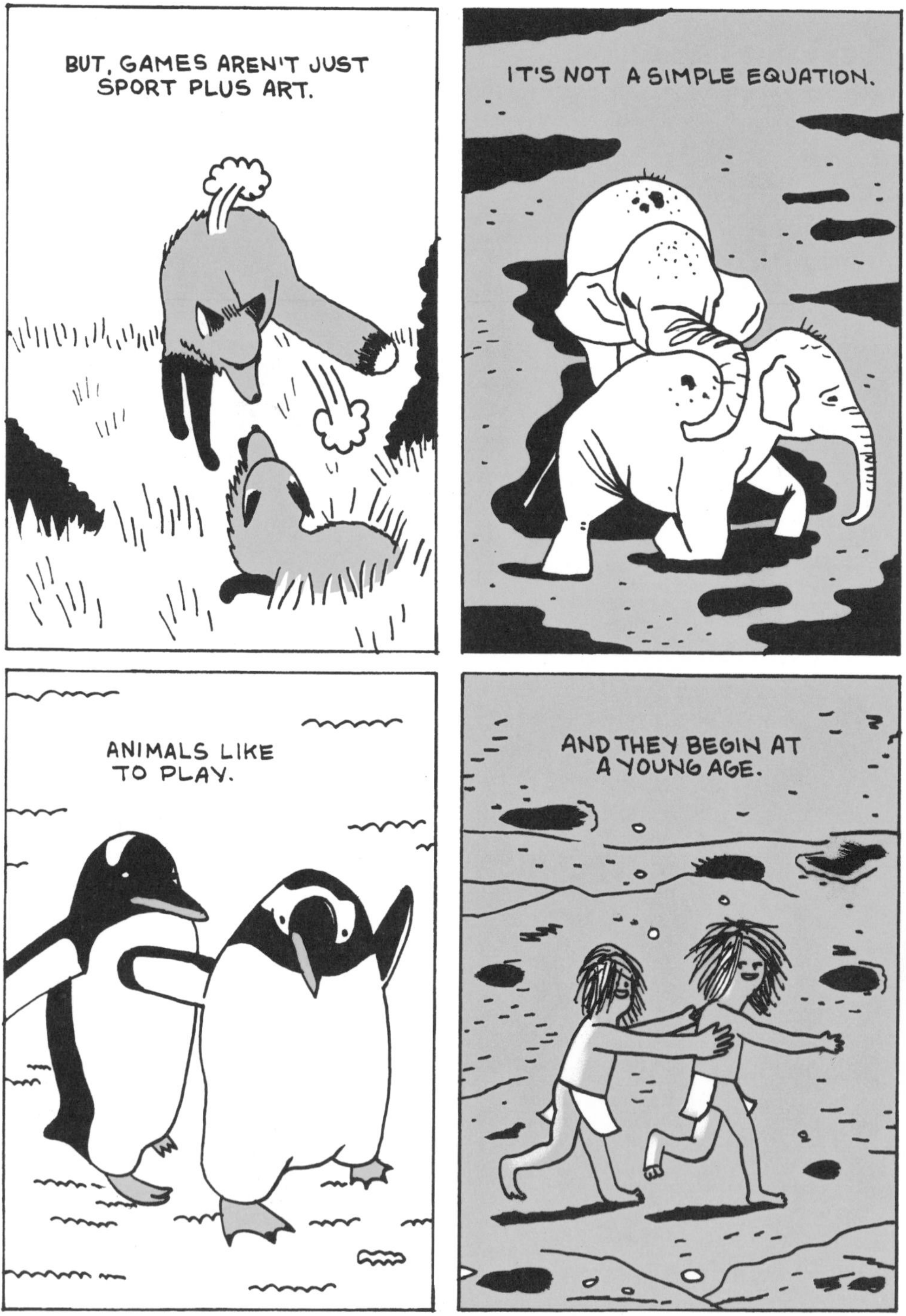
BUT, GAMES AREN'T JUST SPORT PLUS ART.
IT'S NOT A SIMPLE EQUATION.
ANIMALS LIKE TO PLAY.
AND THEY BEGIN AT A YOUNG AGE.

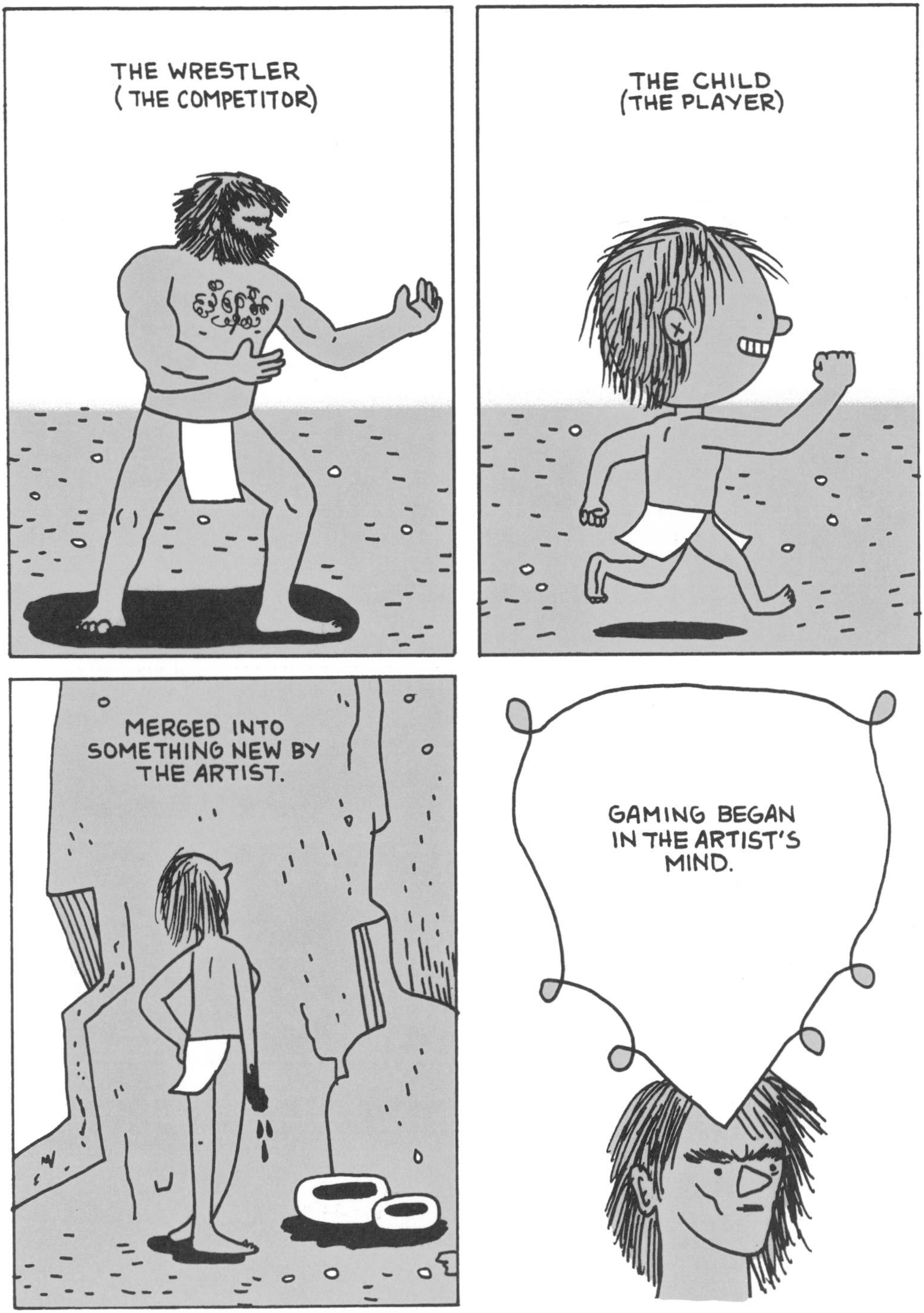
THE WRESTLER
(THE COMPETITOR)
THE CHILD
(THE PLAYER)
MERGED INTO
SOMETHING NEW BY
THE ARTIST.
GAMING BEGAN
IN THE ARTIST'S
MIND.

THE ARTISTS MADE THE IDEAS MANIFEST.

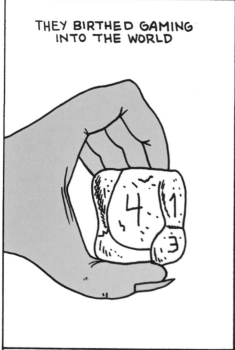

THEY BIRTHED GAMING INTO THE WORLD

AND WE BECAME PLAYERS.

THE FIRST GAME PIECES WERE
MADE FROM SHEEP AND GOAT BONES.

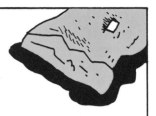

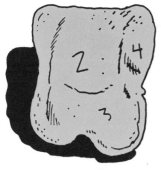

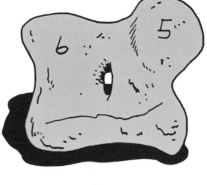

KNUCKLES AND ANKLES

CARVED INTO SOMETHING NEW

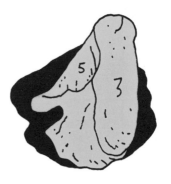

FOR THE PURPOSE OF FUN.

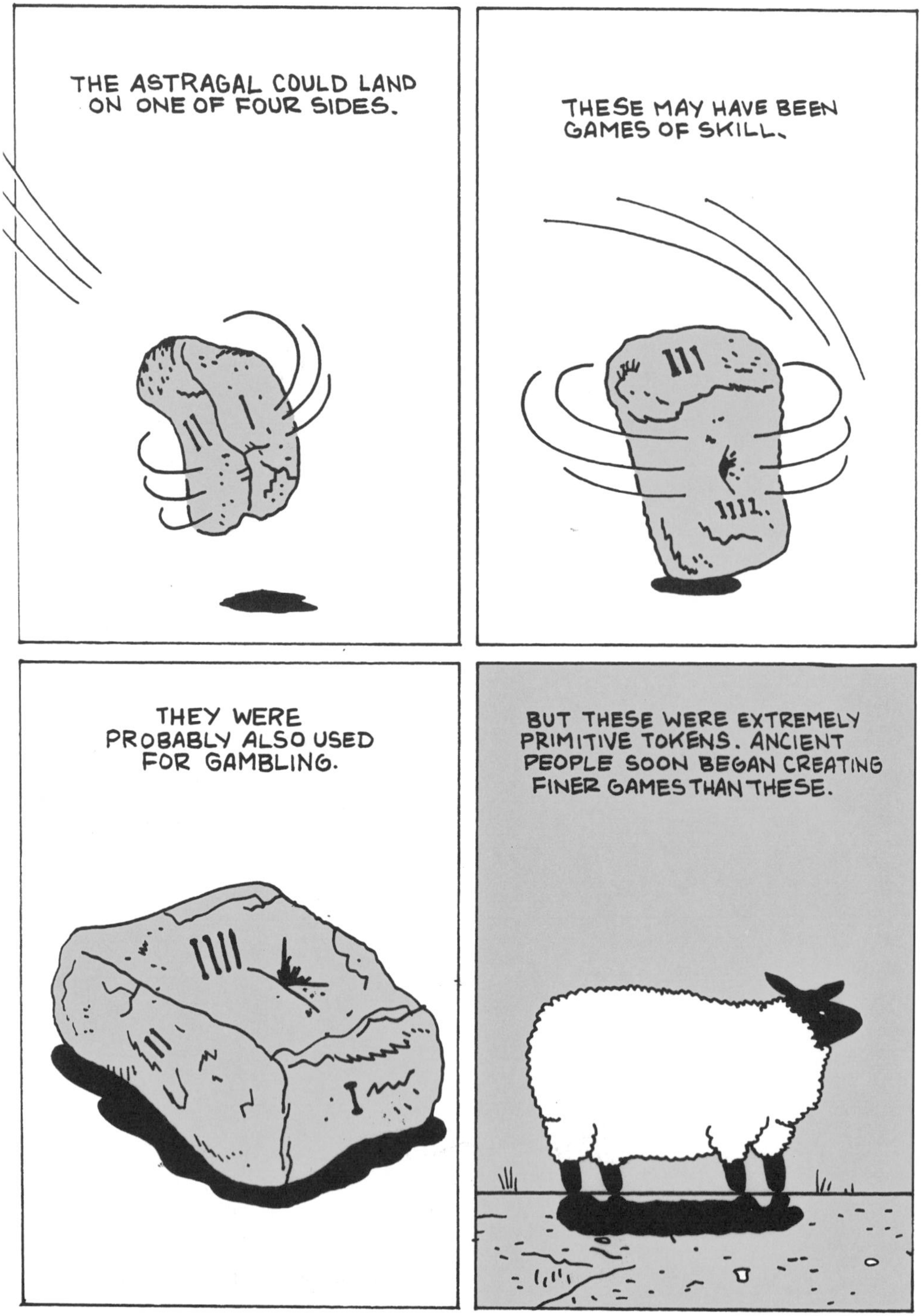
THE ASTRAGAL COULD LAND ON ONE OF FOUR SIDES.
THESE MAY HAVE BEEN GAMES OF SKILL.
THEY WERE PROBABLY ALSO USED FOR GAMBLING.
BUT THESE WERE EXTREMELY PRIMITIVE TOKENS. ANCIENT PEOPLE SOON BEGAN CREATING FINER GAMES THAN THESE.

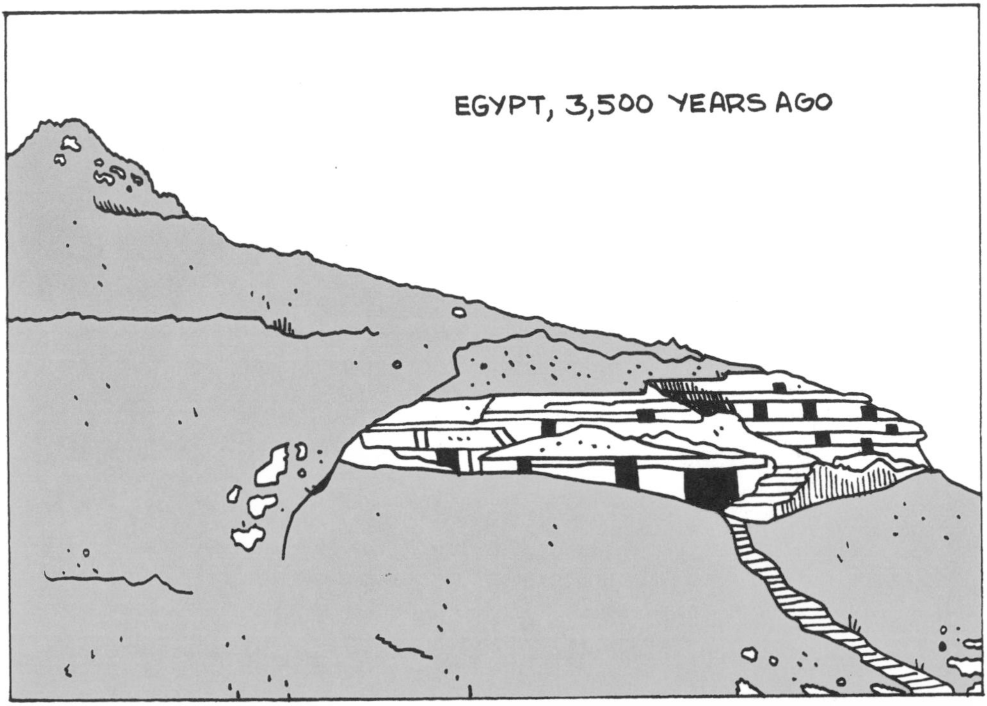
EGYPT, 3,500 YEARS AGO

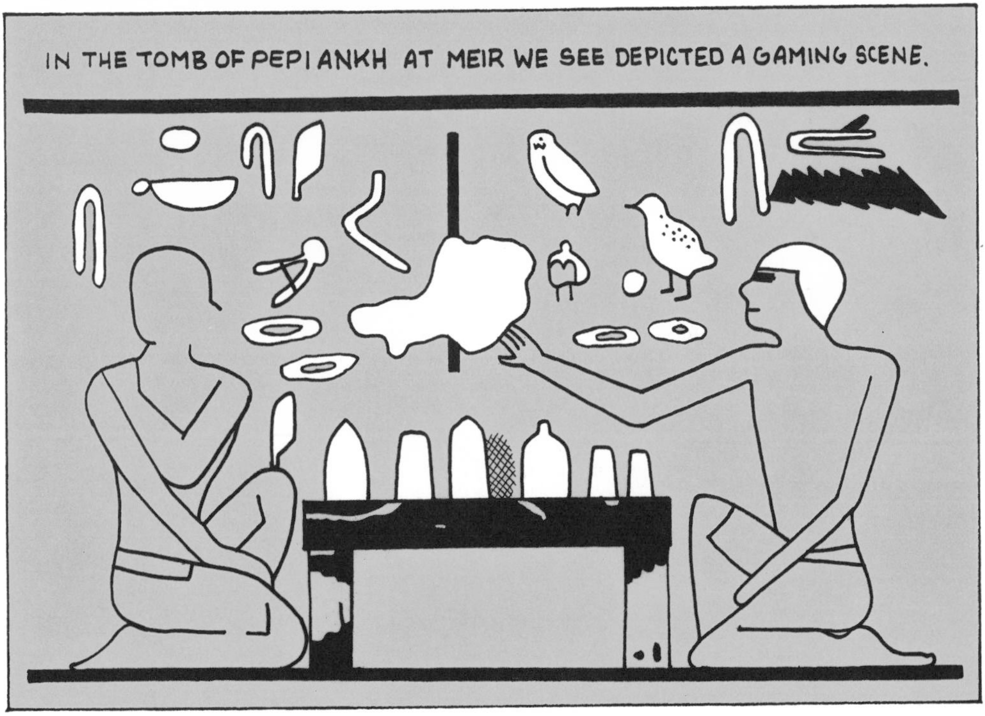
IN THE TOMB OF PEPI ANKH AT MEIR WE SEE DEPICTED A GAMING SCENE.

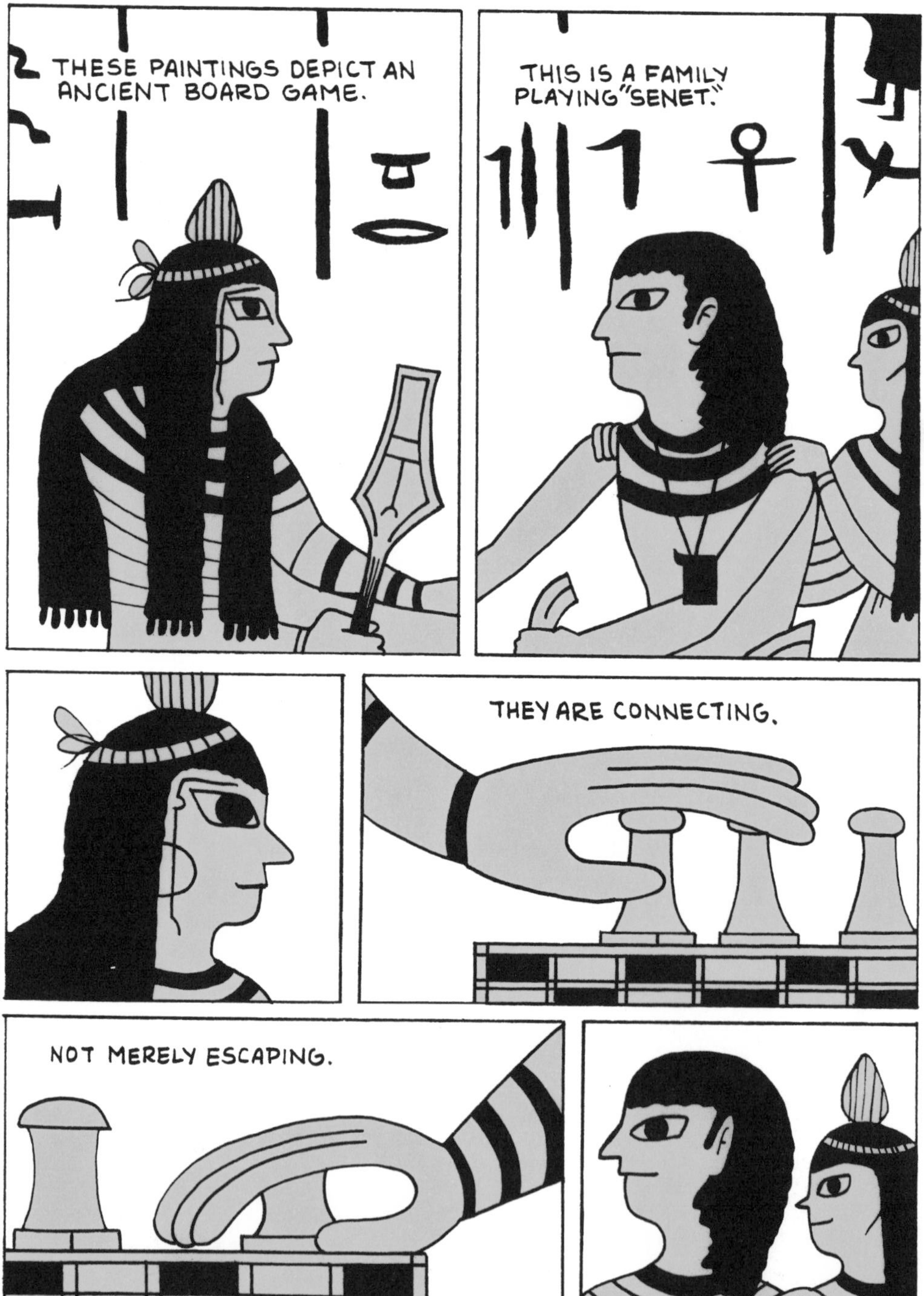
THESE PAINTINGS DEPICT AN ANCIENT BOARD GAME.
THIS IS A FAMILY PLAYING "SENET."
THEY ARE CONNECTING.
NOT MERELY ESCAPING.

SENET WAS A RITUALISTIC GAME AS WELL.

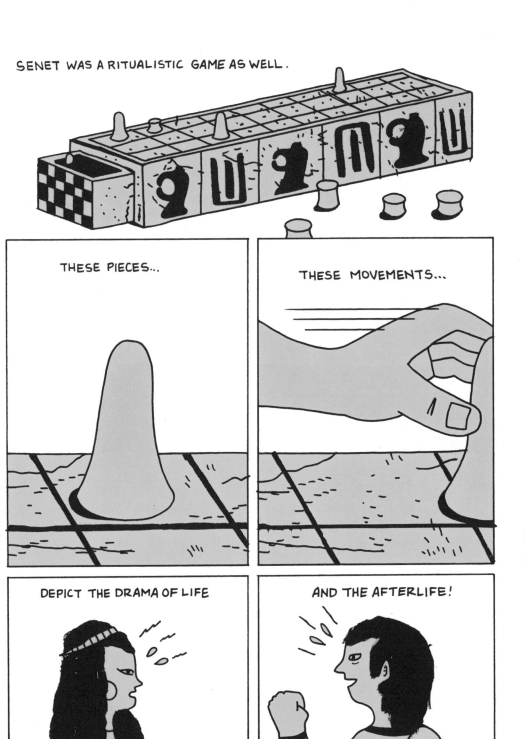

THESE PIECES...

THESE MOVEMENTS...

DEPICT THE DRAMA OF LIFE

AND THE AFTERLIFE!

BUT SENET WAS NOT
CONCEIVED TO BE
RITUALISTIC.

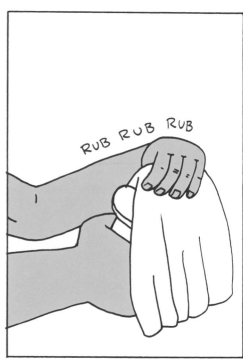

RUB RUB RUB

SENET BEGAN INSIDE
THE MIND OF A NAMELESS
ARTIST.

LOOKING TO PASS THE TIME.
LOOKING TO ENTERTAIN.
LOOKING TO ESCAPE.

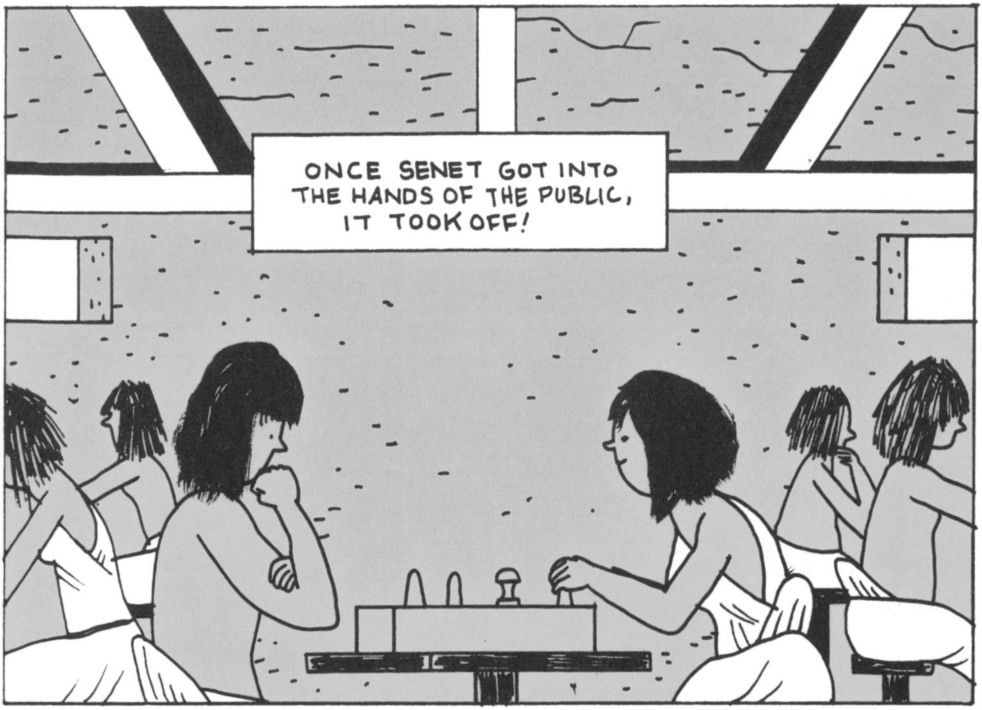
ONCE SENET GOT INTO
THE HANDS OF THE PUBLIC,
IT TOOK OFF!

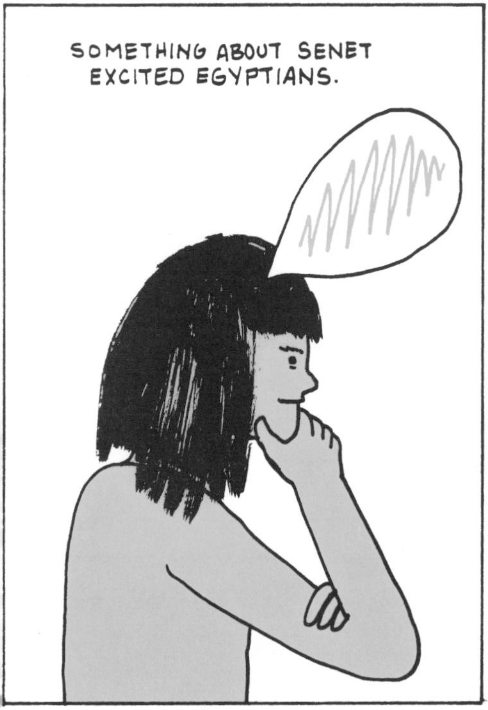
SOMETHING ABOUT SENET
EXCITED EGYPTIANS.

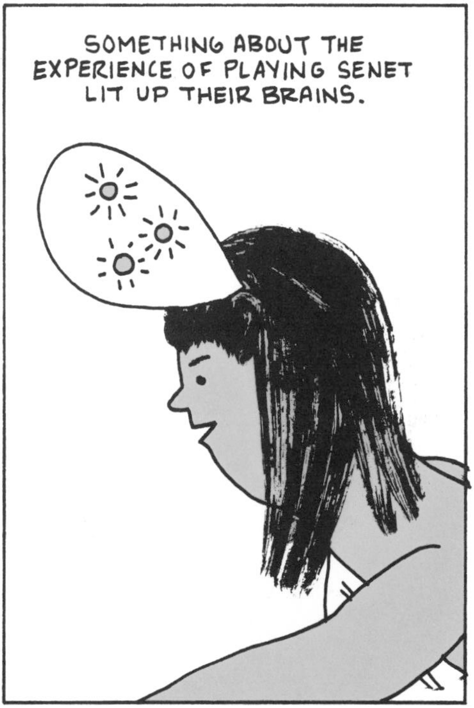
SOMETHING ABOUT THE
EXPERIENCE OF PLAYING SENET
LIT UP THEIR BRAINS.

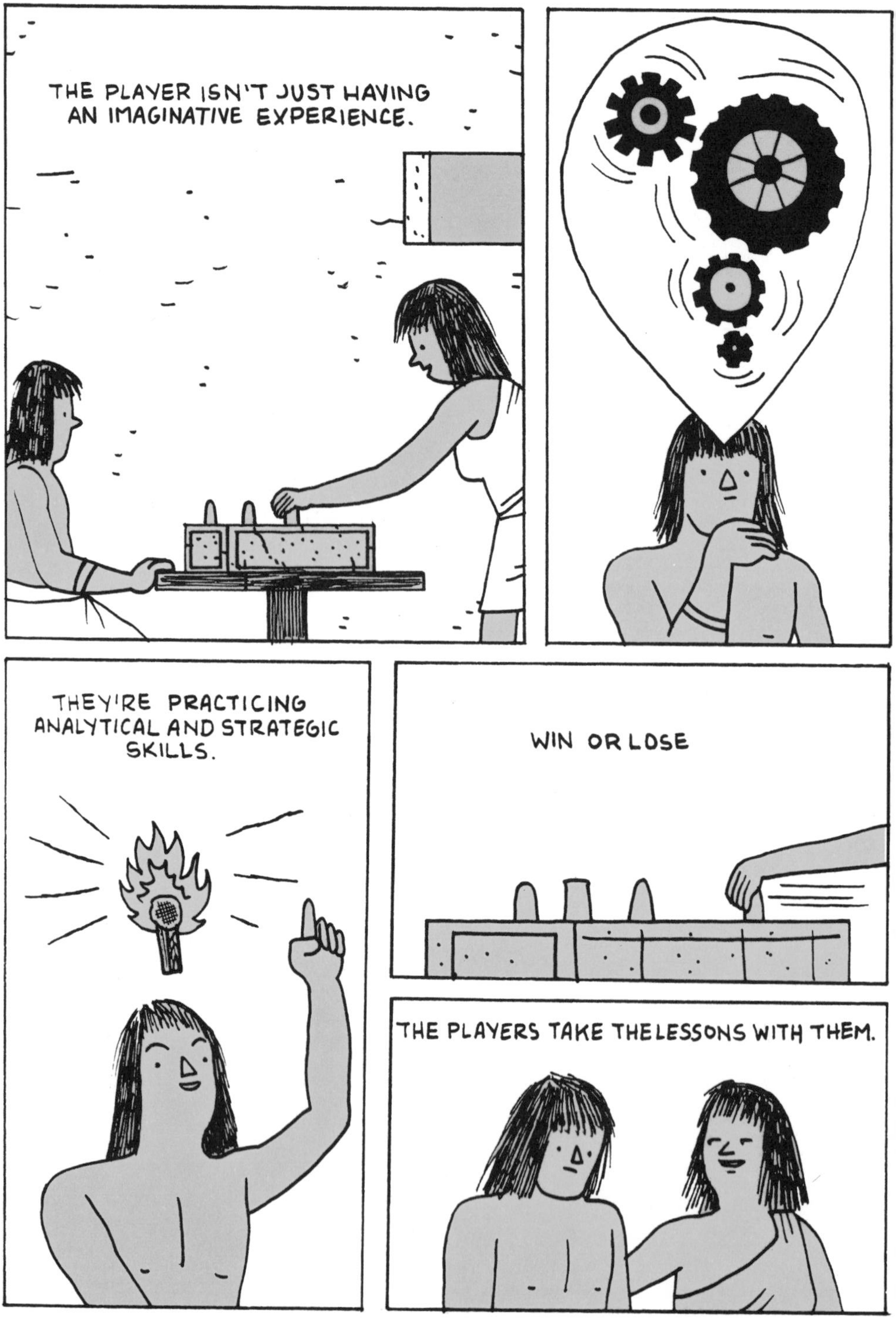
THE PLAYER ISN'T JUST HAVING AN IMAGINATIVE EXPERIENCE.
THEY'RE PRACTICING ANALYTICAL AND STRATEGIC SKILLS.
WIN OR LOSE
THE PLAYERS TAKE THE LESSONS WITH THEM.

PLAYING SENET EXCITES THE PRE-FRONTAL CORTEX.

THE PRE-FRONTAL CORTEX IS THE BRAIN'S COMMAND CENTER.

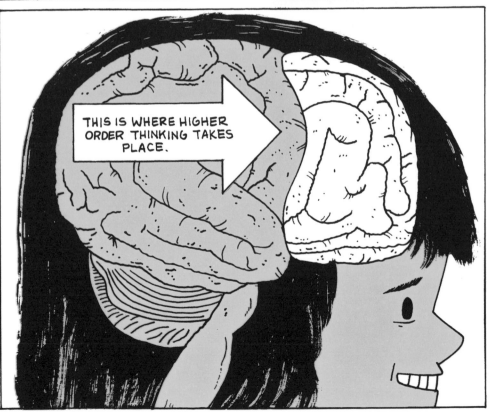

THIS IS WHERE HIGHER ORDER THINKING TAKES PLACE.

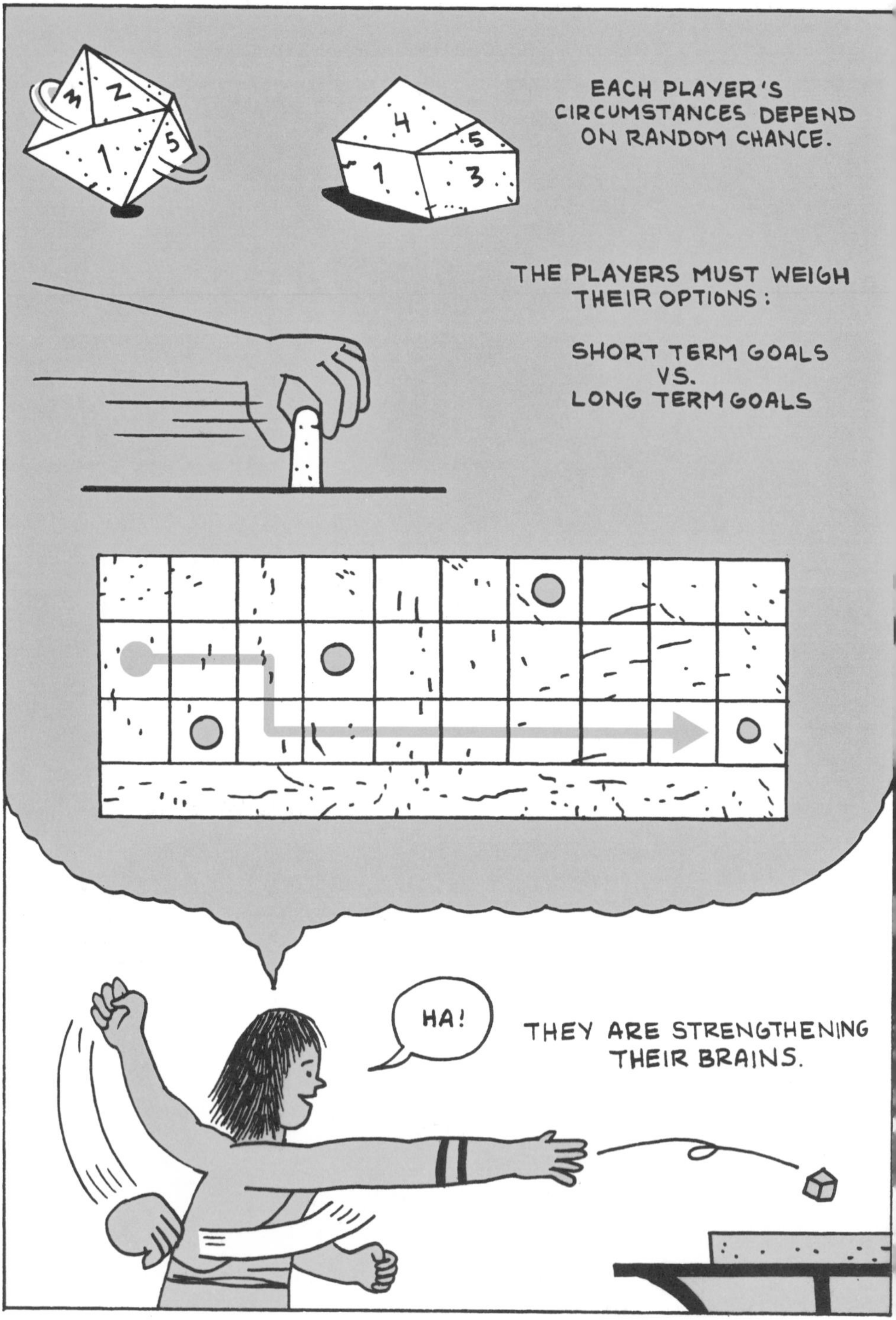
EACH PLAYER'S CIRCUMSTANCES DEPEND ON RANDOM CHANCE.
THE PLAYERS MUST WEIGH THEIR OPTIONS:
SHORT TERM GOALS VS. LONG TERM GOALS
HA!
THEY ARE STRENGTHENING THEIR BRAINS.

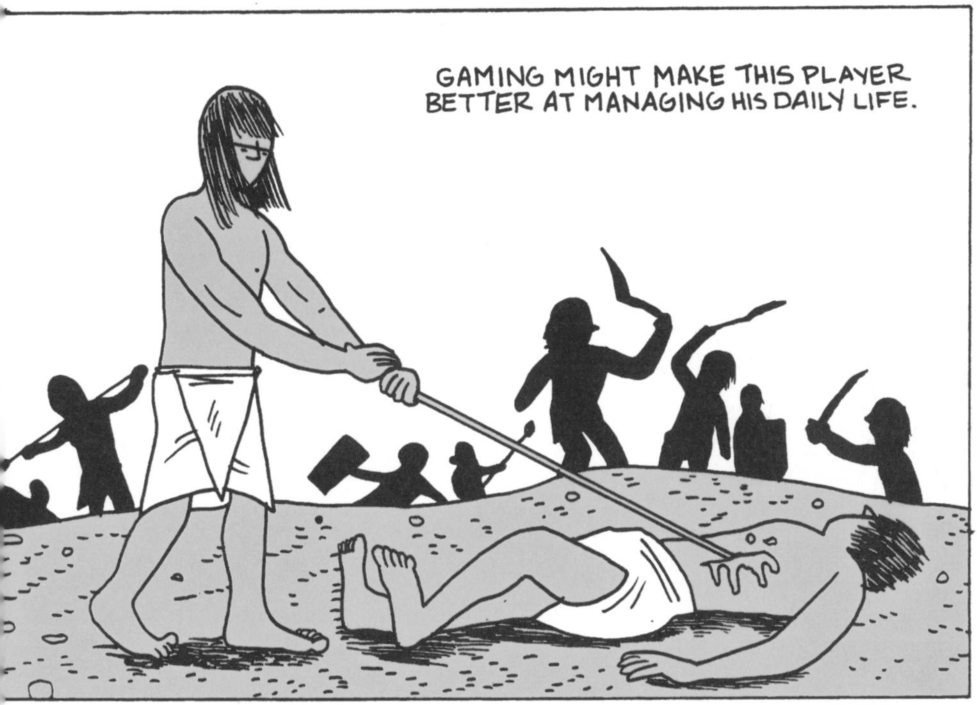
GAMING MIGHT MAKE THIS PLAYER BETTER AT MANAGING HIS DAILY LIFE.

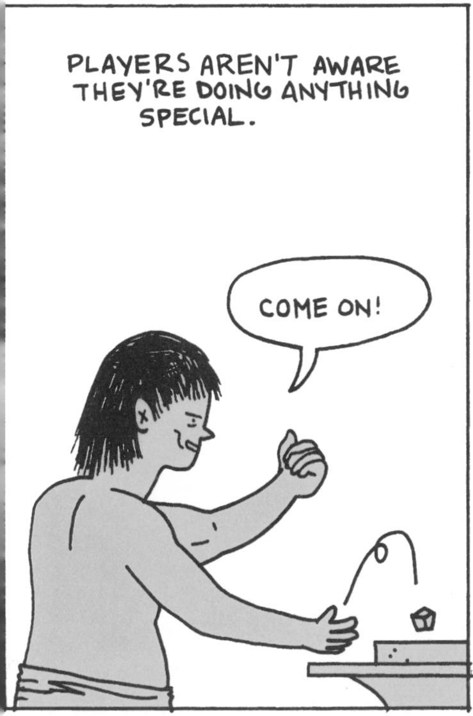
PLAYERS AREN'T AWARE THEY'RE DOING ANYTHING SPECIAL.
COME ON!

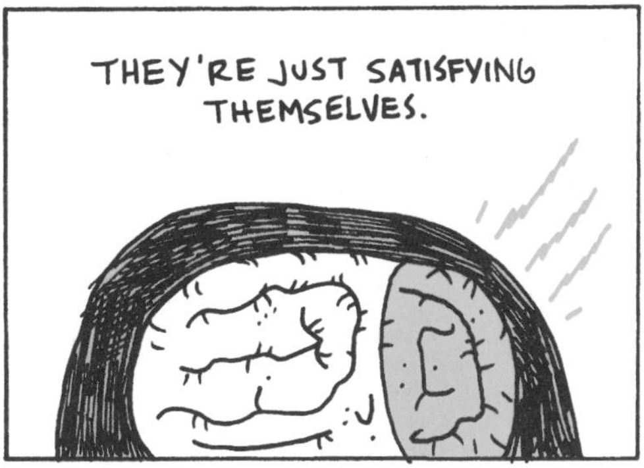
THEY'RE JUST SATISFYING THEMSELVES.

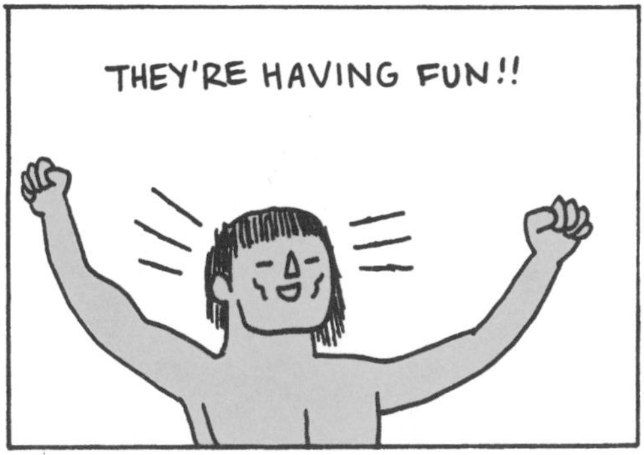
THEY'RE HAVING FUN!!

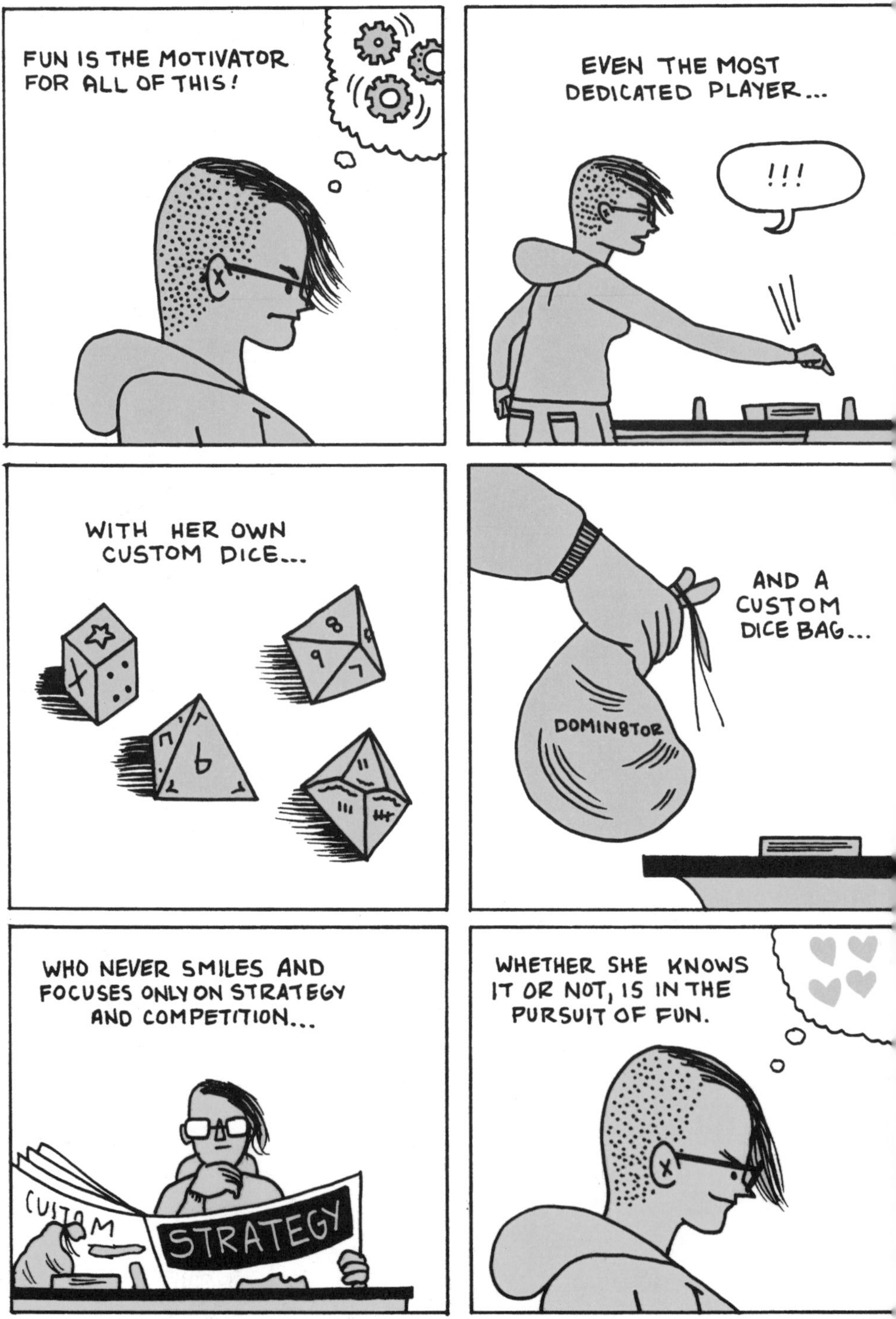
FUN IS THE MOTIVATOR FOR ALL OF THIS!
EVEN THE MOST DEDICATED PLAYER...
!!!
WITH HER OWN CUSTOM DICE...
AND A CUSTOM DICE BAG...
DOMIN8TOR
WHO NEVER SMILES AND FOCUSES ONLY ON STRATEGY AND COMPETITION...
CUSTOM
STRATEGY
WHETHER SHE KNOWS IT OR NOT, IS IN THE PURSUIT OF FUN.

FUSAJIRO YAMAUCHI,
FOUNDER OF NINTENDO

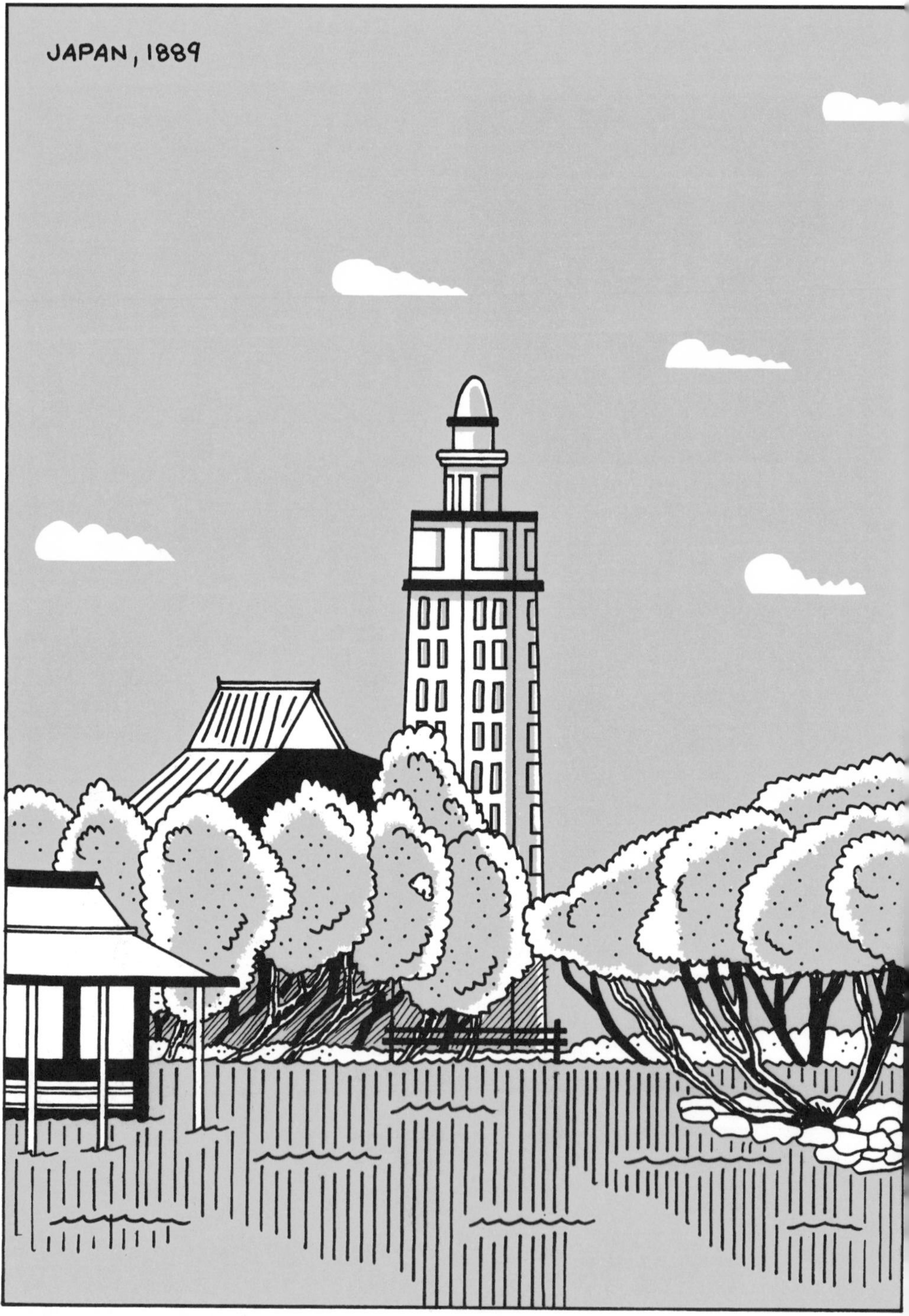
JAPAN, 1889

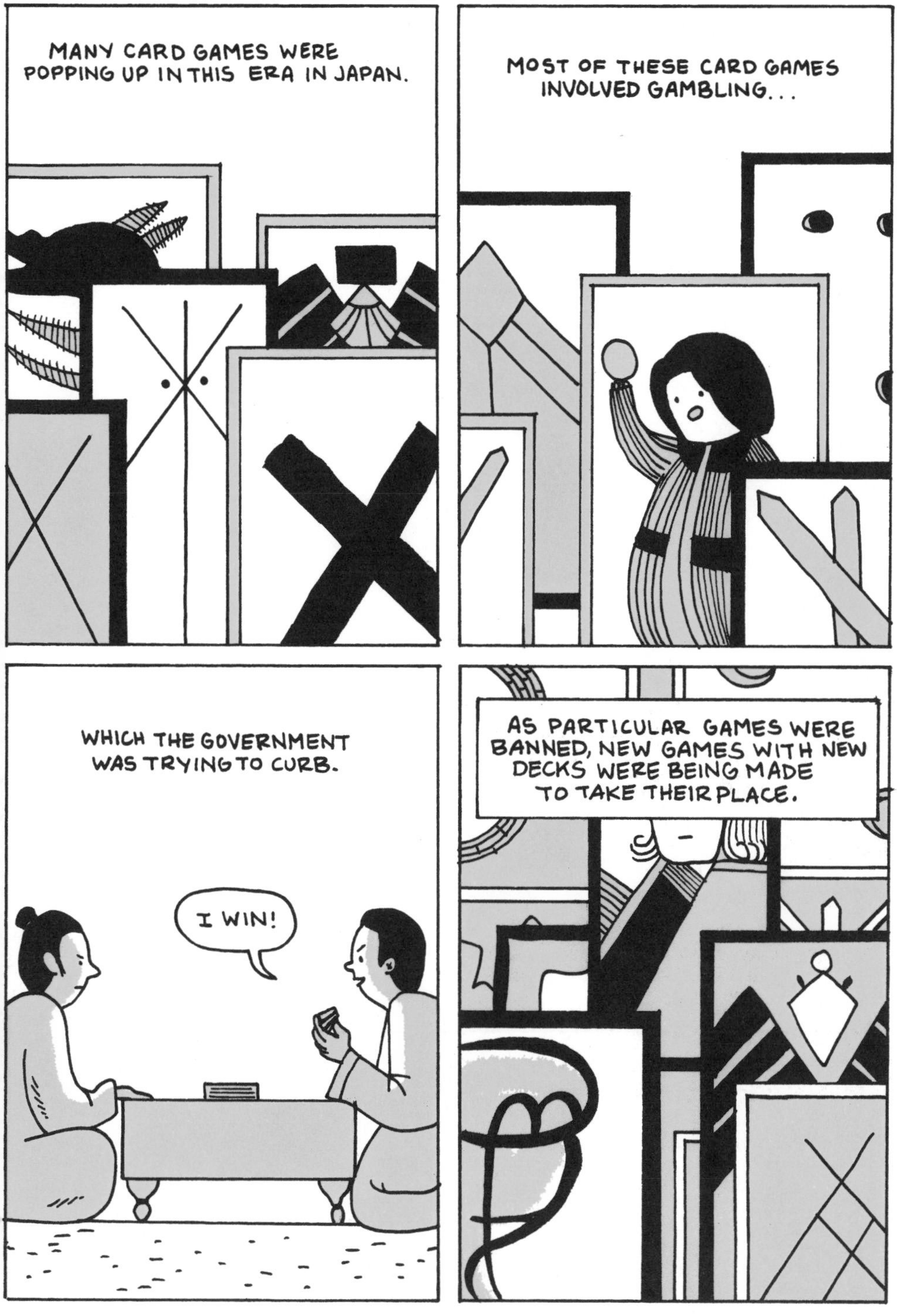
MANY CARD GAMES WERE POPPING UP IN THIS ERA IN JAPAN.
MOST OF THESE CARD GAMES INVOLVED GAMBLING...
WHICH THE GOVERNMENT WAS TRYING TO CURB.
I WIN!
AS PARTICULAR GAMES WERE BANNED, NEW GAMES WITH NEW DECKS WERE BEING MADE TO TAKE THEIR PLACE.

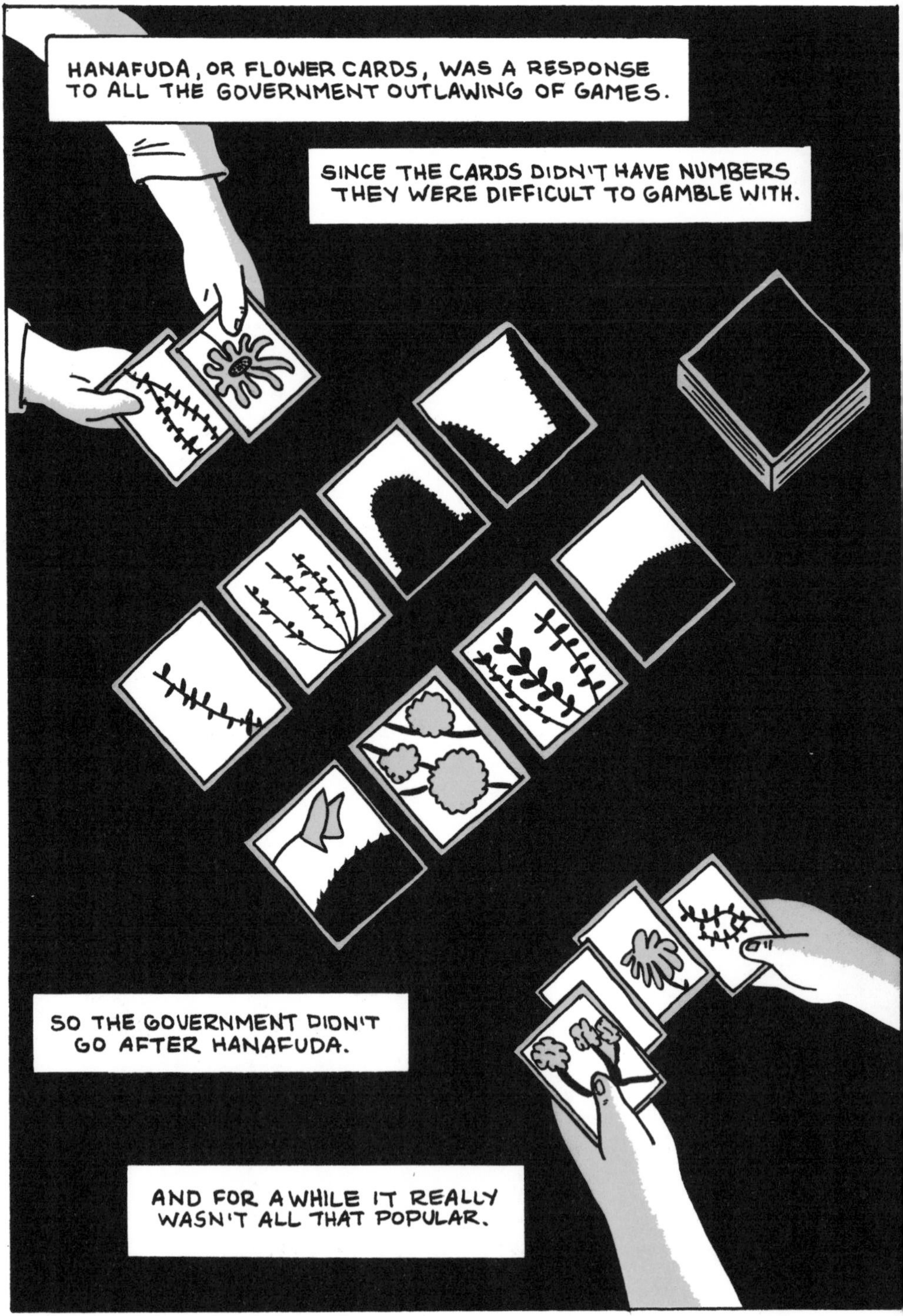

HANAFUDA, OR FLOWER CARDS, WAS A RESPONSE TO ALL THE GOVERNMENT OUTLAWING OF GAMES.
SINCE THE CARDS DIDN'T HAVE NUMBERS THEY WERE DIFFICULT TO GAMBLE WITH.
SO THE GOVERNMENT DIDN'T GO AFTER HANAFUDA.
AND FOR A WHILE IT REALLY WASN'T ALL THAT POPULAR.

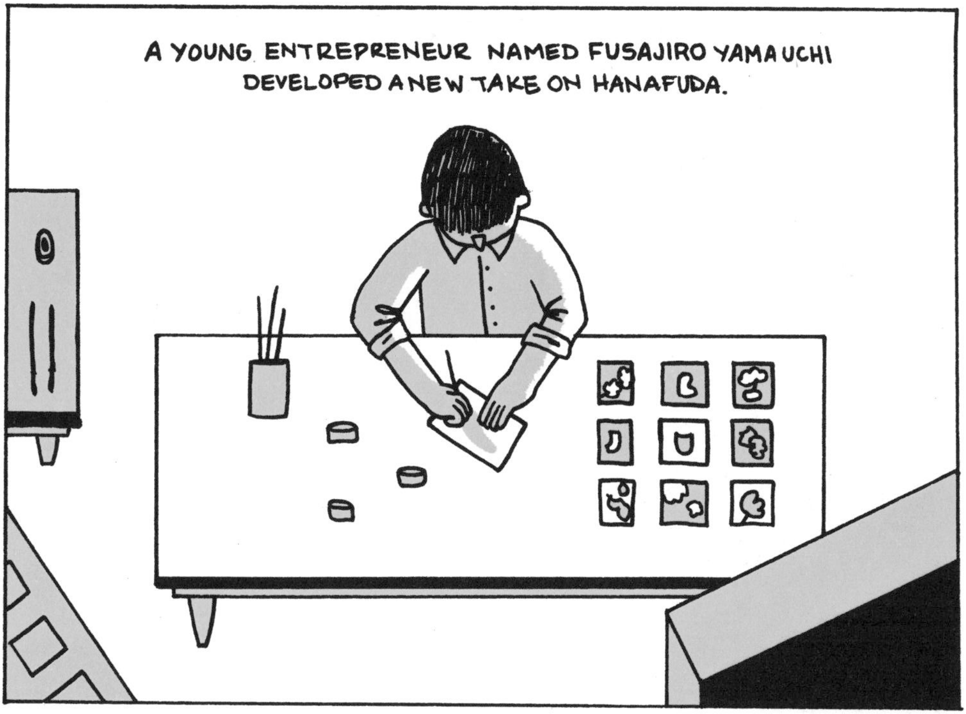
A YOUNG ENTREPRENEUR NAMED FUSAJIRO YAMAUCHI DEVELOPED A NEW TAKE ON HANAFUDA.

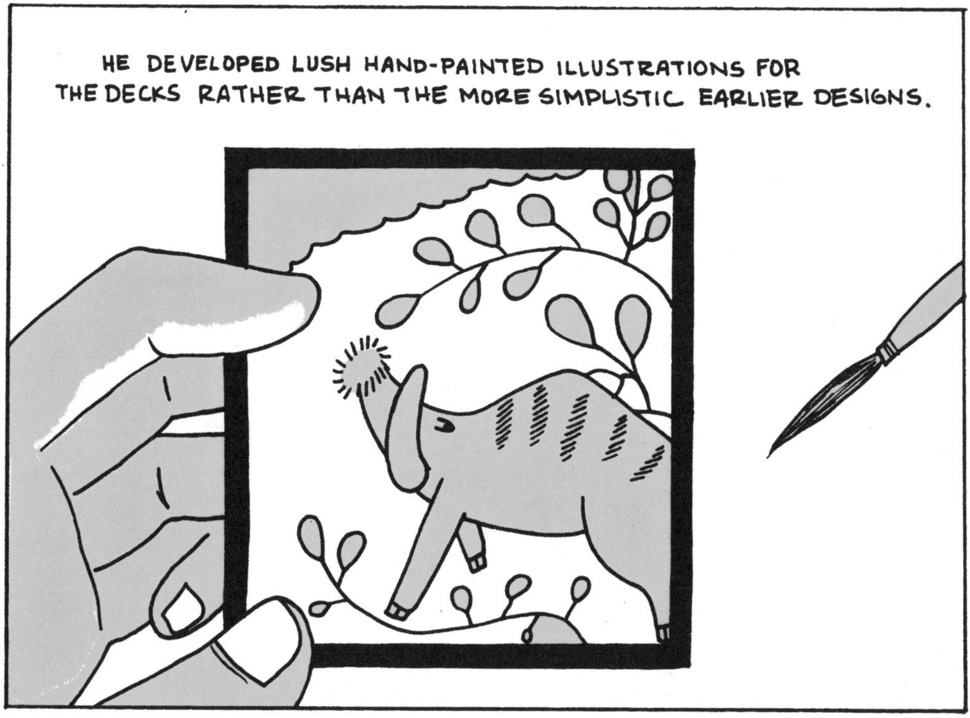
HE DEVELOPED LUSH HAND-PAINTED ILLUSTRATIONS FOR THE DECKS RATHER THAN THE MORE SIMPLISTIC EARLIER DESIGNS.

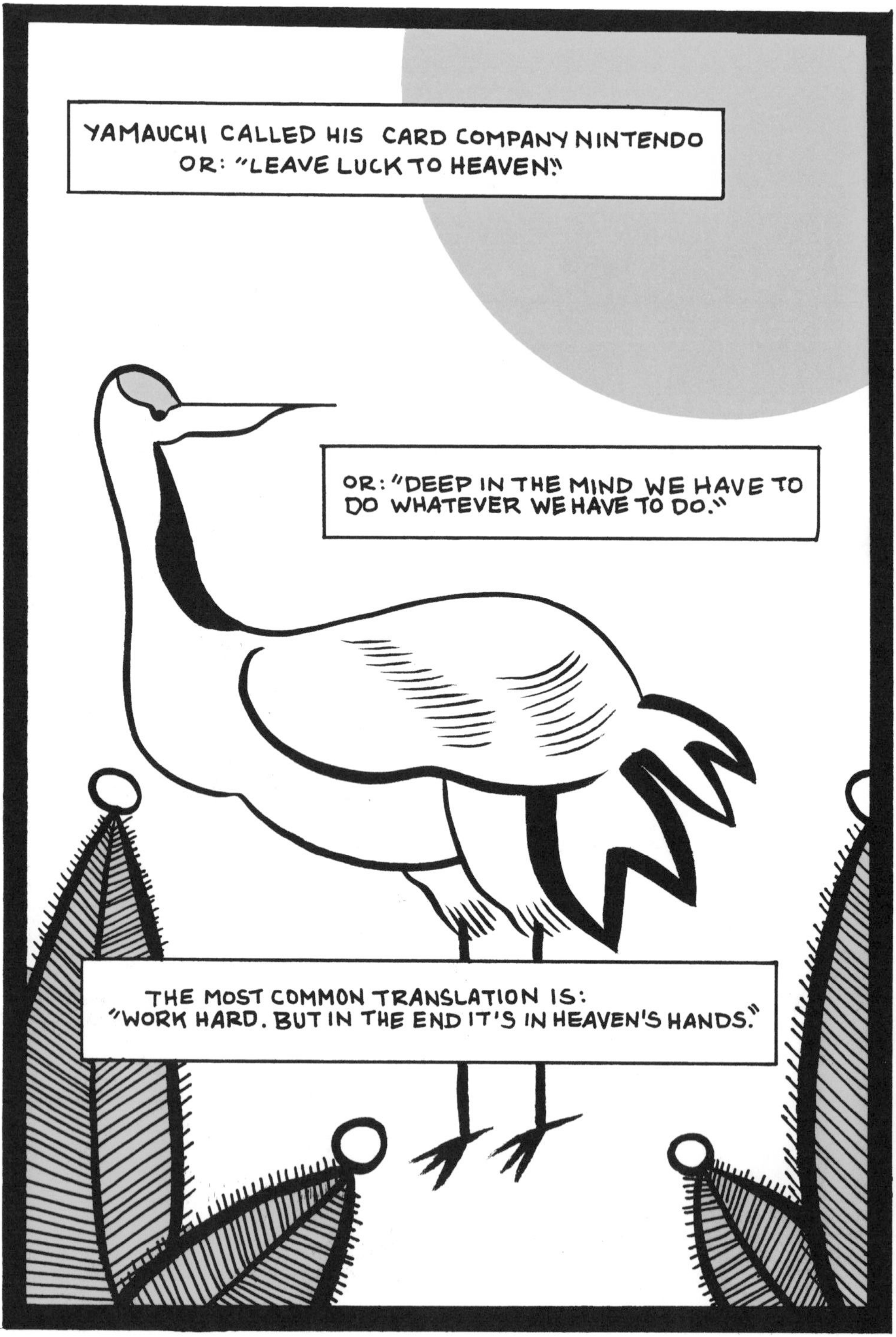
YAMAUCHI CALLED HIS CARD COMPANY NINTENDO OR: "LEAVE LUCK TO HEAVEN."
OR: "DEEP IN THE MIND WE HAVE TO DO WHATEVER WE HAVE TO DO."
THE MOST COMMON TRANSLATION IS: "WORK HARD. BUT IN THE END IT'S IN HEAVEN'S HANDS."

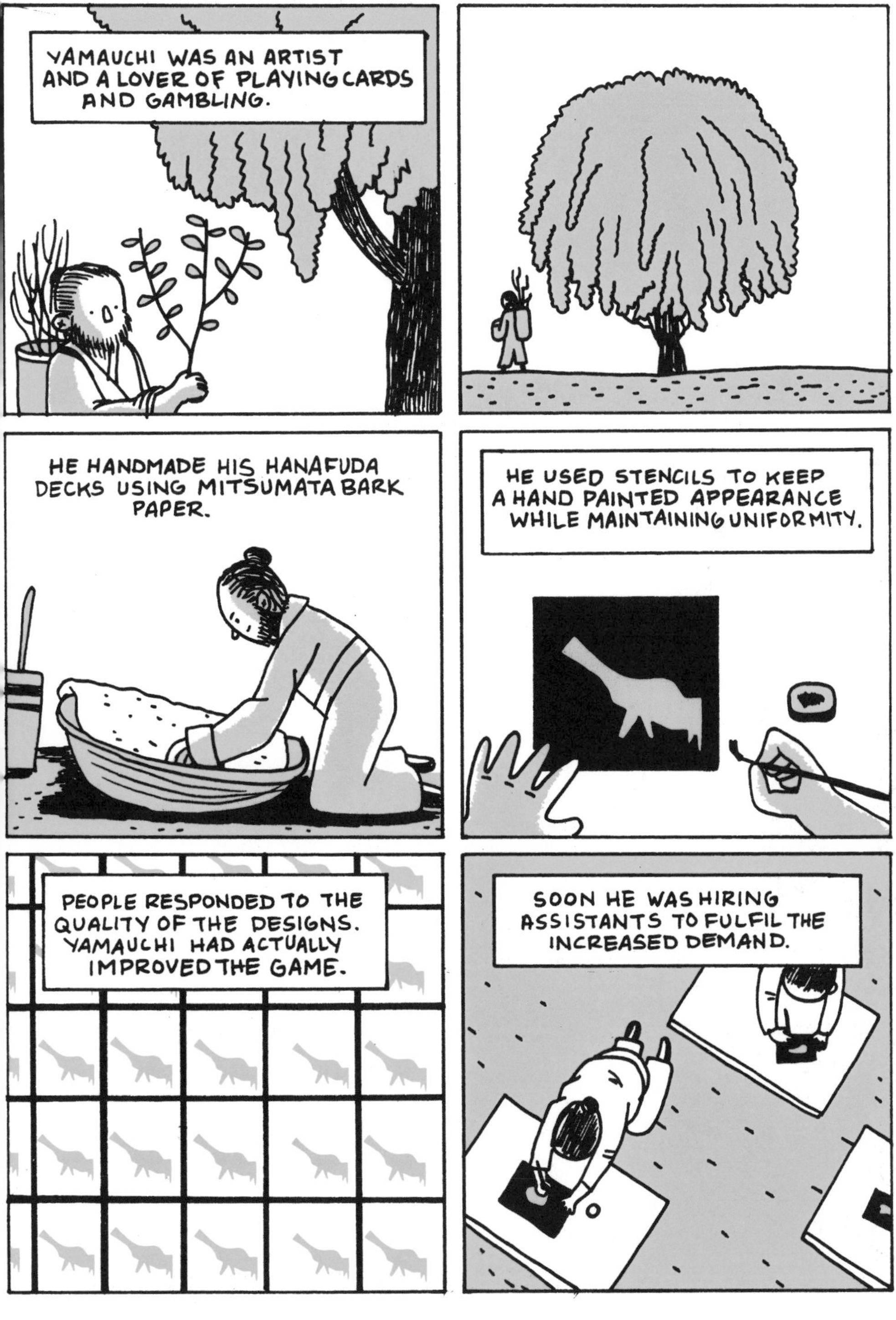
YAMAUCHI WAS AN ARTIST AND A LOVER OF PLAYING CARDS AND GAMBLING.
HE HANDMADE HIS HANAFUDA DECKS USING MITSUMATA BARK PAPER.
HE USED STENCILS TO KEEP A HAND PAINTED APPEARANCE WHILE MAINTAINING UNIFORMITY.
PEOPLE RESPONDED TO THE QUALITY OF THE DESIGNS. YAMAUCHI HAD ACTUALLY IMPROVED THE GAME.
SOON HE WAS HIRING ASSISTANTS TO FULFIL THE INCREASED DEMAND.

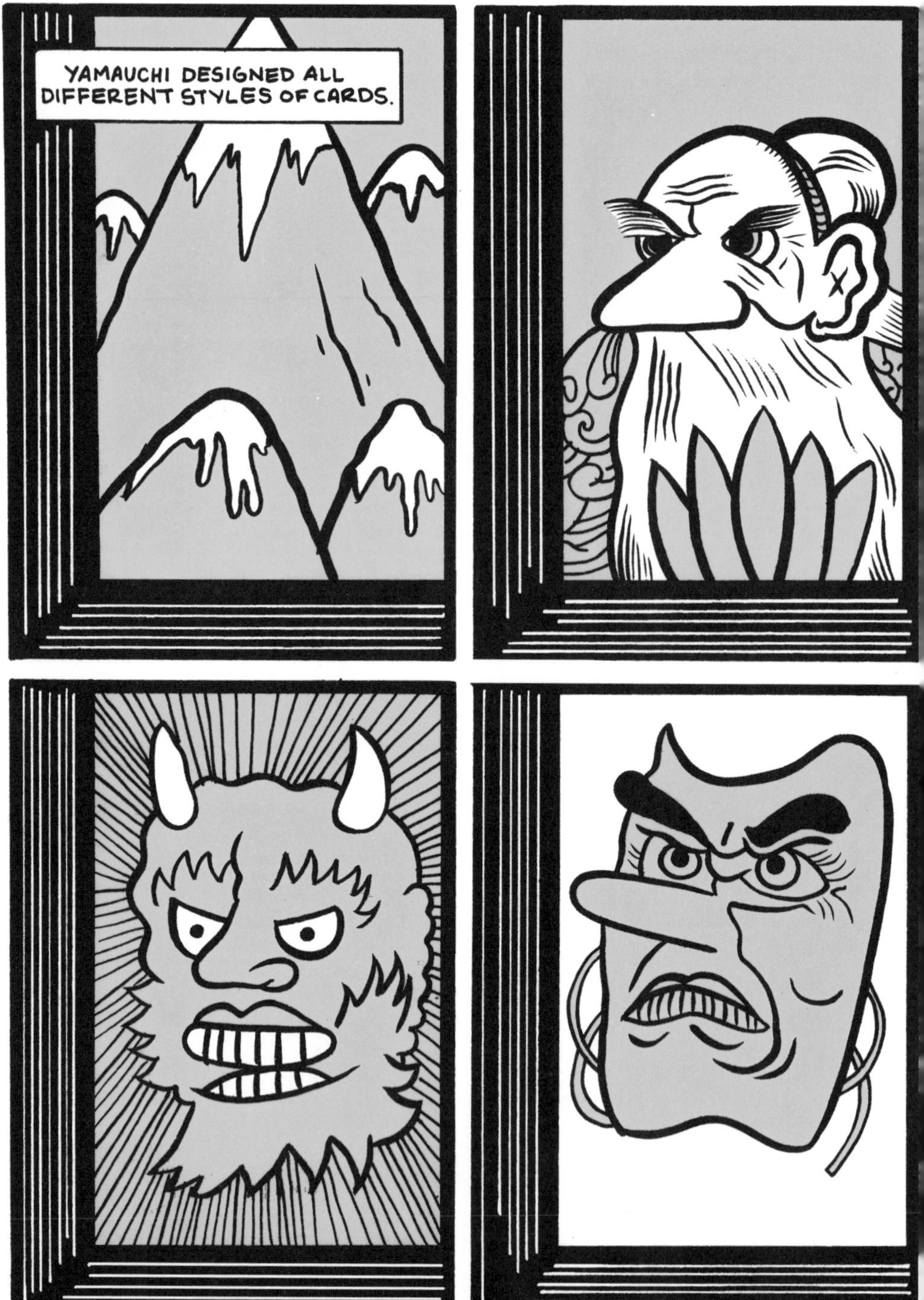
YAMAUCHI DESIGNED ALL DIFFERENT STYLES OF CARDS.

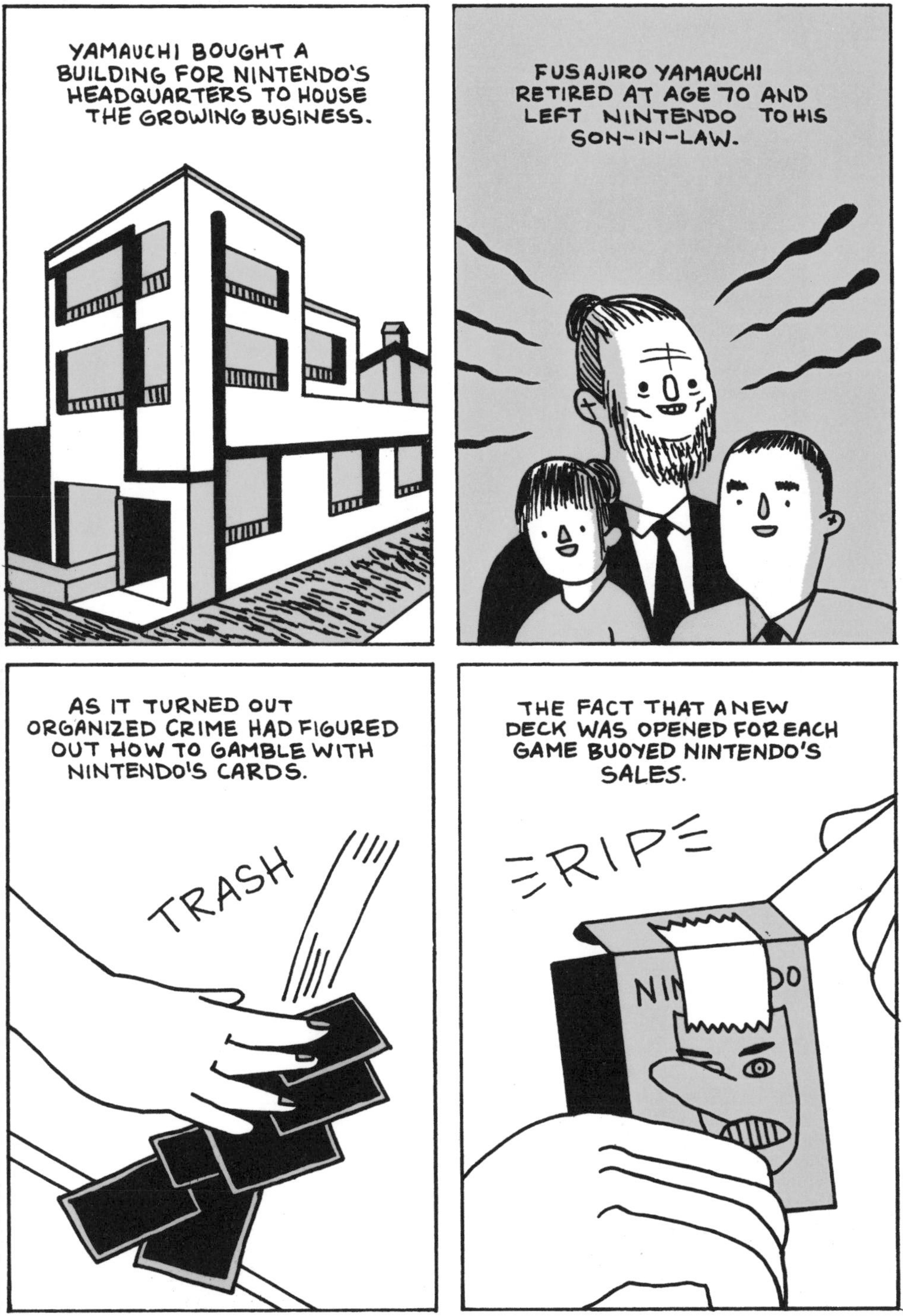
YAMAUCHI BOUGHT A BUILDING FOR NINTENDO'S HEADQUARTERS TO HOUSE THE GROWING BUSINESS.
FUSAJIRO YAMAUCHI RETIRED AT AGE 70 AND LEFT NINTENDO TO HIS SON-IN-LAW.
AS IT TURNED OUT ORGANIZED CRIME HAD FIGURED OUT HOW TO GAMBLE WITH NINTENDO'S CARDS.
TRASH
THE FACT THAT A NEW DECK WAS OPENED FOR EACH GAME BUOYED NINTENDO'S SALES.
RIP

GUNPEI YOKOI
NINTENDO FACTORY ENGINEER
TURNED TOY INVENTOR

HIROSHI YAMAUCHI
PRESIDENT AND CHAIRMAN
OF NINTENDO (1949-2005)

NINTENDO CONTINUED TO MAKE PLAYING CARDS EXCLUSIVELY WELL INTO THE 1960s.

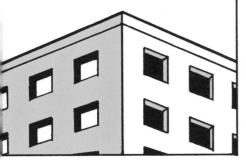

BUT UNDER THE HELM OF HIROSHI YAMAUCHI, GRANDSON OF FUSAJIRO, THE COMPANY BEGAN EXPANDING INTO OTHER AREAS.

ONE DAY IN 1970 HE NOTICED AN ENGINEER NAMED GUNPEI YOKOI.

GUNPEI WAS USING A TOOL HIROSHI HAD NOT SEEN BEFORE.

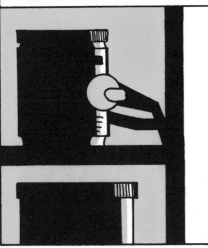

AS IT TURNED OUT GUNPEI HAD INVENTED IT HIMSELF.

SPROING!

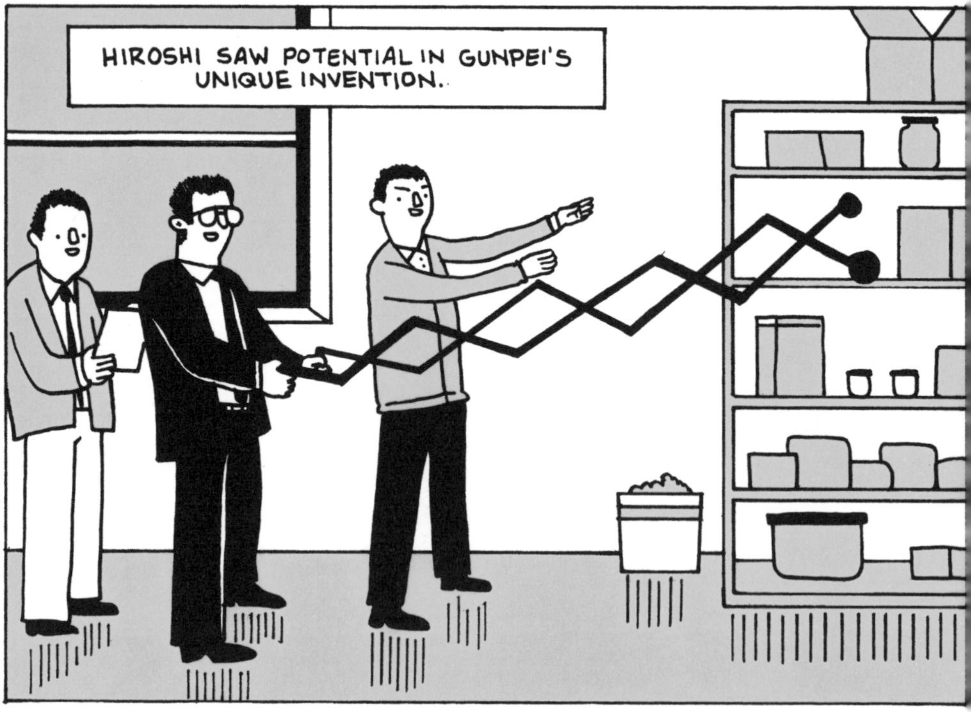
HIROSHI SAW POTENTIAL IN GUNPEI'S UNIQUE INVENTION.

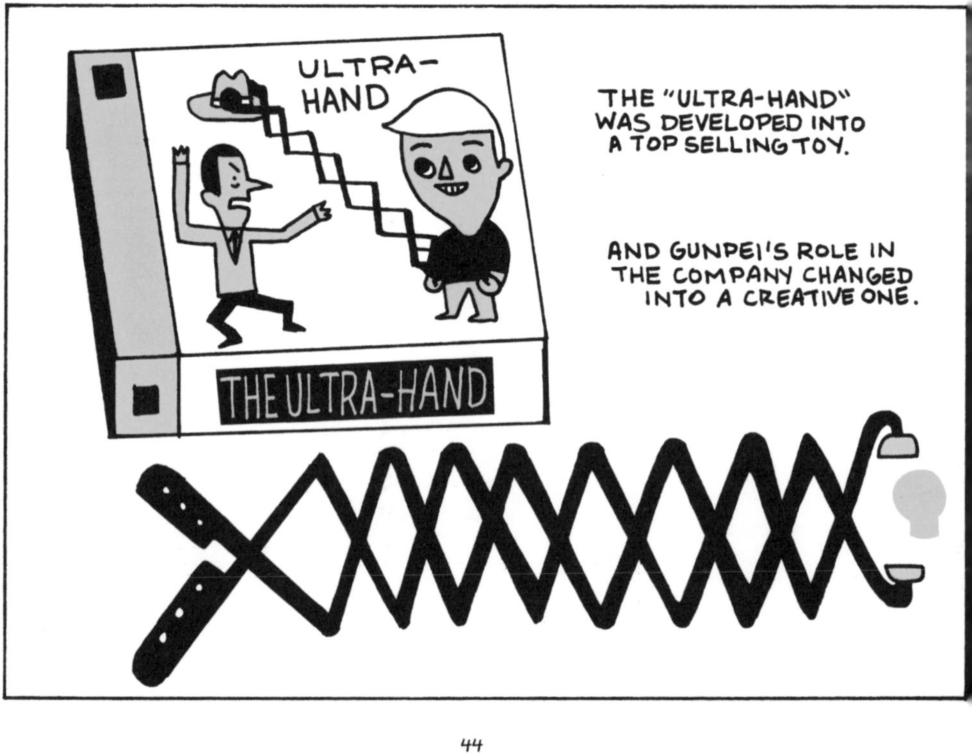
ULTRA-HAND
THE ULTRA-HAND
THE "ULTRA-HAND" WAS DEVELOPED INTO A TOP SELLING TOY.
AND GUNPEI'S ROLE IN THE COMPANY CHANGED INTO A CREATIVE ONE.

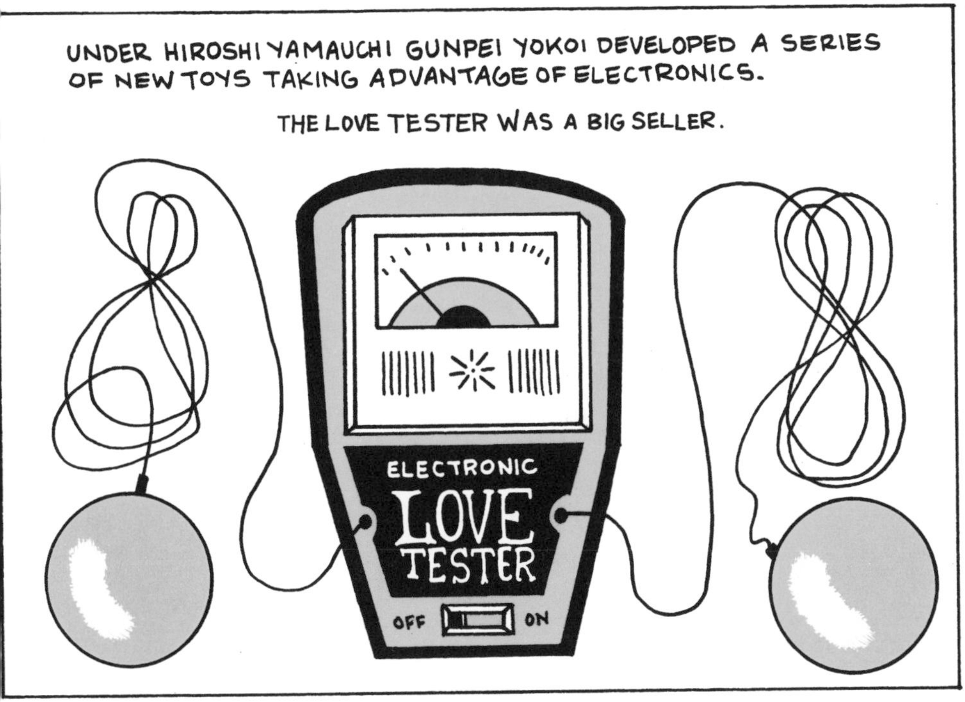
UNDER HIROSHI YAMAUCHI GUNPEI YOKOI DEVELOPED A SERIES OF NEW TOYS TAKING ADVANTAGE OF ELECTRONICS.
THE LOVE TESTER WAS A BIG SELLER.
ELECTRONIC
LOVE
TESTER
OFF
ON

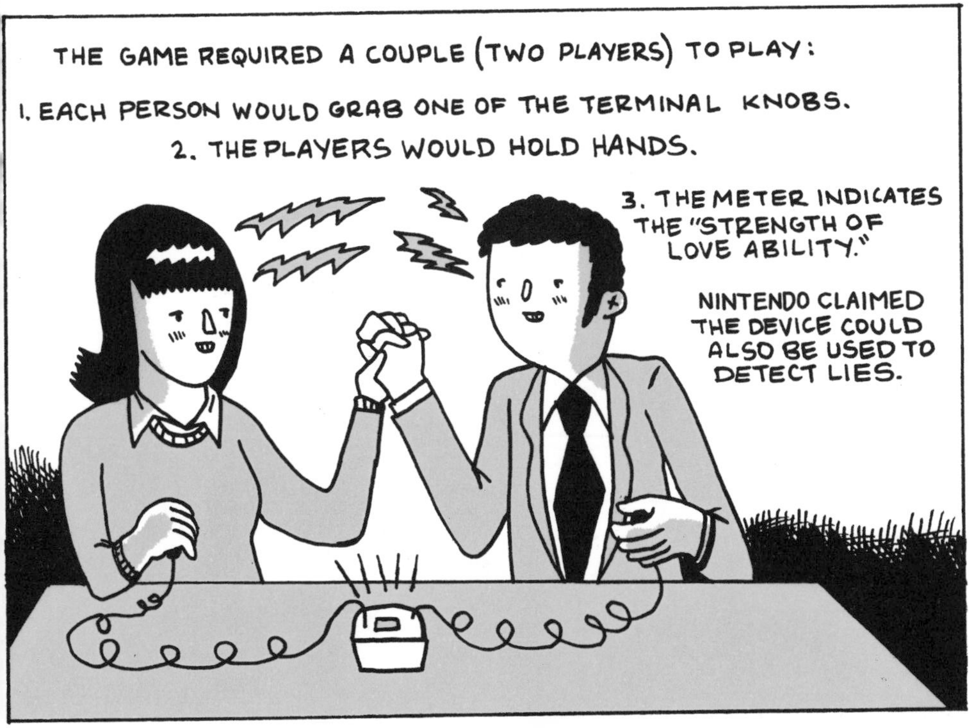
THE GAME REQUIRED A COUPLE (TWO PLAYERS) TO PLAY:
1. EACH PERSON WOULD GRAB ONE OF THE TERMINAL KNOBS.
2. THE PLAYERS WOULD HOLD HANDS.
3. THE METER INDICATES THE "STRENGTH OF LOVE ABILITY."
NINTENDO CLAIMED THE DEVICE COULD ALSO BE USED TO DETECT LIES.

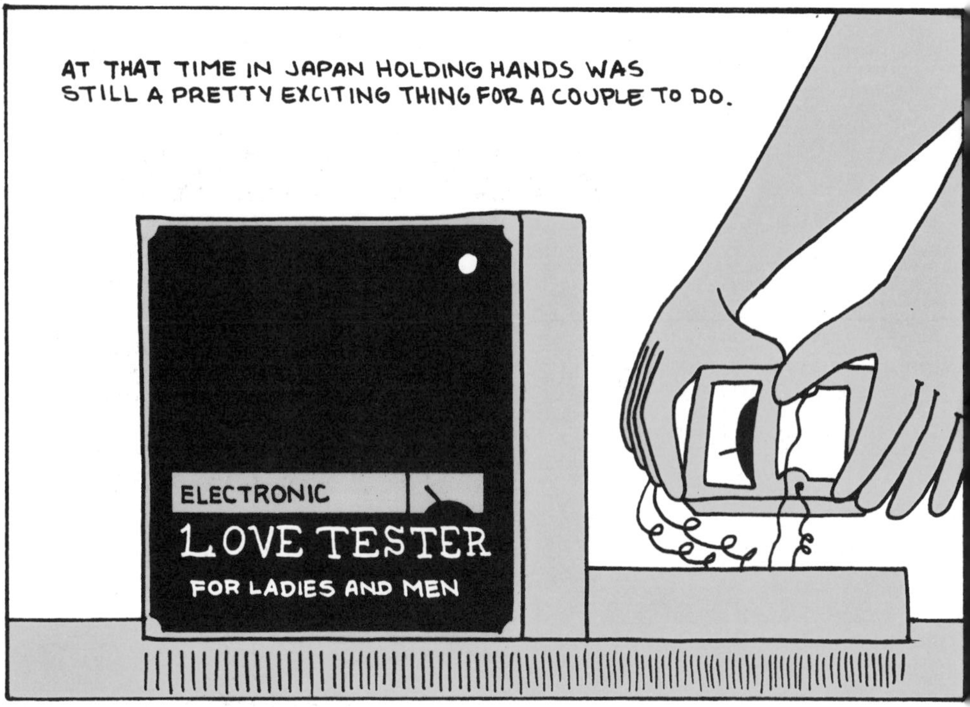
AT THAT TIME IN JAPAN HOLDING HANDS WAS STILL A PRETTY EXCITING THING FOR A COUPLE TO DO.
ELECTRONIC
LOVE TESTER
FOR LADIES AND MEN

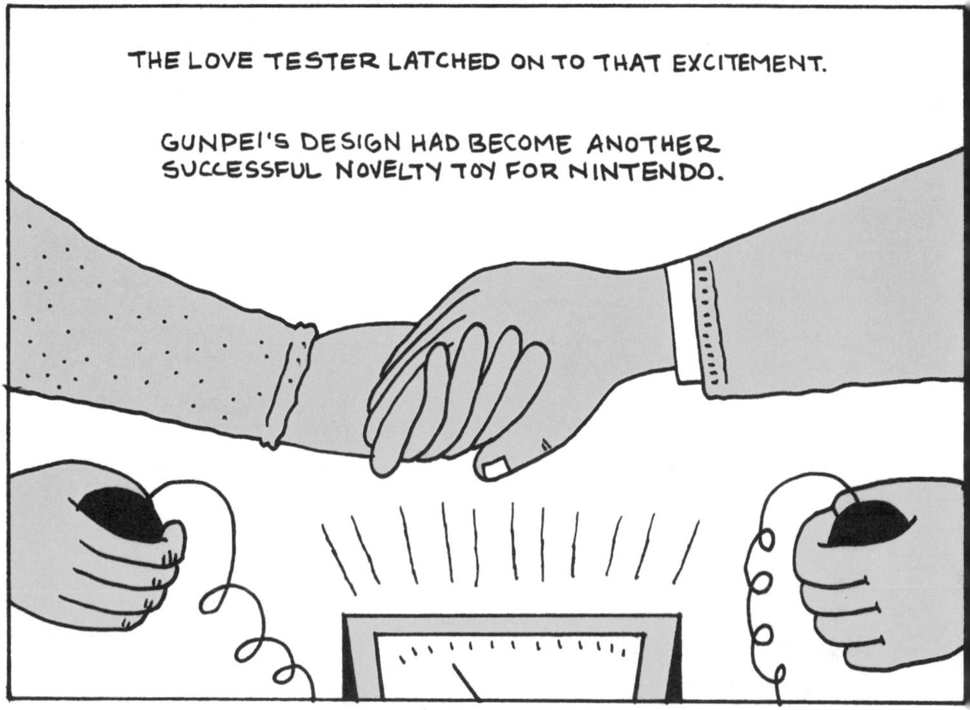
THE LOVE TESTER LATCHED ON TO THAT EXCITEMENT.
GUNPEI'S DESIGN HAD BECOME ANOTHER SUCCESSFUL NOVELTY TOY FOR NINTENDO.

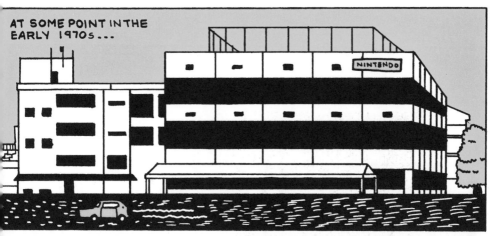

AT SOME POINT IN THE EARLY 1970s...

MASAYUKI UEMURA, A SALES-MAN FOR SHARP, SHOWED UP ON A ROUTINE SALES CALL.

WE'VE DEVELOPED THIS PHOTOCELL TECHNOLOGY.*

WHAT DO YOU THINK, GUNPEI?

HMMMM...

*DEVICES THAT DETECT LIGHT.

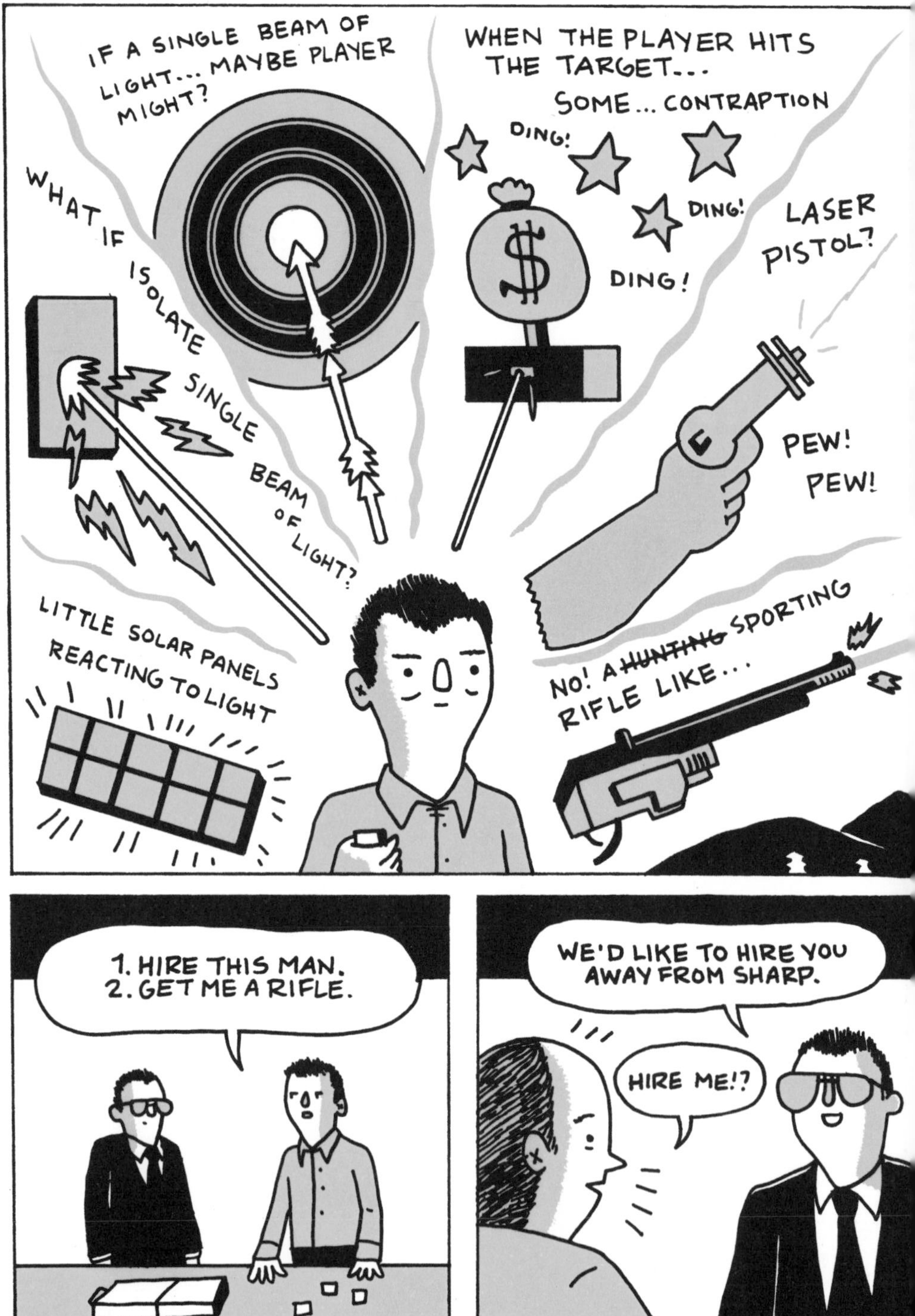
IF A SINGLE BEAM OF LIGHT... MAYBE PLAYER MIGHT?
WHEN THE PLAYER HITS THE TARGET...
SOME... CONTRAPTION
DING!
DING!
DING!
WHAT IF ISOLATE SINGLE BEAM OF LIGHT?
LASER PISTOL?
PEW! PEW!
LITTLE SOLAR PANELS REACTING TO LIGHT
NO! A ~~HUNTING~~ SPORTING RIFLE LIKE...
1. HIRE THIS MAN.
2. GET ME A RIFLE.
WE'D LIKE TO HIRE YOU AWAY FROM SHARP.
HIRE ME!?

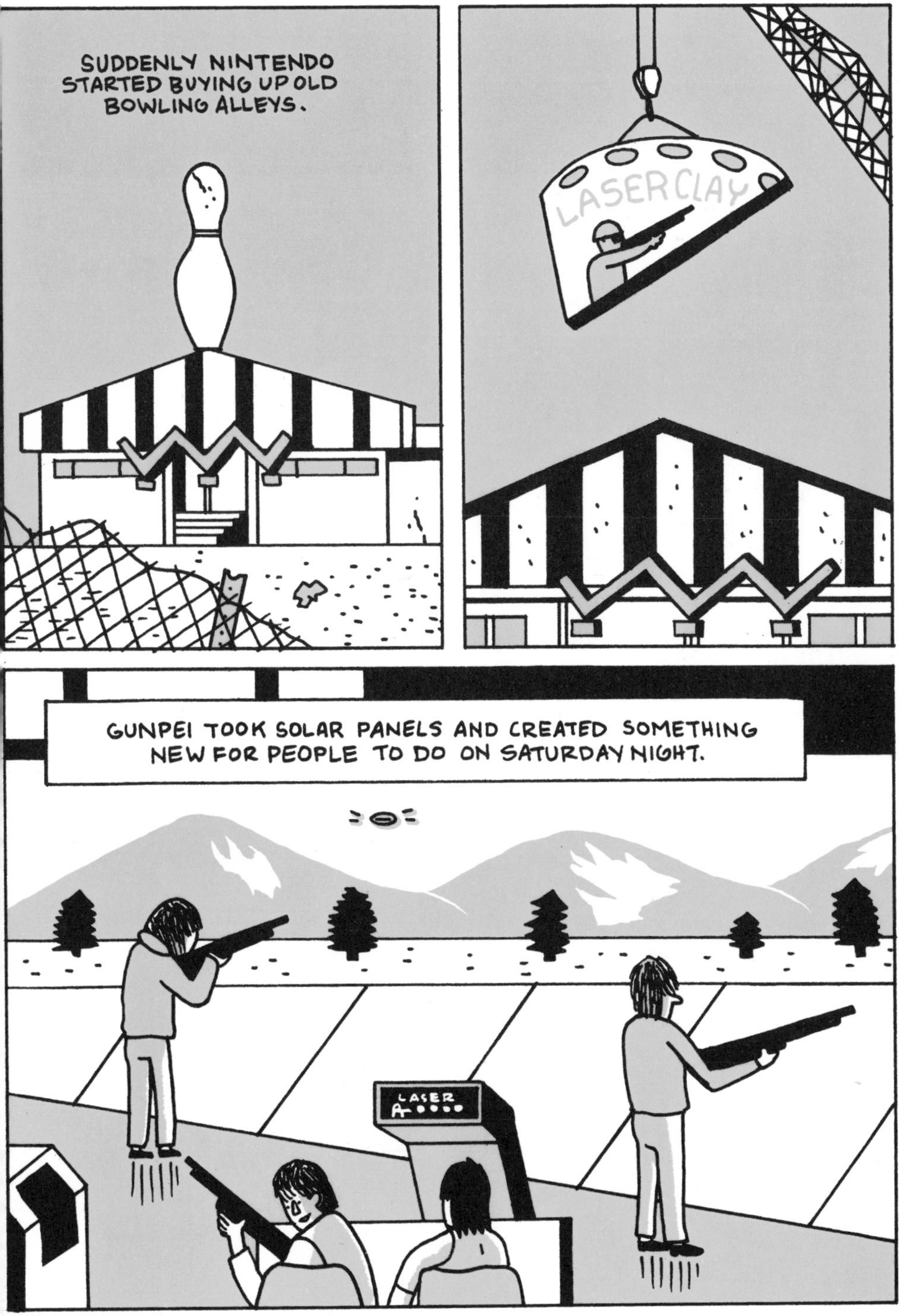
SUDDENLY NINTENDO STARTED BUYING UP OLD BOWLING ALLEYS.
LASER CLAY
GUNPEI TOOK SOLAR PANELS AND CREATED SOMETHING NEW FOR PEOPLE TO DO ON SATURDAY NIGHT.
LASER

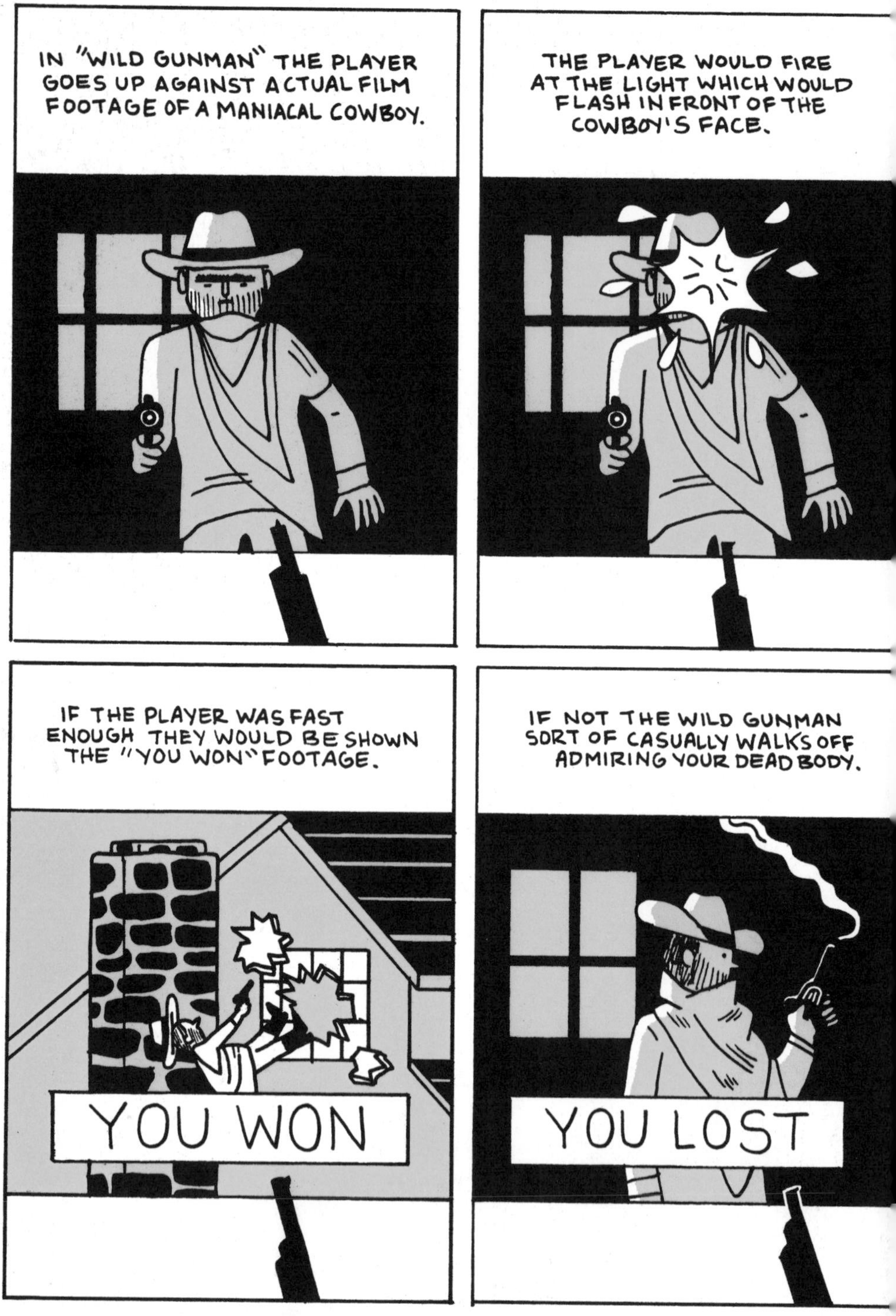
IN "WILD GUNMAN" THE PLAYER GOES UP AGAINST ACTUAL FILM FOOTAGE OF A MANIACAL COWBOY.
THE PLAYER WOULD FIRE AT THE LIGHT WHICH WOULD FLASH IN FRONT OF THE COWBOY'S FACE.
IF THE PLAYER WAS FAST ENOUGH THEY WOULD BE SHOWN THE "YOU WON" FOOTAGE.
YOU WON
IF NOT THE WILD GUNMAN SORT OF CASUALLY WALKS OFF ADMIRING YOUR DEAD BODY.
YOU LOST

MINORU ARAKAWA
FOUNDER AND FIRST
PRESIDENT OF
NINTENDO OF AMERICA

HOWARD LINCOLN
NINTENDO LAWYER TURNED
SENIOR VICE PRESIDENT
AND GENERAL COUNSEL OF
NINTENDO OF AMERICA

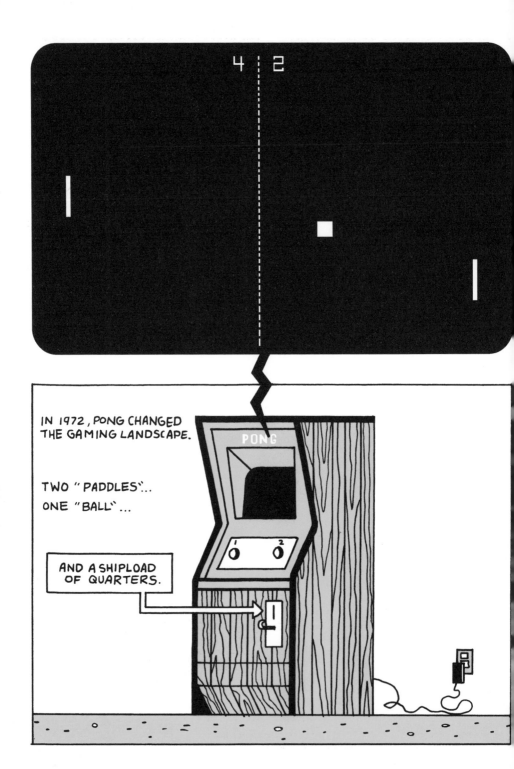

4 ¦ 2

IN 1972, PONG CHANGED
THE GAMING LANDSCAPE.

TWO "PADDLES"...
ONE "BALL"...

AND A SHIPLOAD
OF QUARTERS.

PONG

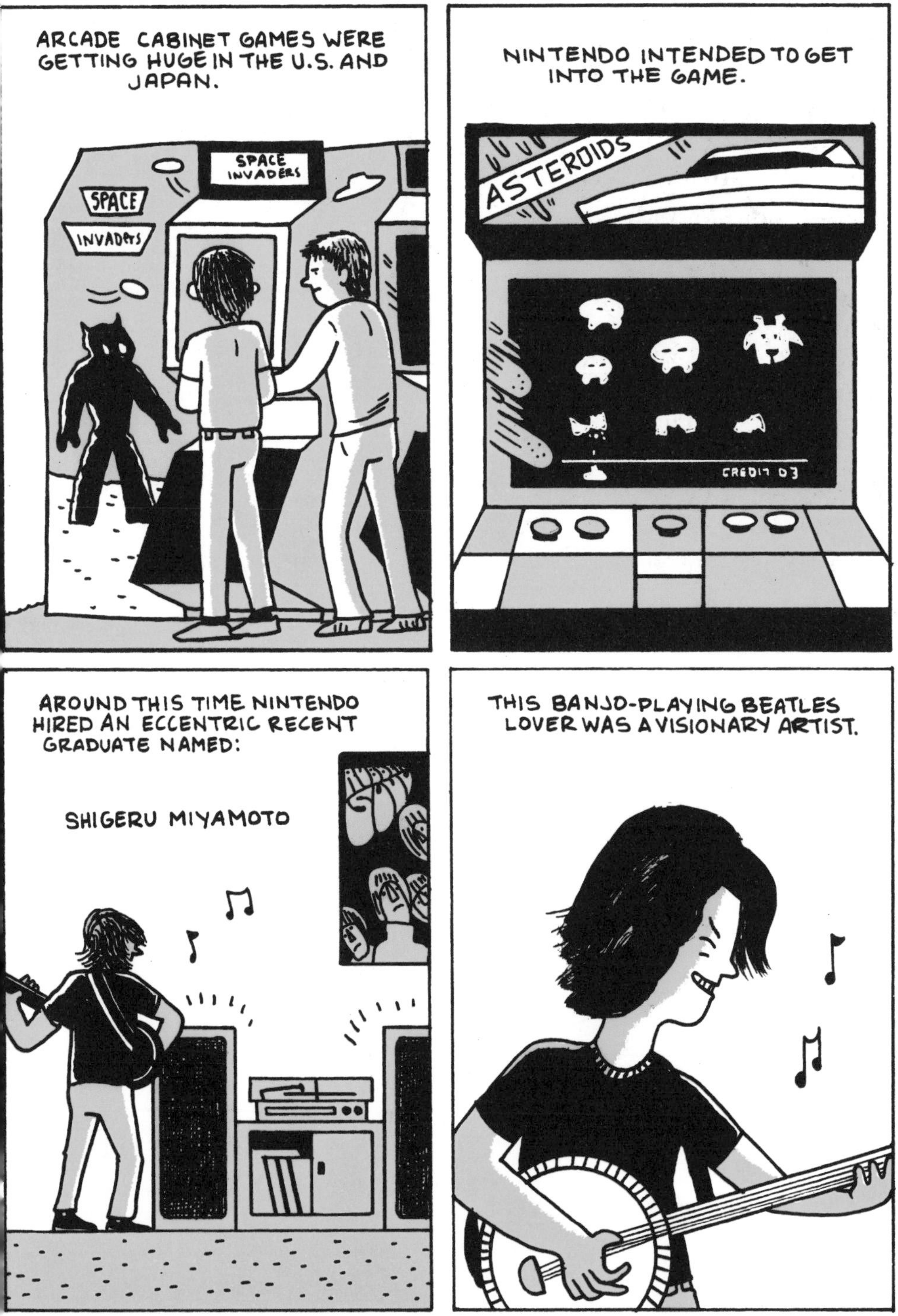
ARCADE CABINET GAMES WERE GETTING HUGE IN THE U.S. AND JAPAN.
SPACE INVADERS
SPACE
INVADERS
NINTENDO INTENDED TO GET INTO THE GAME.
ASTEROIDS
CREDIT 03
AROUND THIS TIME NINTENDO HIRED AN ECCENTRIC RECENT GRADUATE NAMED:
SHIGERU MIYAMOTO
THIS BANJO-PLAYING BEATLES LOVER WAS A VISIONARY ARTIST.

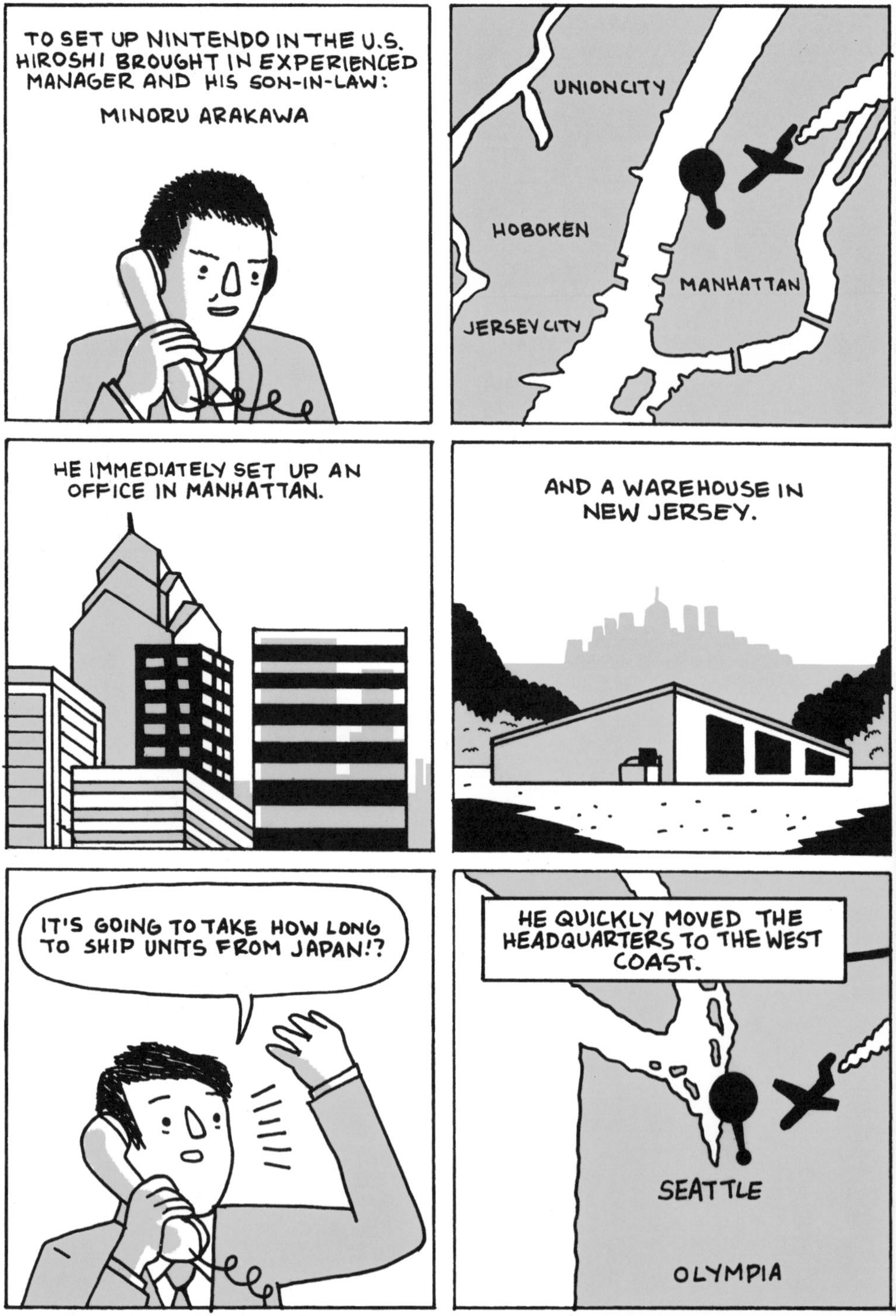
TO SET UP NINTENDO IN THE U.S. HIROSHI BROUGHT IN EXPERIENCED MANAGER AND HIS SON-IN-LAW:
MINORU ARAKAWA
UNION CITY
HOBOKEN
MANHATTAN
JERSEY CITY
HE IMMEDIATELY SET UP AN OFFICE IN MANHATTAN.
AND A WAREHOUSE IN NEW JERSEY.
IT'S GOING TO TAKE HOW LONG TO SHIP UNITS FROM JAPAN!?
HE QUICKLY MOVED THE HEADQUARTERS TO THE WEST COAST.
SEATTLE
OLYMPIA

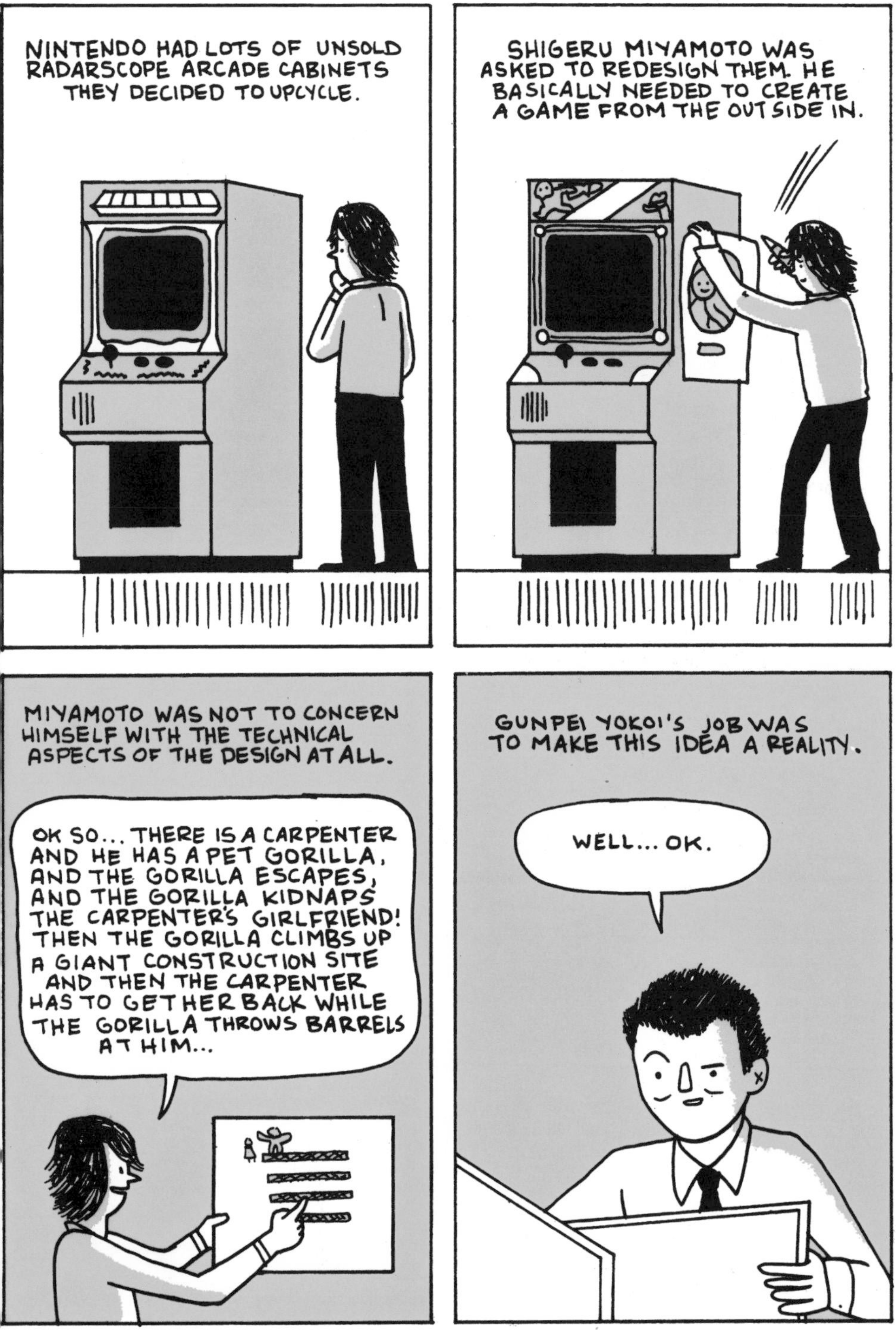
NINTENDO HAD LOTS OF UNSOLD RADARSCOPE ARCADE CABINETS THEY DECIDED TO UPCYCLE.
SHIGERU MIYAMOTO WAS ASKED TO REDESIGN THEM. HE BASICALLY NEEDED TO CREATE A GAME FROM THE OUTSIDE IN.
MIYAMOTO WAS NOT TO CONCERN HIMSELF WITH THE TECHNICAL ASPECTS OF THE DESIGN AT ALL.
OK SO... THERE IS A CARPENTER AND HE HAS A PET GORILLA, AND THE GORILLA ESCAPES, AND THE GORILLA KIDNAPS THE CARPENTER'S GIRLFRIEND! THEN THE GORILLA CLIMBS UP A GIANT CONSTRUCTION SITE AND THEN THE CARPENTER HAS TO GET HER BACK WHILE THE GORILLA THROWS BARRELS AT HIM...
GUNPEI YOKOI'S JOB WAS TO MAKE THIS IDEA A REALITY.
WELL... OK.

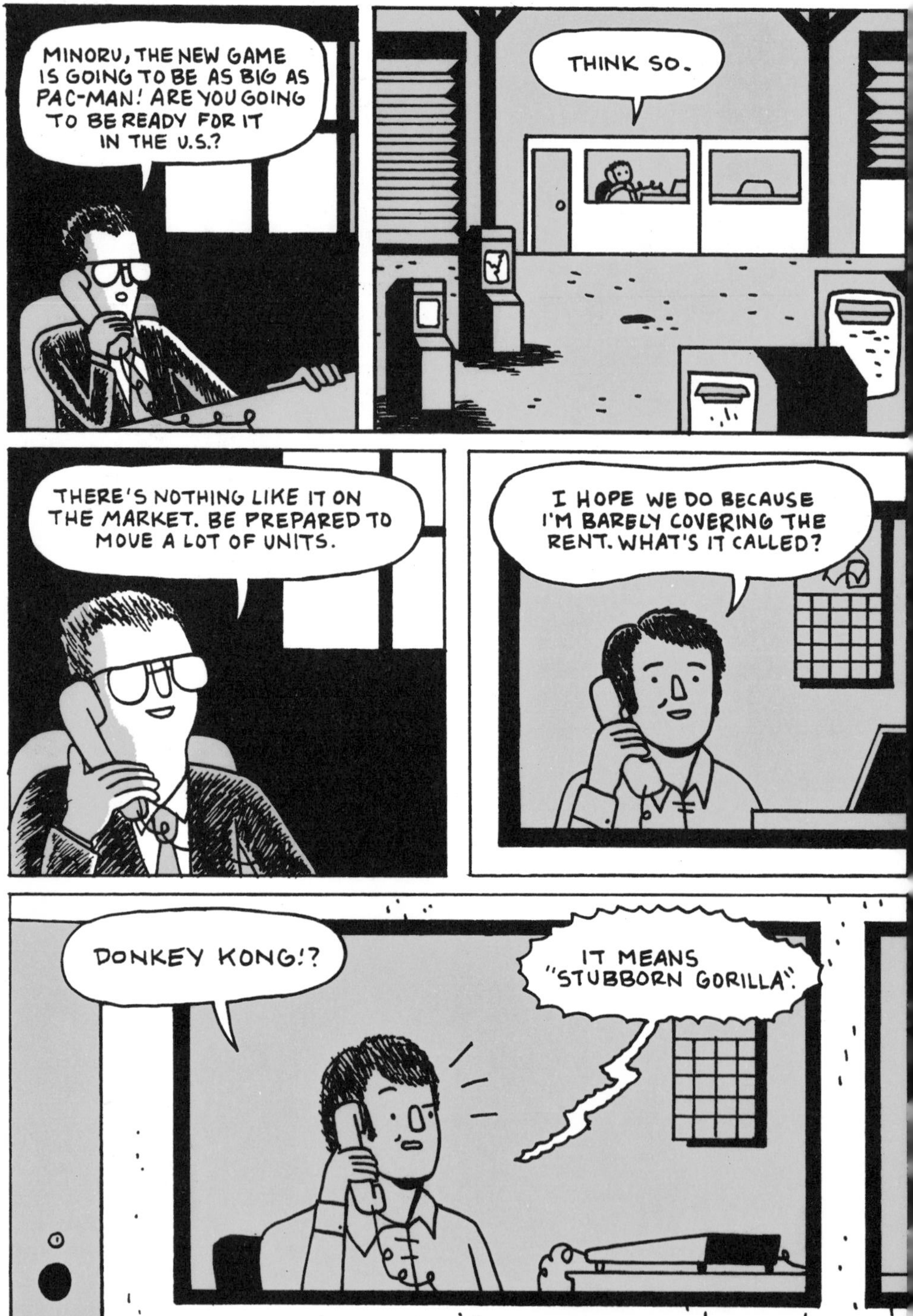
MINORU, THE NEW GAME IS GOING TO BE AS BIG AS PAC-MAN! ARE YOU GOING TO BE READY FOR IT IN THE U.S.?
THINK SO.
THERE'S NOTHING LIKE IT ON THE MARKET. BE PREPARED TO MOVE A LOT OF UNITS.
I HOPE WE DO BECAUSE I'M BARELY COVERING THE RENT. WHAT'S IT CALLED?
DONKEY KONG!?
IT MEANS "STUBBORN GORILLA".

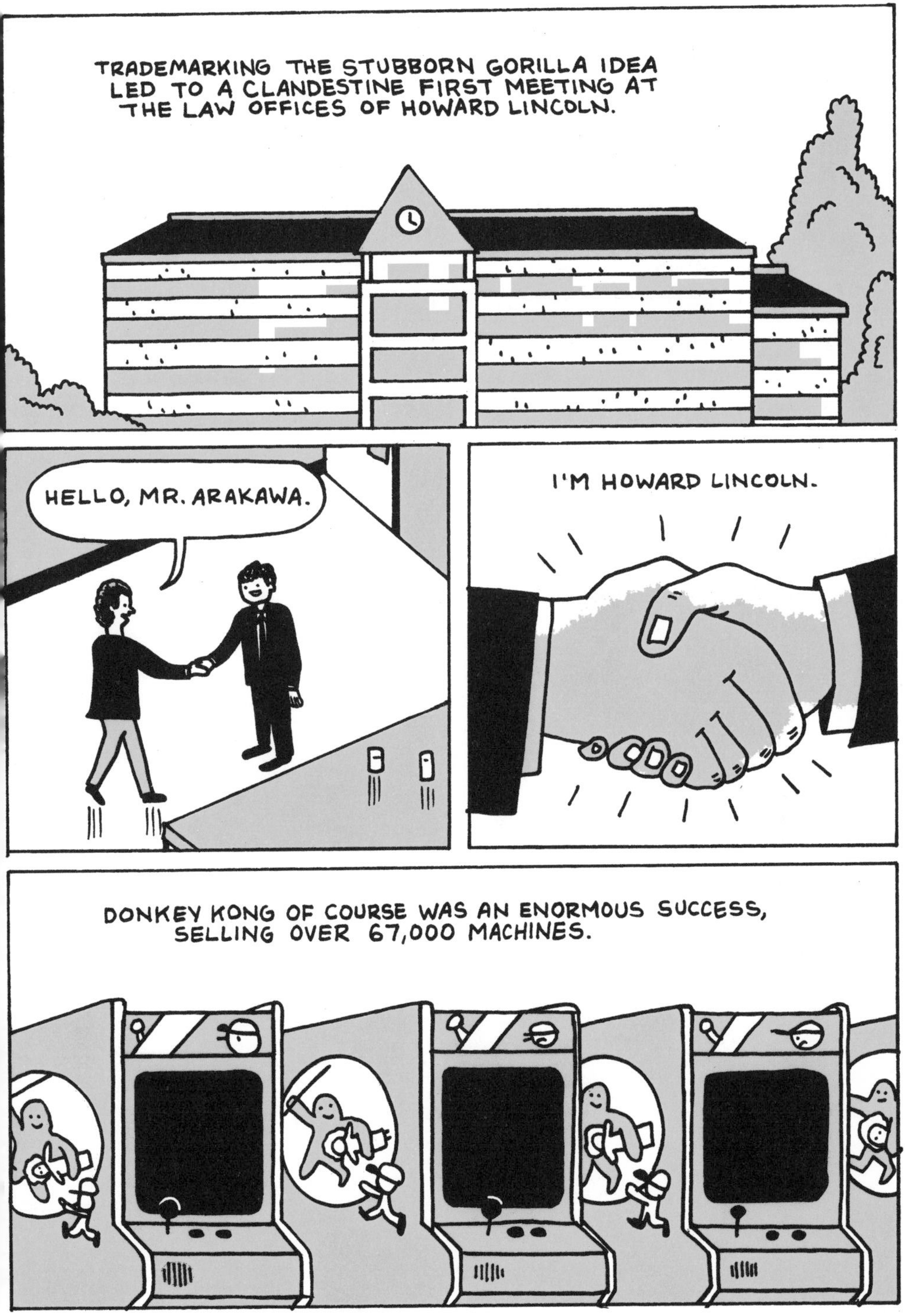

TRADEMARKING THE STUBBORN GORILLA IDEA LED TO A CLANDESTINE FIRST MEETING AT THE LAW OFFICES OF HOWARD LINCOLN.
HELLO, MR. ARAKAWA.
I'M HOWARD LINCOLN.
DONKEY KONG OF COURSE WAS AN ENORMOUS SUCCESS, SELLING OVER 67,000 MACHINES.

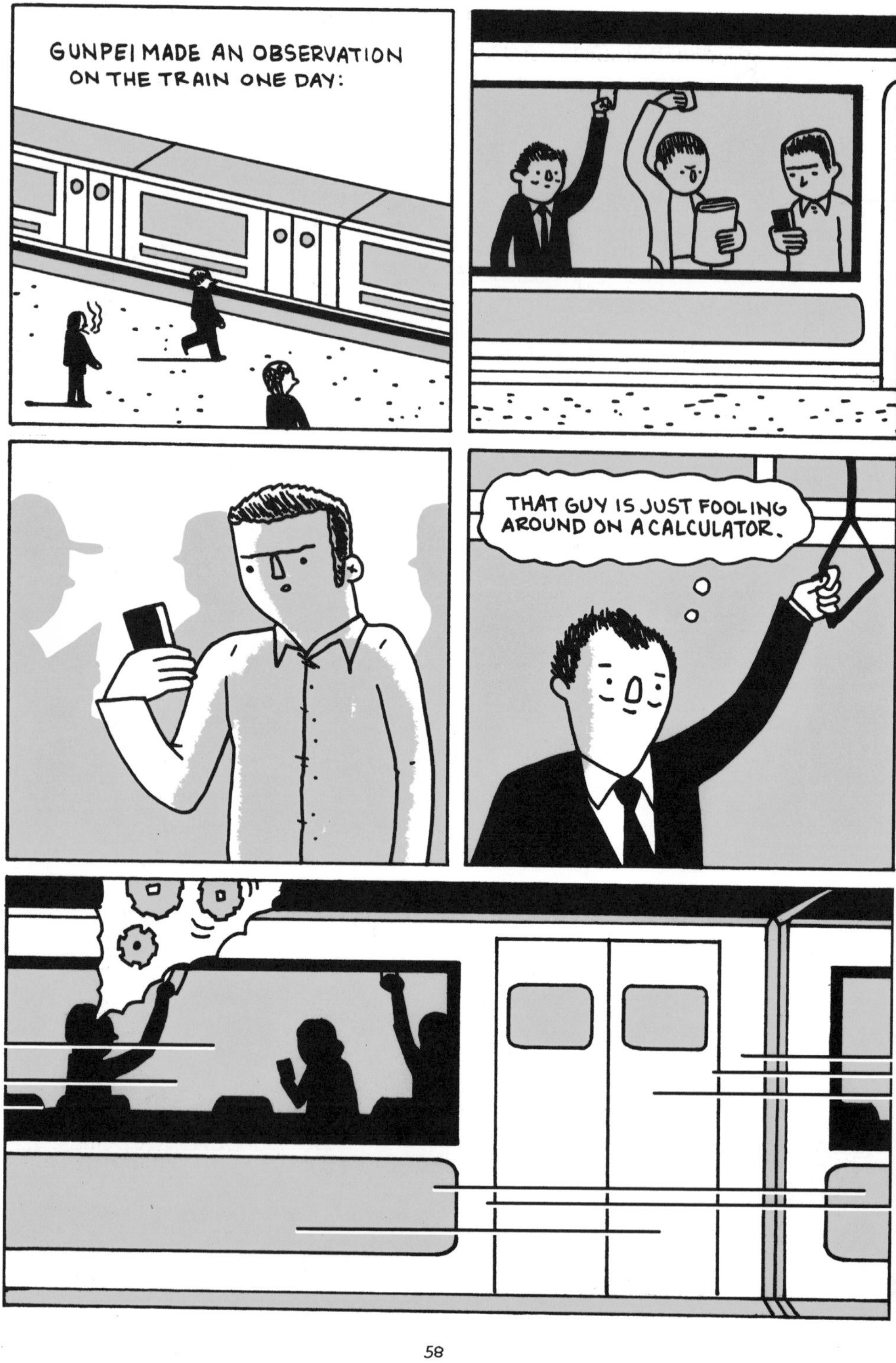
GUNPEI MADE AN OBSERVATION ON THE TRAIN ONE DAY:
THAT GUY IS JUST FOOLING AROUND ON A CALCULATOR.

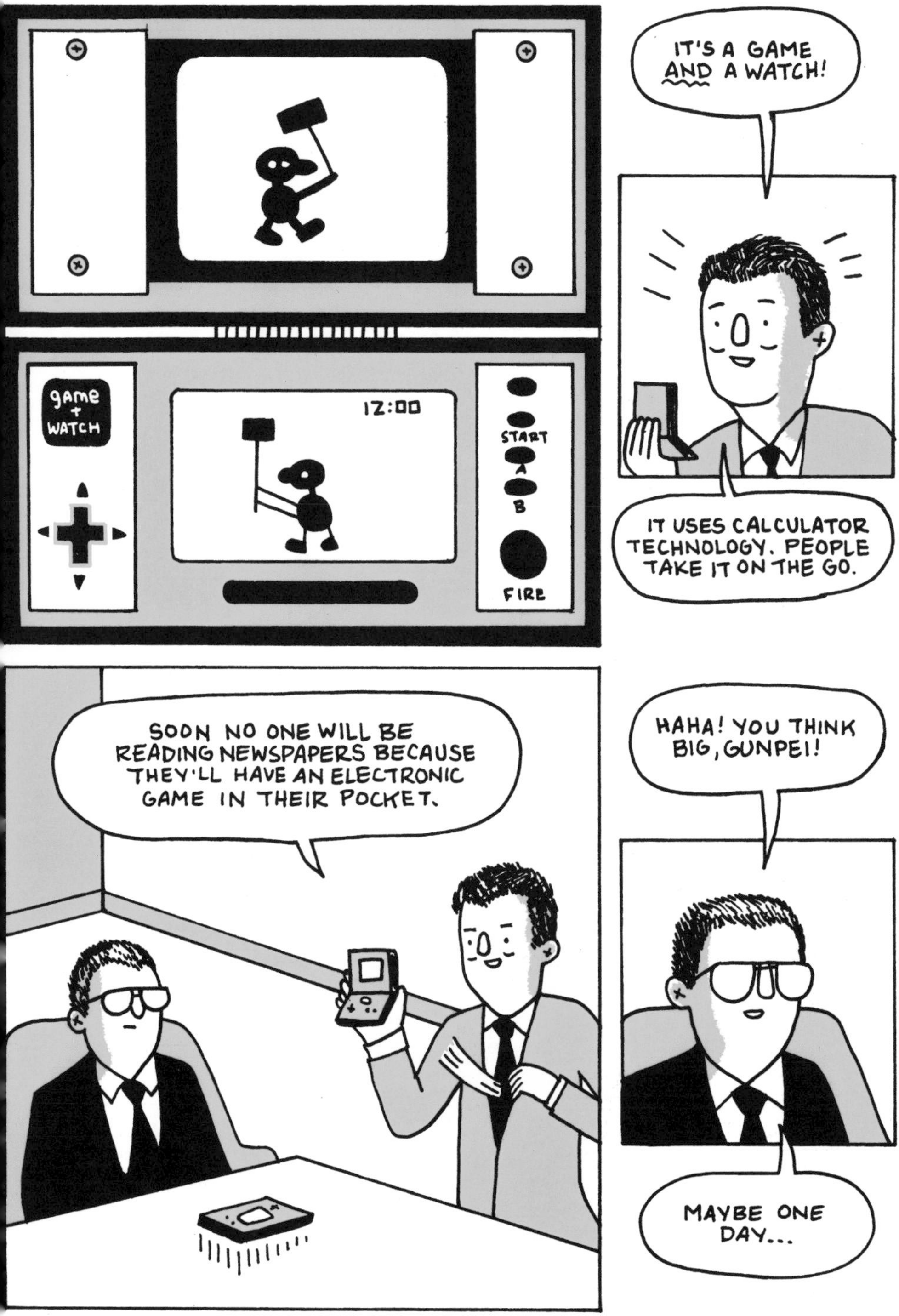
game + WATCH
12:00
START
A
B
FIRE
IT'S A GAME AND A WATCH!
IT USES CALCULATOR TECHNOLOGY. PEOPLE TAKE IT ON THE GO.
SOON NO ONE WILL BE READING NEWSPAPERS BECAUSE THEY'LL HAVE AN ELECTRONIC GAME IN THEIR POCKET.
HAHA! YOU THINK BIG, GUNPEI!
MAYBE ONE DAY...

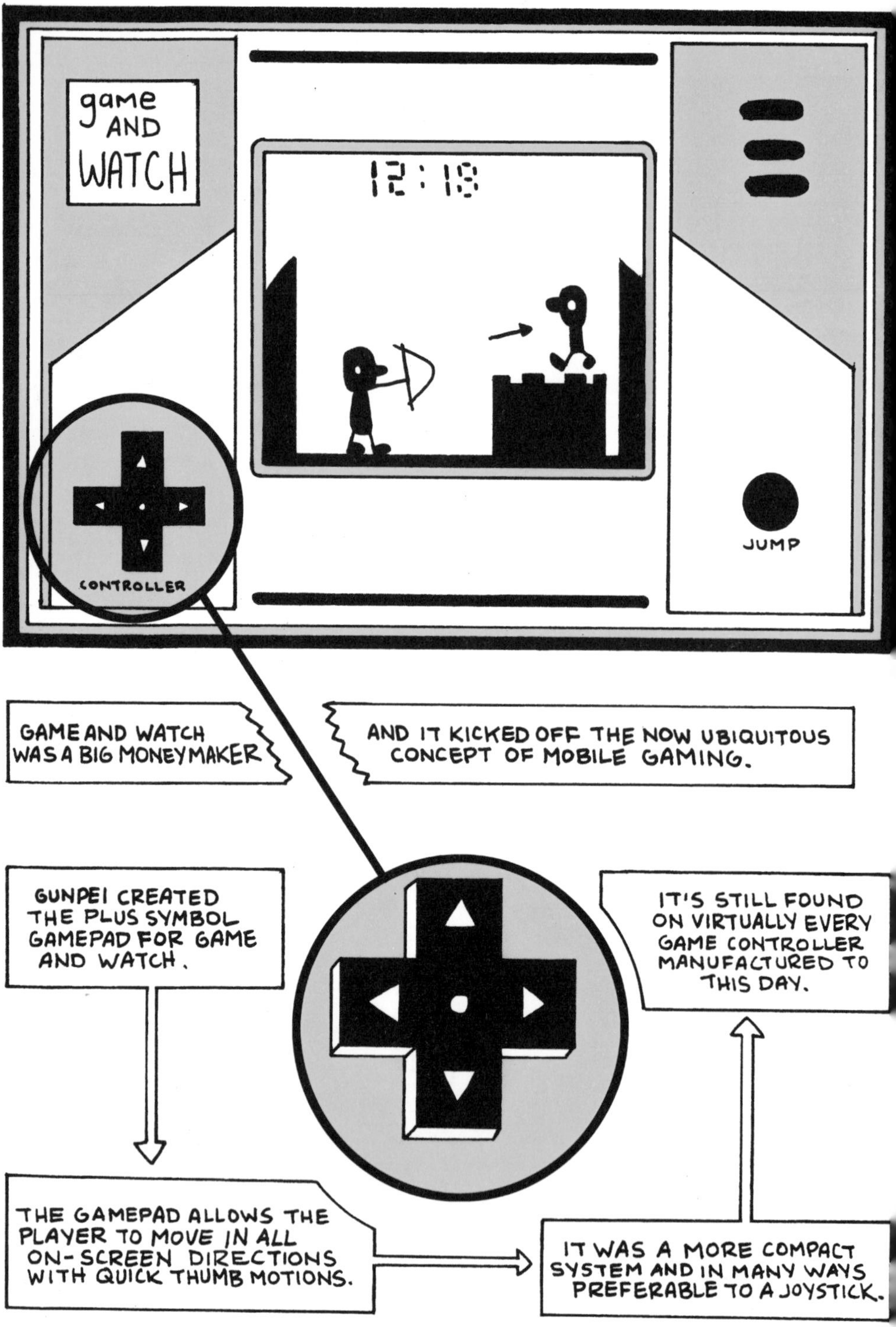

game AND WATCH
12:19
CONTROLLER
JUMP
GAME AND WATCH WAS A BIG MONEYMAKER
AND IT KICKED OFF THE NOW UBIQUITOUS CONCEPT OF MOBILE GAMING.
GUNPEI CREATED THE PLUS SYMBOL GAMEPAD FOR GAME AND WATCH.
IT'S STILL FOUND ON VIRTUALLY EVERY GAME CONTROLLER MANUFACTURED TO THIS DAY.
THE GAMEPAD ALLOWS THE PLAYER TO MOVE IN ALL ON-SCREEN DIRECTIONS WITH QUICK THUMB MOTIONS.
IT WAS A MORE COMPACT SYSTEM AND IN MANY WAYS PREFERABLE TO A JOYSTICK.

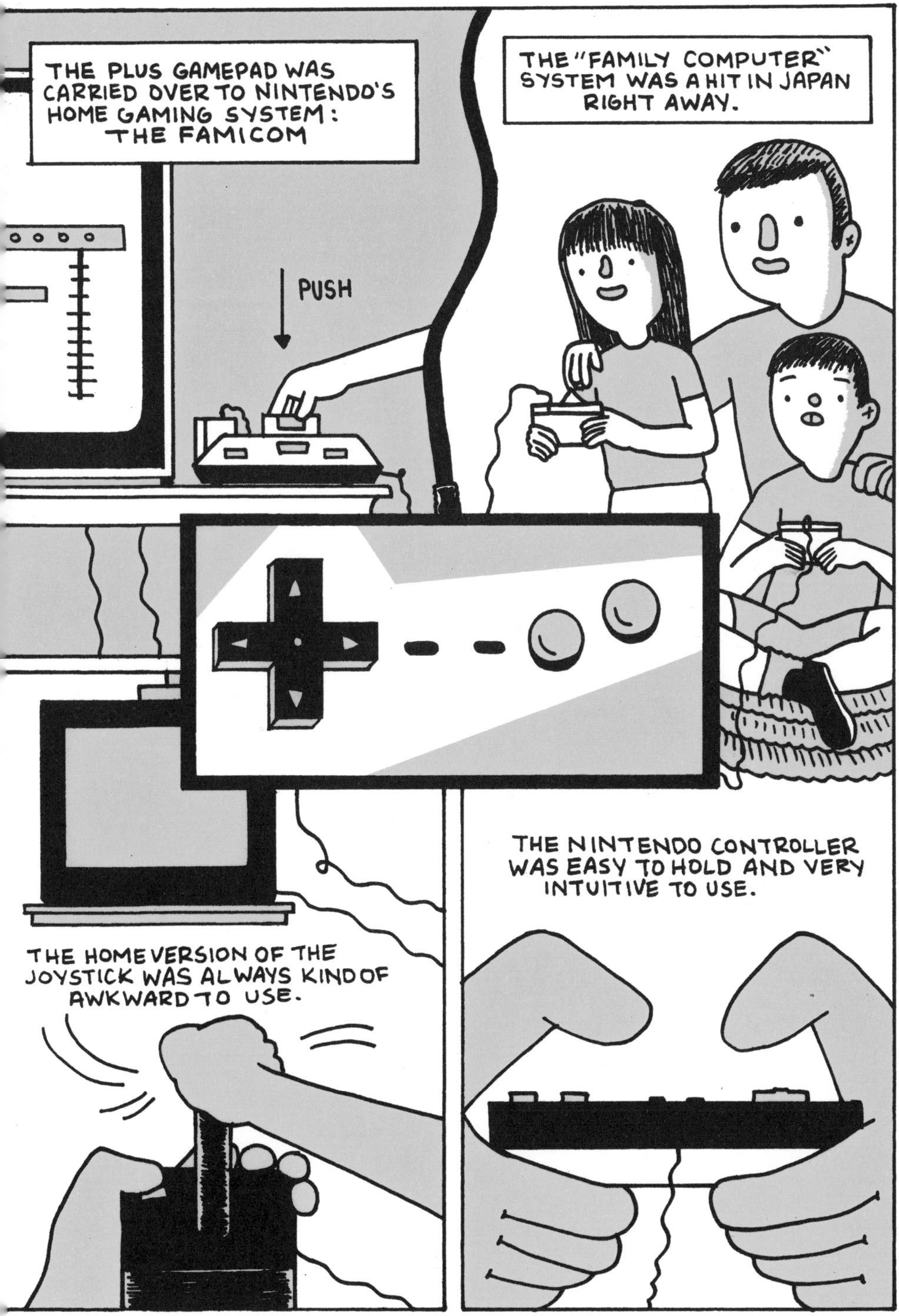
THE PLUS GAMEPAD WAS CARRIED OVER TO NINTENDO'S HOME GAMING SYSTEM: THE FAMICOM
PUSH
THE "FAMILY COMPUTER" SYSTEM WAS A HIT IN JAPAN RIGHT AWAY.
THE HOME VERSION OF THE JOYSTICK WAS ALWAYS KIND OF AWKWARD TO USE.
THE NINTENDO CONTROLLER WAS EASY TO HOLD AND VERY INTUITIVE TO USE.

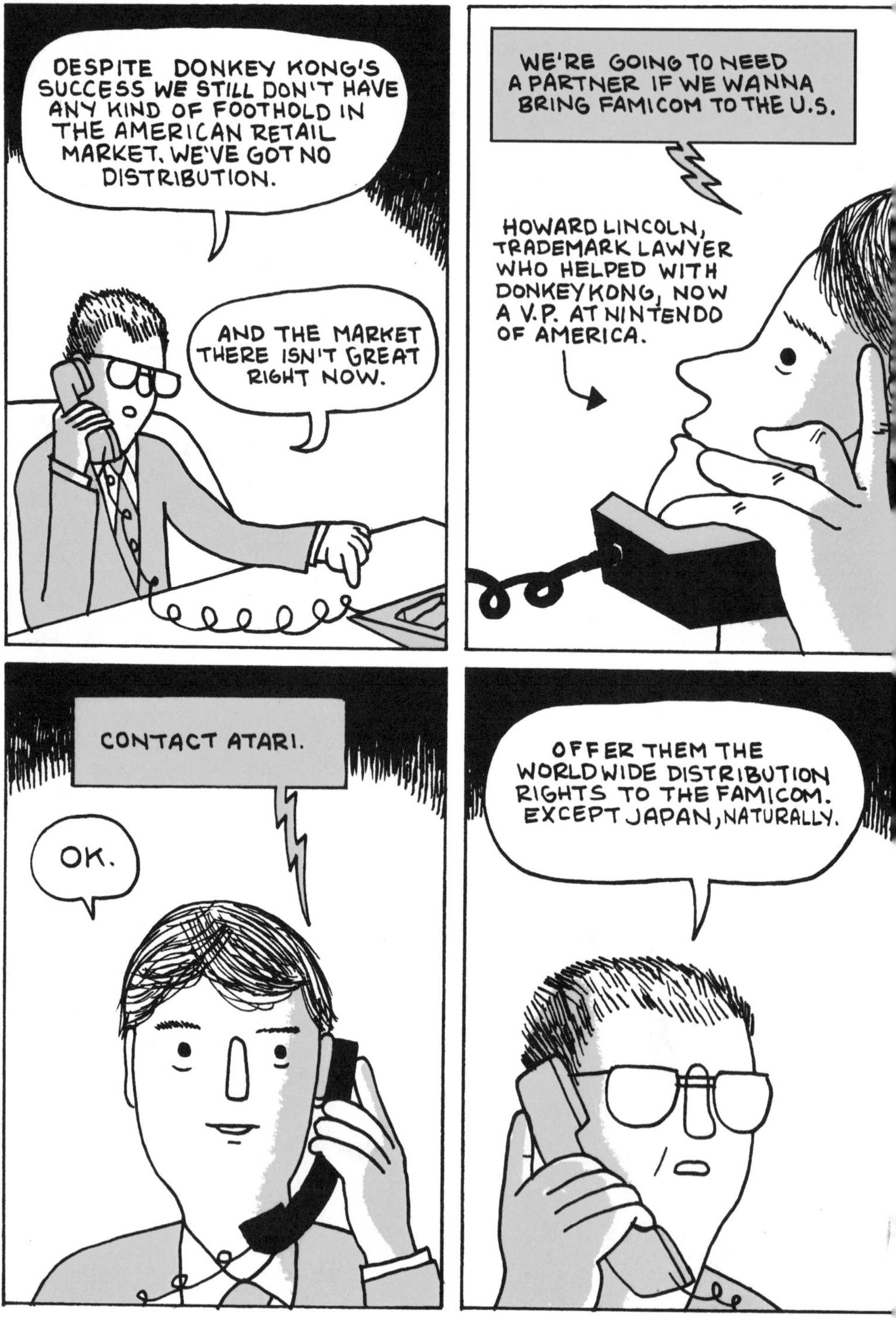
DESPITE DONKEY KONG'S SUCCESS WE STILL DON'T HAVE ANY KIND OF FOOTHOLD IN THE AMERICAN RETAIL MARKET. WE'VE GOT NO DISTRIBUTION.
AND THE MARKET THERE ISN'T GREAT RIGHT NOW.
WE'RE GOING TO NEED A PARTNER IF WE WANNA BRING FAMICOM TO THE U.S.
HOWARD LINCOLN, TRADEMARK LAWYER WHO HELPED WITH DONKEY KONG, NOW A V.P. AT NINTENDO OF AMERICA.
CONTACT ATARI.
OK.
OFFER THEM THE WORLDWIDE DISTRIBUTION RIGHTS TO THE FAMICOM. EXCEPT JAPAN, NATURALLY.

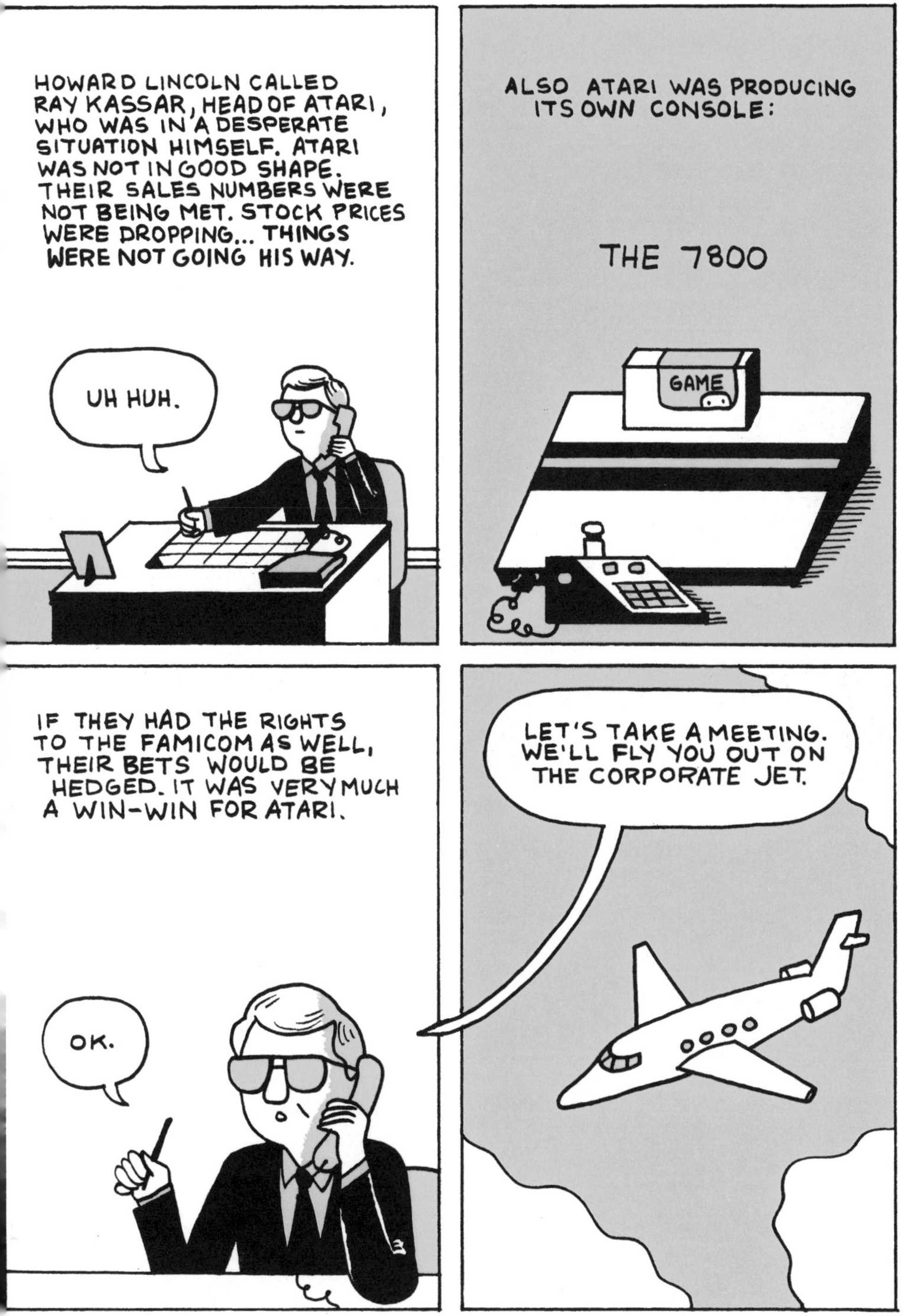
HOWARD LINCOLN CALLED RAY KASSAR, HEAD OF ATARI, WHO WAS IN A DESPERATE SITUATION HIMSELF. ATARI WAS NOT IN GOOD SHAPE. THEIR SALES NUMBERS WERE NOT BEING MET. STOCK PRICES WERE DROPPING... THINGS WERE NOT GOING HIS WAY.
UH HUH.
ALSO ATARI WAS PRODUCING ITS OWN CONSOLE:
THE 7800
GAME
IF THEY HAD THE RIGHTS TO THE FAMICOM AS WELL, THEIR BETS WOULD BE HEDGED. IT WAS VERY MUCH A WIN-WIN FOR ATARI.
OK.
LET'S TAKE A MEETING. WE'LL FLY YOU OUT ON THE CORPORATE JET.

IT WAS JUST LINCOLN AND ARAKAWA ON THE WARNER CORPORATE JET.

POACHED SALMON PÂTÉ.

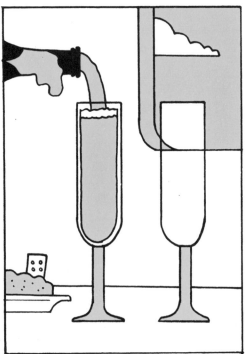

THEY'RE REALLY LAYING IT ON THICK.

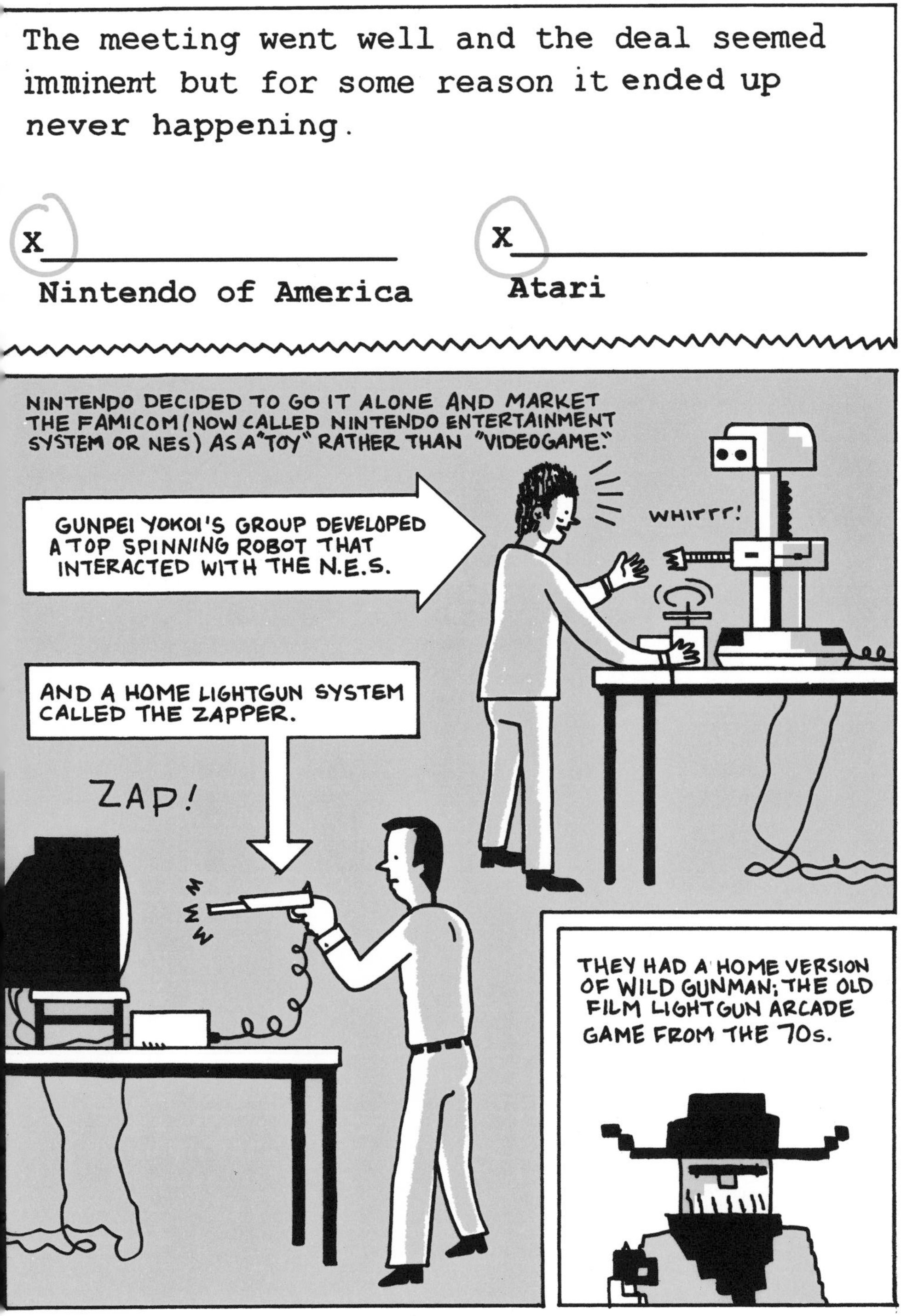
The meeting went well and the deal seemed imminent but for some reason it ended up never happening.
X
Nintendo of America
X
Atari
NINTENDO DECIDED TO GO IT ALONE AND MARKET THE FAMICOM (NOW CALLED NINTENDO ENTERTAINMENT SYSTEM OR NES) AS A "TOY" RATHER THAN "VIDEOGAME."
GUNPEI YOKOI'S GROUP DEVELOPED A TOP SPINNING ROBOT THAT INTERACTED WITH THE N.E.S.
WHIrrr!
AND A HOME LIGHTGUN SYSTEM CALLED THE ZAPPER.
ZAP!
THEY HAD A HOME VERSION OF WILD GUNMAN; THE OLD FILM LIGHTGUN ARCADE GAME FROM THE 70s.

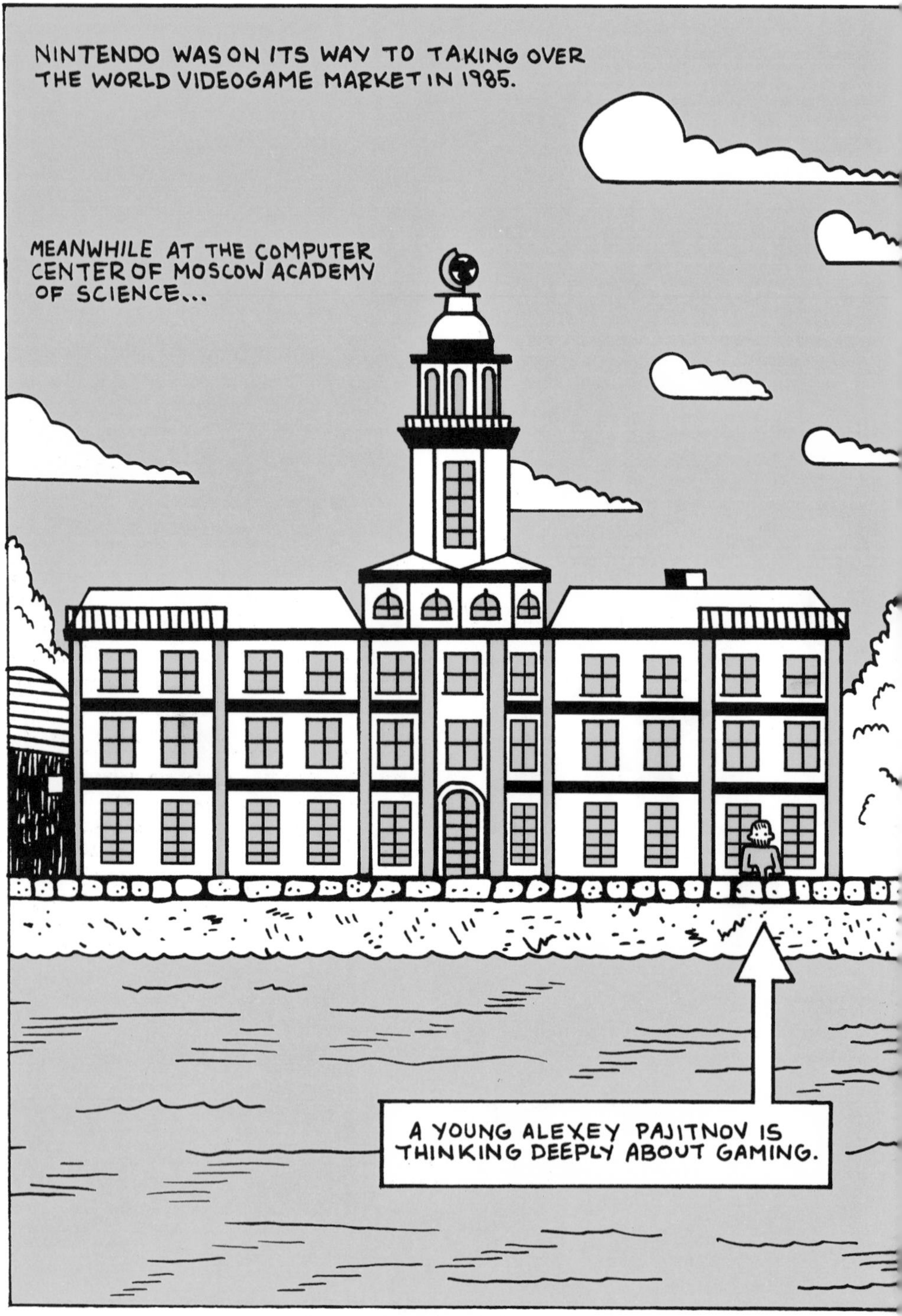
NINTENDO WAS ON ITS WAY TO TAKING OVER THE WORLD VIDEOGAME MARKET IN 1985.
MEANWHILE AT THE COMPUTER CENTER OF MOSCOW ACADEMY OF SCIENCE...
A YOUNG ALEXEY PAJITNOV IS THINKING DEEPLY ABOUT GAMING.

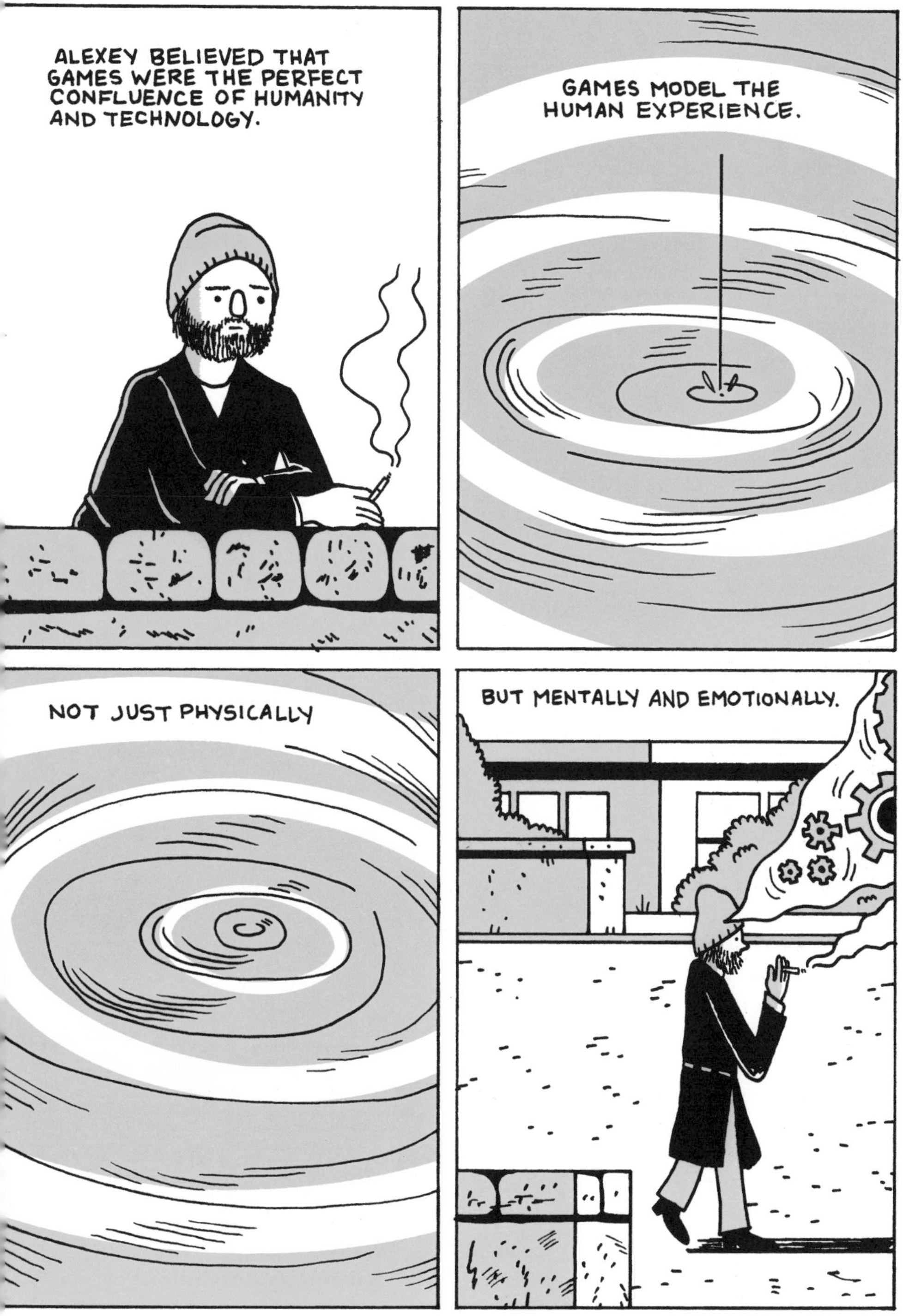
ALEXEY BELIEVED THAT GAMES WERE THE PERFECT CONFLUENCE OF HUMANITY AND TECHNOLOGY.
GAMES MODEL THE HUMAN EXPERIENCE.
NOT JUST PHYSICALLY
BUT MENTALLY AND EMOTIONALLY.

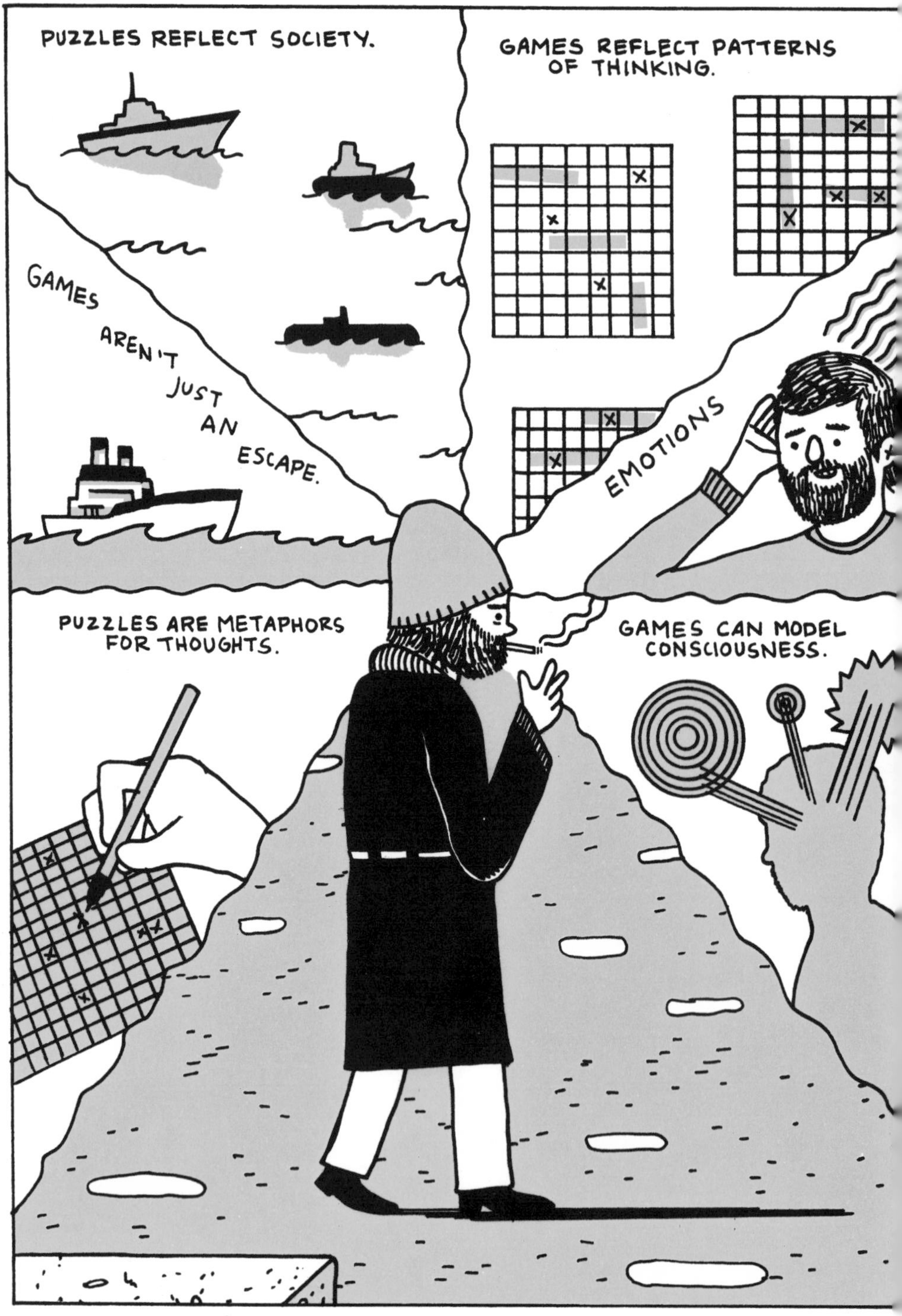
PUZZLES REFLECT SOCIETY.
GAMES AREN'T JUST AN ESCAPE.
GAMES REFLECT PATTERNS OF THINKING.
EMOTIONS
PUZZLES ARE METAPHORS FOR THOUGHTS.
GAMES CAN MODEL CONSCIOUSNESS.

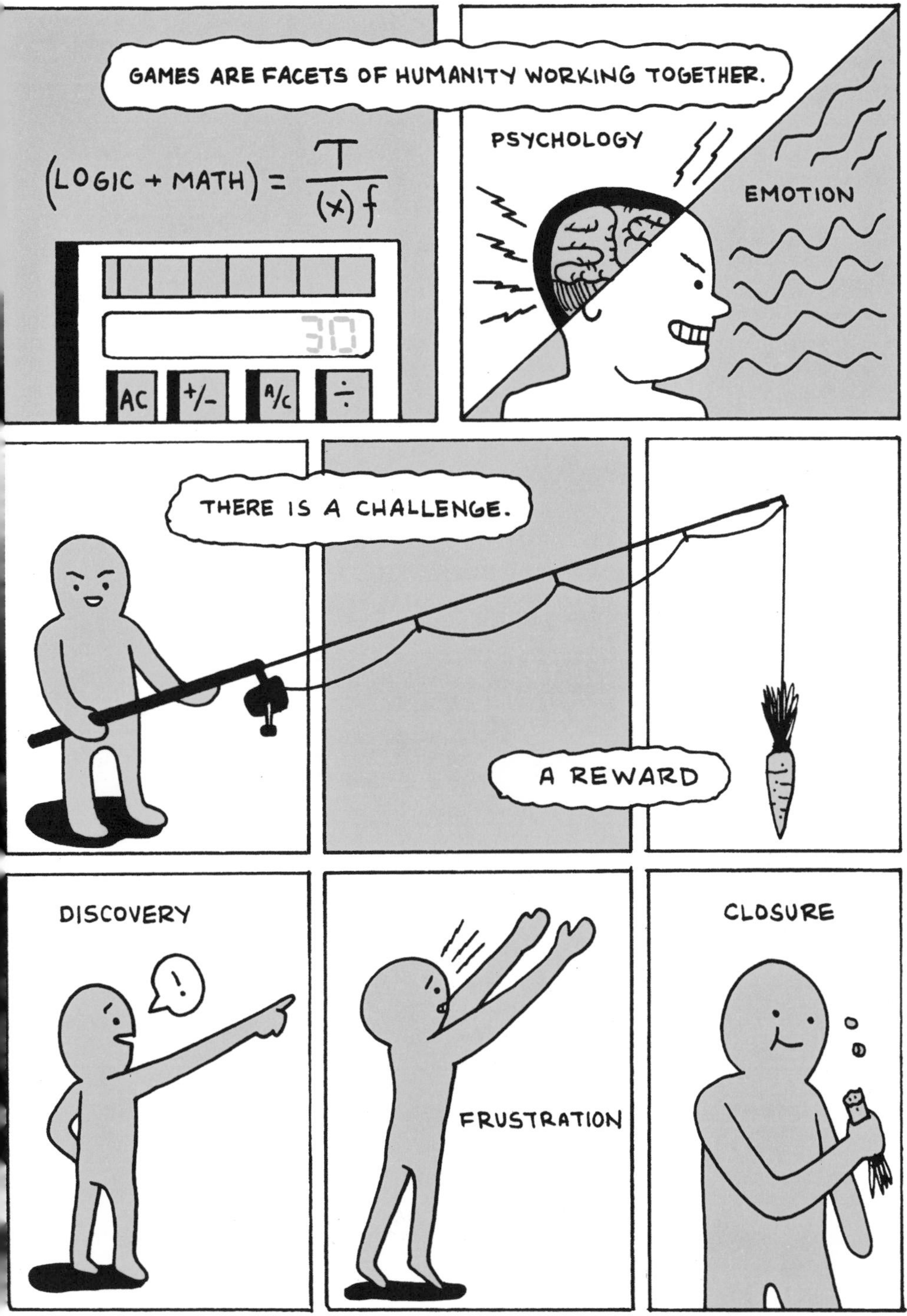
GAMES ARE FACETS OF HUMANITY WORKING TOGETHER.
(LOGIC + MATH) = T / (x) f
30
AC
+/-
A/C
÷
PSYCHOLOGY
EMOTION
THERE IS A CHALLENGE.
A REWARD
DISCOVERY
!
FRUSTRATION
CLOSURE

ALEXEY WORKED ON AN ELECTRONIKA 60
MOSTLY USING A MATHEMATICS PROGRAM.

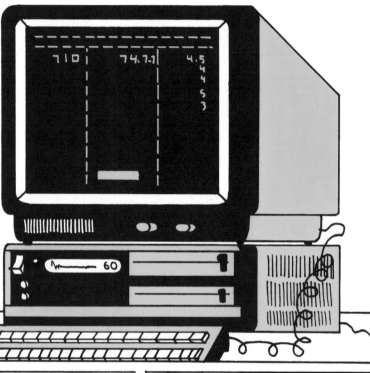

SPECS

SPEED:
250,000
OPERATIONS
PER SECOND

RAM: 8KB

NO GRAPHICS
CAPABILITIES

HIS JOB WAS TO CREATE
ARTIFICIAL INTELLIGENCE AND
VOICE RECOGNITION SOFTWARE.

HIS PREDECESSORS SENT
SPUTNIK INTO ORBIT.

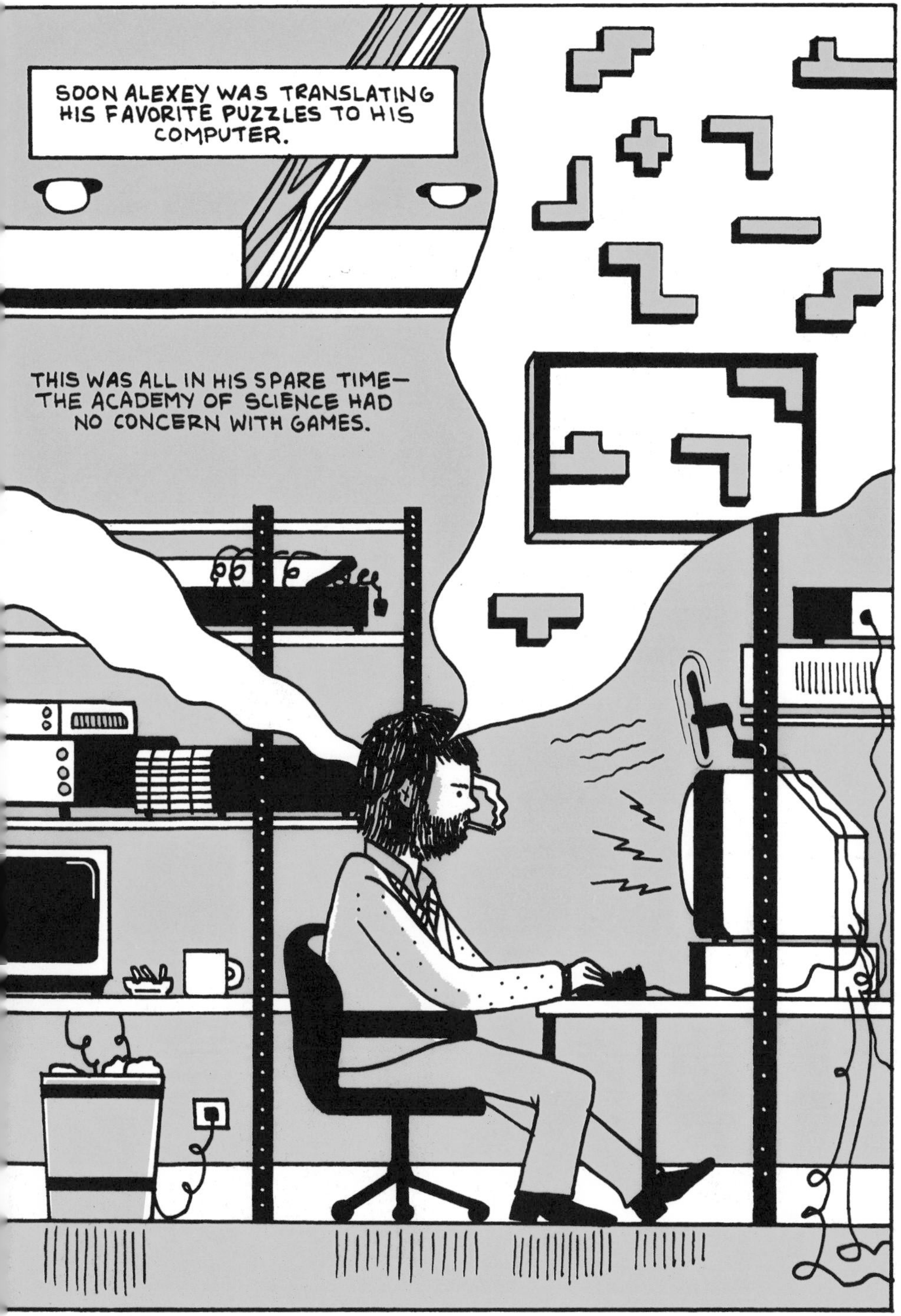
SOON ALEXEY WAS TRANSLATING HIS FAVORITE PUZZLES TO HIS COMPUTER.
THIS WAS ALL IN HIS SPARE TIME— THE ACADEMY OF SCIENCE HAD NO CONCERN WITH GAMES.

ALEXEY WAS THINKING ABOUT A PUZZLE HE LOVED.

IT WAS A DECEPTIVELY SIMPLE GAME CALLED PENTOMINOES.

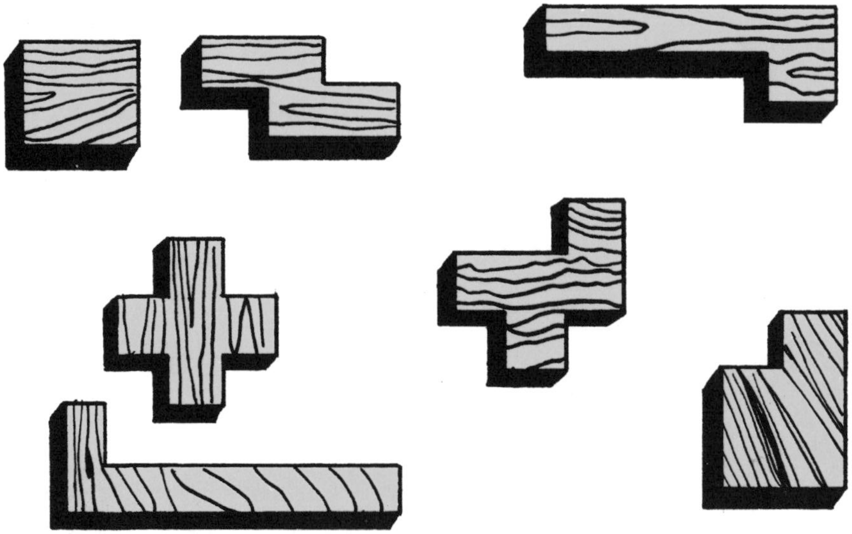

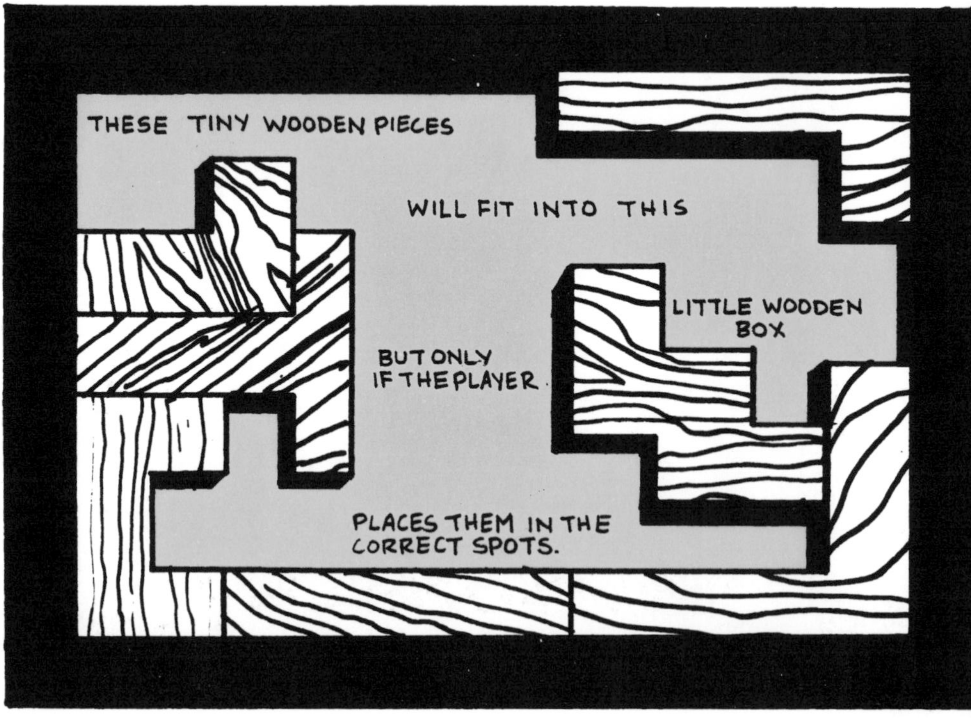
THESE TINY WOODEN PIECES
WILL FIT INTO THIS
LITTLE WOODEN BOX
BUT ONLY IF THE PLAYER
PLACES THEM IN THE CORRECT SPOTS.

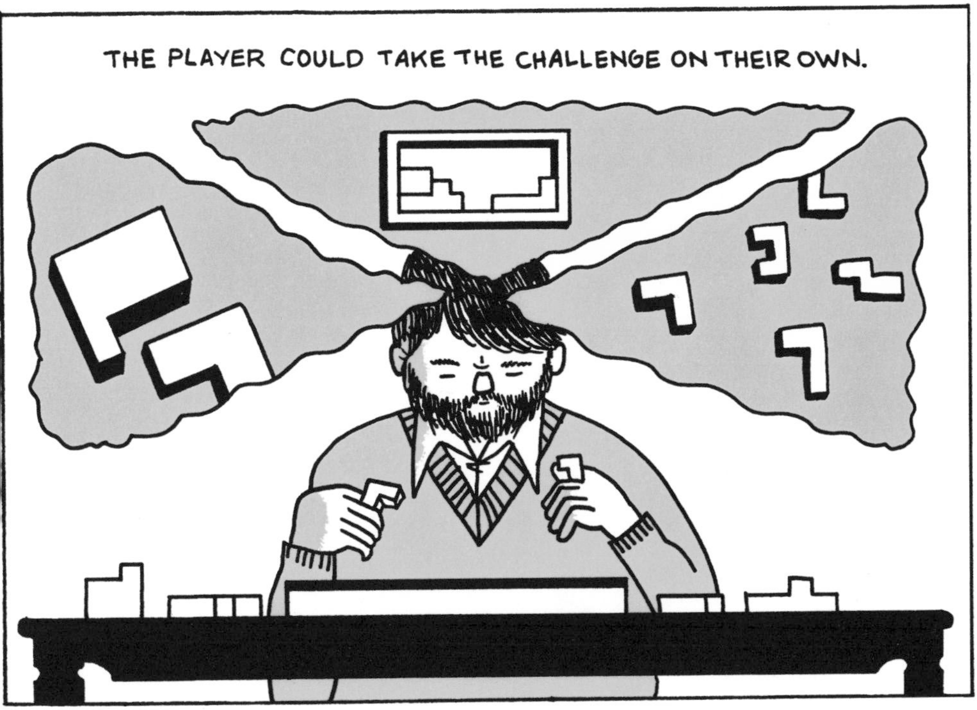
THE PLAYER COULD TAKE THE CHALLENGE ON THEIR OWN.

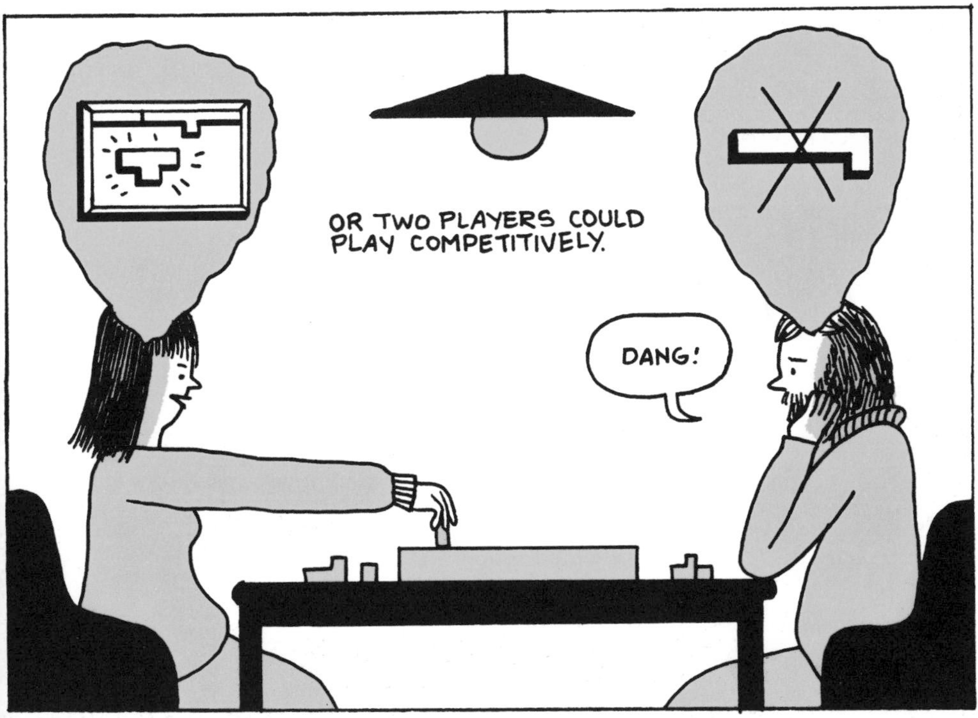
OR TWO PLAYERS COULD PLAY COMPETITIVELY.
DANG!

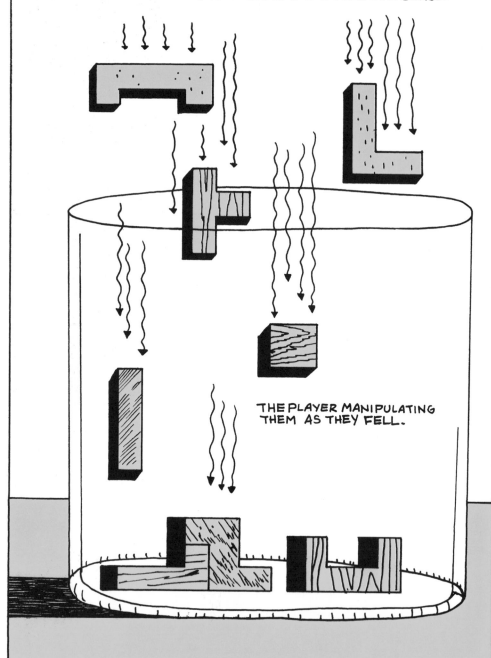

ALEXEY IMAGINED THE PENTOMINOES FALLING FROM THE SKY AND BEING COLLECTED IN A GLASS.

THE PLAYER MANIPULATING THEM AS THEY FELL.

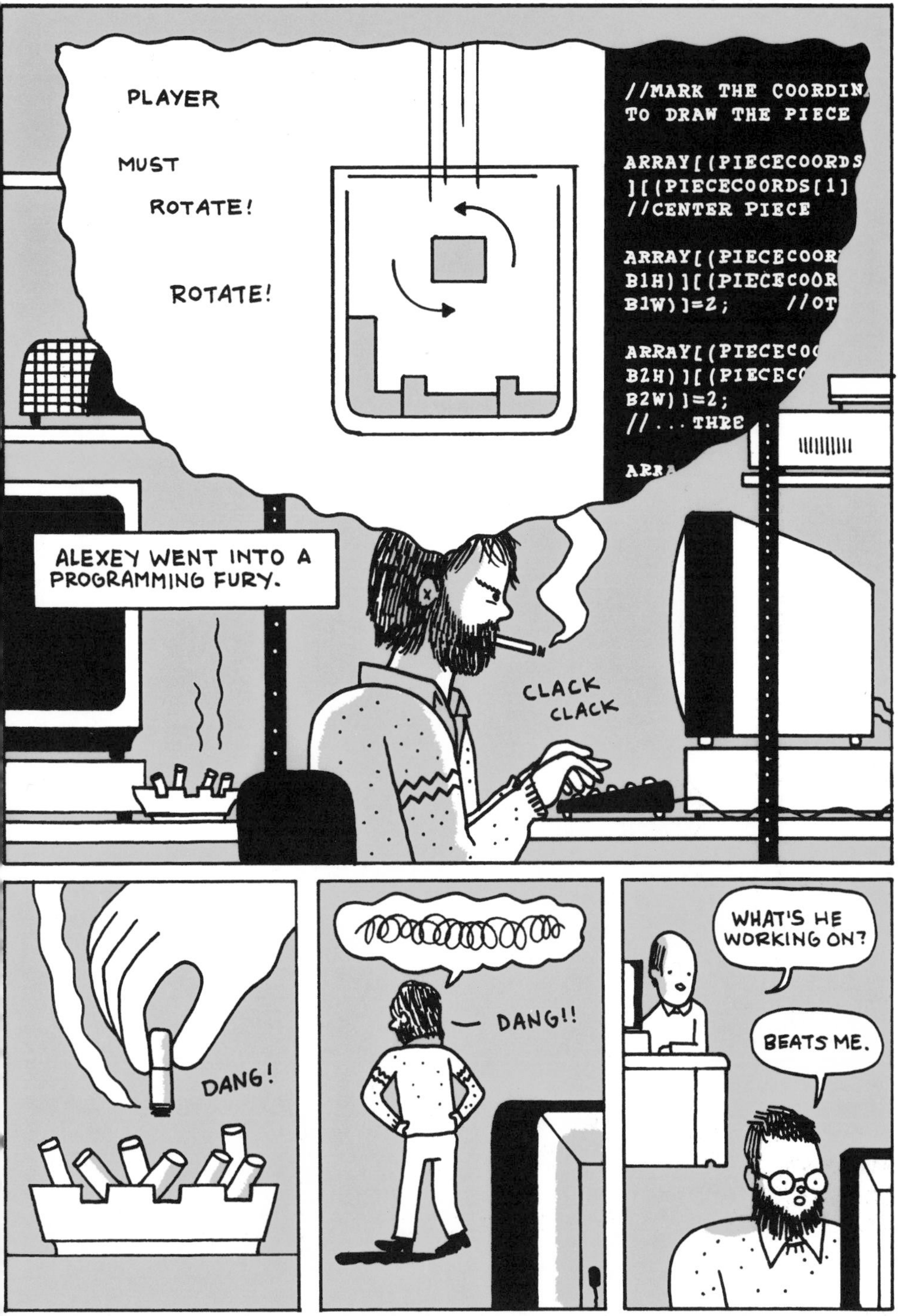
PLAYER
MUST
ROTATE!
ROTATE!
//MARK THE COORDIN
TO DRAW THE PIECE
ARRAY[(PIECECOORDS
][(PIECECOORDS[1]
//CENTER PIECE
ARRAY[(PIECECOOR
B1H)][(PIECECOOR
B1W)]=2; //OT
ARRAY[(PIECECO
B2H)][(PIECEC
B2W)]=2;
//...THRE
ARR
ALEXEY WENT INTO A PROGRAMMING FURY.
CLACK
CLACK
DANG!
DANG!!
WHAT'S HE WORKING ON?
BEATS ME.

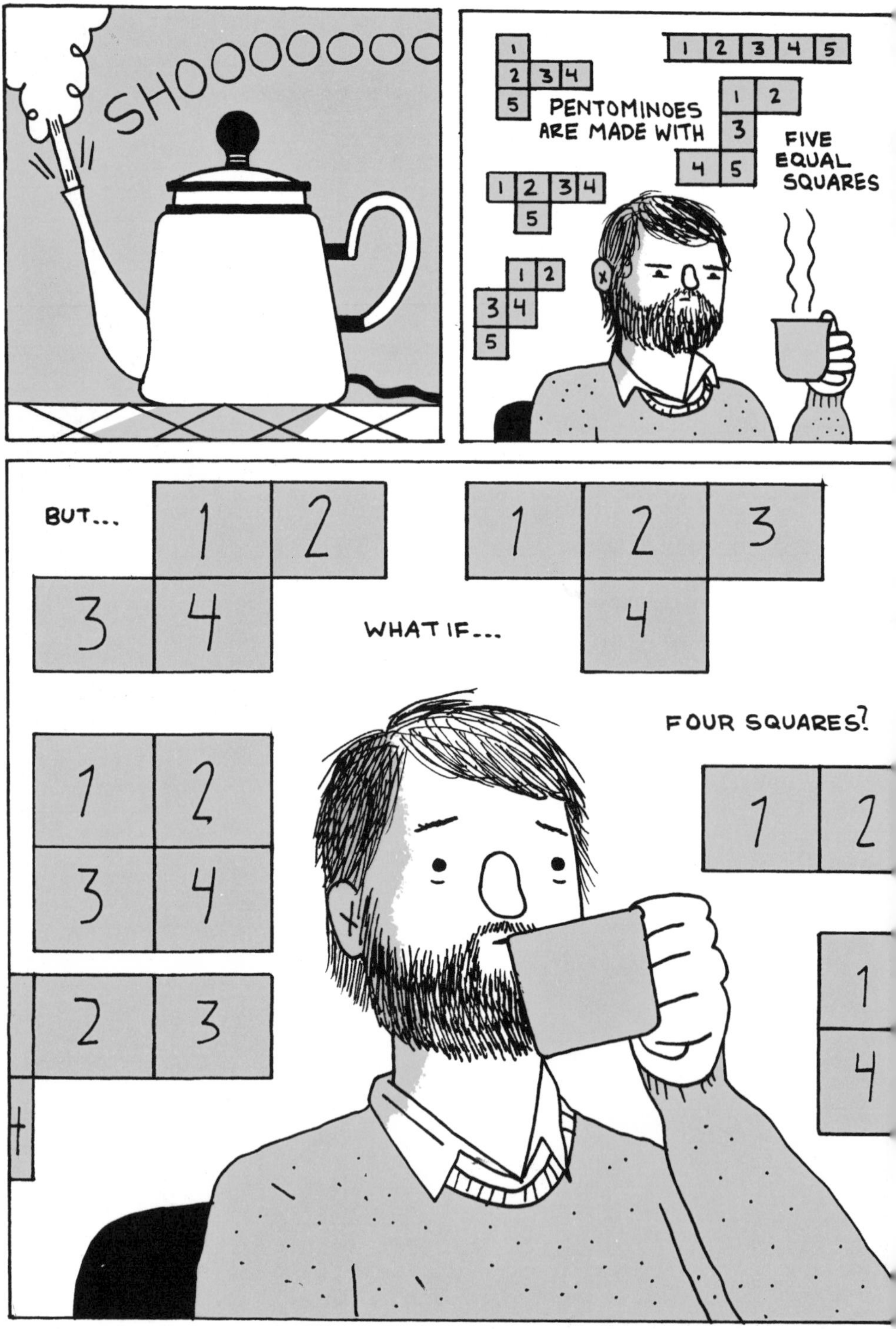
SHOOOOOOO
PENTOMINOES ARE MADE WITH
FIVE EQUAL SQUARES
BUT...
WHAT IF...
FOUR SQUARES?

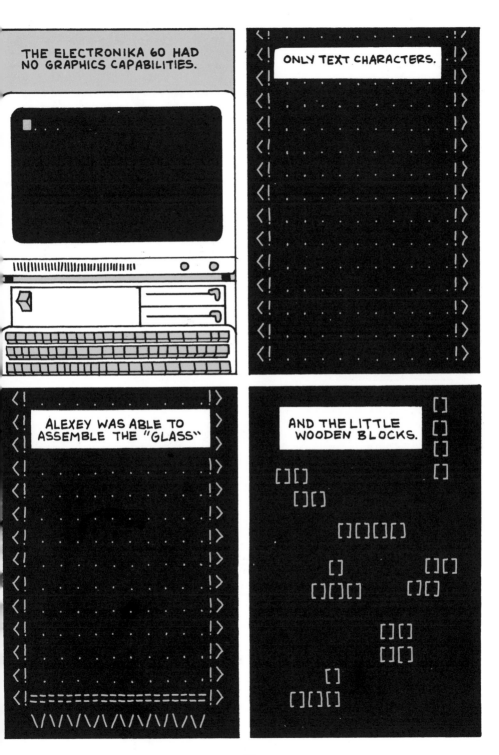

THE ELECTRONIKA 60 HAD NO GRAPHICS CAPABILITIES.

ONLY TEXT CHARACTERS.

ALEXEY WAS ABLE TO ASSEMBLE THE "GLASS"

AND THE LITTLE WOODEN BLOCKS.

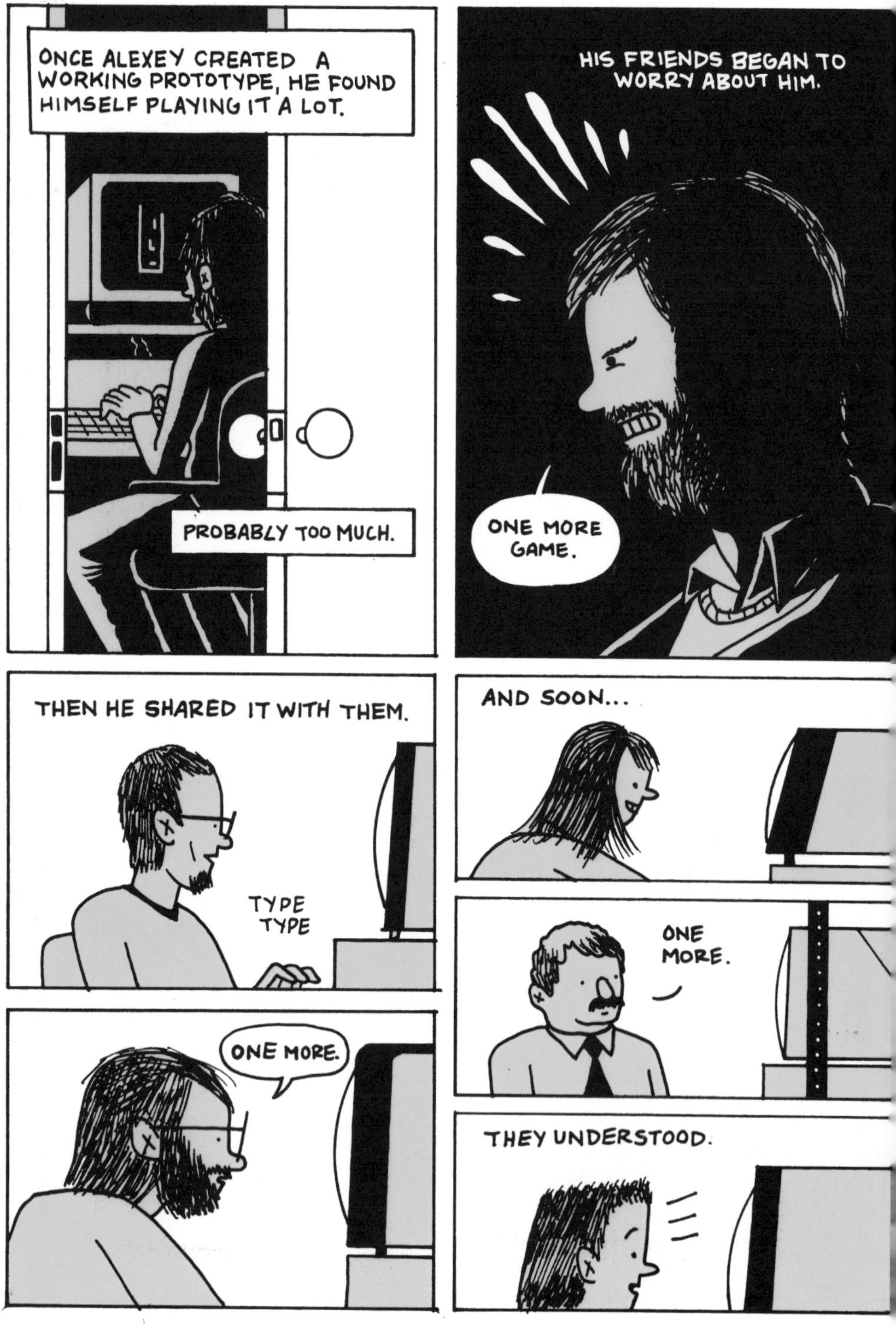
ONCE ALEXEY CREATED A WORKING PROTOTYPE, HE FOUND HIMSELF PLAYING IT A LOT.
PROBABLY TOO MUCH.
HIS FRIENDS BEGAN TO WORRY ABOUT HIM.
ONE MORE GAME.
THEN HE SHARED IT WITH THEM.
TYPE TYPE
ONE MORE.
AND SOON...
ONE MORE.
THEY UNDERSTOOD.

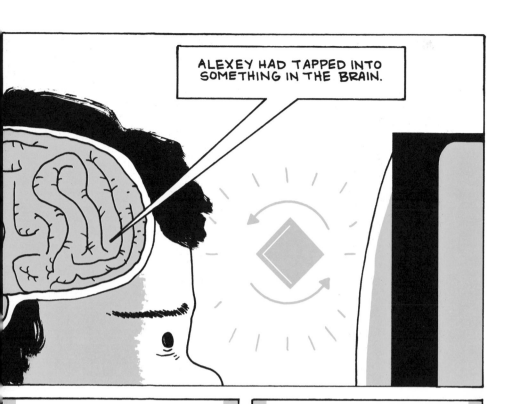

ALEXEY HAD TAPPED INTO SOMETHING IN THE BRAIN.

THE NATURE OF THE GAMEPLAY CAUSES THE PLAYER'S PRE-FRONTAL CORTEX TO BE STIMULATED CONSTANTLY.

LINE CLEARED!

PEOPLE REMAINED MOTIVATED TO CONTINUE TO PLAY ON AND ON.

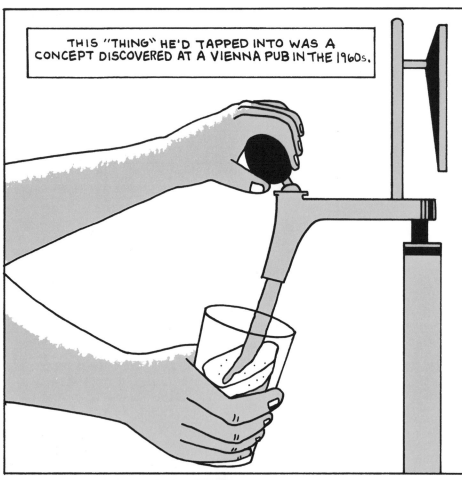

THIS "THING" HE'D TAPPED INTO WAS A CONCEPT DISCOVERED AT A VIENNA PUB IN THE 1960s.

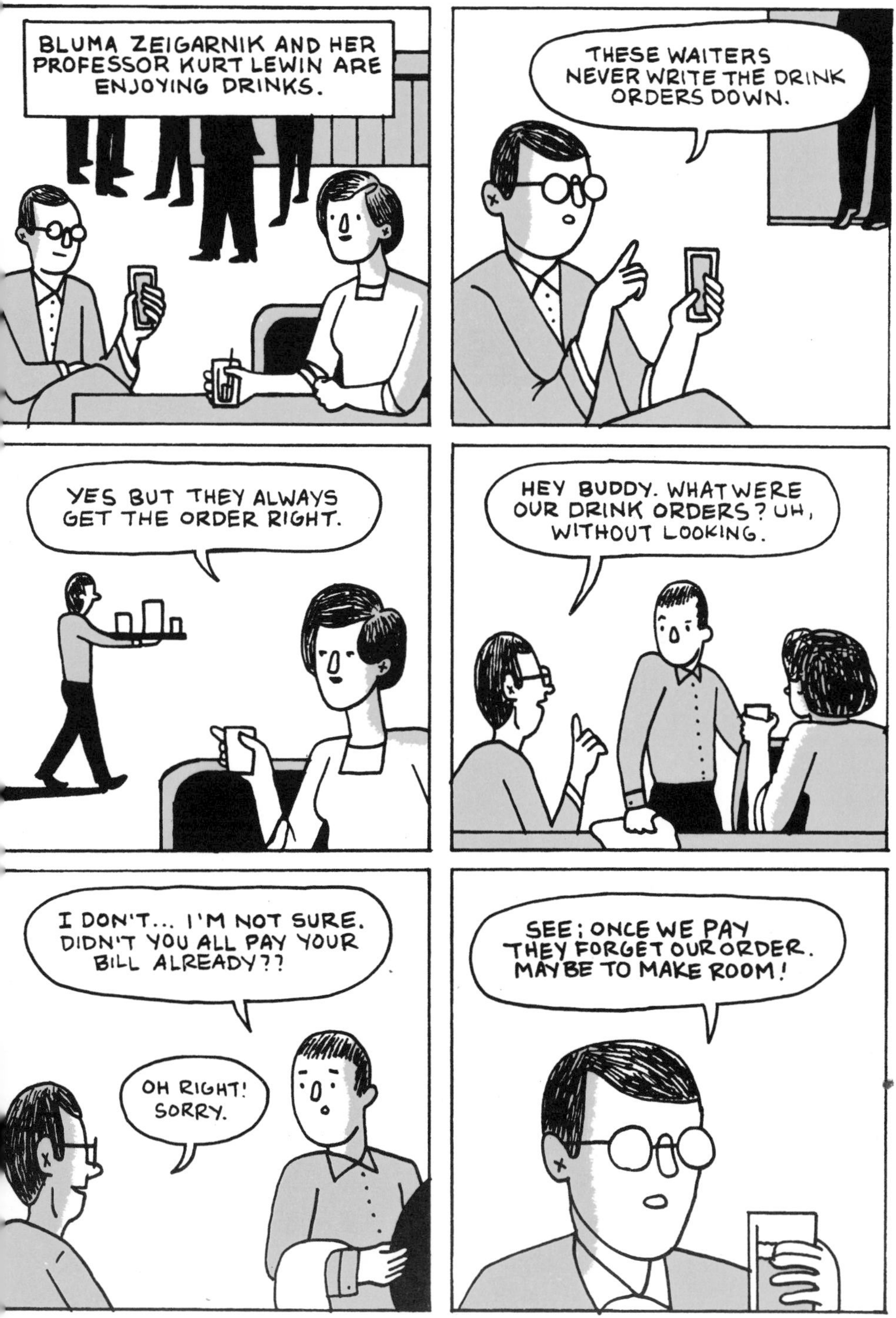
BLUMA ZEIGARNIK AND HER PROFESSOR KURT LEWIN ARE ENJOYING DRINKS.
THESE WAITERS NEVER WRITE THE DRINK ORDERS DOWN.
YES BUT THEY ALWAYS GET THE ORDER RIGHT.
HEY BUDDY. WHAT WERE OUR DRINK ORDERS? UH, WITHOUT LOOKING.
I DON'T... I'M NOT SURE. DIDN'T YOU ALL PAY YOUR BILL ALREADY??
OH RIGHT! SORRY.
SEE; ONCE WE PAY THEY FORGET OUR ORDER. MAYBE TO MAKE ROOM!

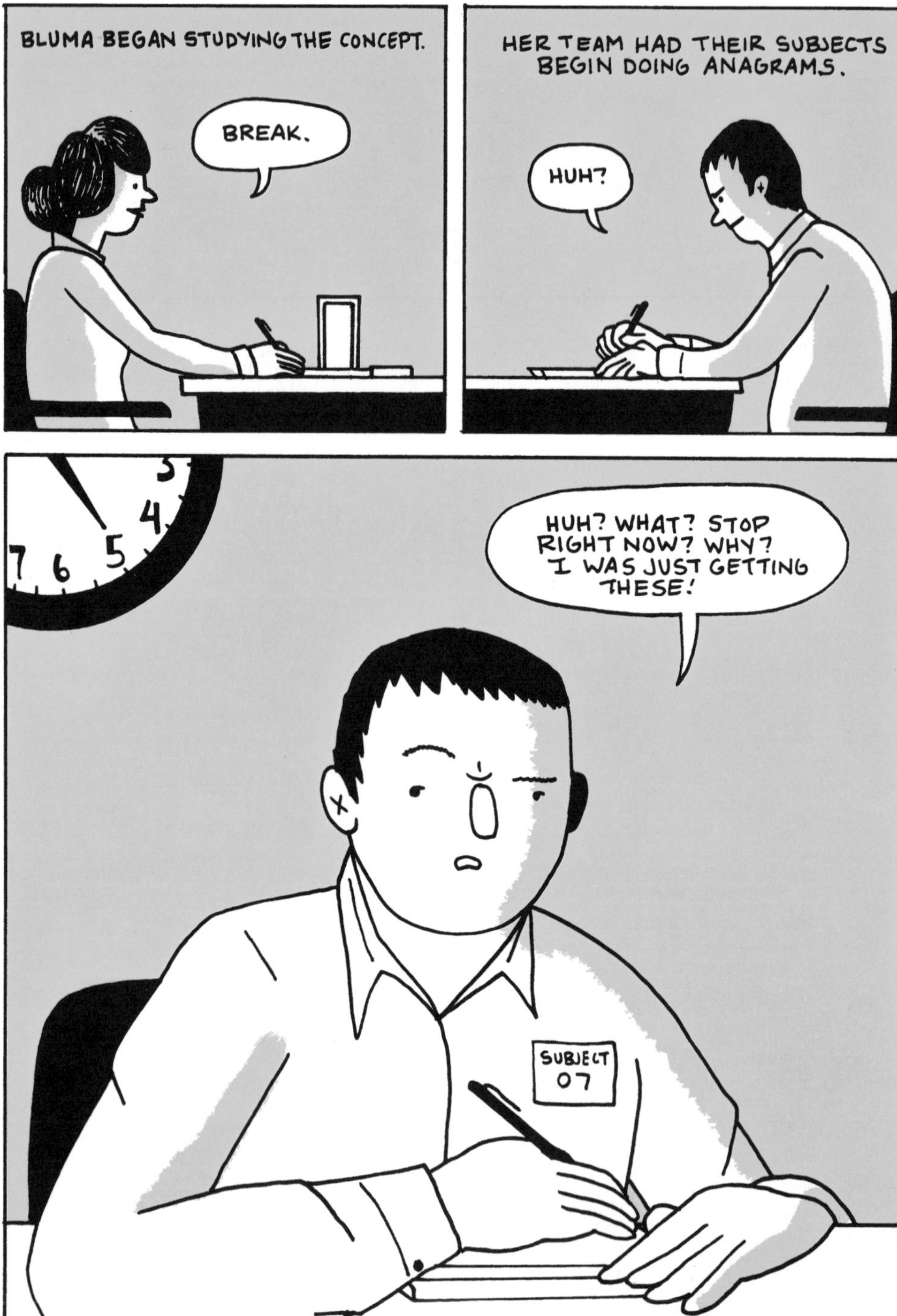
BLUMA BEGAN STUDYING THE CONCEPT.
BREAK.
HER TEAM HAD THEIR SUBJECTS BEGIN DOING ANAGRAMS.
HUH?
HUH? WHAT? STOP RIGHT NOW? WHY? I WAS JUST GETTING THESE!
SUBJECT 07

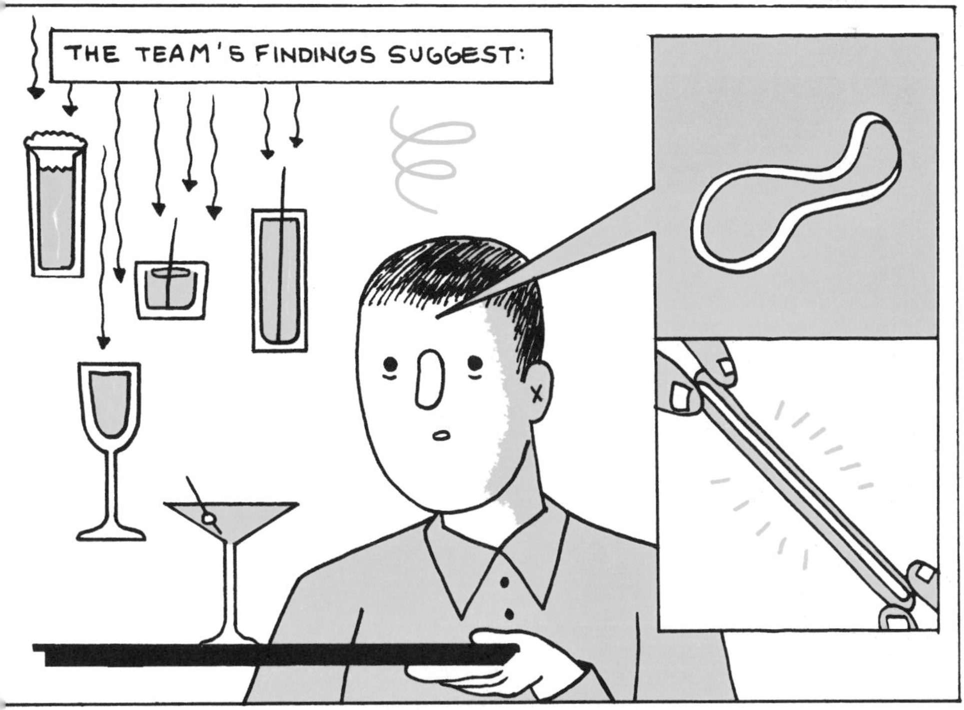
THE TEAM'S FINDINGS SUGGEST:

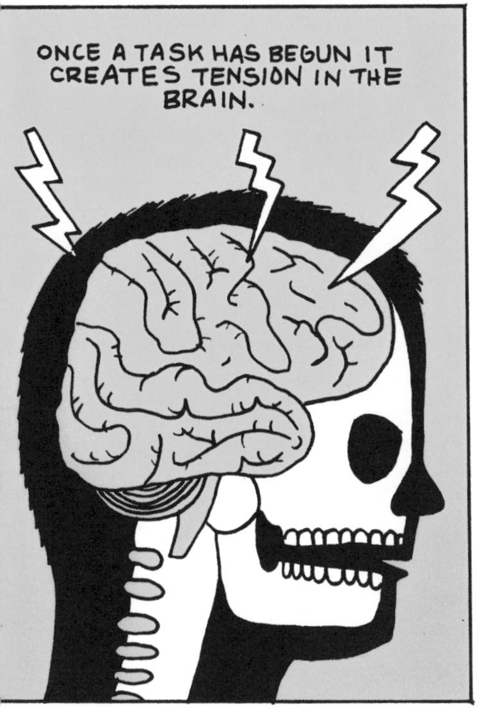
ONCE A TASK HAS BEGUN IT CREATES TENSION IN THE BRAIN.

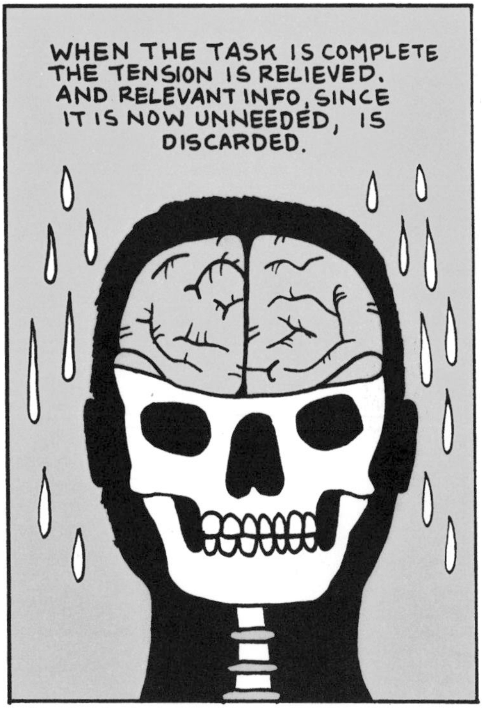
WHEN THE TASK IS COMPLETE THE TENSION IS RELIEVED. AND RELEVANT INFO, SINCE IT IS NOW UNNEEDED, IS DISCARDED.

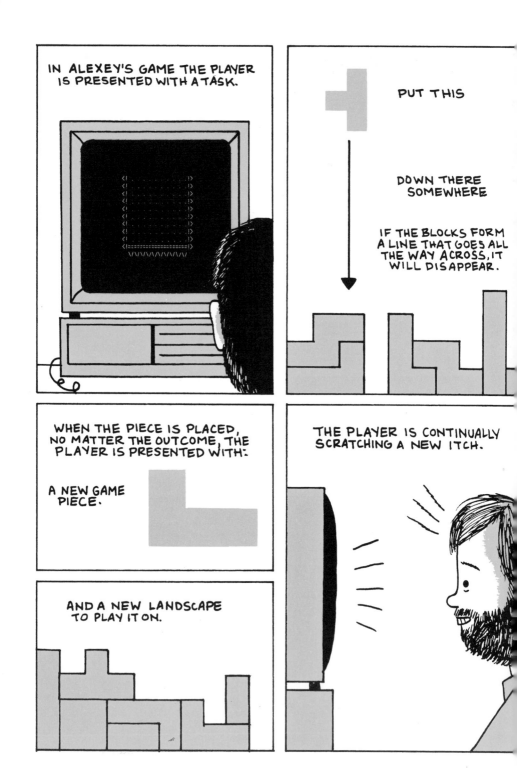

IN ALEXEY'S GAME THE PLAYER IS PRESENTED WITH A TASK.

PUT THIS

DOWN THERE SOMEWHERE

IF THE BLOCKS FORM A LINE THAT GOES ALL THE WAY ACROSS, IT WILL DISAPPEAR.

WHEN THE PIECE IS PLACED, NO MATTER THE OUTCOME, THE PLAYER IS PRESENTED WITH:

A NEW GAME PIECE.

AND A NEW LANDSCAPE TO PLAY IT ON.

THE PLAYER IS CONTINUALLY SCRATCHING A NEW ITCH.

THE PLAYER FIRST VIEWS THE GAME PIECE.

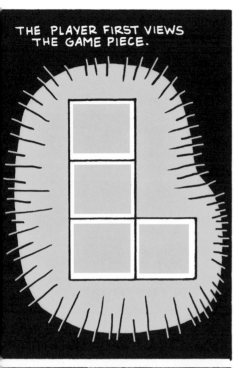

THEN THE PLAYER HAS TO VISUALIZE HOW TO ROTATE THE PIECE TO SUIT THEIR NEEDS.

BUT THIS VISUALIZATION IS ACTUALLY OCCURING ON SCREEN AT THE SAME TIME.

THE PLAYER'S BRAIN HAS TO BE IN SYNCH WITH THE GAME.

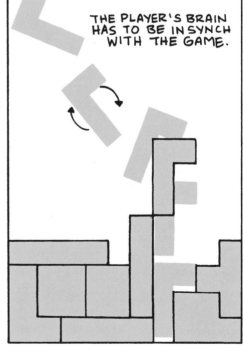

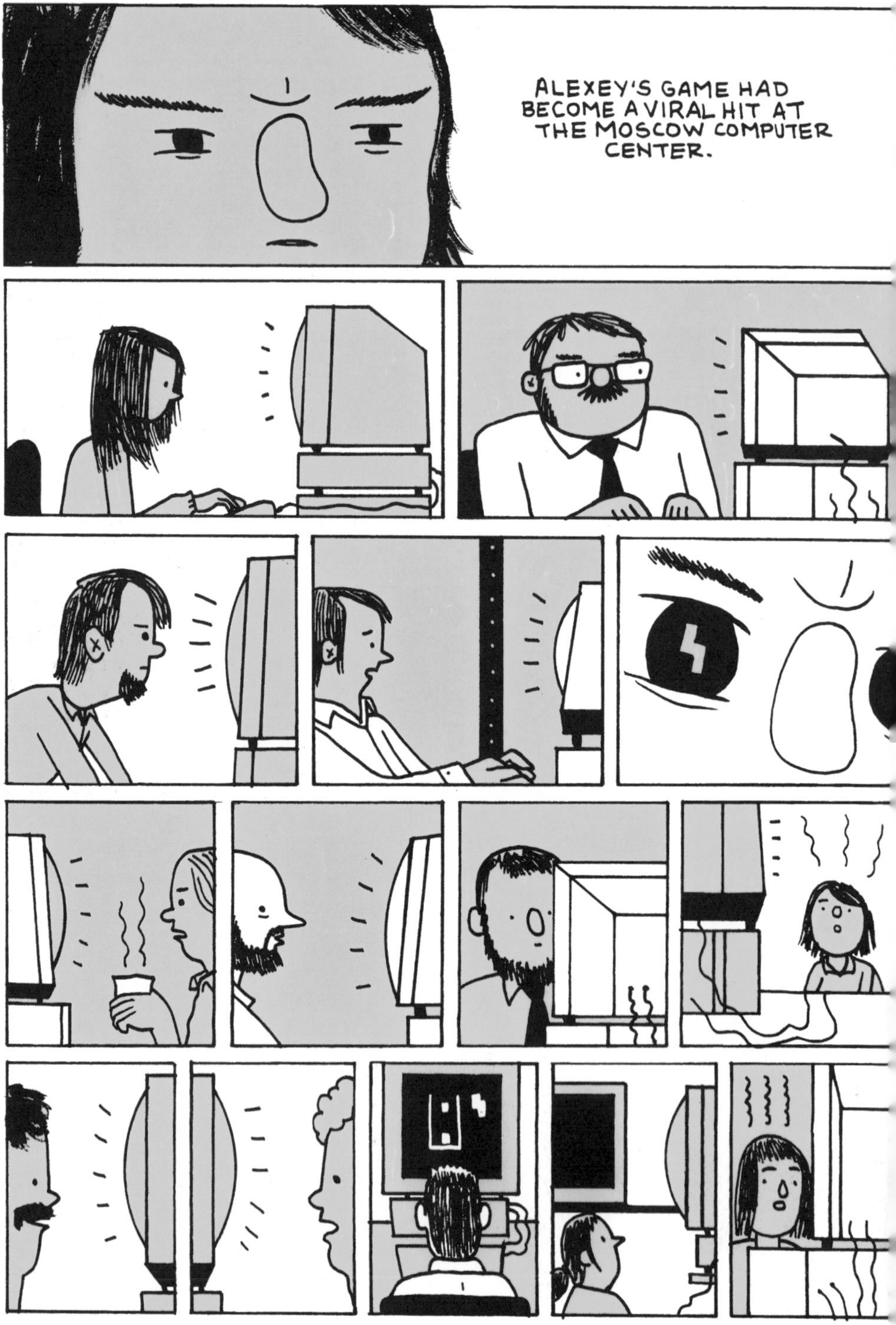
ALEXEY'S GAME HAD BECOME A VIRAL HIT AT THE MOSCOW COMPUTER CENTER.

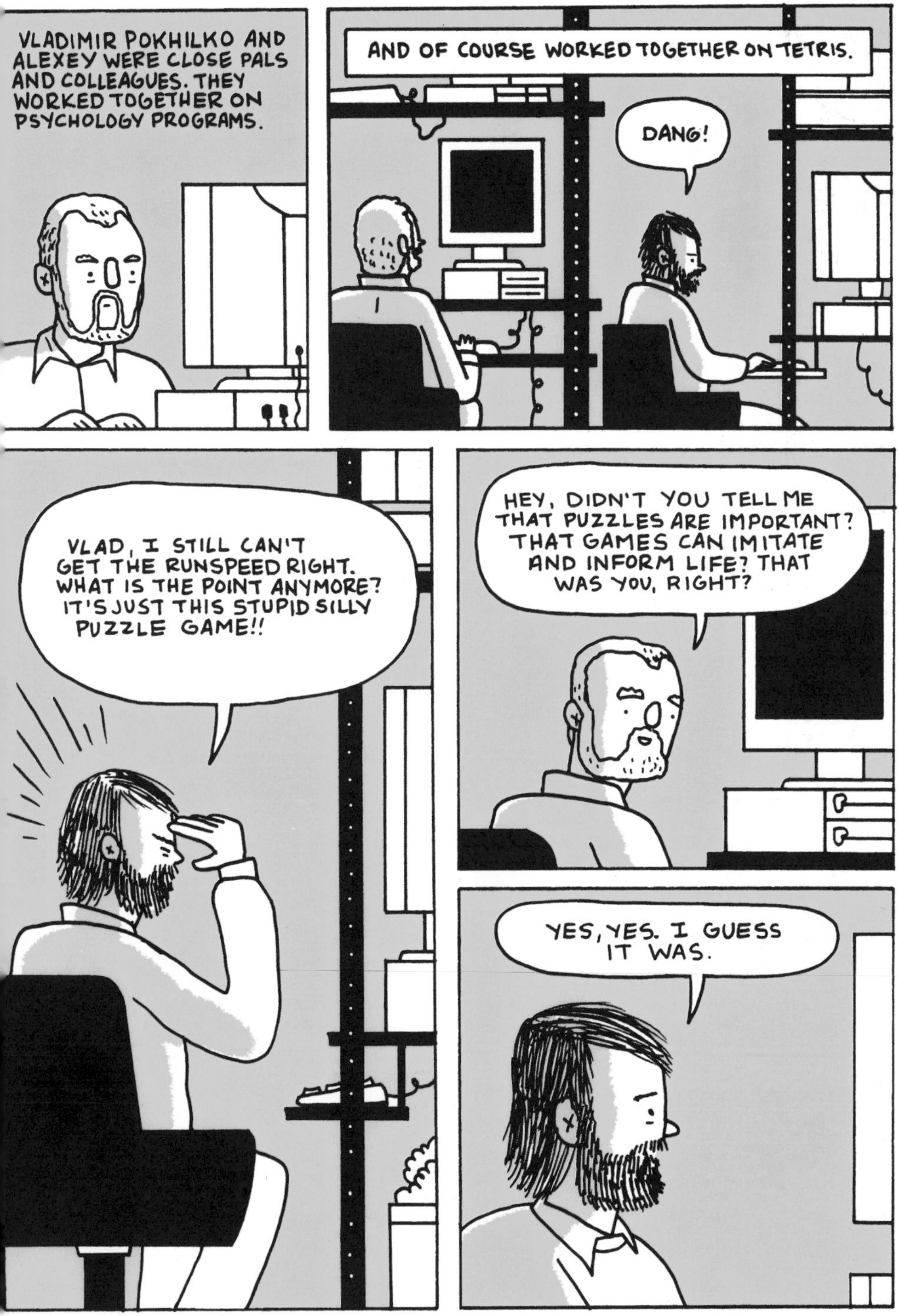
VLADIMIR POKHILKO AND ALEXEY WERE CLOSE PALS AND COLLEAGUES. THEY WORKED TOGETHER ON PSYCHOLOGY PROGRAMS.
AND OF COURSE WORKED TOGETHER ON TETRIS.
DANG!
VLAD, I STILL CAN'T GET THE RUNSPEED RIGHT. WHAT IS THE POINT ANYMORE? IT'S JUST THIS STUPID SILLY PUZZLE GAME!!
HEY, DIDN'T YOU TELL ME THAT PUZZLES ARE IMPORTANT? THAT GAMES CAN IMITATE AND INFORM LIFE? THAT WAS YOU, RIGHT?
YES, YES. I GUESS IT WAS.

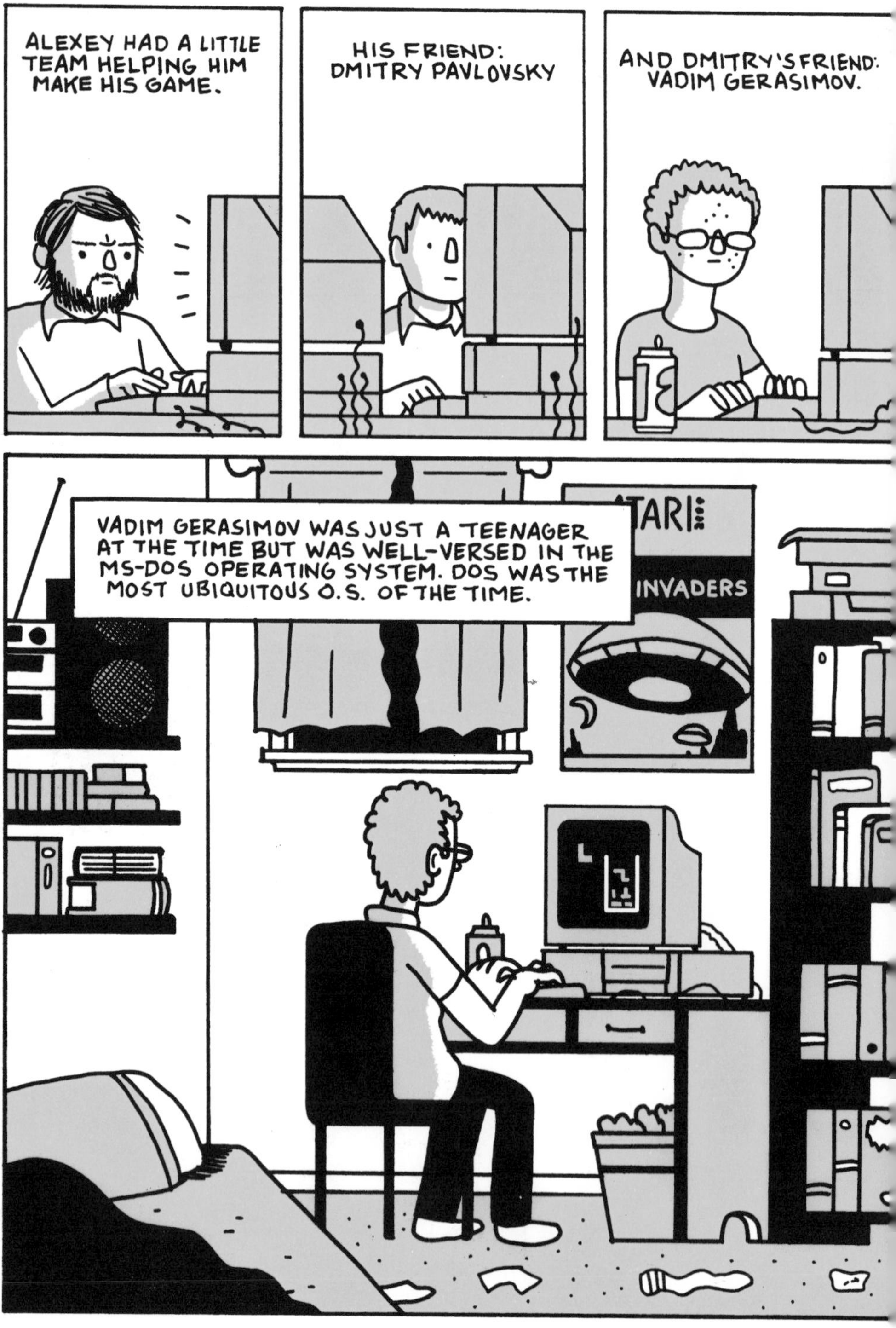
ALEXEY HAD A LITTLE TEAM HELPING HIM MAKE HIS GAME.
HIS FRIEND: DMITRY PAVLOVSKY
AND DMITRY'S FRIEND: VADIM GERASIMOV.
VADIM GERASIMOV WAS JUST A TEENAGER AT THE TIME BUT WAS WELL-VERSED IN THE MS-DOS OPERATING SYSTEM. DOS WAS THE MOST UBIQUITOUS O.S. OF THE TIME.
ATARI
INVADERS

TOGETHER THEY DEVELOPED A GRAPHICAL VERSION OF ALEXEY'S GAME THAT RAN ON MS-DOS.

THIS VERSION RAN ON THE TYPE OF COMPUTER EVERYONE USED.

THE GAME FIT ON A 5.25 INCH FLOPPY DISC.

ALEXEY'S LITTLE GAME PIECES WERE NOW CALLED "TETRAMINOES"

NAMED FOR THE FOUR LITTLE BLOCKS THAT MAKE UP EACH PIECE.

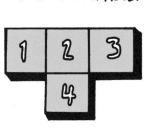

I'M CALLING THE GAME "TETRIS"!!

IT IS "TETRA" PLUS "TENNIS."

UH, OK. THAT'S A WEIRD NAME.

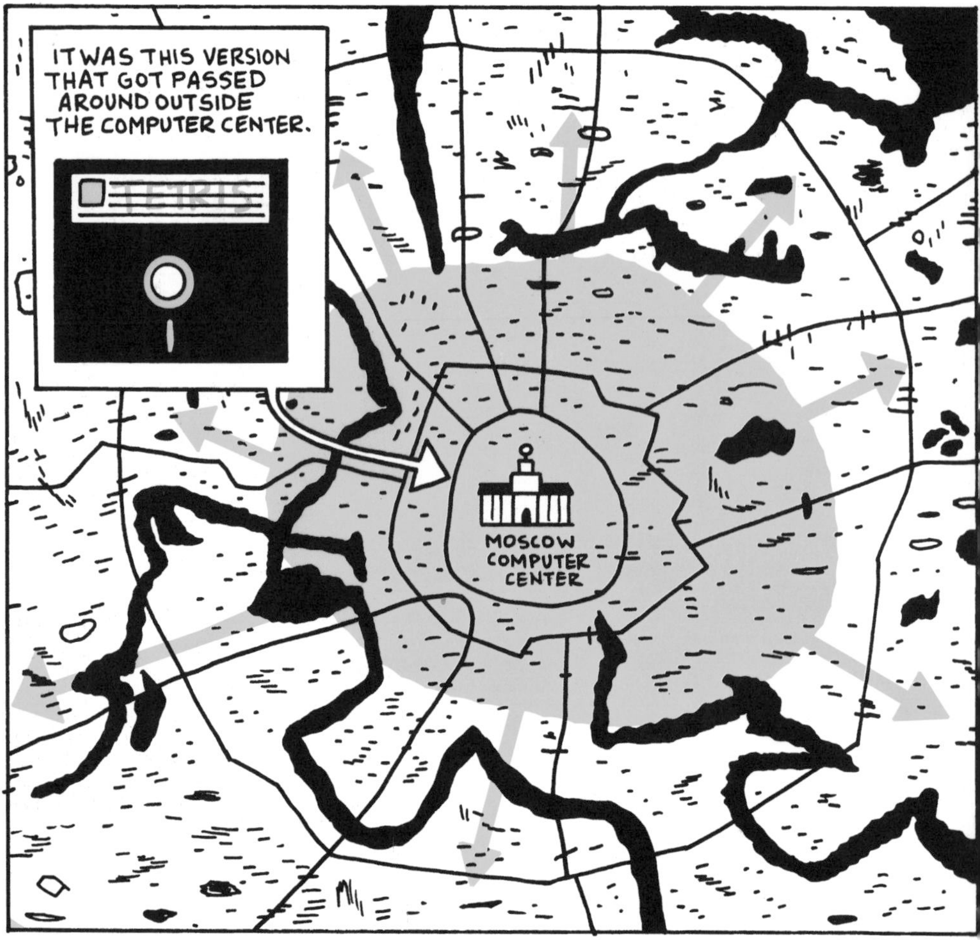
IT WAS THIS VERSION THAT GOT PASSED AROUND OUTSIDE THE COMPUTER CENTER.
TETRIS
MOSCOW COMPUTER CENTER

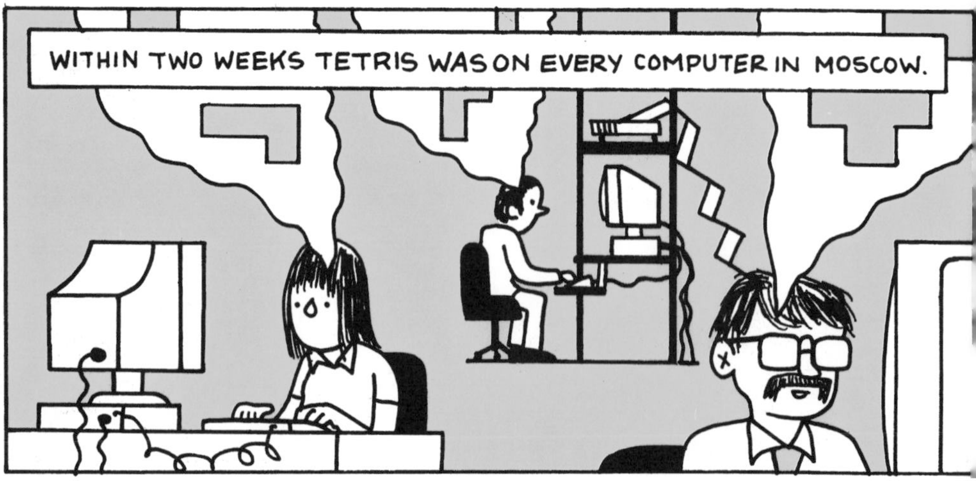
WITHIN TWO WEEKS TETRIS WAS ON EVERY COMPUTER IN MOSCOW.

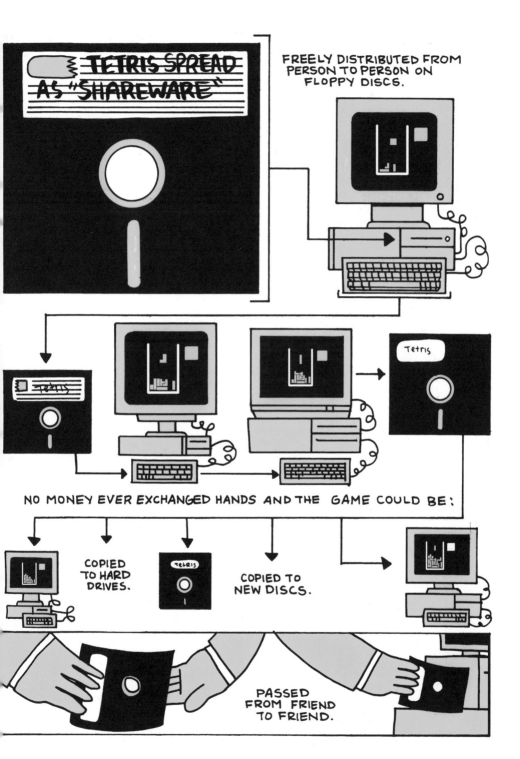

TETRIS SPREAD AS "SHAREWARE"

FREELY DISTRIBUTED FROM PERSON TO PERSON ON FLOPPY DISCS.

Tetris

NO MONEY EVER EXCHANGED HANDS AND THE GAME COULD BE:

COPIED TO HARD DRIVES.

COPIED TO NEW DISCS.

PASSED FROM FRIEND TO FRIEND.

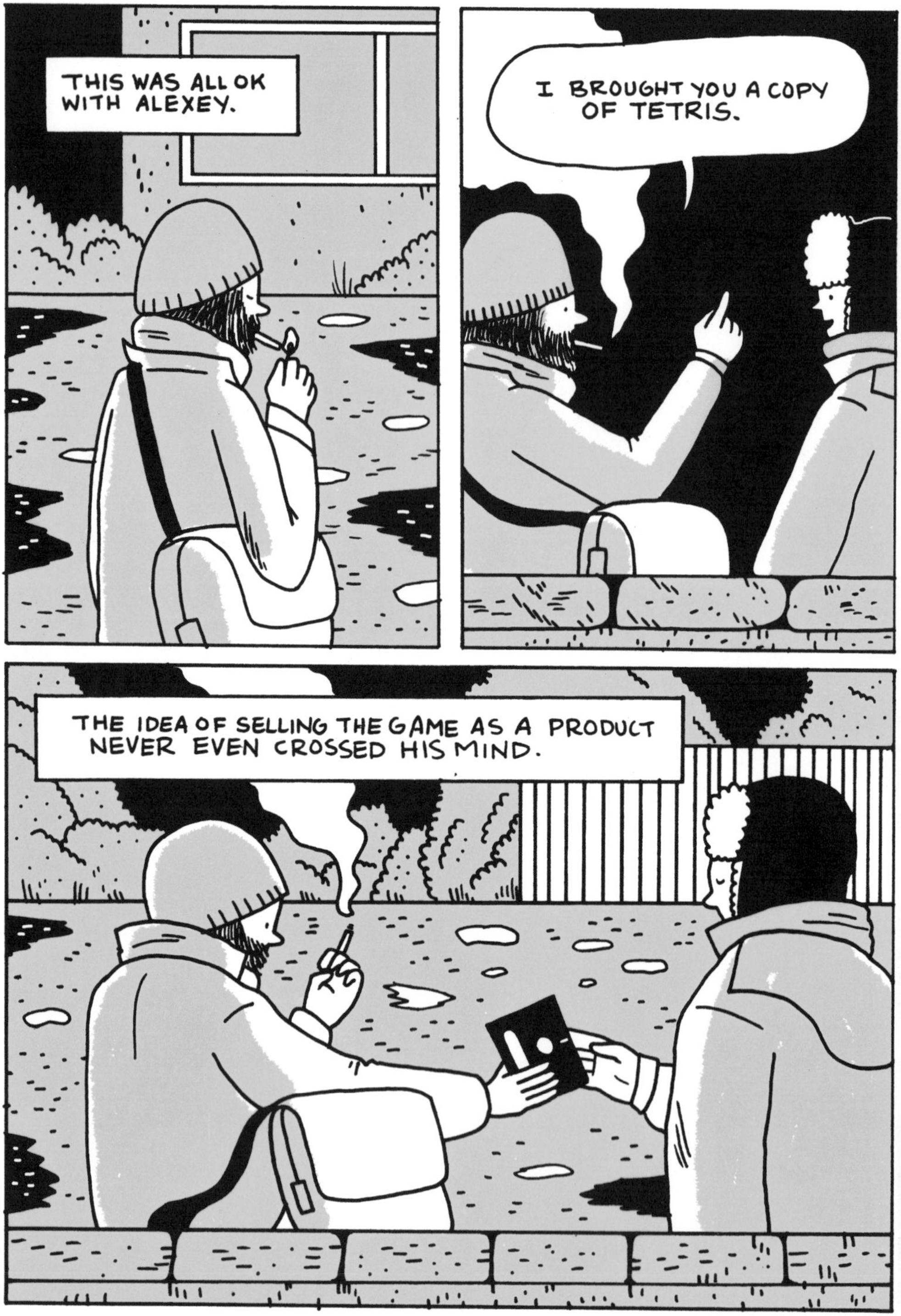
THIS WAS ALL OK WITH ALEXEY.
I BROUGHT YOU A COPY OF TETRIS.
THE IDEA OF SELLING THE GAME AS A PRODUCT NEVER EVEN CROSSED HIS MIND.

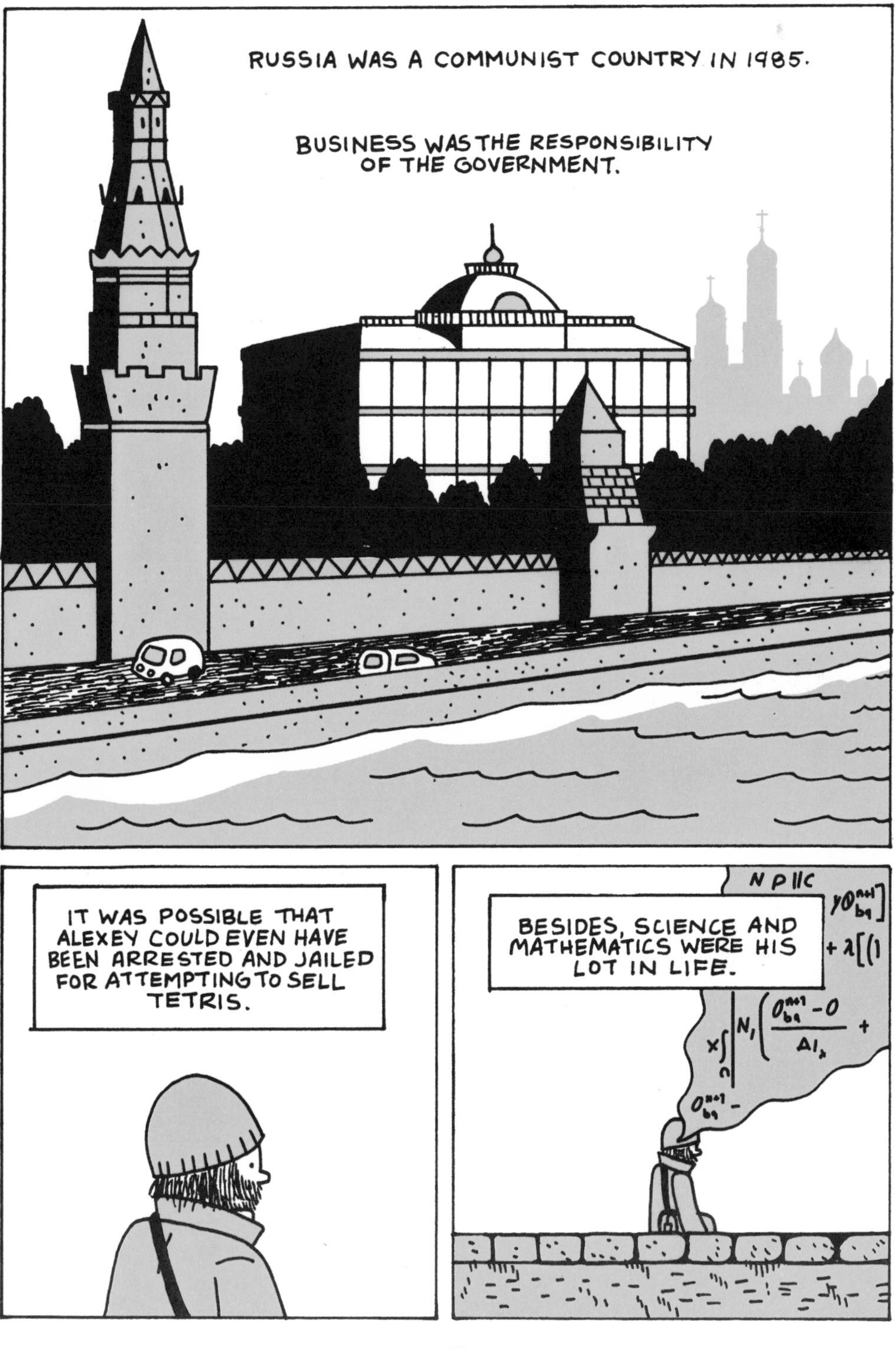
RUSSIA WAS A COMMUNIST COUNTRY IN 1985.
BUSINESS WAS THE RESPONSIBILITY OF THE GOVERNMENT.
IT WAS POSSIBLE THAT ALEXEY COULD EVEN HAVE BEEN ARRESTED AND JAILED FOR ATTEMPTING TO SELL TETRIS.
BESIDES, SCIENCE AND MATHEMATICS WERE HIS LOT IN LIFE.

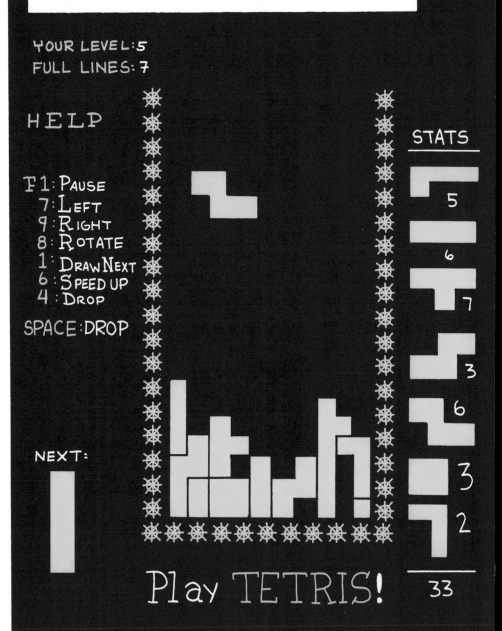

THIS WAS THE VERSION OF TETRIS THAT WAS GIVEN FREE REIN TO TAKE OVER MOSCOW.

YOUR LEVEL: 5
FULL LINES: 7

HELP

F1: Pause
7: Left
9: Right
8: Rotate
1: Draw Next
6: Speed Up
4: Drop

SPACE: DROP

NEXT:

STATS

5
6
7
3
6
3
2

Play TETRIS!

33

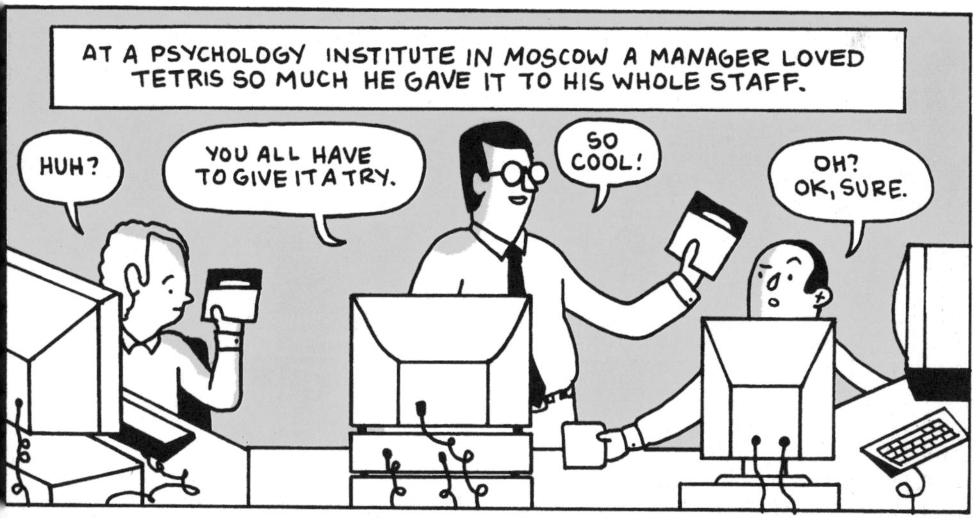
AT A PSYCHOLOGY INSTITUTE IN MOSCOW A MANAGER LOVED TETRIS SO MUCH HE GAVE IT TO HIS WHOLE STAFF.
HUH?
YOU ALL HAVE TO GIVE IT A TRY.
SO COOL!
OH? OK, SURE.

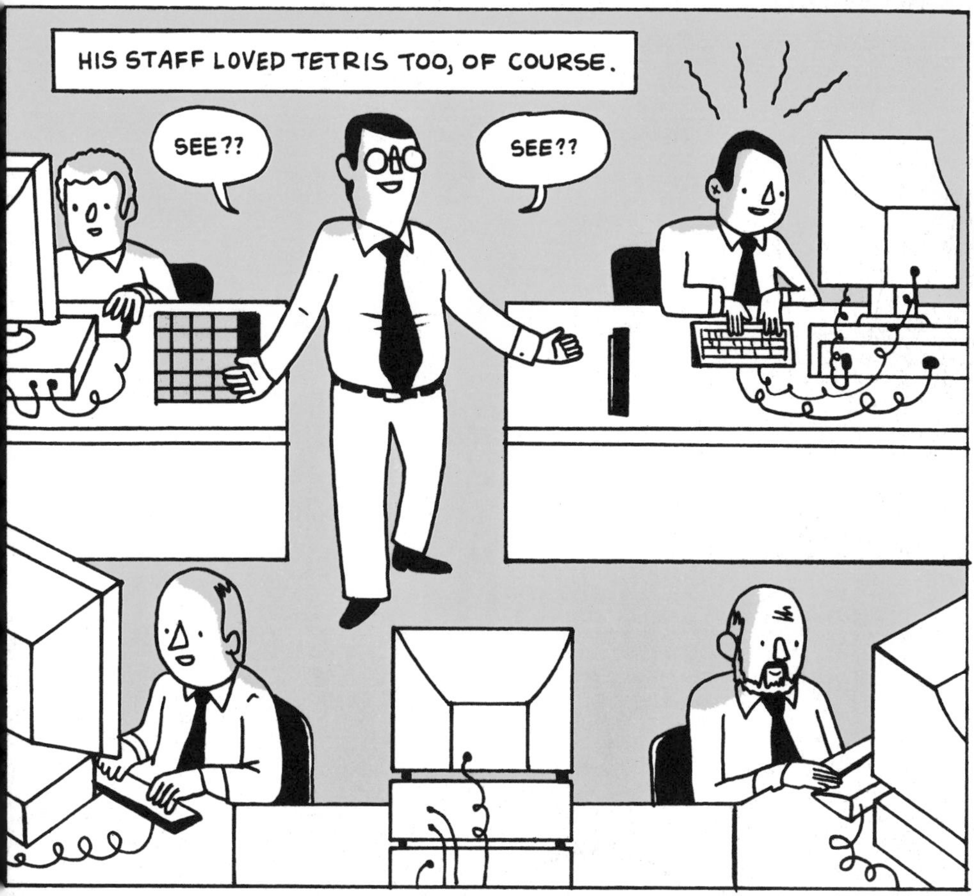
HIS STAFF LOVED TETRIS TOO, OF COURSE.
SEE??
SEE??

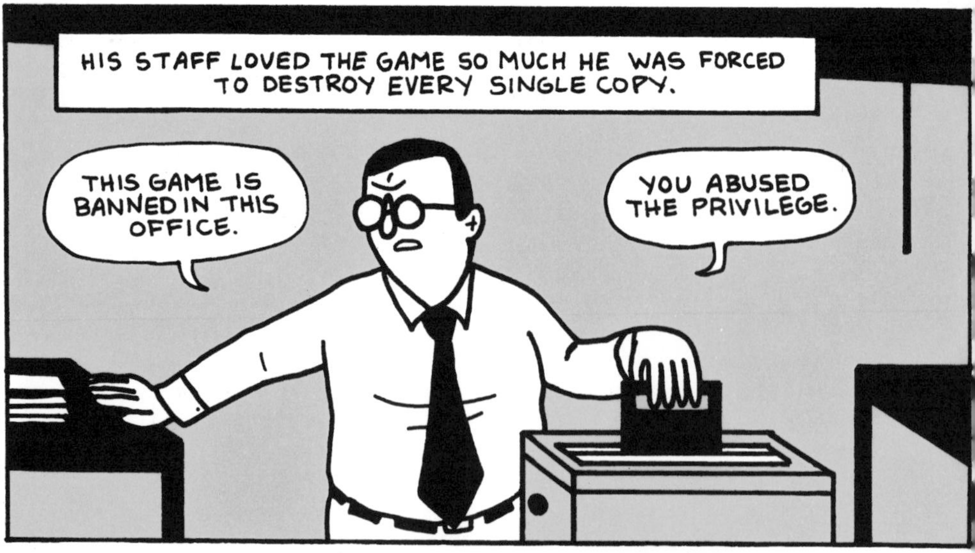
HIS STAFF LOVED THE GAME SO MUCH HE WAS FORCED TO DESTROY EVERY SINGLE COPY.
THIS GAME IS BANNED IN THIS OFFICE.
YOU ABUSED THE PRIVILEGE.

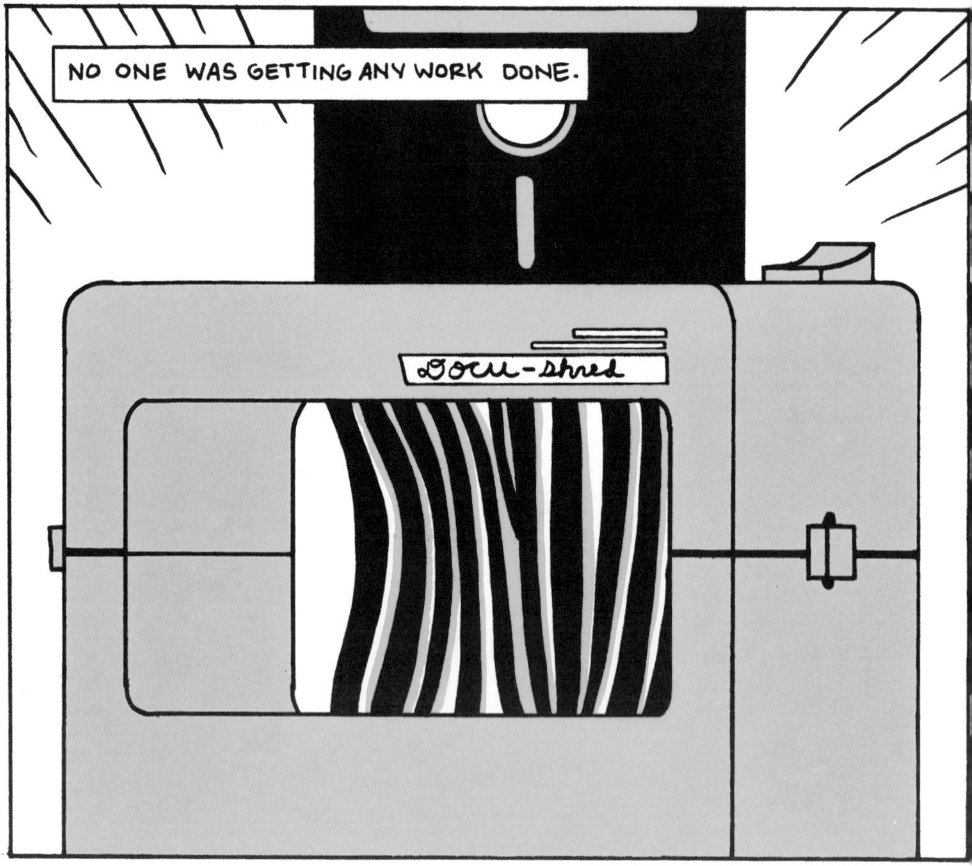
NO ONE WAS GETTING ANY WORK DONE.
Docu-Shred

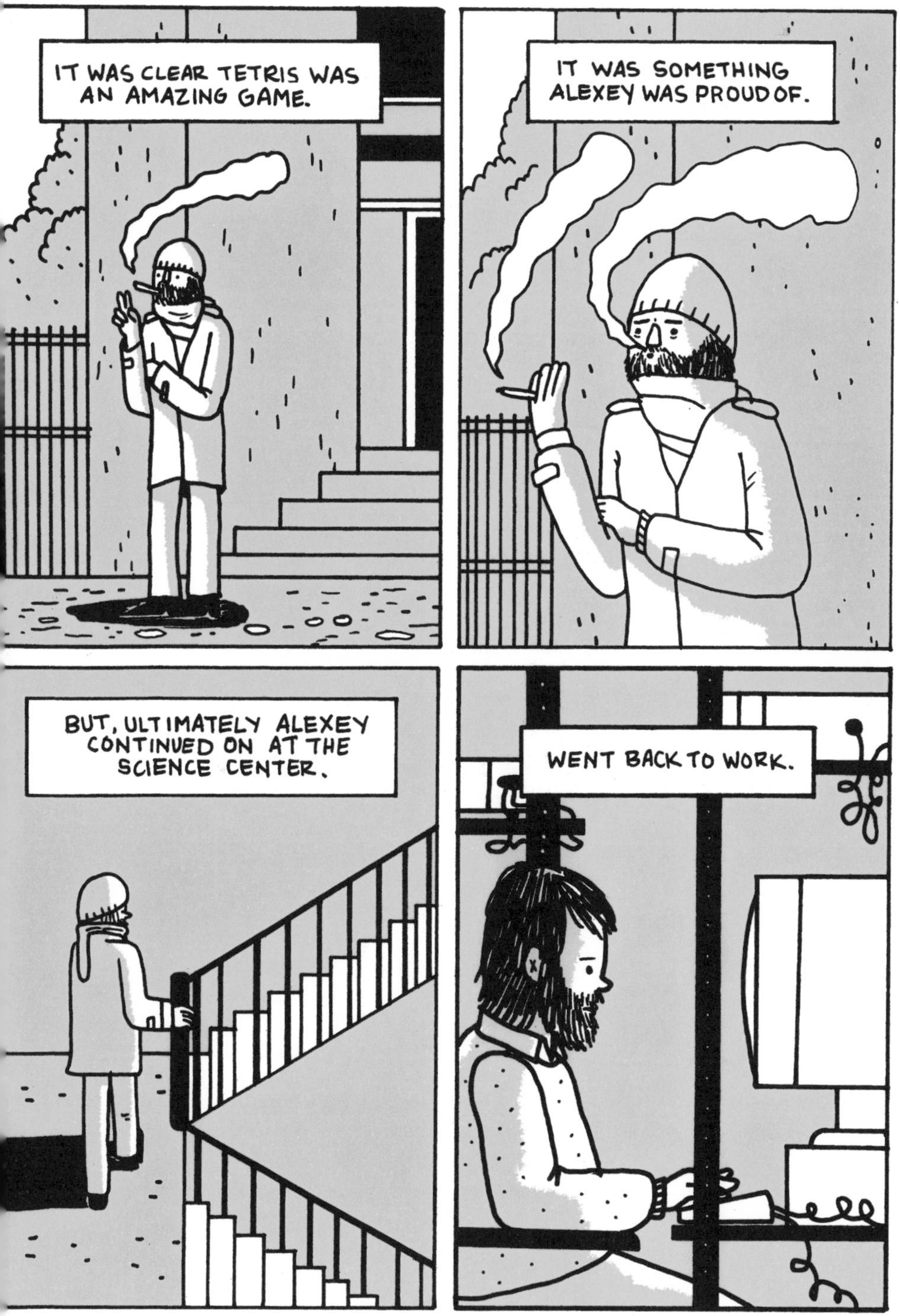
IT WAS CLEAR TETRIS WAS AN AMAZING GAME.
IT WAS SOMETHING ALEXEY WAS PROUD OF.
BUT, ULTIMATELY ALEXEY CONTINUED ON AT THE SCIENCE CENTER.
WENT BACK TO WORK.

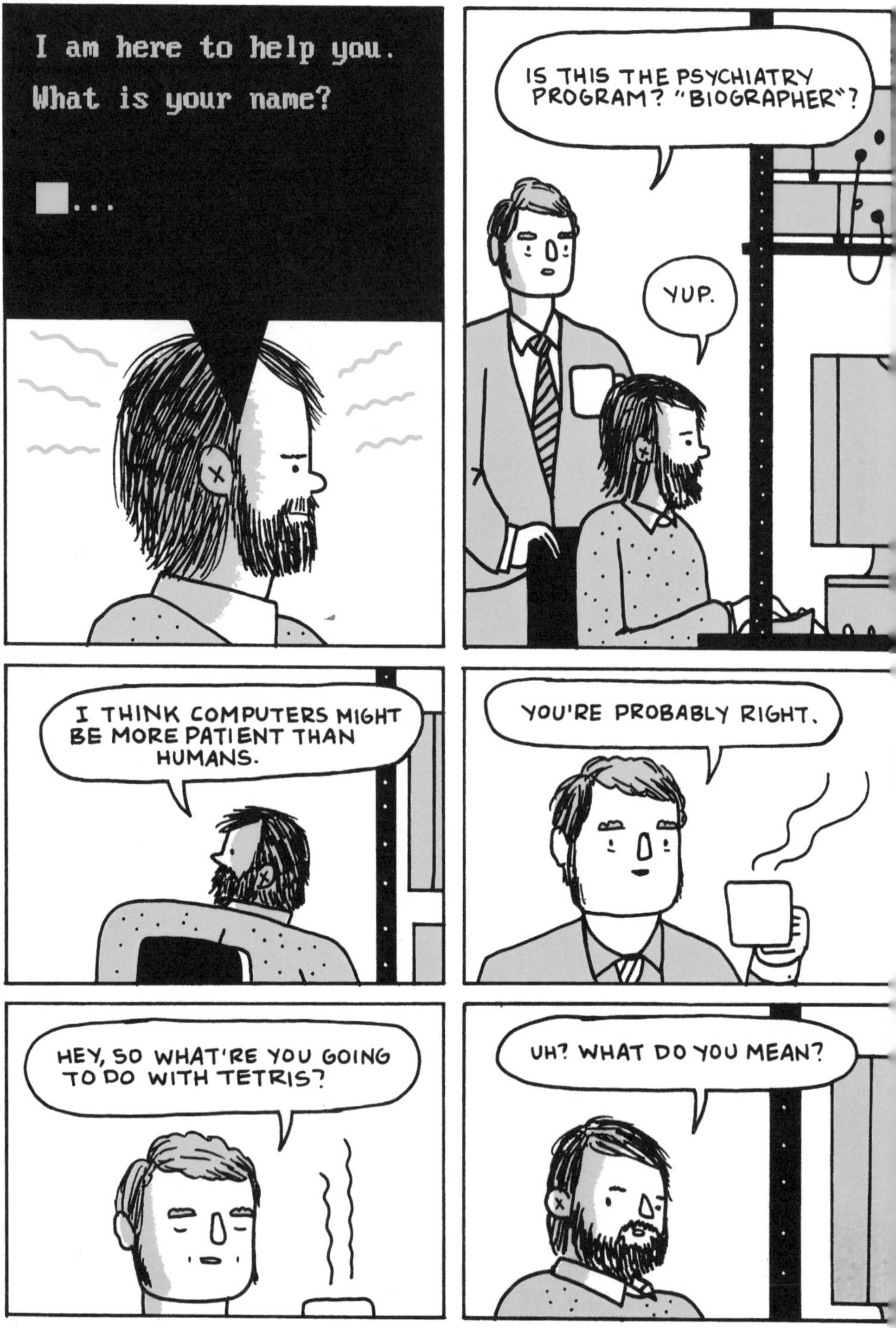
I am here to help you.
What is your name?
...
IS THIS THE PSYCHIATRY PROGRAM? "BIOGRAPHER"?
YUP.
I THINK COMPUTERS MIGHT BE MORE PATIENT THAN HUMANS.
YOU'RE PROBABLY RIGHT.
HEY, SO WHAT'RE YOU GOING TO DO WITH TETRIS?
UH? WHAT DO YOU MEAN?

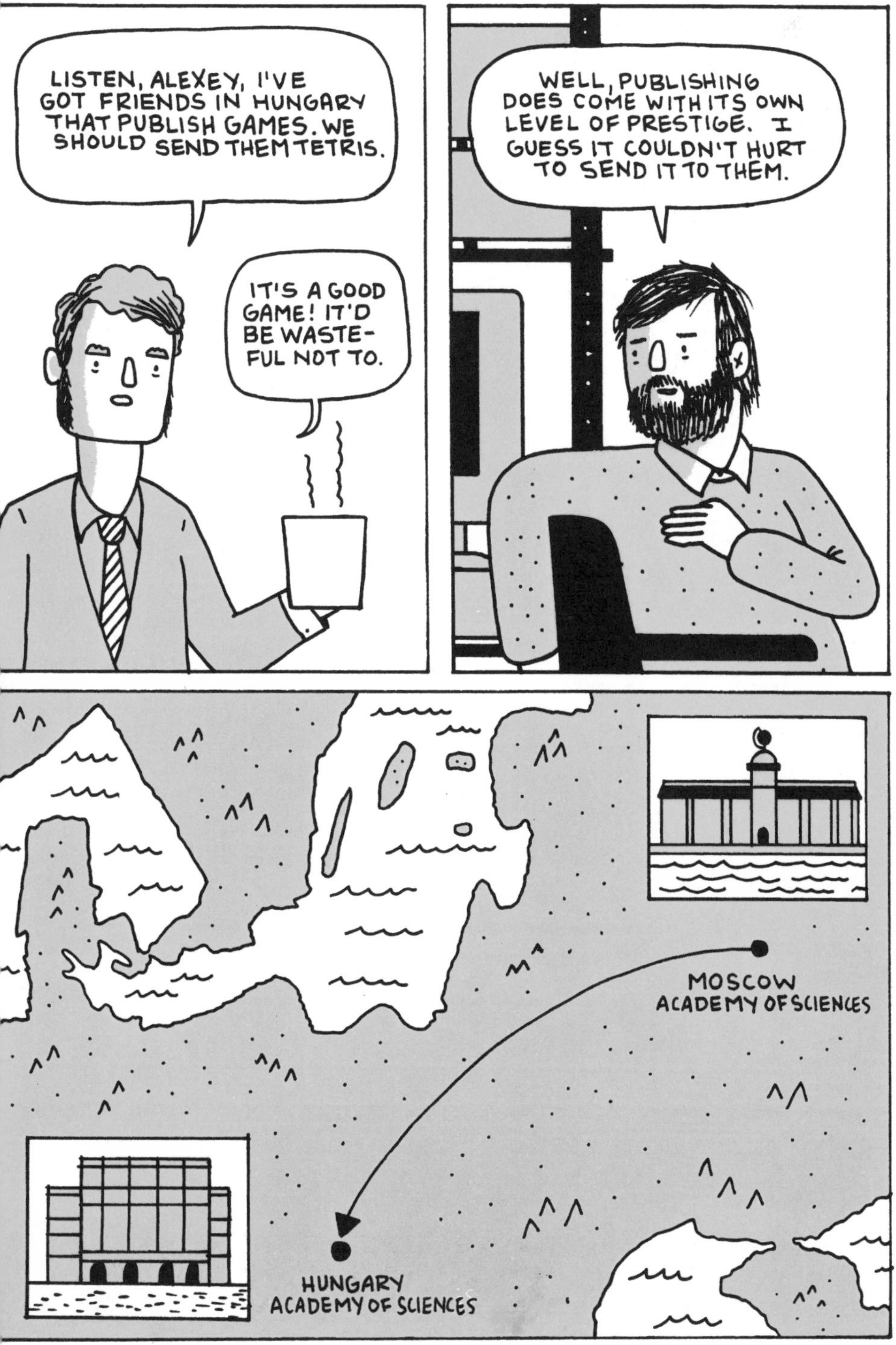

LISTEN, ALEXEY, I'VE GOT FRIENDS IN HUNGARY THAT PUBLISH GAMES. WE SHOULD SEND THEM TETRIS.
IT'S A GOOD GAME! IT'D BE WASTE-FUL NOT TO.
WELL, PUBLISHING DOES COME WITH ITS OWN LEVEL OF PRESTIGE. I GUESS IT COULDN'T HURT TO SEND IT TO THEM.
MOSCOW ACADEMY OF SCIENCES
HUNGARY ACADEMY OF SCIENCES

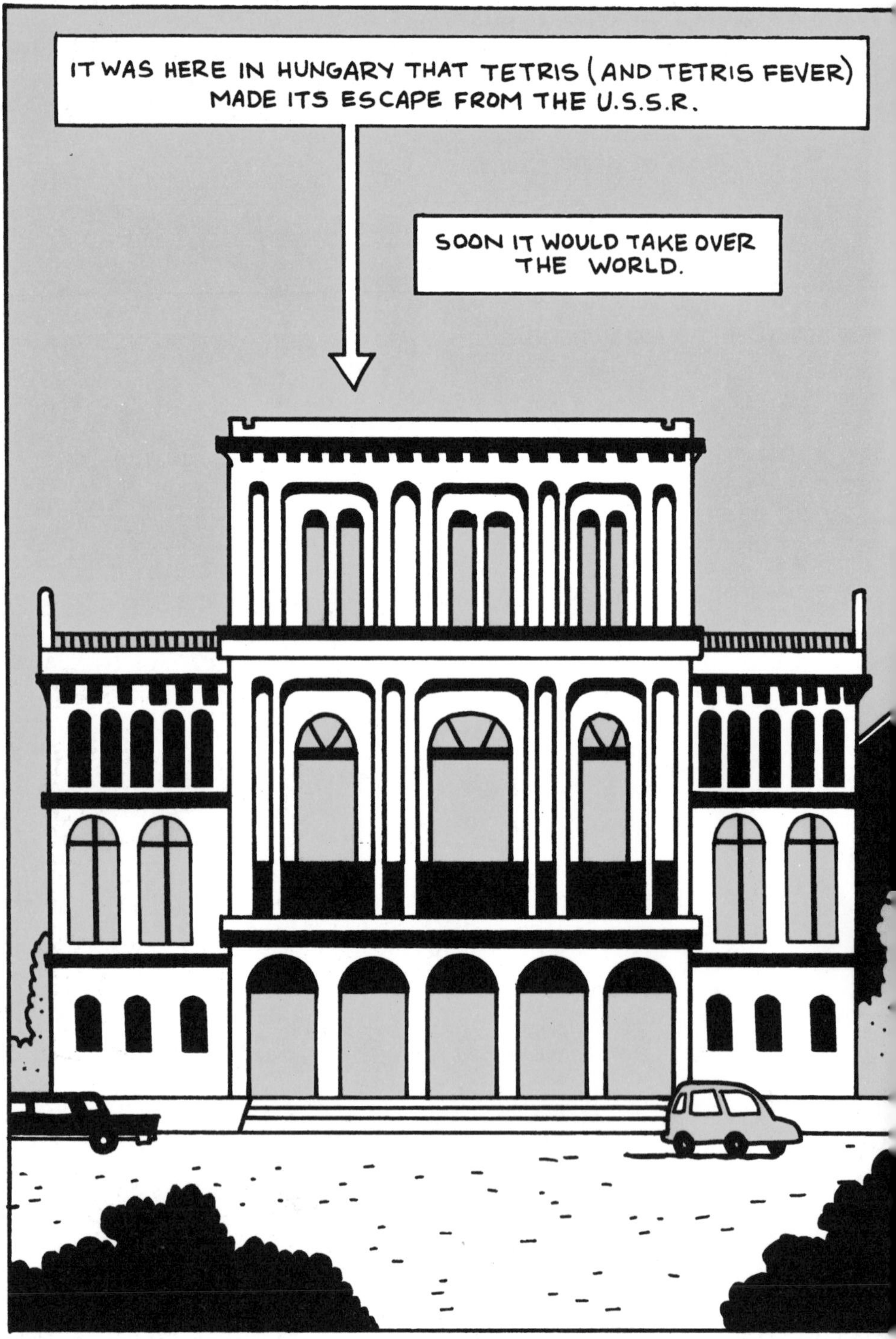
IT WAS HERE IN HUNGARY THAT TETRIS (AND TETRIS FEVER) MADE ITS ESCAPE FROM THE U.S.S.R.
SOON IT WOULD TAKE OVER THE WORLD.

ROBERT STEIN
ANDROMEDA SOFTWARE

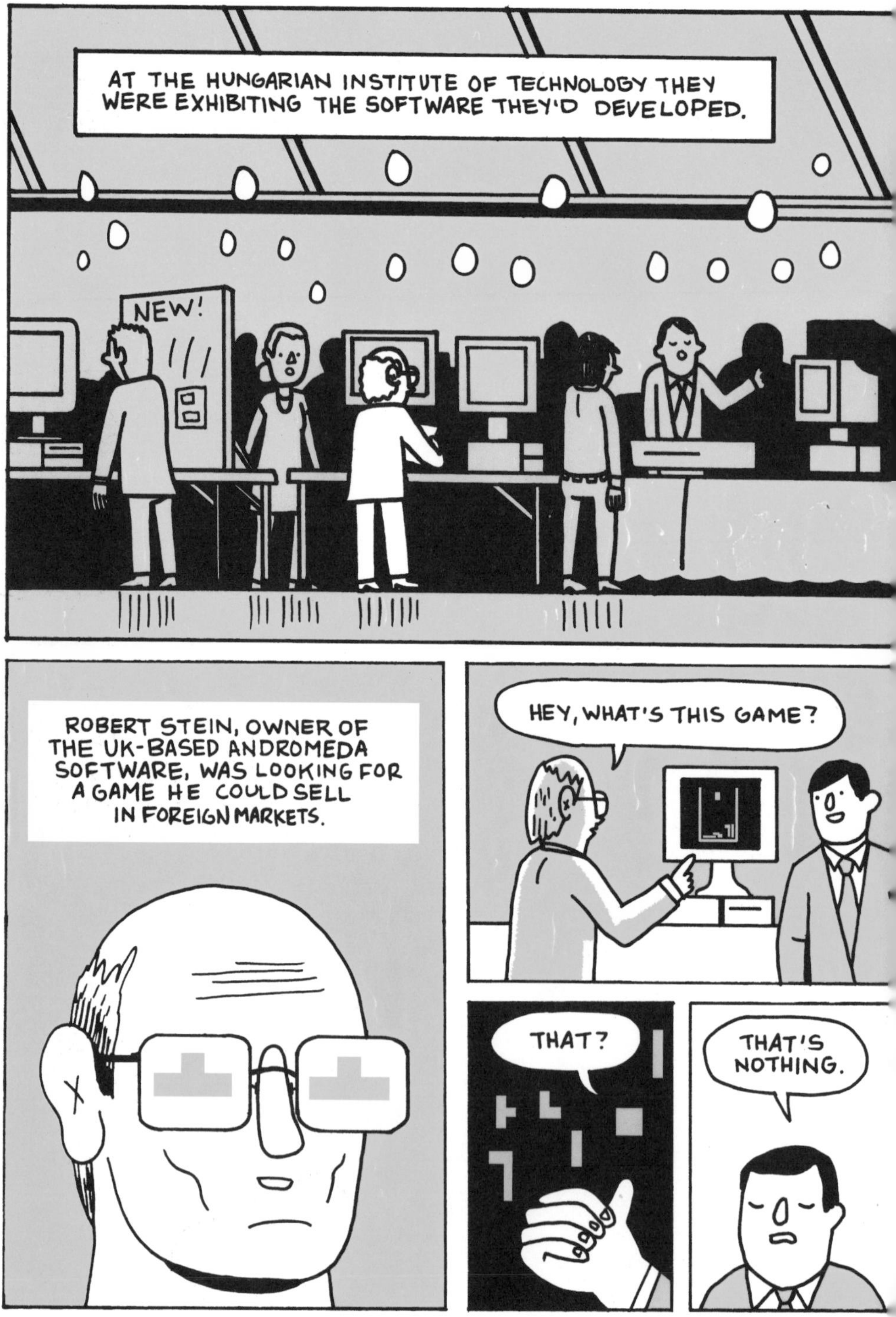
AT THE HUNGARIAN INSTITUTE OF TECHNOLOGY THEY WERE EXHIBITING THE SOFTWARE THEY'D DEVELOPED.
NEW!
ROBERT STEIN, OWNER OF THE UK-BASED ANDROMEDA SOFTWARE, WAS LOOKING FOR A GAME HE COULD SELL IN FOREIGN MARKETS.
HEY, WHAT'S THIS GAME?
THAT?
THAT'S NOTHING.

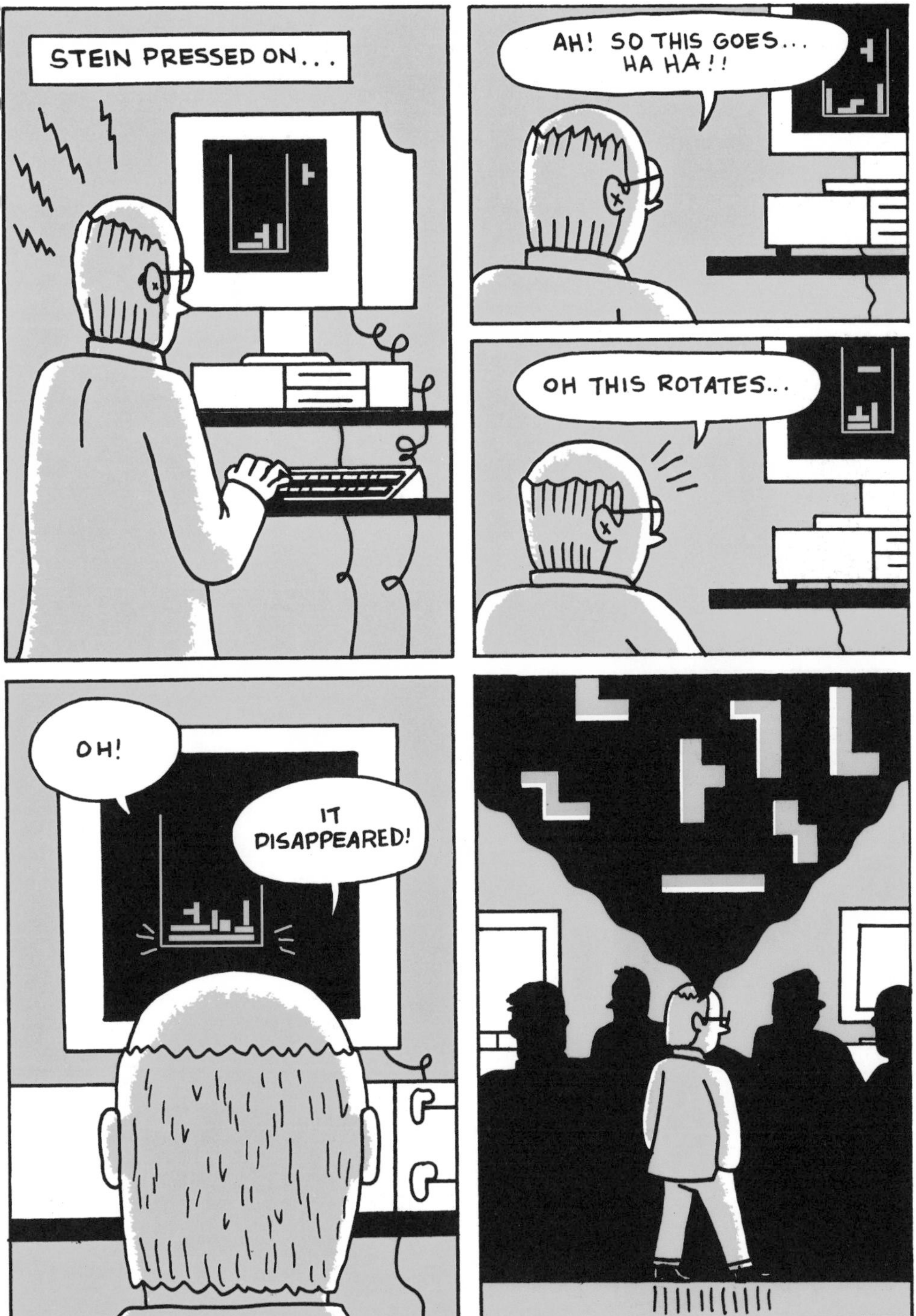
STEIN PRESSED ON...
AH! SO THIS GOES... HA HA!!
OH THIS ROTATES...
OH!
IT DISAPPEARED!

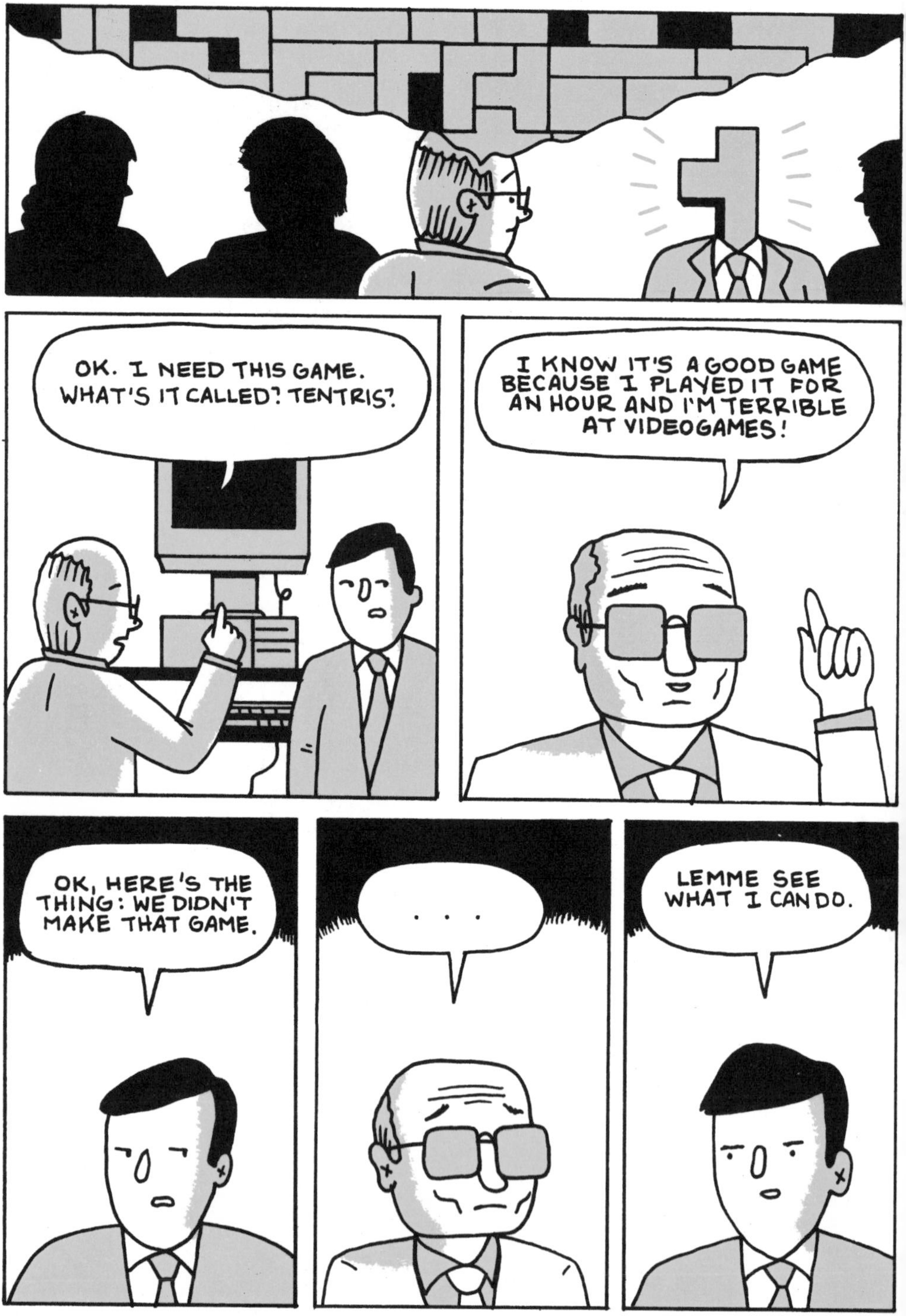
OK. I NEED THIS GAME.
WHAT'S IT CALLED? TENTRIS?
I KNOW IT'S A GOOD GAME BECAUSE I PLAYED IT FOR AN HOUR AND I'M TERRIBLE AT VIDEOGAMES!
OK, HERE'S THE THING: WE DIDN'T MAKE THAT GAME.
. . .
LEMME SEE WHAT I CAN DO.

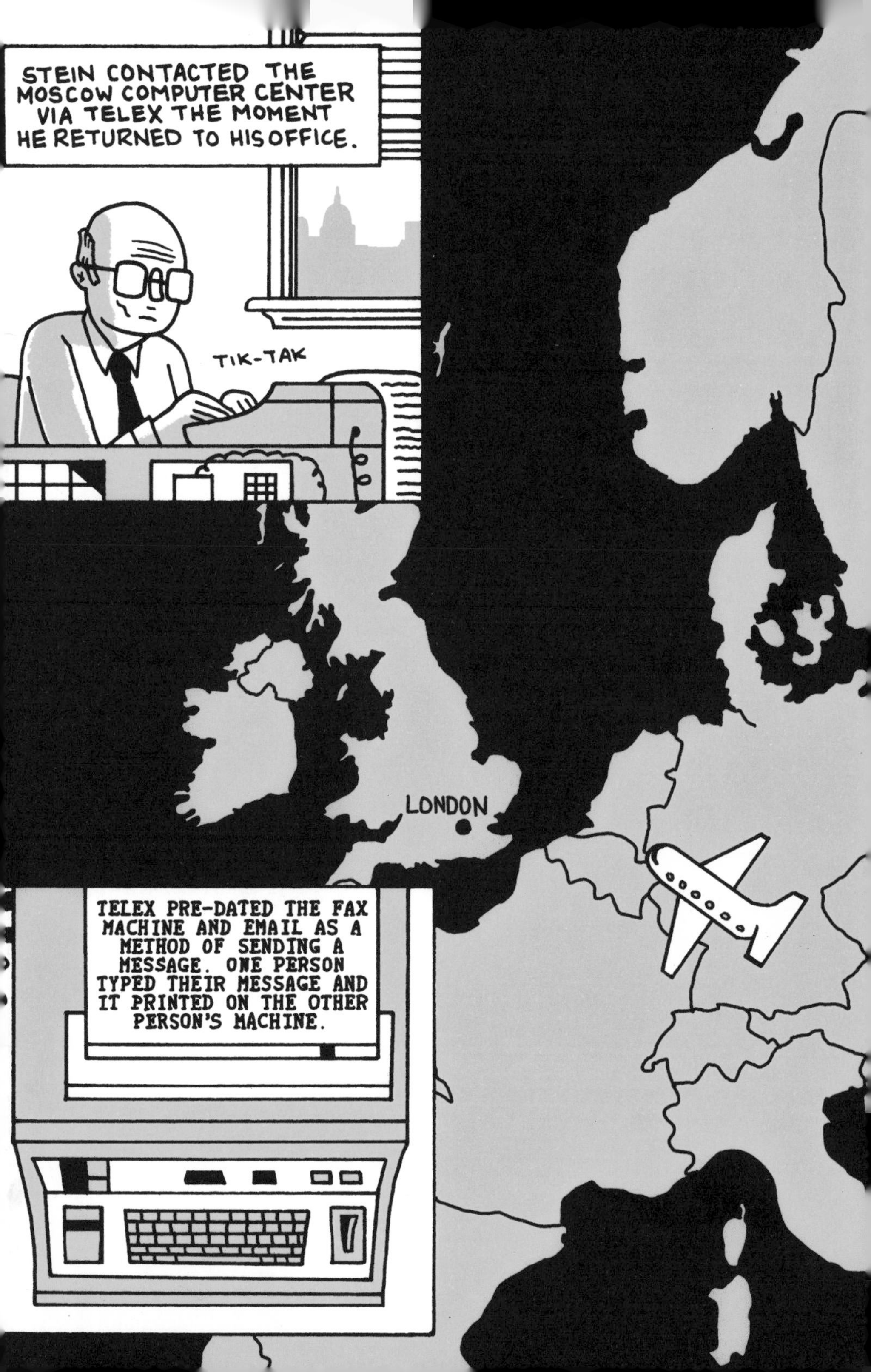
STEIN CONTACTED THE MOSCOW COMPUTER CENTER VIA TELEX THE MOMENT HE RETURNED TO HIS OFFICE.
TIK-TAK
LONDON
TELEX PRE-DATED THE FAX MACHINE AND EMAIL AS A METHOD OF SENDING A MESSAGE. ONE PERSON TYPED THEIR MESSAGE AND IT PRINTED ON THE OTHER PERSON'S MACHINE.

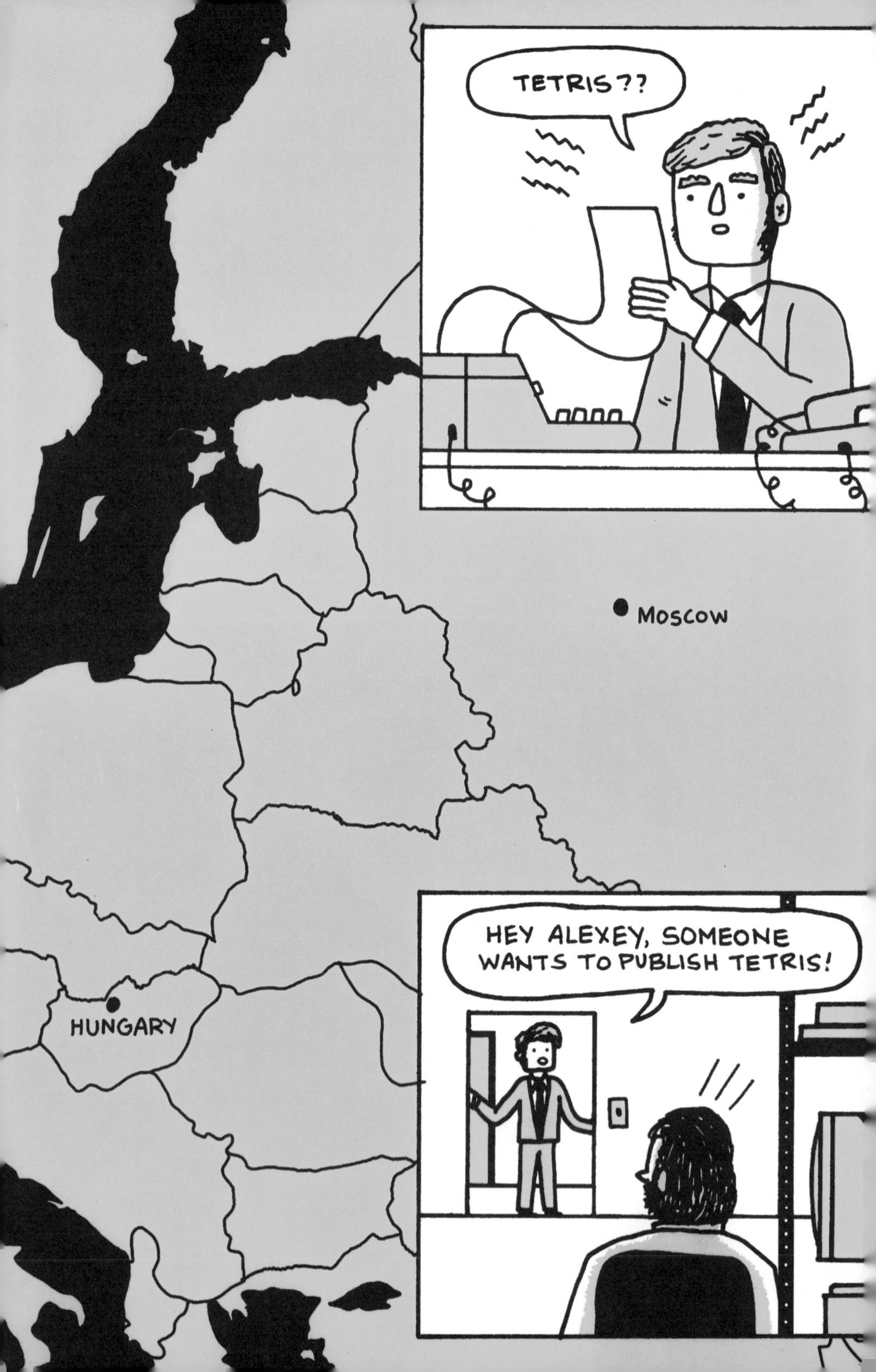
TETRIS??
MOSCOW
HEY ALEXEY, SOMEONE WANTS TO PUBLISH TETRIS!
HUNGARY

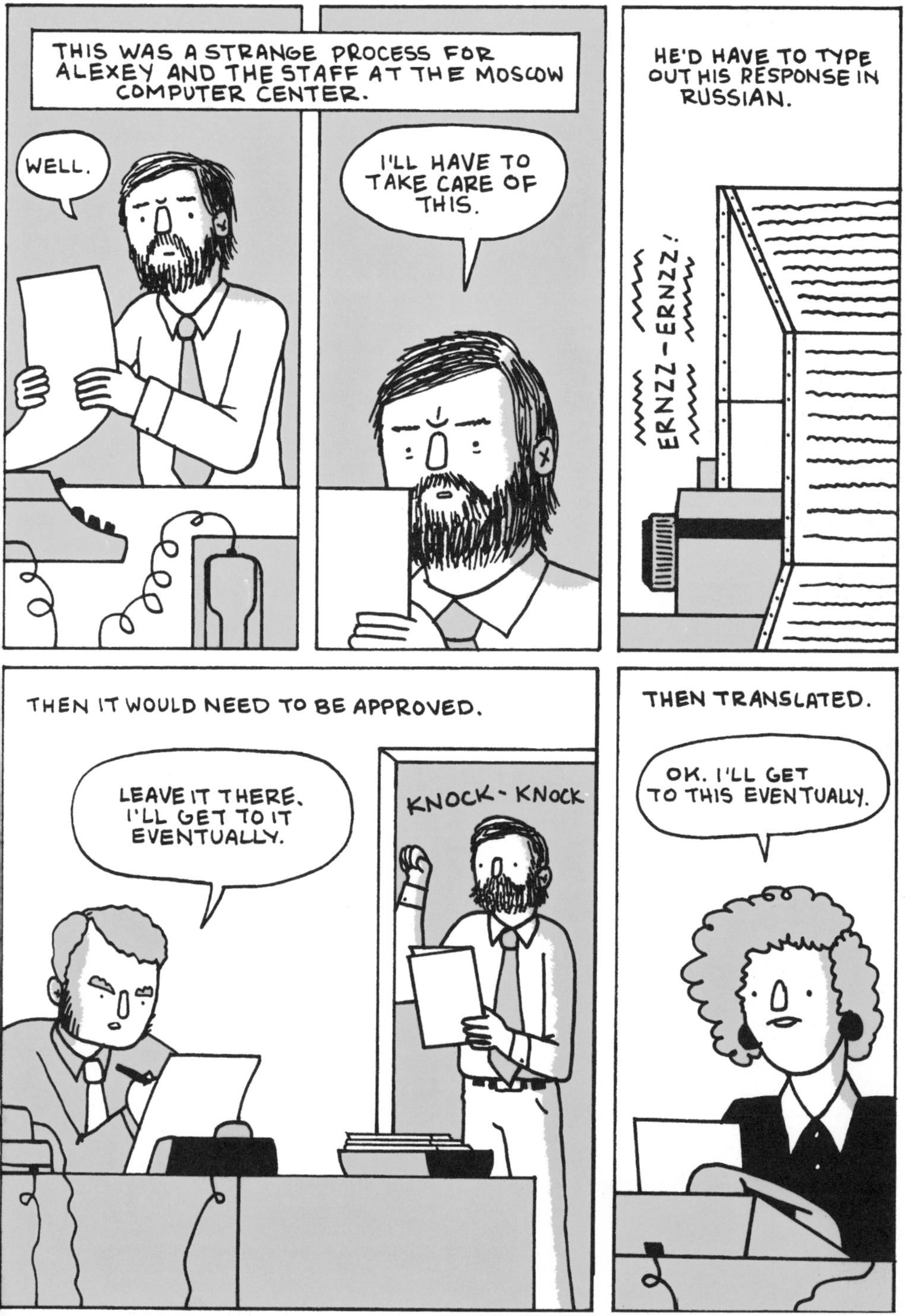
THIS WAS A STRANGE PROCESS FOR ALEXEY AND THE STAFF AT THE MOSCOW COMPUTER CENTER.
WELL.
I'LL HAVE TO TAKE CARE OF THIS.
HE'D HAVE TO TYPE OUT HIS RESPONSE IN RUSSIAN.
ERNZZ-ERNZZ!
THEN IT WOULD NEED TO BE APPROVED.
LEAVE IT THERE. I'LL GET TO IT EVENTUALLY.
KNOCK-KNOCK
THEN TRANSLATED.
OK. I'LL GET TO THIS EVENTUALLY.

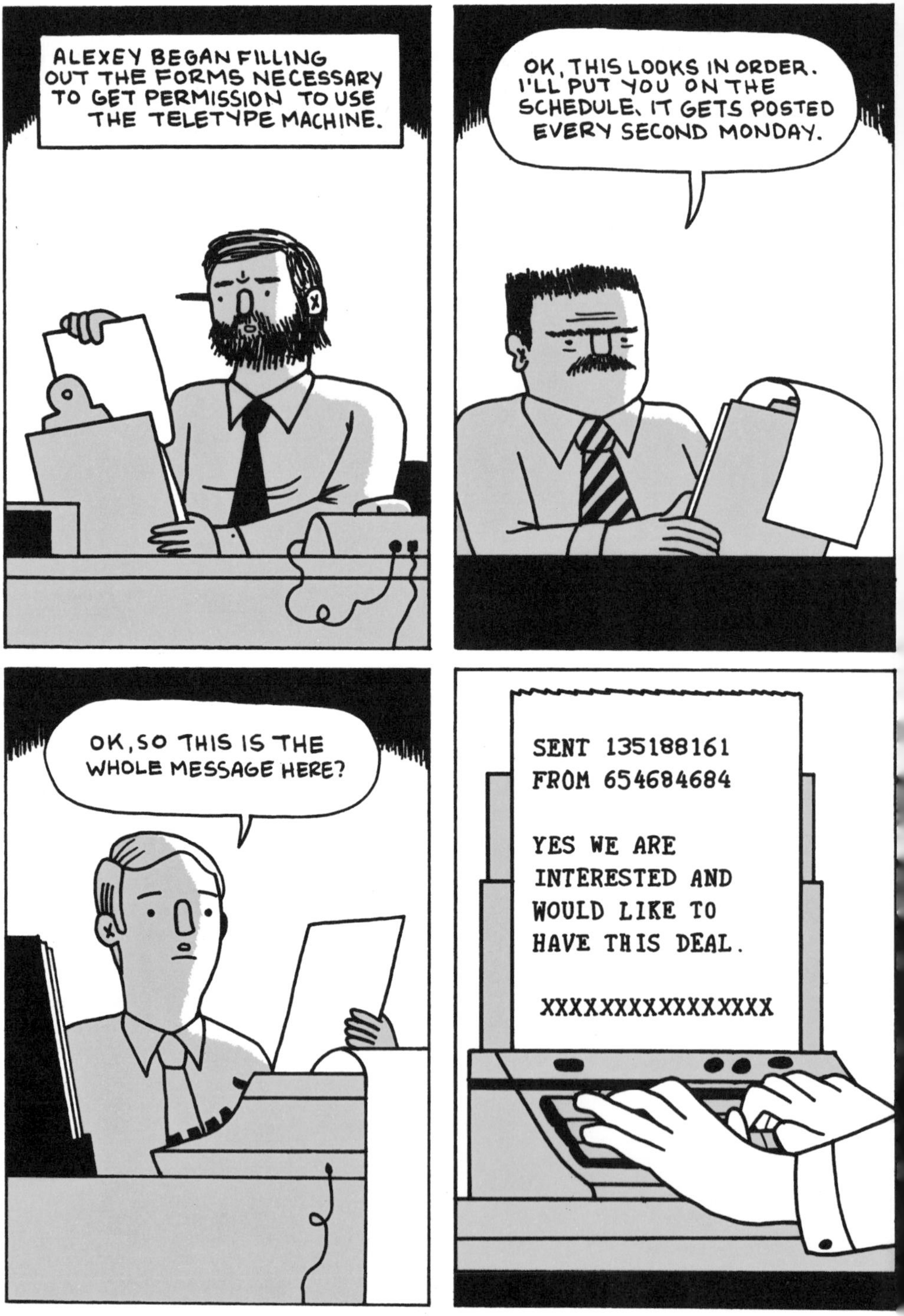
ALEXEY BEGAN FILLING OUT THE FORMS NECESSARY TO GET PERMISSION TO USE THE TELETYPE MACHINE.
OK, THIS LOOKS IN ORDER. I'LL PUT YOU ON THE SCHEDULE. IT GETS POSTED EVERY SECOND MONDAY.
OK, SO THIS IS THE WHOLE MESSAGE HERE?
SENT 135188161
FROM 654684684
YES WE ARE INTERESTED AND WOULD LIKE TO HAVE THIS DEAL.
XXXXXXXXXXXXXXXX

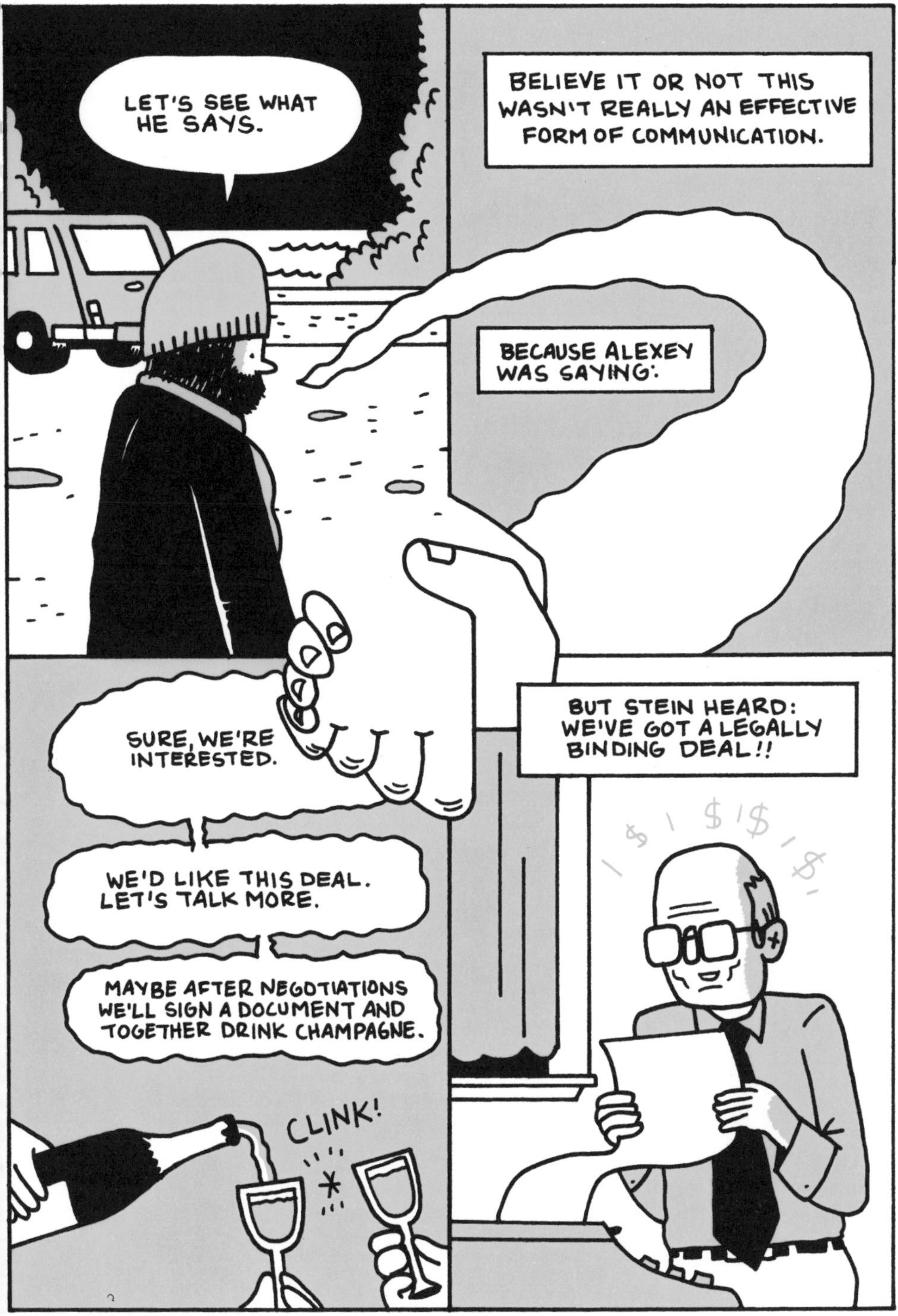
LET'S SEE WHAT HE SAYS.
BELIEVE IT OR NOT THIS WASN'T REALLY AN EFFECTIVE FORM OF COMMUNICATION.
BECAUSE ALEXEY WAS SAYING:
SURE, WE'RE INTERESTED.
WE'D LIKE THIS DEAL. LET'S TALK MORE.
MAYBE AFTER NEGOTIATIONS WE'LL SIGN A DOCUMENT AND TOGETHER DRINK CHAMPAGNE.
CLINK!
BUT STEIN HEARD: WE'VE GOT A LEGALLY BINDING DEAL!!

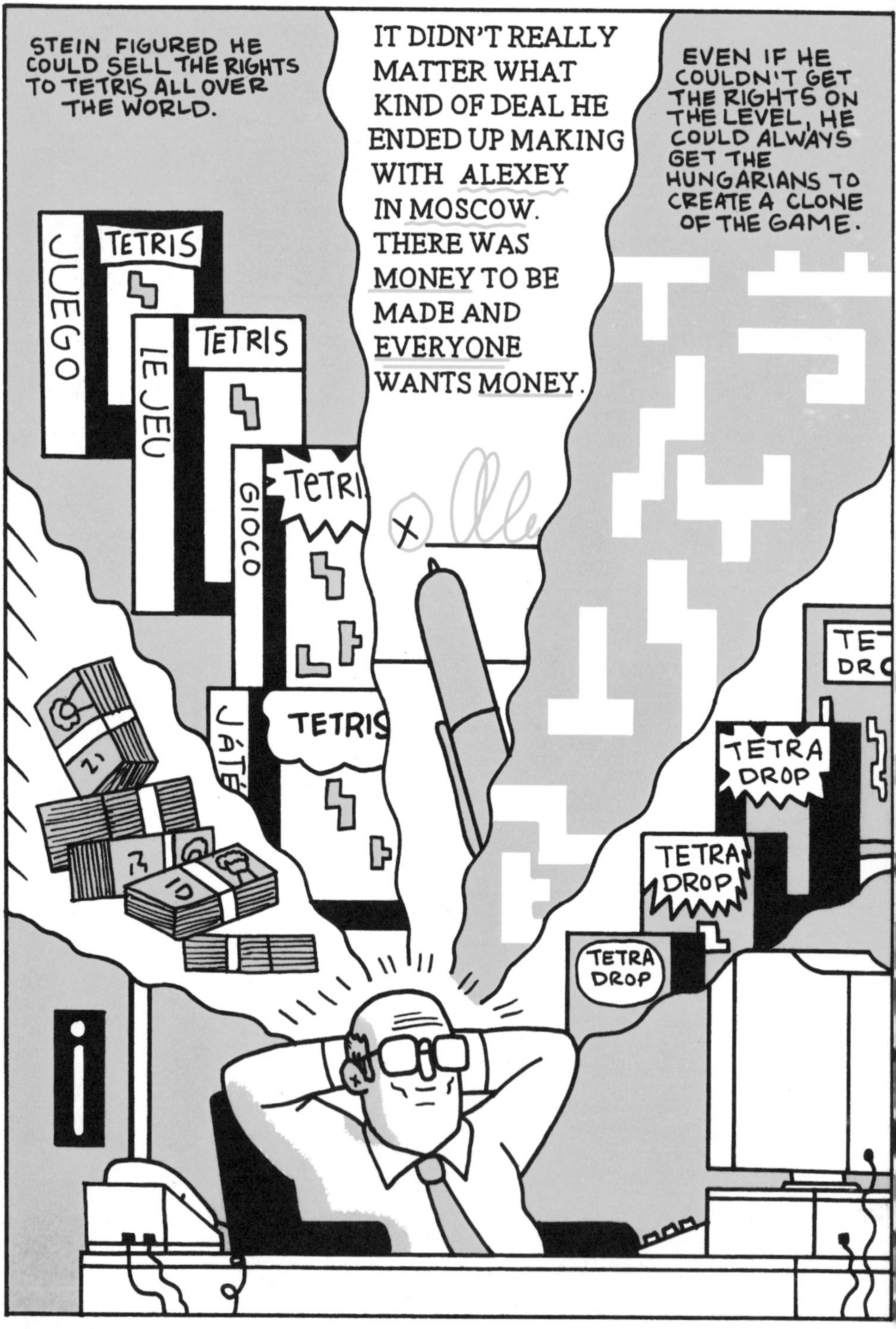
STEIN FIGURED HE COULD SELL THE RIGHTS TO TETRIS ALL OVER THE WORLD.
IT DIDN'T REALLY MATTER WHAT KIND OF DEAL HE ENDED UP MAKING WITH ALEXEY IN MOSCOW. THERE WAS MONEY TO BE MADE AND EVERYONE WANTS MONEY.
EVEN IF HE COULDN'T GET THE RIGHTS ON THE LEVEL, HE COULD ALWAYS GET THE HUNGARIANS TO CREATE A CLONE OF THE GAME.
JUEGO
TETRIS
LE JEU
TETRIS
GIOCO
TETRIS
TETRA DROP
TETRA DROP
TETRA DROP

ROBERT MAXWELL
PRESIDENT OF MIRROR GROUP
PARENT COMPANY OF MIRRORSOFT

JIM MACKONOCHIE
MIRRORSOFT

GILMAN LOUIE
SPECTRUM HOLOBYTE

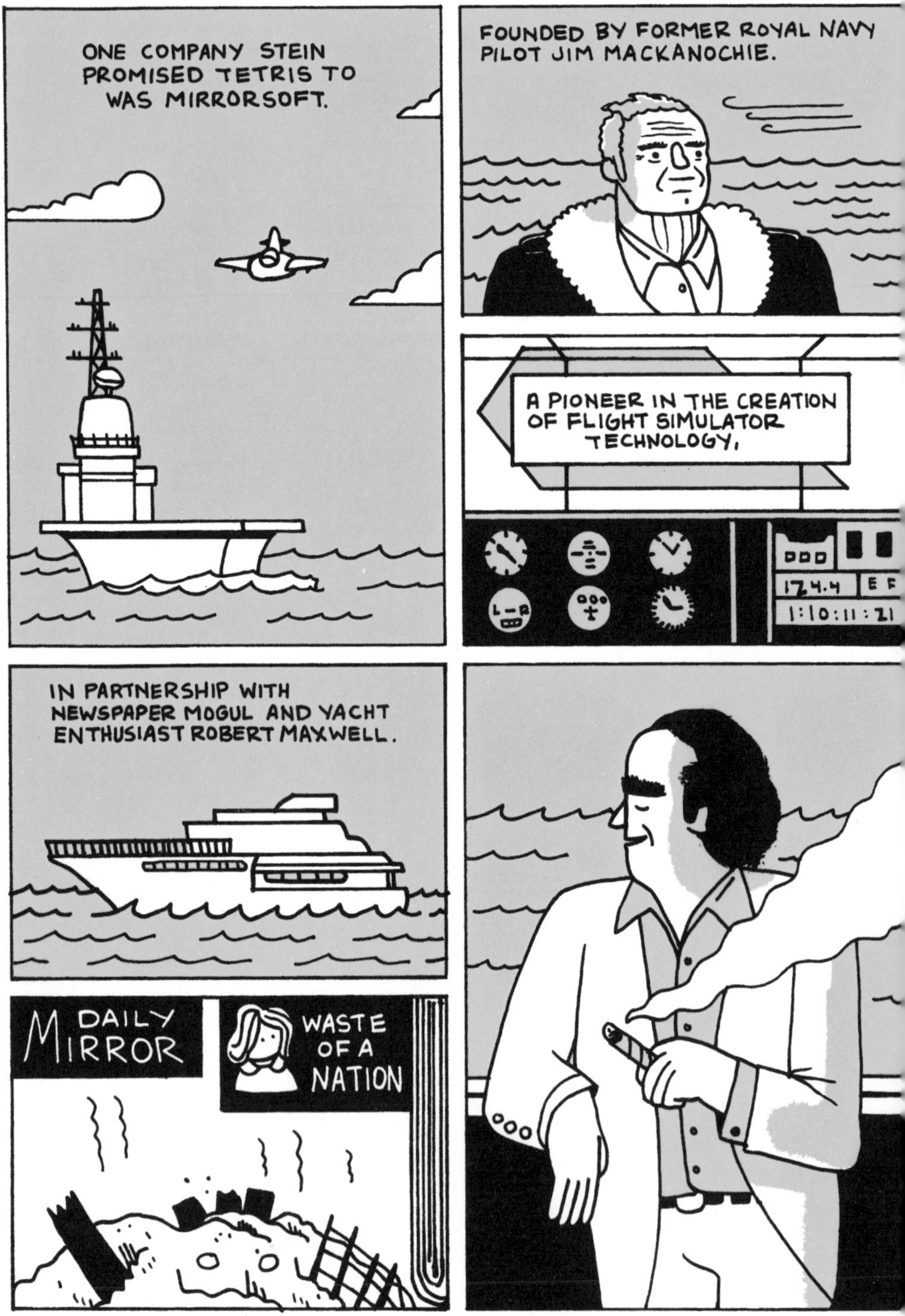
ONE COMPANY STEIN PROMISED TETRIS TO WAS MIRRORSOFT.
FOUNDED BY FORMER ROYAL NAVY PILOT JIM MACKANOCHIE.
A PIONEER IN THE CREATION OF FLIGHT SIMULATOR TECHNOLOGY,
124.4
1:10:11:21
IN PARTNERSHIP WITH NEWSPAPER MOGUL AND YACHT ENTHUSIAST ROBERT MAXWELL.
DAILY MIRROR
WASTE OF A NATION

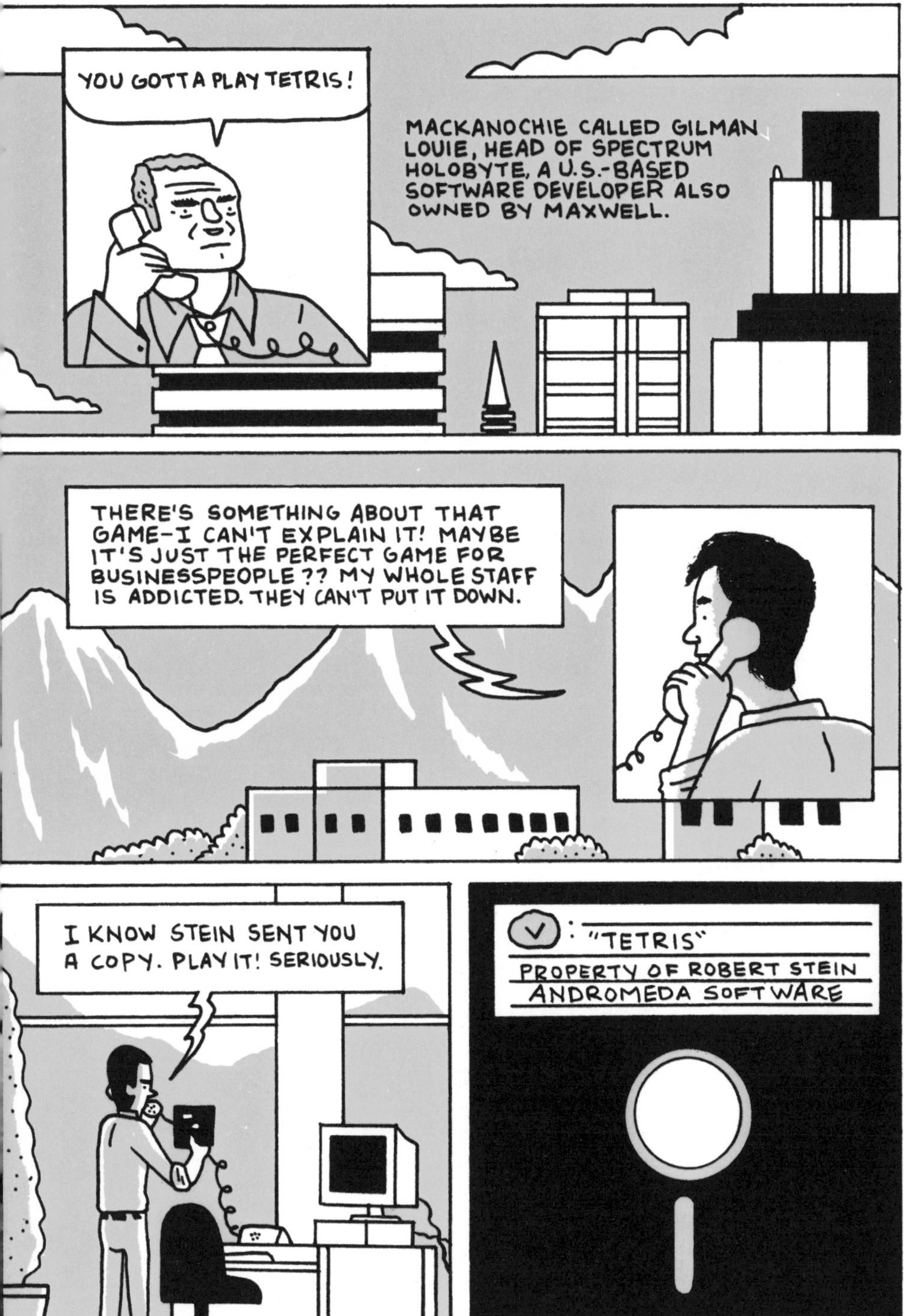
YOU GOTTA PLAY TETRIS!
MACKANOCHIE CALLED GILMAN LOUIE, HEAD OF SPECTRUM HOLOBYTE, A U.S.-BASED SOFTWARE DEVELOPER ALSO OWNED BY MAXWELL.
THERE'S SOMETHING ABOUT THAT GAME—I CAN'T EXPLAIN IT! MAYBE IT'S JUST THE PERFECT GAME FOR BUSINESSPEOPLE?? MY WHOLE STAFF IS ADDICTED. THEY CAN'T PUT IT DOWN.
I KNOW STEIN SENT YOU A COPY. PLAY IT! SERIOUSLY.
"TETRIS"
PROPERTY OF ROBERT STEIN
ANDROMEDA SOFTWARE

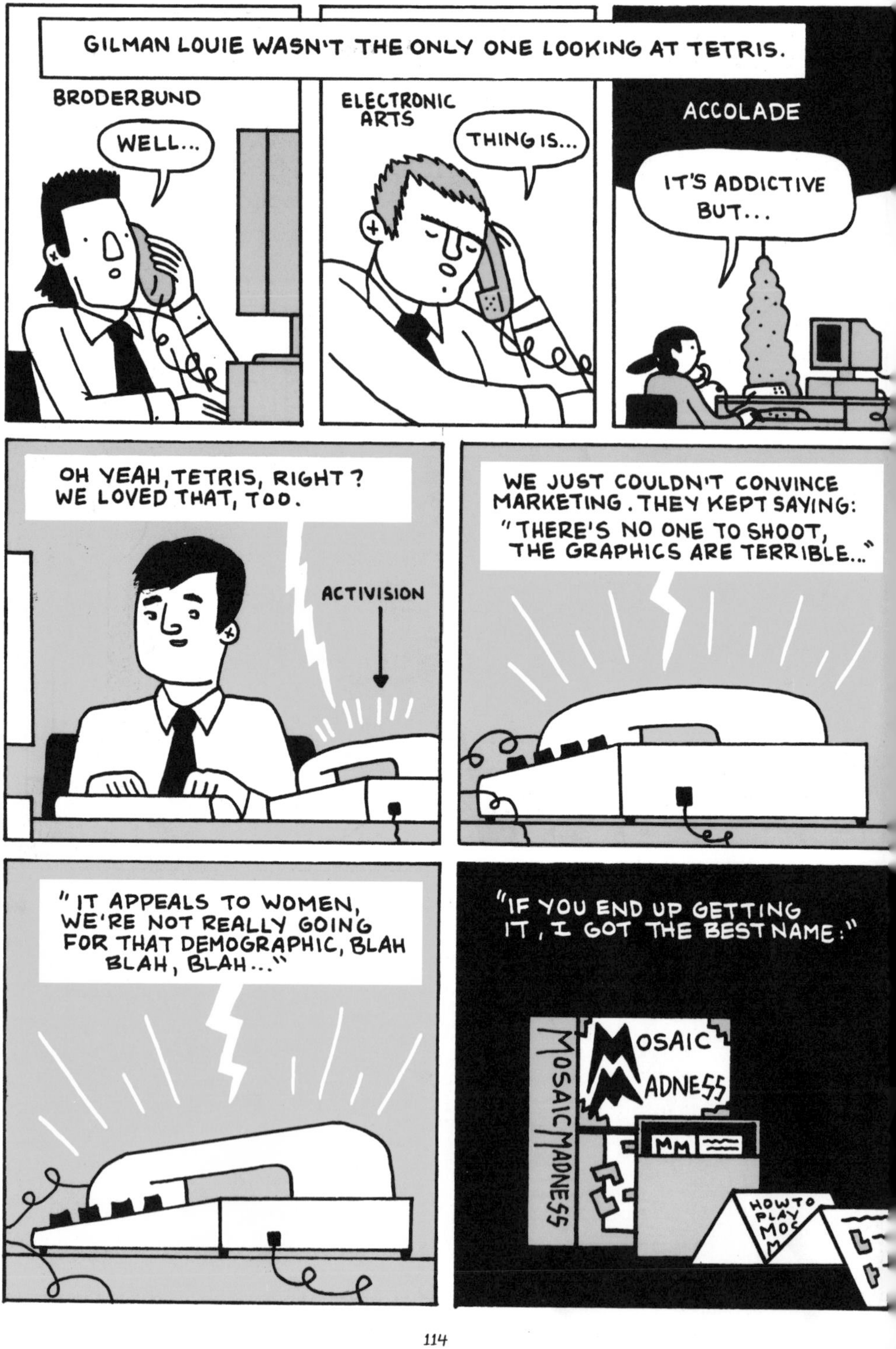
GILMAN LOUIE WASN'T THE ONLY ONE LOOKING AT TETRIS.
BRODERBUND
WELL...
ELECTRONIC ARTS
THING IS...
ACCOLADE
IT'S ADDICTIVE BUT...
OH YEAH, TETRIS, RIGHT? WE LOVED THAT, TOO.
ACTIVISION
WE JUST COULDN'T CONVINCE MARKETING. THEY KEPT SAYING: "THERE'S NO ONE TO SHOOT, THE GRAPHICS ARE TERRIBLE..."
"IT APPEALS TO WOMEN, WE'RE NOT REALLY GOING FOR THAT DEMOGRAPHIC, BLAH BLAH, BLAH..."
"IF YOU END UP GETTING IT, I GOT THE BEST NAME:"
MOSAIC MADNESS
MOSAIC MADNESS
MM
HOW TO PLAY MOS

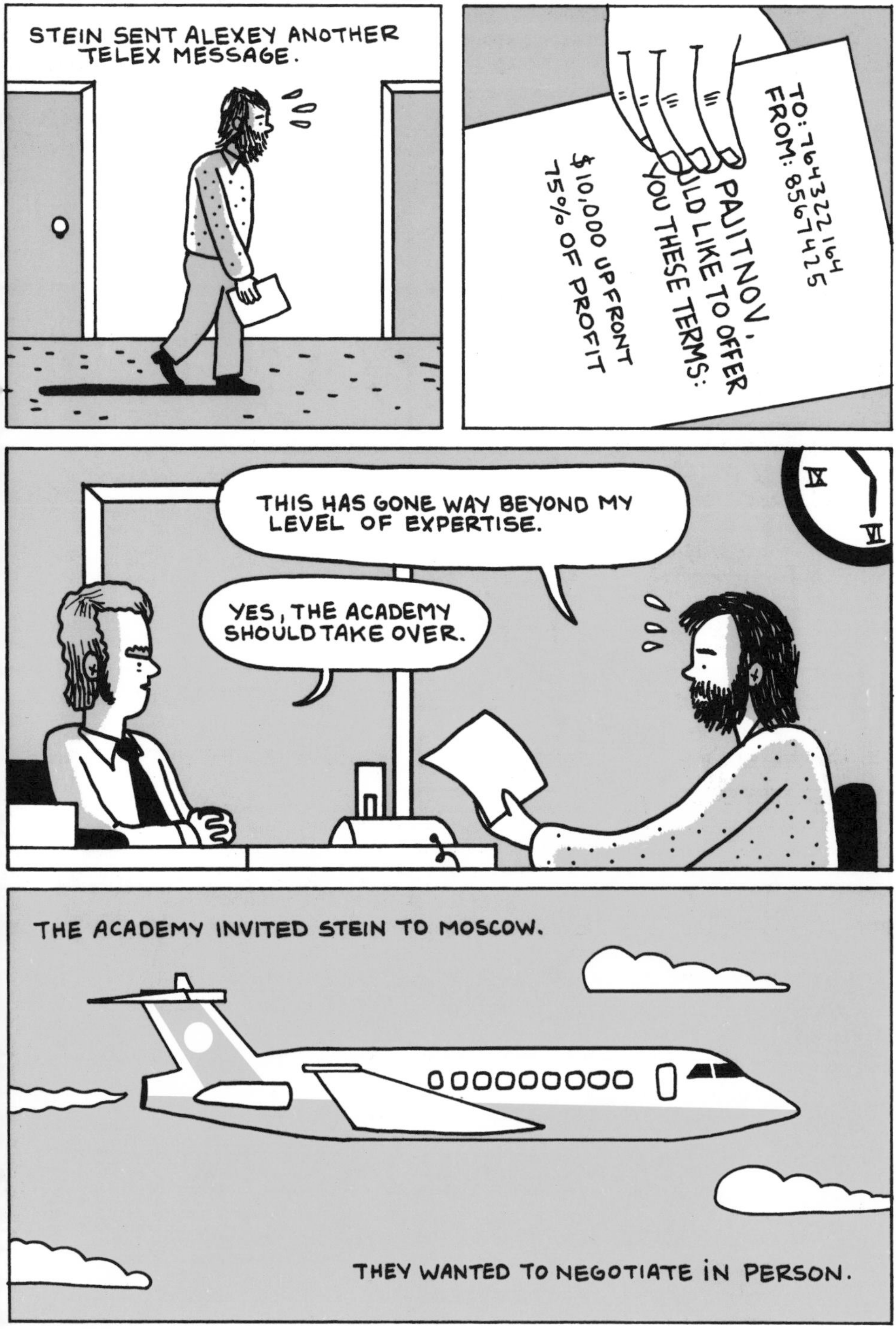
STEIN SENT ALEXEY ANOTHER TELEX MESSAGE.
TO: 7643322164
FROM: 8567425
PAJITNOV,
...ULD LIKE TO OFFER
YOU THESE TERMS:
$10,000 UPFRONT
75% OF PROFIT
THIS HAS GONE WAY BEYOND MY LEVEL OF EXPERTISE.
YES, THE ACADEMY SHOULD TAKE OVER.
THE ACADEMY INVITED STEIN TO MOSCOW.
THEY WANTED TO NEGOTIATE IN PERSON.

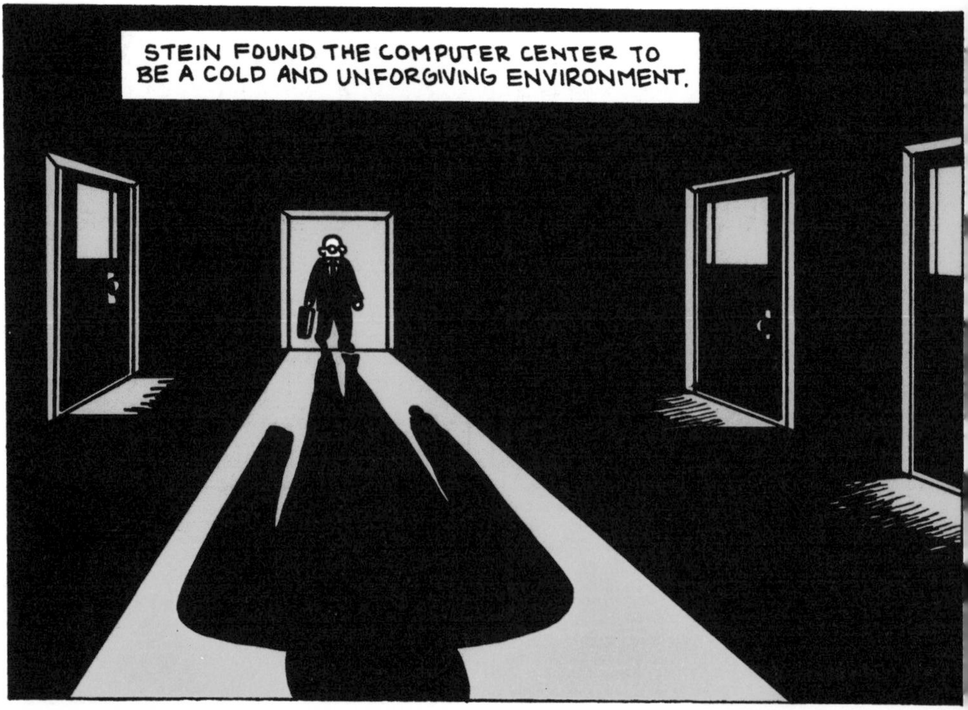
STEIN FOUND THE COMPUTER CENTER TO BE A COLD AND UNFORGIVING ENVIRONMENT.

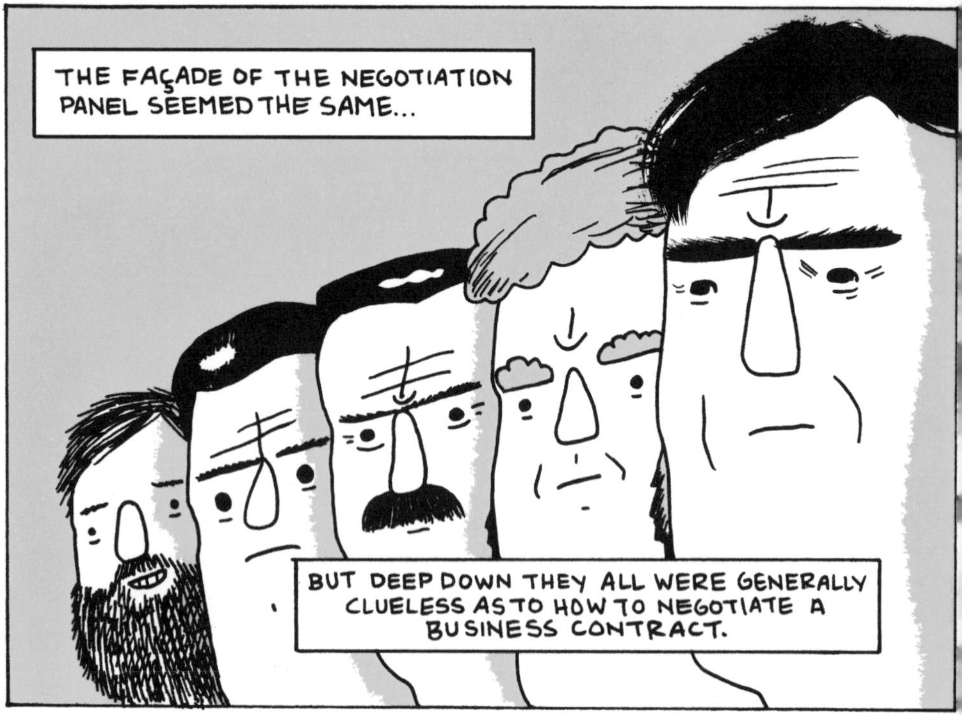
THE FAÇADE OF THE NEGOTIATION PANEL SEEMED THE SAME...
BUT DEEP DOWN THEY ALL WERE GENERALLY CLUELESS AS TO HOW TO NEGOTIATE A BUSINESS CONTRACT.

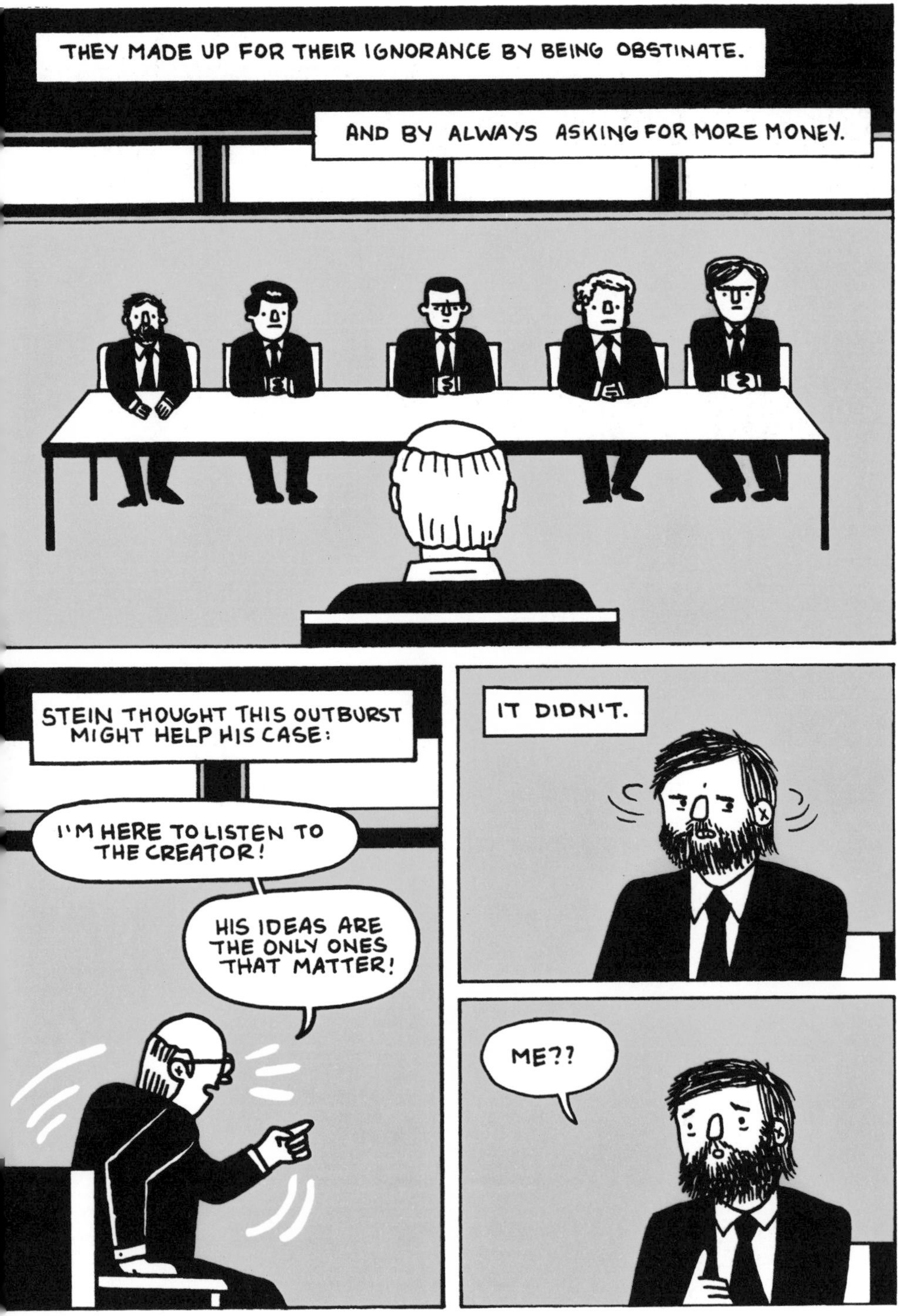
THEY MADE UP FOR THEIR IGNORANCE BY BEING OBSTINATE.
AND BY ALWAYS ASKING FOR MORE MONEY.
STEIN THOUGHT THIS OUTBURST MIGHT HELP HIS CASE:
I'M HERE TO LISTEN TO THE CREATOR!
HIS IDEAS ARE THE ONLY ONES THAT MATTER!
IT DIDN'T.
ME??

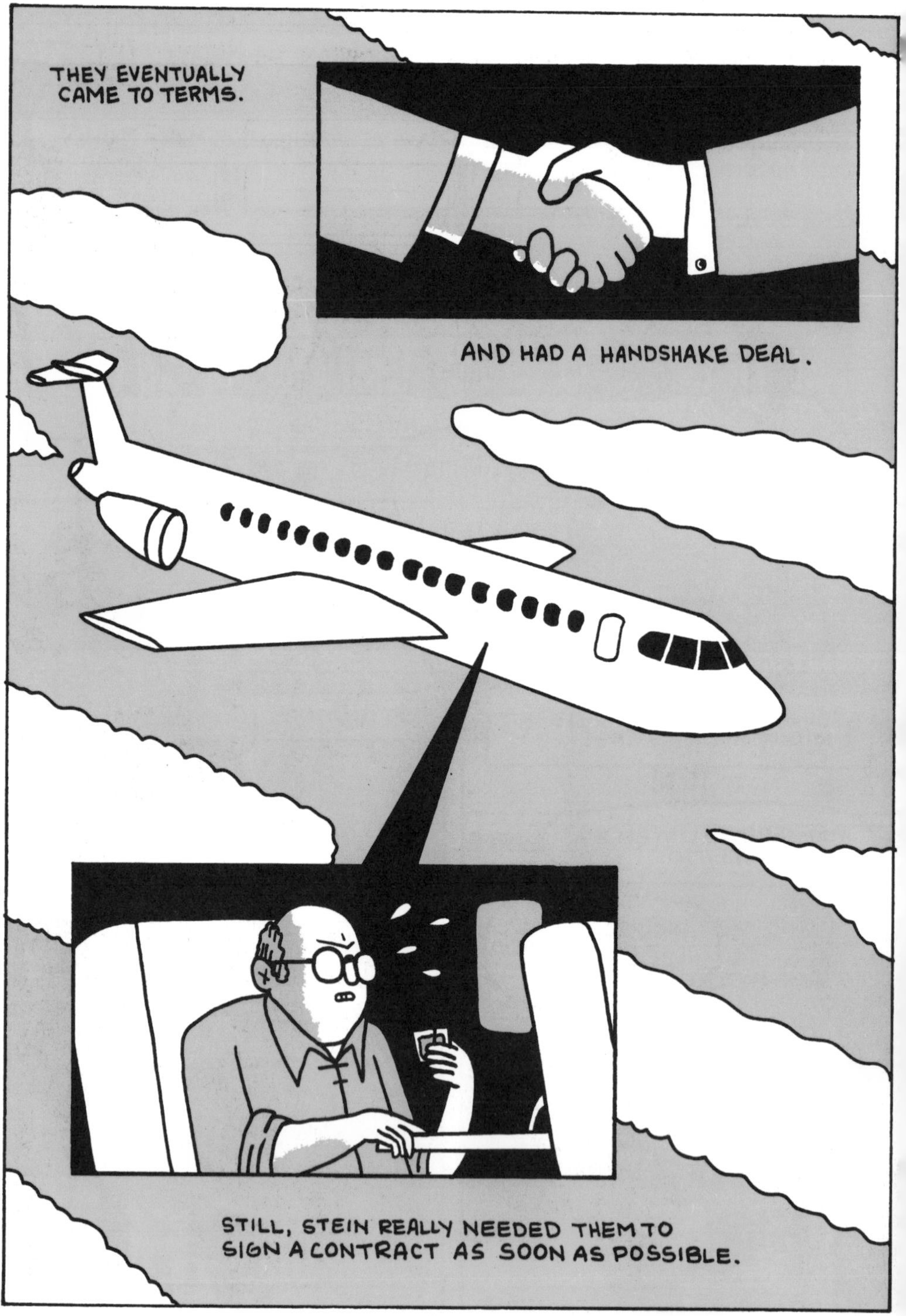
THEY EVENTUALLY CAME TO TERMS.
AND HAD A HANDSHAKE DEAL.
STILL, STEIN REALLY NEEDED THEM TO SIGN A CONTRACT AS SOON AS POSSIBLE.

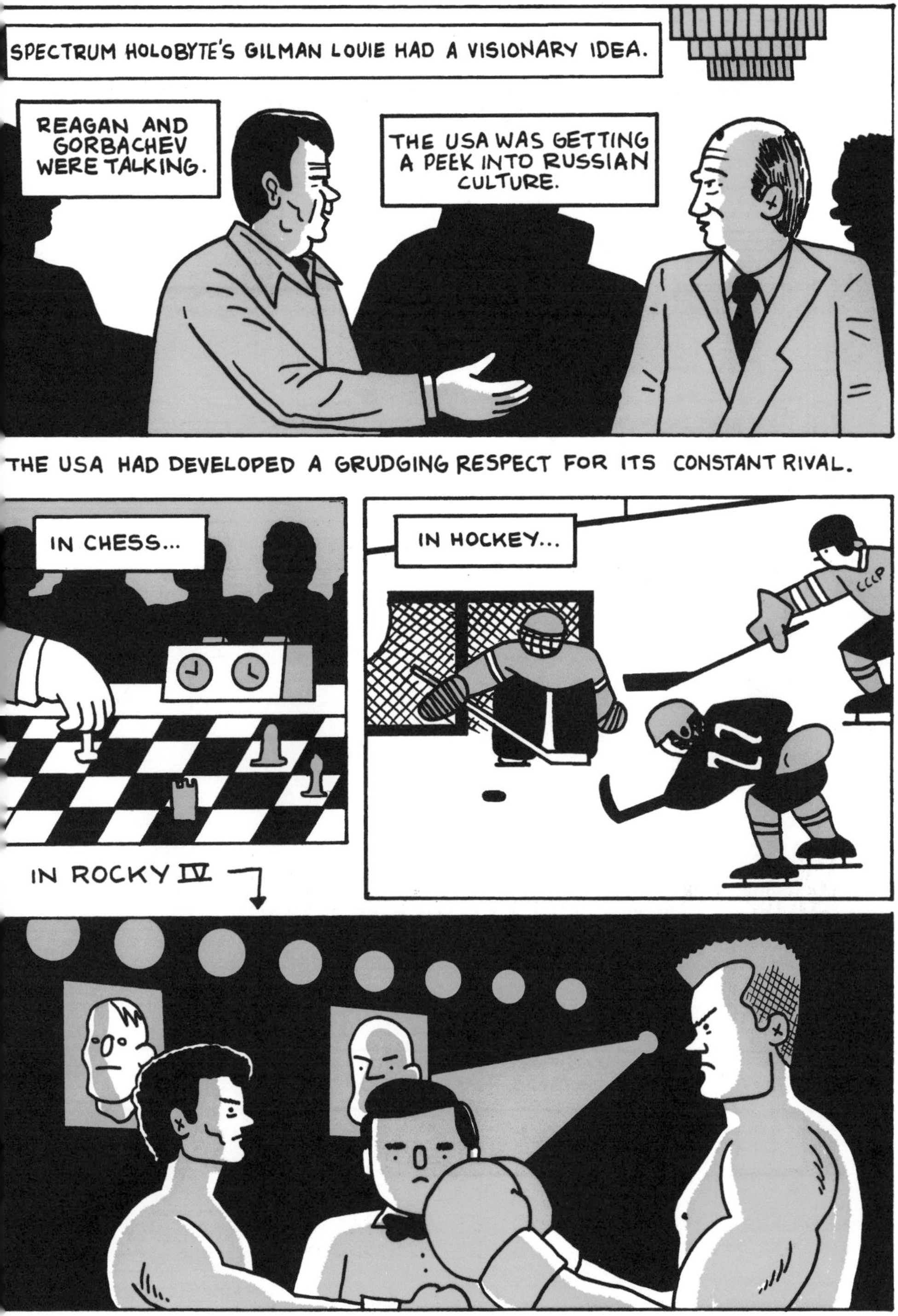
SPECTRUM HOLOBYTE'S GILMAN LOUIE HAD A VISIONARY IDEA.
REAGAN AND GORBACHEV WERE TALKING.
THE USA WAS GETTING A PEEK INTO RUSSIAN CULTURE.
THE USA HAD DEVELOPED A GRUDGING RESPECT FOR ITS CONSTANT RIVAL.
IN CHESS...
IN HOCKEY...
CCCP
IN ROCKY IV

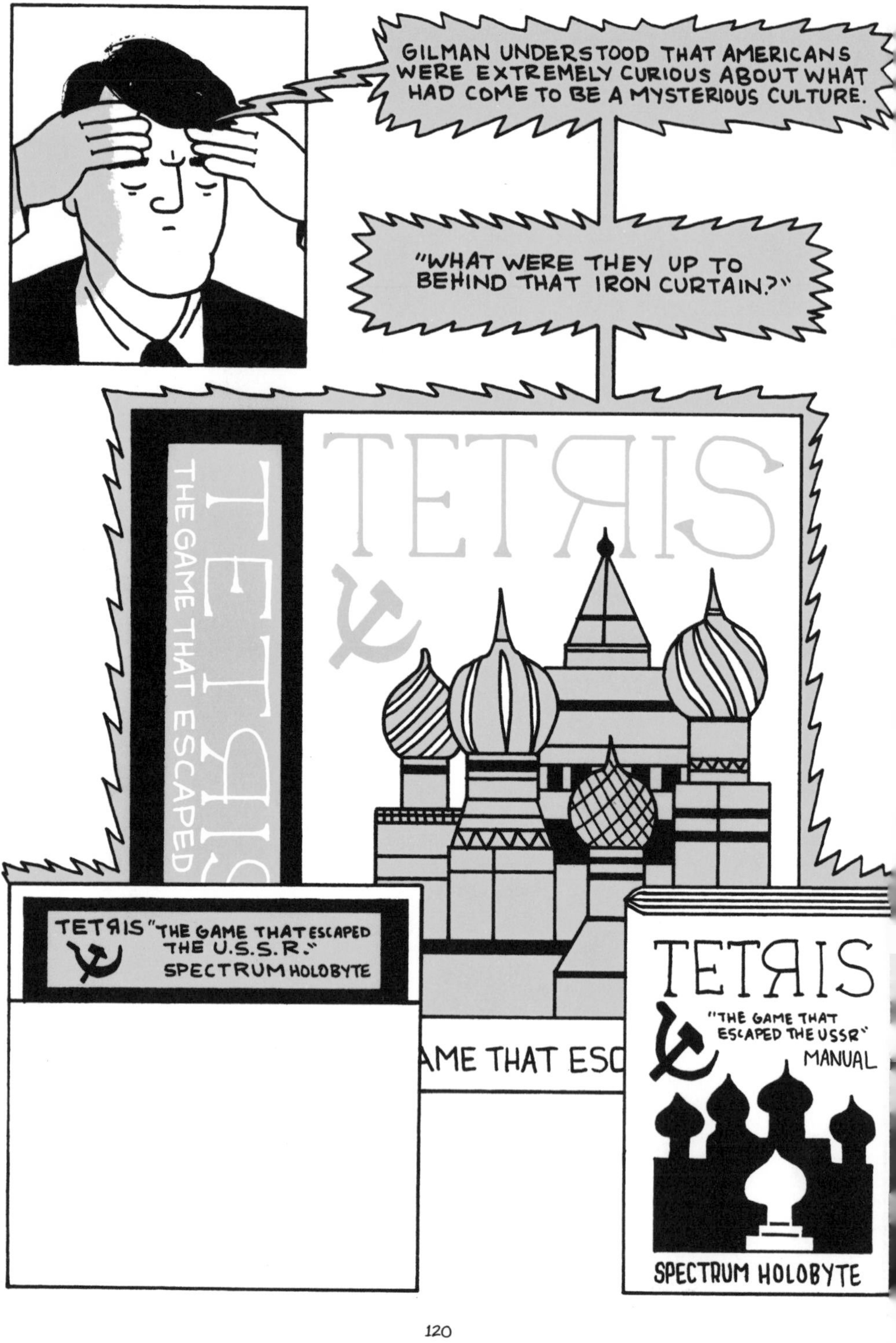
GILMAN UNDERSTOOD THAT AMERICANS WERE EXTREMELY CURIOUS ABOUT WHAT HAD COME TO BE A MYSTERIOUS CULTURE.
"WHAT WERE THEY UP TO BEHIND THAT IRON CURTAIN?"
TETRIS
THE GAME THAT ESCAPED
TETRIS
TETRIS "THE GAME THAT ESCAPED THE U.S.S.R."
SPECTRUM HOLOBYTE
AME THAT ESC
TETRIS
"THE GAME THAT ESCAPED THE USSR"
MANUAL
SPECTRUM HOLOBYTE

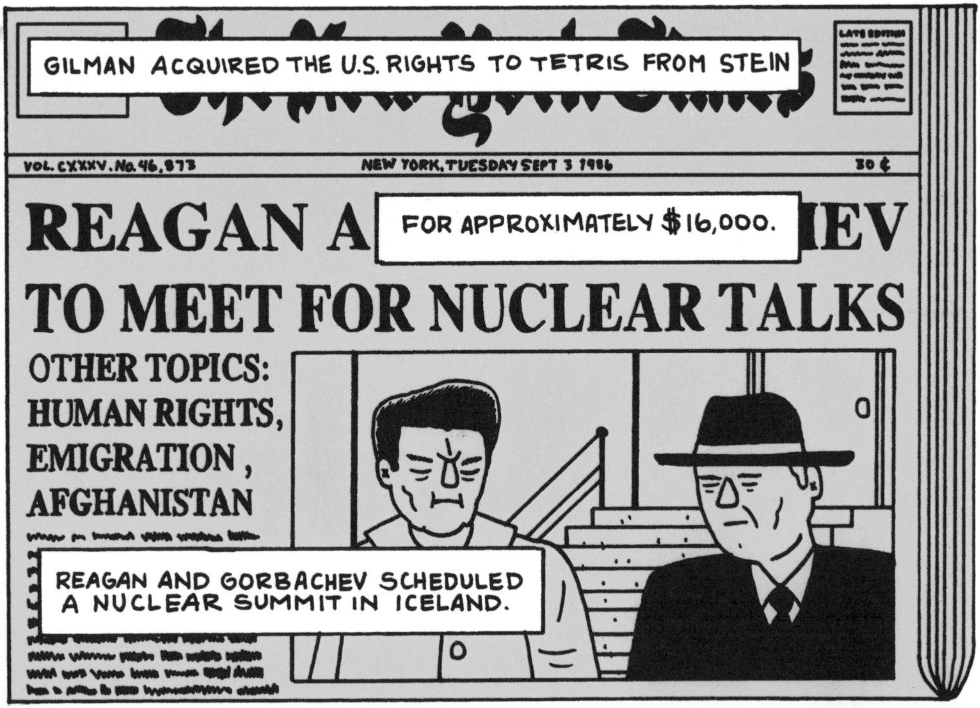
GILMAN ACQUIRED THE U.S. RIGHTS TO TETRIS FROM STEIN
VOL. CXXXV. No. 46,373
NEW YORK, TUESDAY SEPT 3 1986
30 ¢
REAGAN A
FOR APPROXIMATELY $16,000.
IEV
TO MEET FOR NUCLEAR TALKS
OTHER TOPICS: HUMAN RIGHTS, EMIGRATION, AFGHANISTAN
REAGAN AND GORBACHEV SCHEDULED A NUCLEAR SUMMIT IN ICELAND.

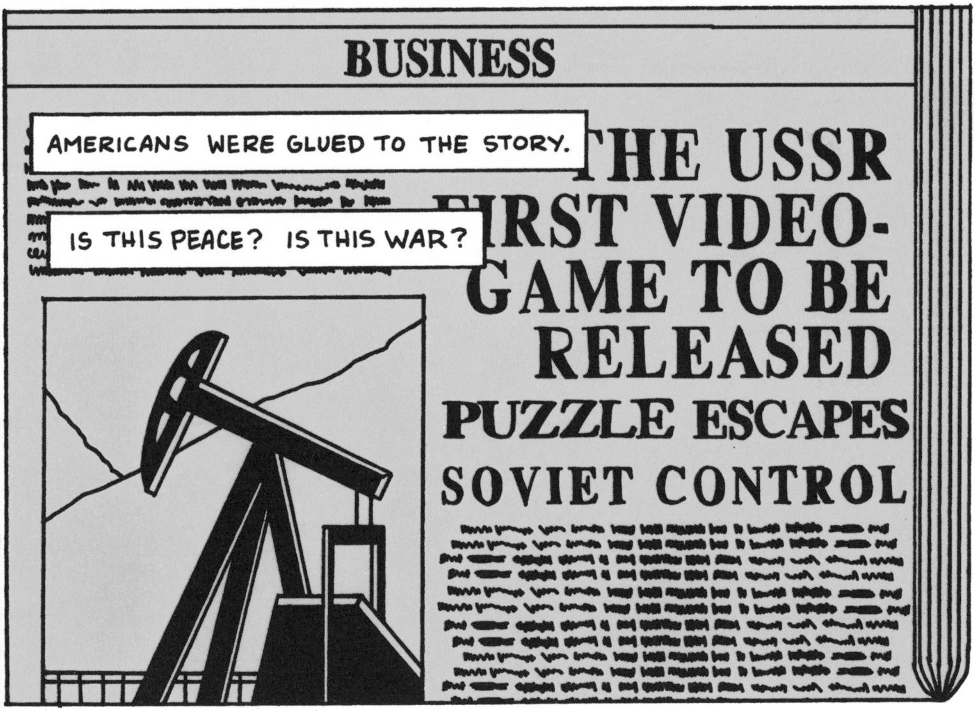
BUSINESS
AMERICANS WERE GLUED TO THE STORY.
HE USSR
IRST VIDEO-
IS THIS PEACE? IS THIS WAR?
GAME TO BE
RELEASED
PUZZLE ESCAPES
SOVIET CONTROL

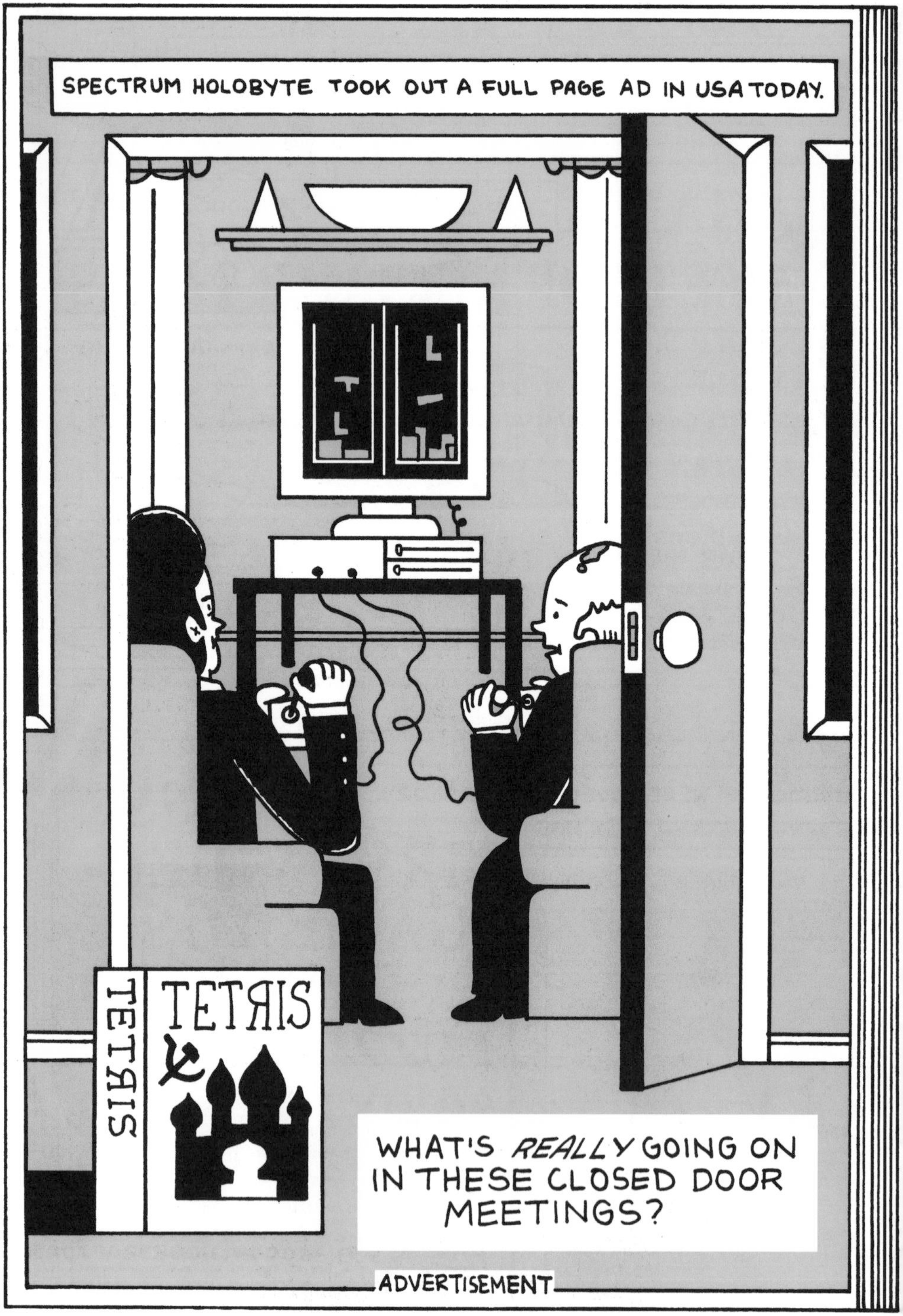
SPECTRUM HOLOBYTE TOOK OUT A FULL PAGE AD IN USA TODAY.
TETRIS
TETRIS
WHAT'S *REALLY* GOING ON IN THESE CLOSED DOOR MEETINGS?
ADVERTISEMENT

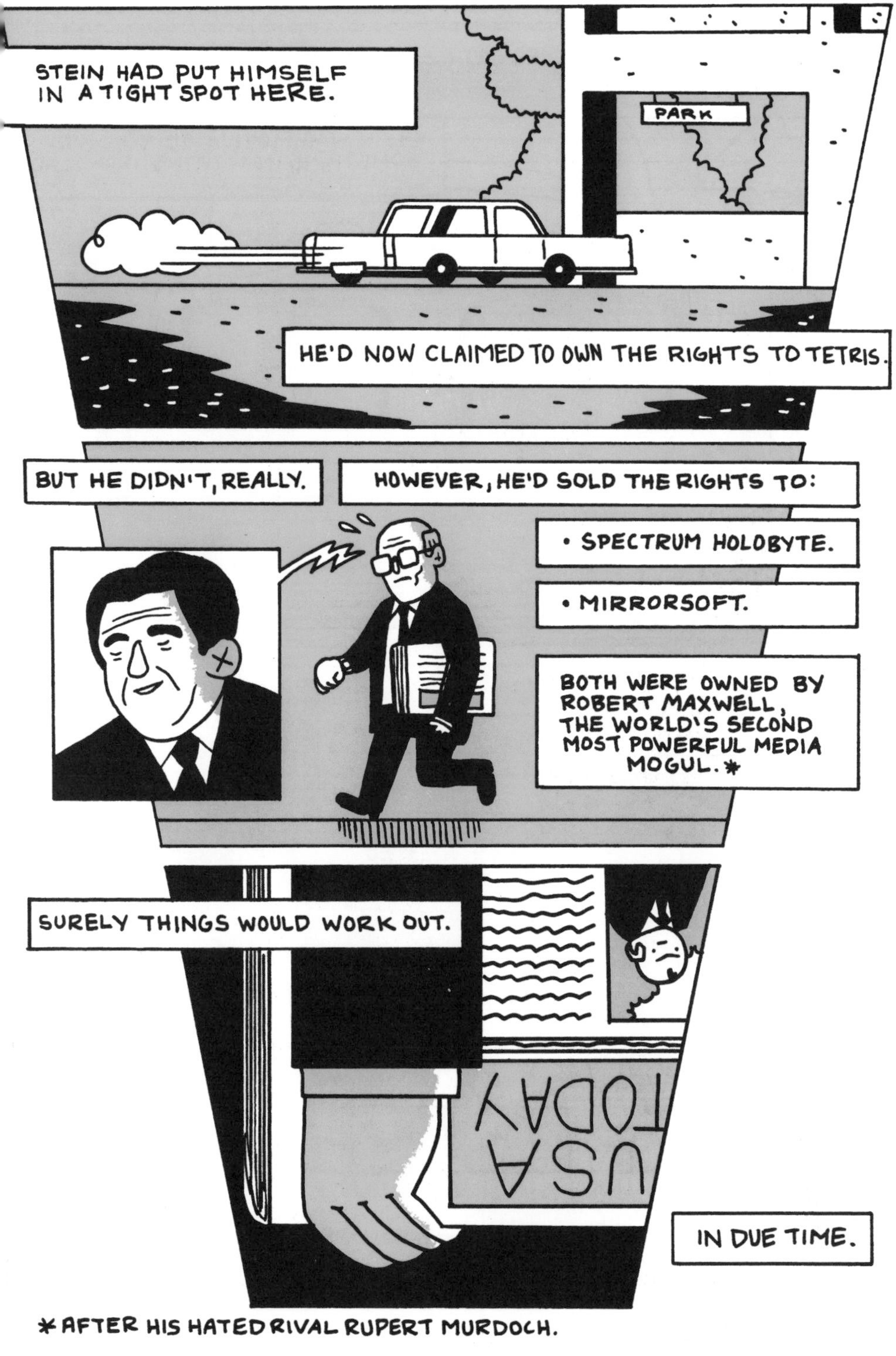
STEIN HAD PUT HIMSELF IN A TIGHT SPOT HERE.
PARK
HE'D NOW CLAIMED TO OWN THE RIGHTS TO TETRIS.
BUT HE DIDN'T, REALLY.
HOWEVER, HE'D SOLD THE RIGHTS TO:
• SPECTRUM HOLOBYTE.
• MIRRORSOFT.
BOTH WERE OWNED BY ROBERT MAXWELL, THE WORLD'S SECOND MOST POWERFUL MEDIA MOGUL. *
SURELY THINGS WOULD WORK OUT.
IN DUE TIME.

* AFTER HIS HATED RIVAL RUPERT MURDOCH.

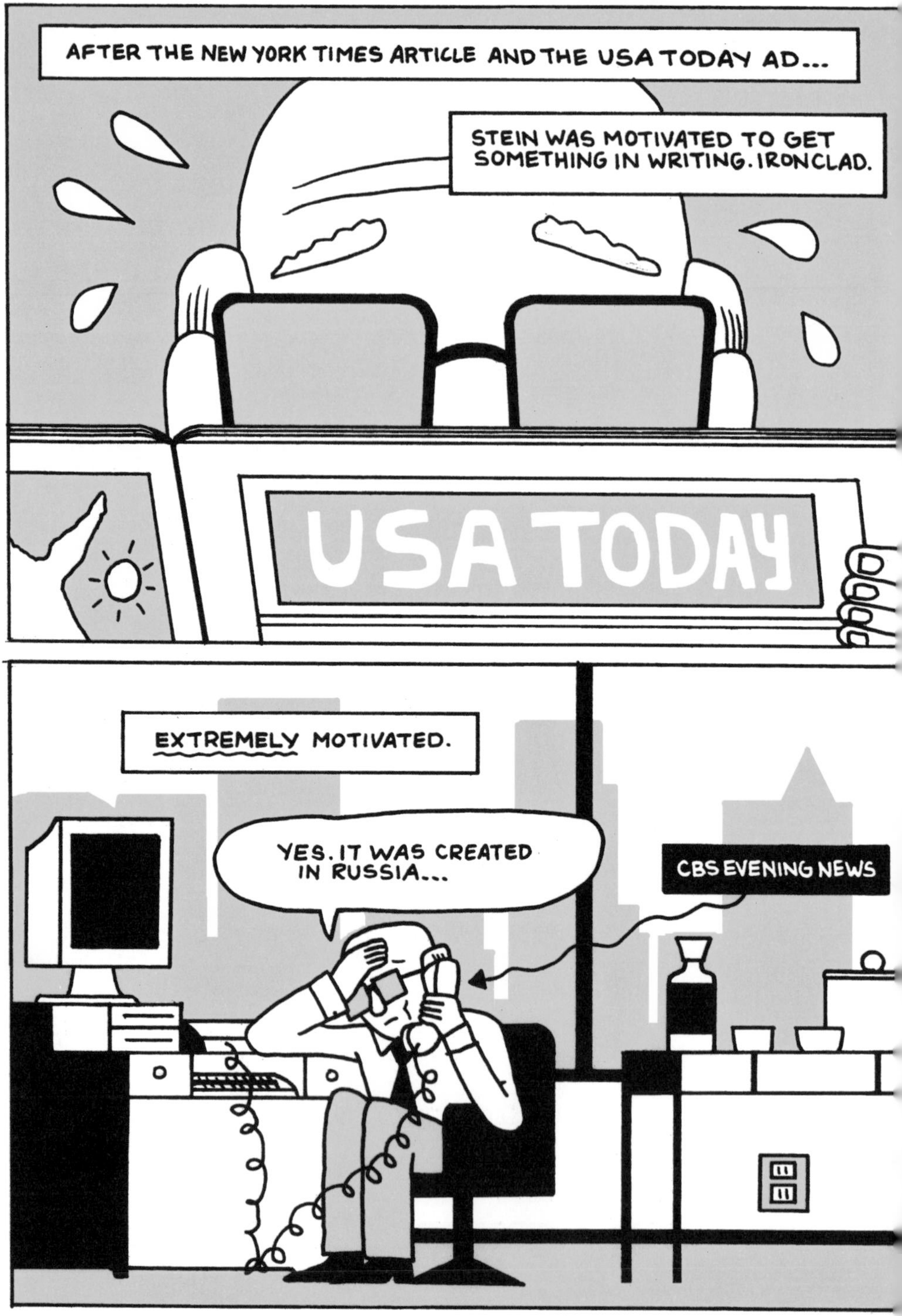
AFTER THE NEW YORK TIMES ARTICLE AND THE USA TODAY AD...
STEIN WAS MOTIVATED TO GET SOMETHING IN WRITING. IRONCLAD.
USA TODAY
EXTREMELY MOTIVATED.
YES. IT WAS CREATED IN RUSSIA...
CBS EVENING NEWS

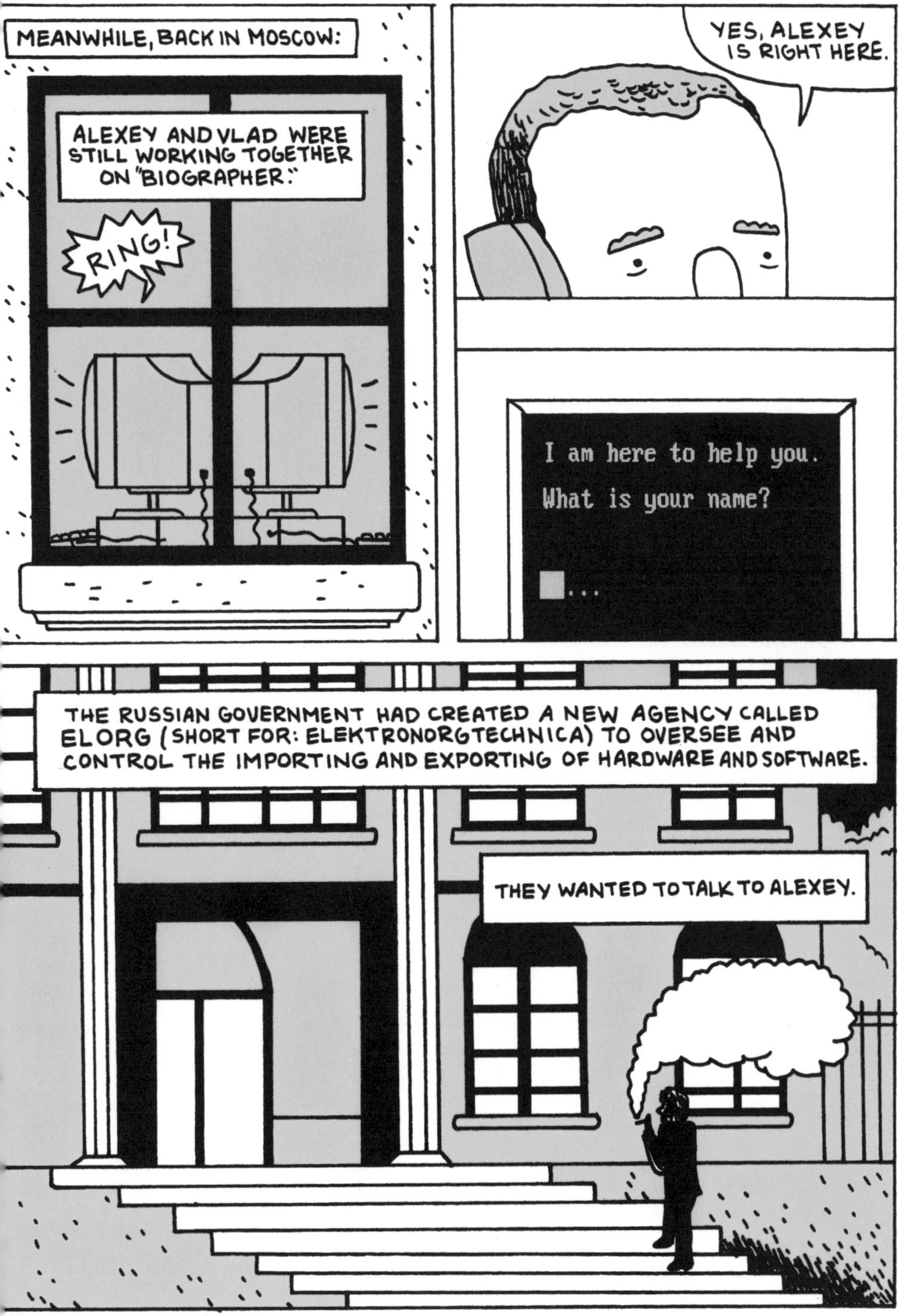
MEANWHILE, BACK IN MOSCOW:
ALEXEY AND VLAD WERE STILL WORKING TOGETHER ON "BIOGRAPHER."
RING!
YES, ALEXEY IS RIGHT HERE.
I am here to help you.
What is your name?
...
THE RUSSIAN GOVERNMENT HAD CREATED A NEW AGENCY CALLED ELORG (SHORT FOR: ELEKTRONORGTECHNICA) TO OVERSEE AND CONTROL THE IMPORTING AND EXPORTING OF HARDWARE AND SOFTWARE.
THEY WANTED TO TALK TO ALEXEY.

ALEXANDER "SASHA" ALEXINKO
ELORG (ELEKTRONORGTECHNICA)

KEVIN MAXWELL
SON OF ROBERT MAXWELL
MIRRORSOFT

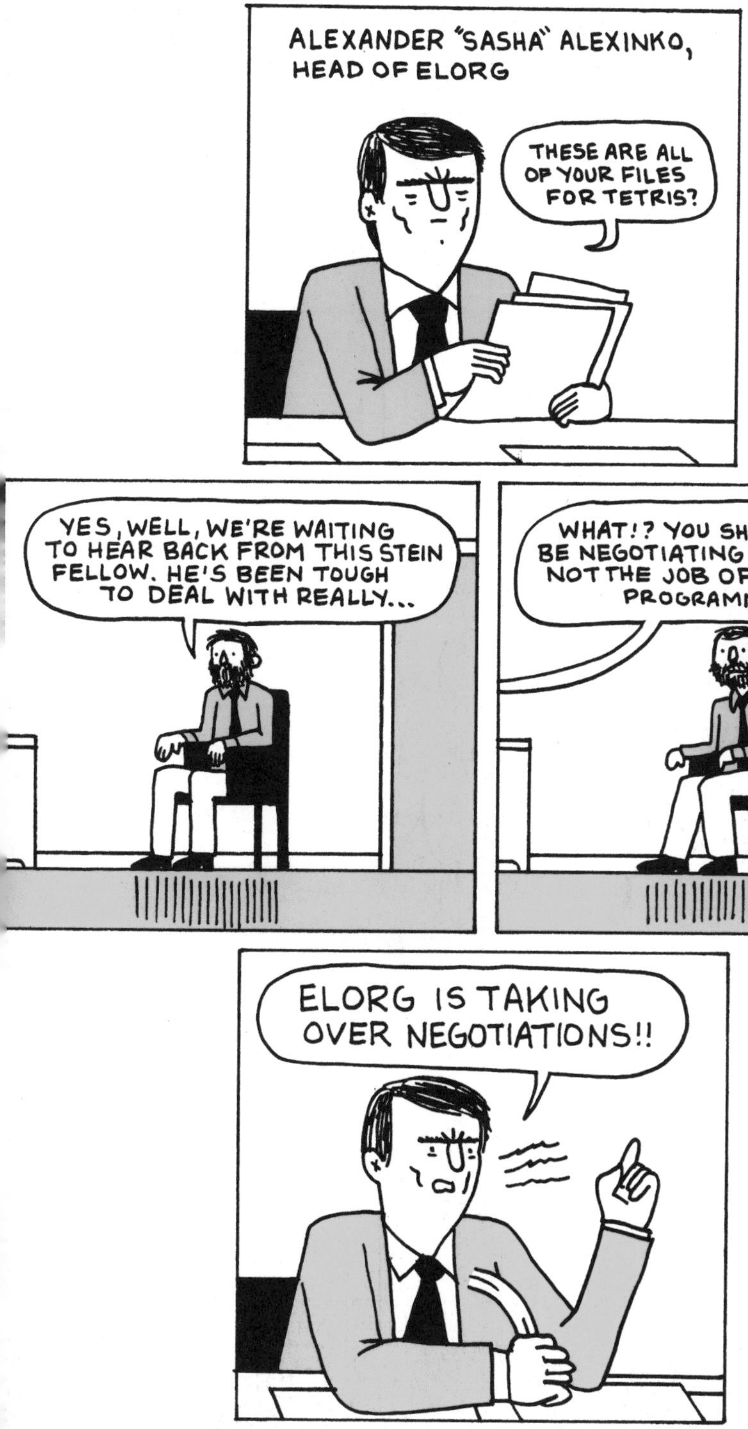
ALEXANDER "SASHA" ALEXINKO, HEAD OF ELORG
THESE ARE ALL OF YOUR FILES FOR TETRIS?
YES, WELL, WE'RE WAITING TO HEAR BACK FROM THIS STEIN FELLOW. HE'S BEEN TOUGH TO DEAL WITH REALLY...
WHAT!? YOU SHOULDN'T BE NEGOTIATING THAT!! THAT'S NOT THE JOB OF A COMPUTER PROGRAMMER!!
ELORG IS TAKING OVER NEGOTIATIONS!!

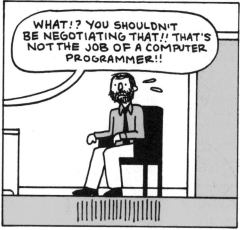

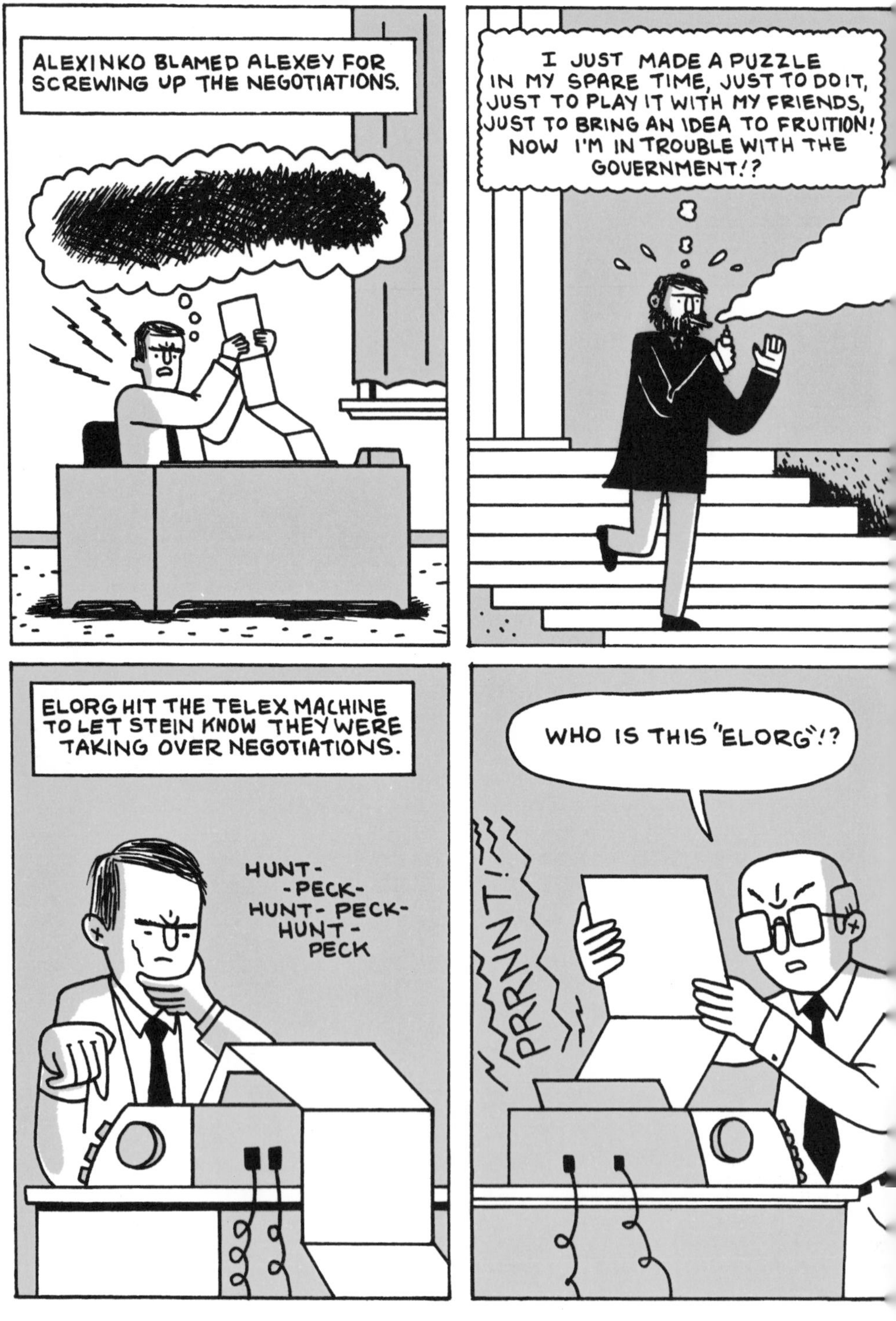
ALEXINKO BLAMED ALEXEY FOR SCREWING UP THE NEGOTIATIONS.
I JUST MADE A PUZZLE IN MY SPARE TIME, JUST TO DO IT, JUST TO PLAY IT WITH MY FRIENDS, JUST TO BRING AN IDEA TO FRUITION! NOW I'M IN TROUBLE WITH THE GOVERNMENT!?
ELORG HIT THE TELEX MACHINE TO LET STEIN KNOW THEY WERE TAKING OVER NEGOTIATIONS.
HUNT- -PECK- HUNT- PECK- HUNT- PECK
WHO IS THIS "ELORG"!?
PRRRNNT!

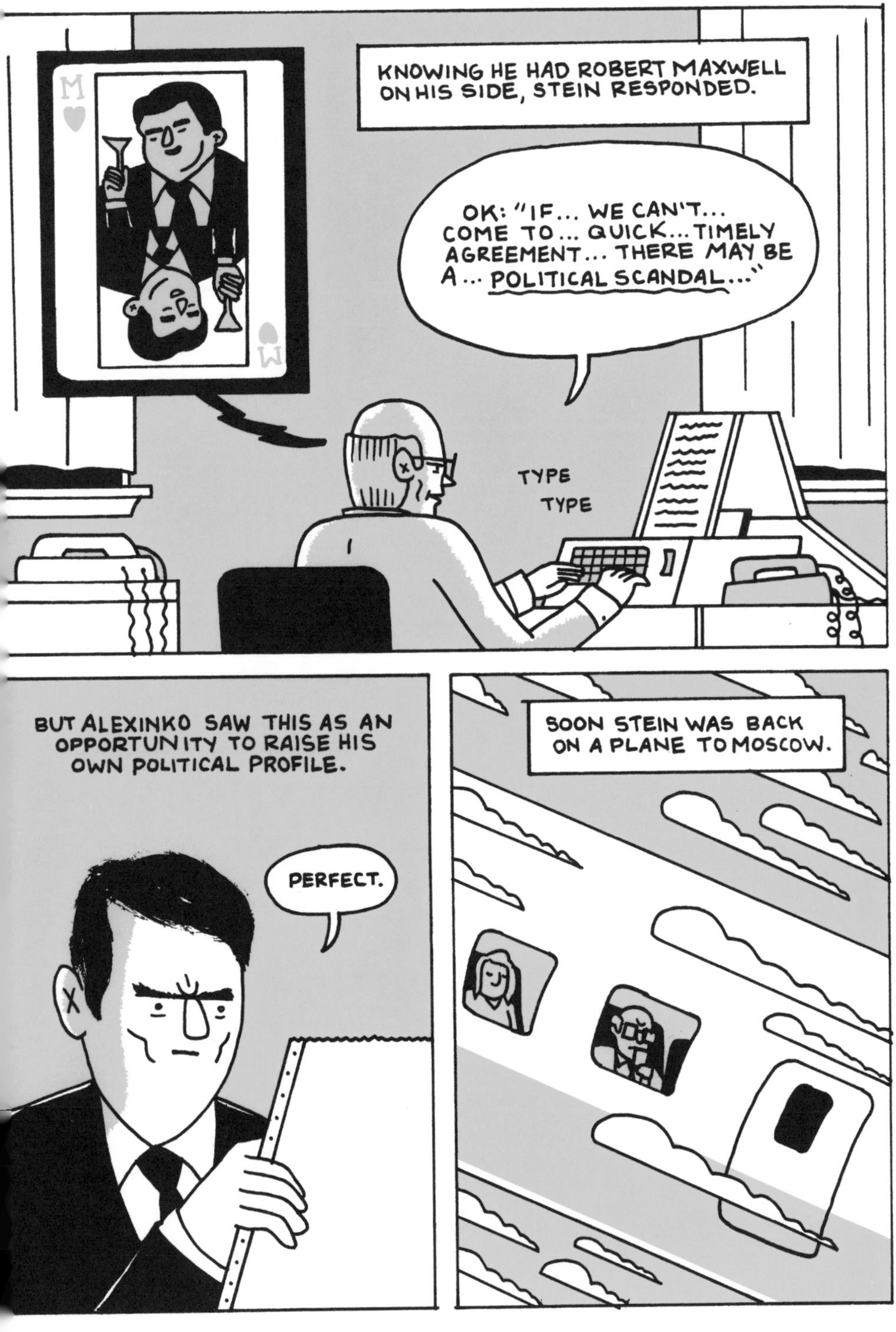
KNOWING HE HAD ROBERT MAXWELL ON HIS SIDE, STEIN RESPONDED.
OK: "IF... WE CAN'T... COME TO... QUICK... TIMELY AGREEMENT... THERE MAY BE A... POLITICAL SCANDAL..."
TYPE
TYPE
BUT ALEXINKO SAW THIS AS AN OPPORTUNITY TO RAISE HIS OWN POLITICAL PROFILE.
PERFECT.
SOON STEIN WAS BACK ON A PLANE TO MOSCOW.

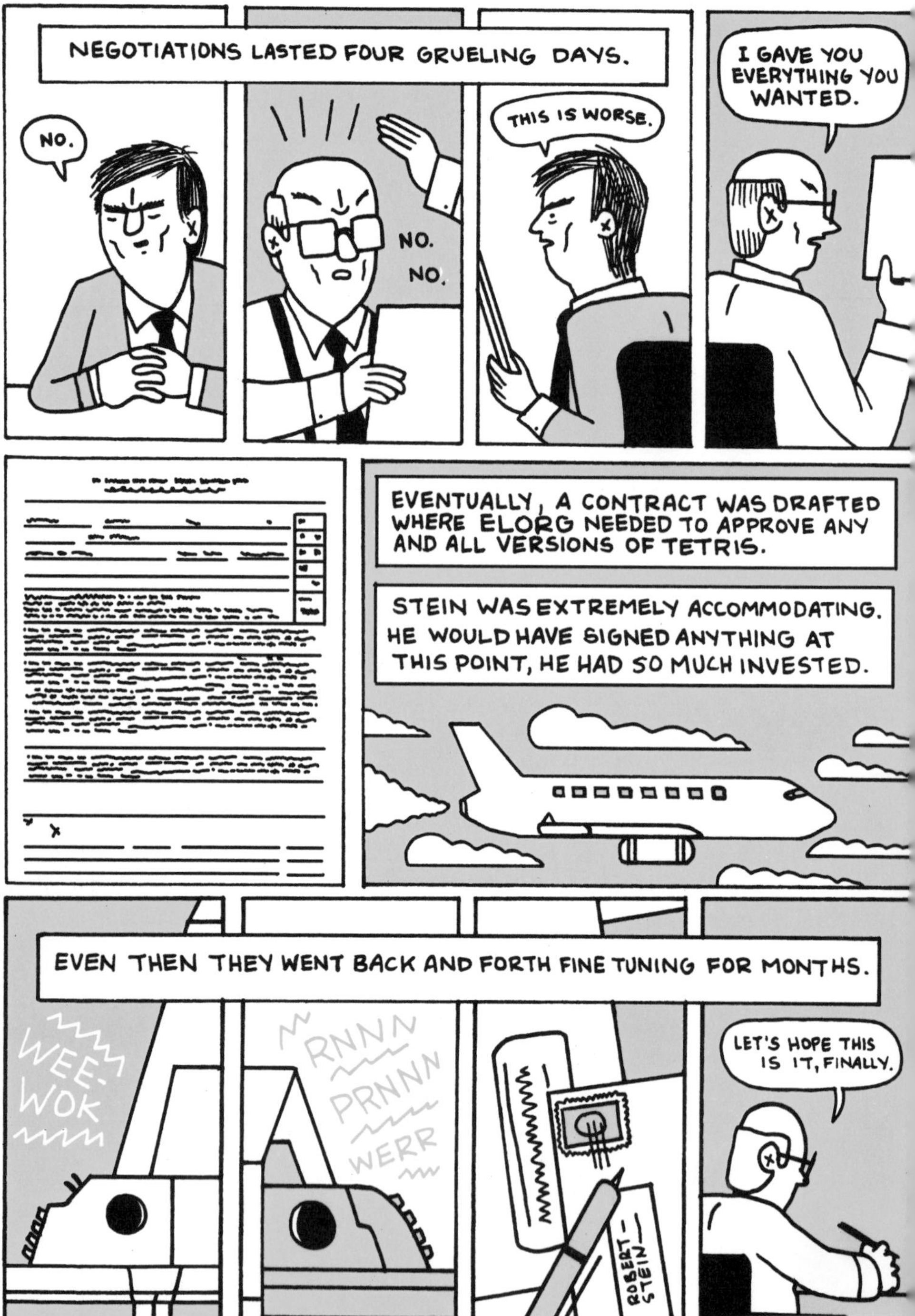
NEGOTIATIONS LASTED FOUR GRUELING DAYS.
NO.
NO.
NO.
THIS IS WORSE.
I GAVE YOU EVERYTHING YOU WANTED.
EVENTUALLY, A CONTRACT WAS DRAFTED WHERE ELORG NEEDED TO APPROVE ANY AND ALL VERSIONS OF TETRIS.
STEIN WAS EXTREMELY ACCOMMODATING. HE WOULD HAVE SIGNED ANYTHING AT THIS POINT, HE HAD SO MUCH INVESTED.
EVEN THEN THEY WENT BACK AND FORTH FINE TUNING FOR MONTHS.
WEE-WOK
RNNN
PRNNN
WERR
ROBERT STEIN
LET'S HOPE THIS IS IT, FINALLY.

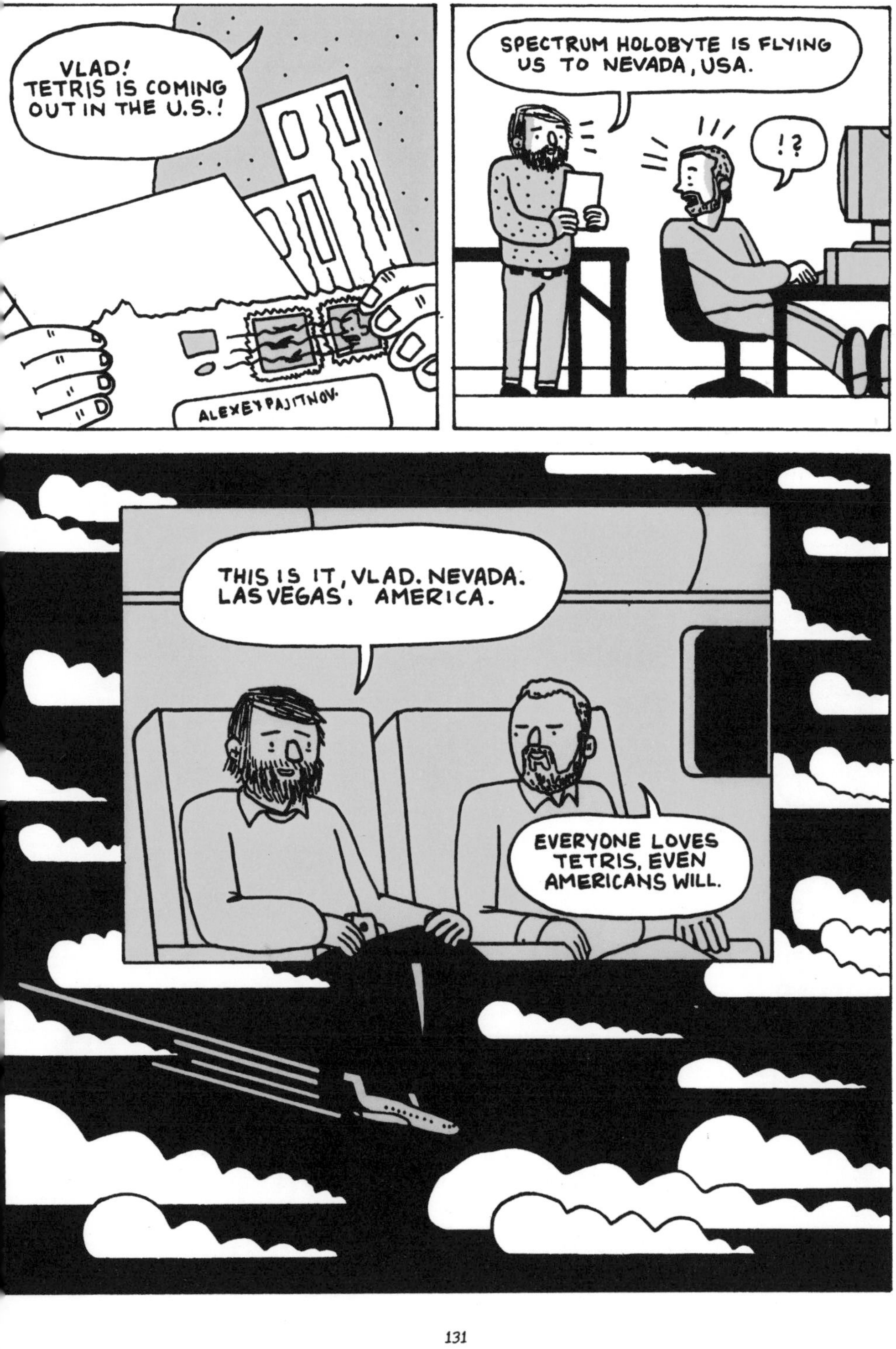
VLAD! TETRIS IS COMING OUT IN THE U.S.!
ALEXEY PAJITNOV.
SPECTRUM HOLOBYTE IS FLYING US TO NEVADA, USA.
!?
THIS IS IT, VLAD. NEVADA. LAS VEGAS. AMERICA.
EVERYONE LOVES TETRIS, EVEN AMERICANS WILL.

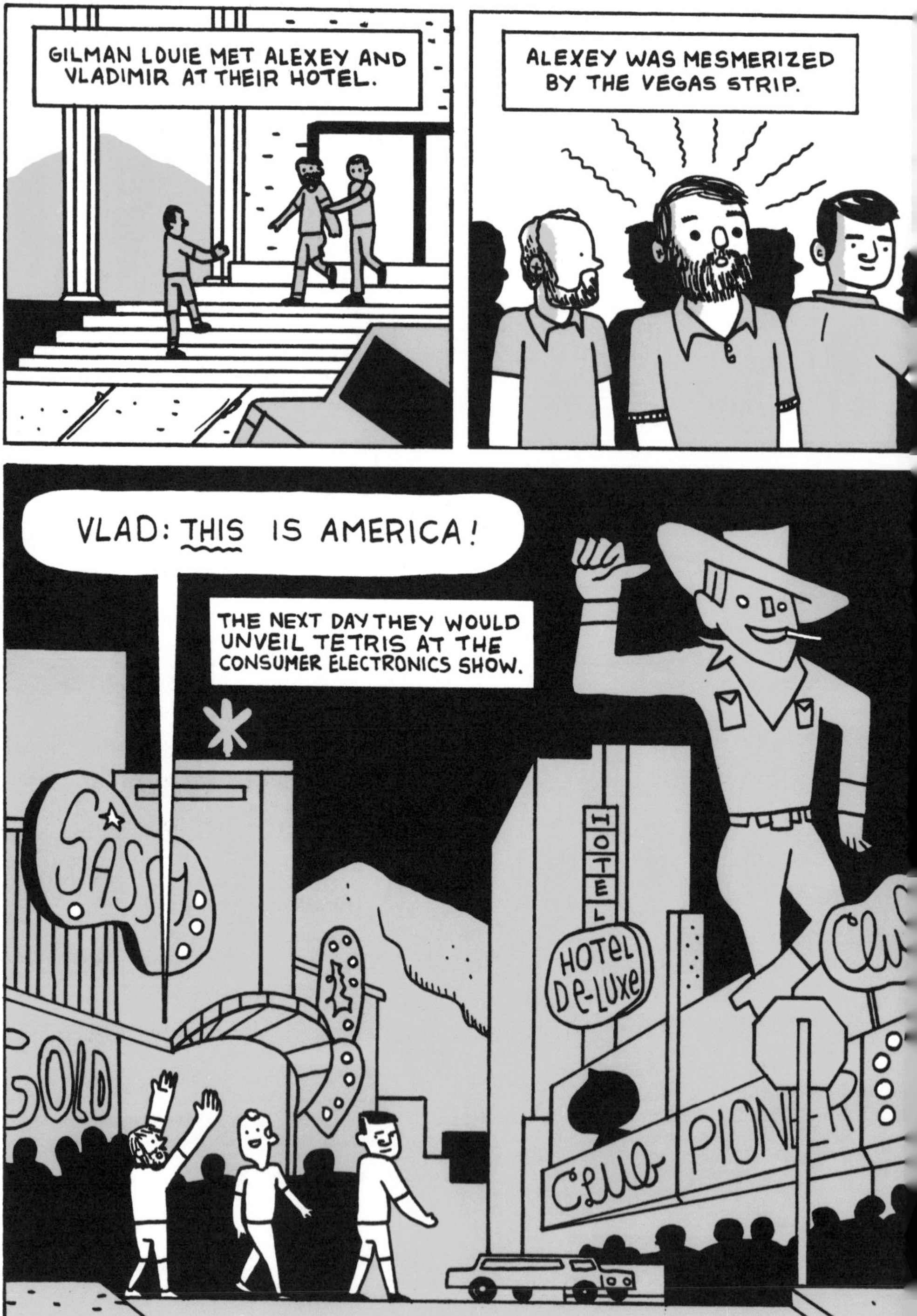
GILMAN LOUIE MET ALEXEY AND VLADIMIR AT THEIR HOTEL.
ALEXEY WAS MESMERIZED BY THE VEGAS STRIP.
VLAD: THIS IS AMERICA!
THE NEXT DAY THEY WOULD UNVEIL TETRIS AT THE CONSUMER ELECTRONICS SHOW.
GOLD
HOTEL
HOTEL DE-LUXE
CLUB

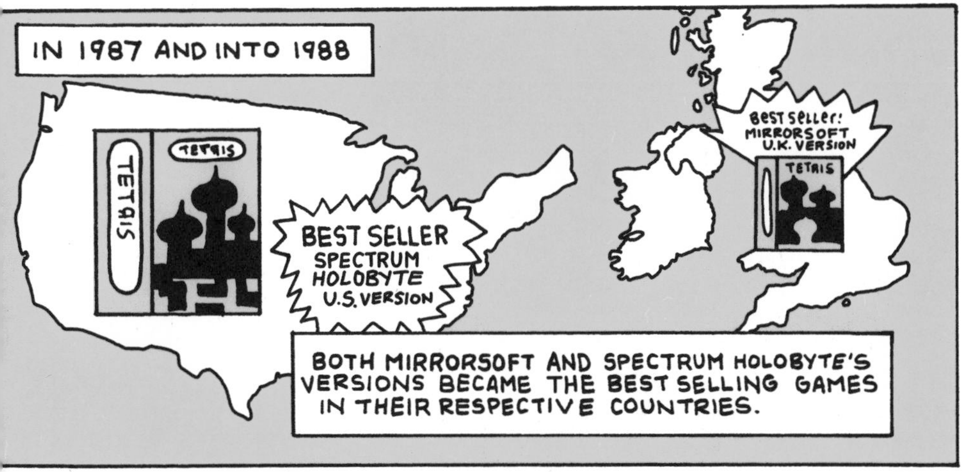
IN 1987 AND INTO 1988
TETRIS
BEST SELLER
SPECTRUM
HOLOBYTE
U.S. VERSION
BEST SELLER!
MIRRORSOFT
U.K. VERSION
TETRIS
BOTH MIRRORSOFT AND SPECTRUM HOLOBYTE'S VERSIONS BECAME THE BEST SELLING GAMES IN THEIR RESPECTIVE COUNTRIES.

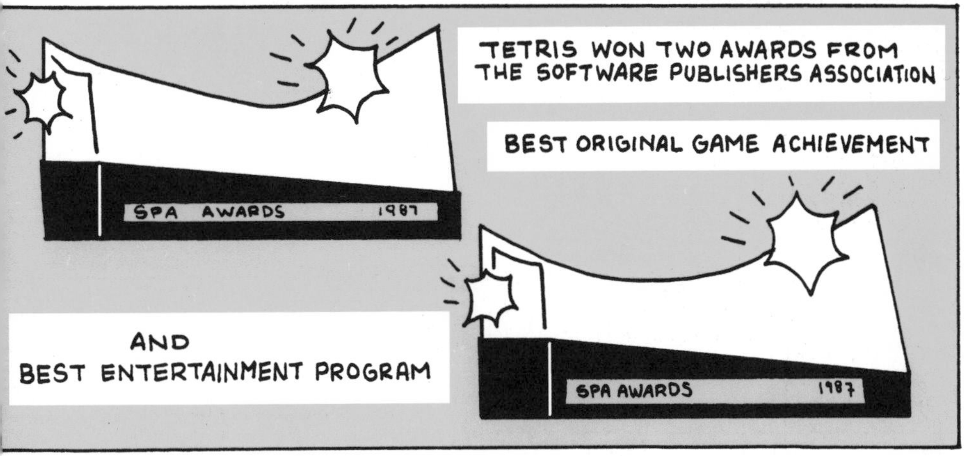
TETRIS WON TWO AWARDS FROM THE SOFTWARE PUBLISHERS ASSOCIATION
BEST ORIGINAL GAME ACHIEVEMENT
SPA AWARDS 1987
AND
BEST ENTERTAINMENT PROGRAM
SPA AWARDS 1987

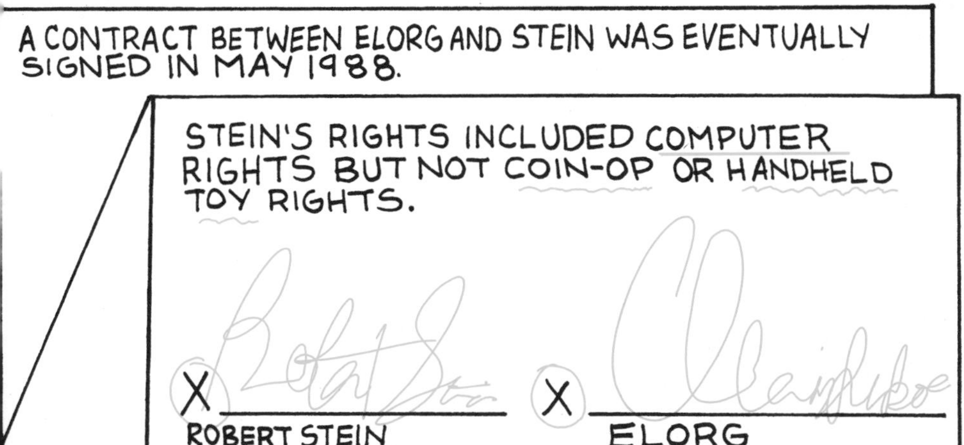
A CONTRACT BETWEEN ELORG AND STEIN WAS EVENTUALLY SIGNED IN MAY 1988.
STEIN'S RIGHTS INCLUDED COMPUTER RIGHTS BUT NOT COIN-OP OR HANDHELD TOY RIGHTS.
X
ROBERT STEIN
ANDROMEDA SOFTWARE
X
ELORG

IN 1987 A GERMAN PILOT NAMED MATTHIAS RUST AIMED TO CREATE AN "IMAGINARY BRIDGE" BETWEEN RUSSIA AND ITS COLD WAR ENEMIES.

HE LANDED A PLANE IN THE MIDDLE OF RED SQUARE IN THE MIDDLE OF THE DAY.

RUST'S JOURNEY WAS IMMORTALIZED IN FLIGHT SIMULATOR.

COM 1	17547	OMI	7403
NAV1	1684	OME	10568
NAV2	1831	XPNDR	679
TIME	10:10:18	MAGS LETS	
FUEL	E		

RUST WAS ARRESTED TWO HOURS AFTER LANDING. HE COULD'VE EASILY BEEN SHOT DOWN.

HE ENDED UP BEING SENTENCED TO FOUR YEARS' HARD LABOR AND NAMED A RADICAL BY THE GOVERNMENT.

TO BEEF UP TETRIS'S GRAPHICS THE PUBLISHERS (MIRRORSOFT AND SPECTRUM HOLOBYTE) ADDED STEREOTYPICAL RUSSIAN IMAGES.

SOMEHOW RUST FOUND HIS WAY INTO ONE OF THESE SCREENS.

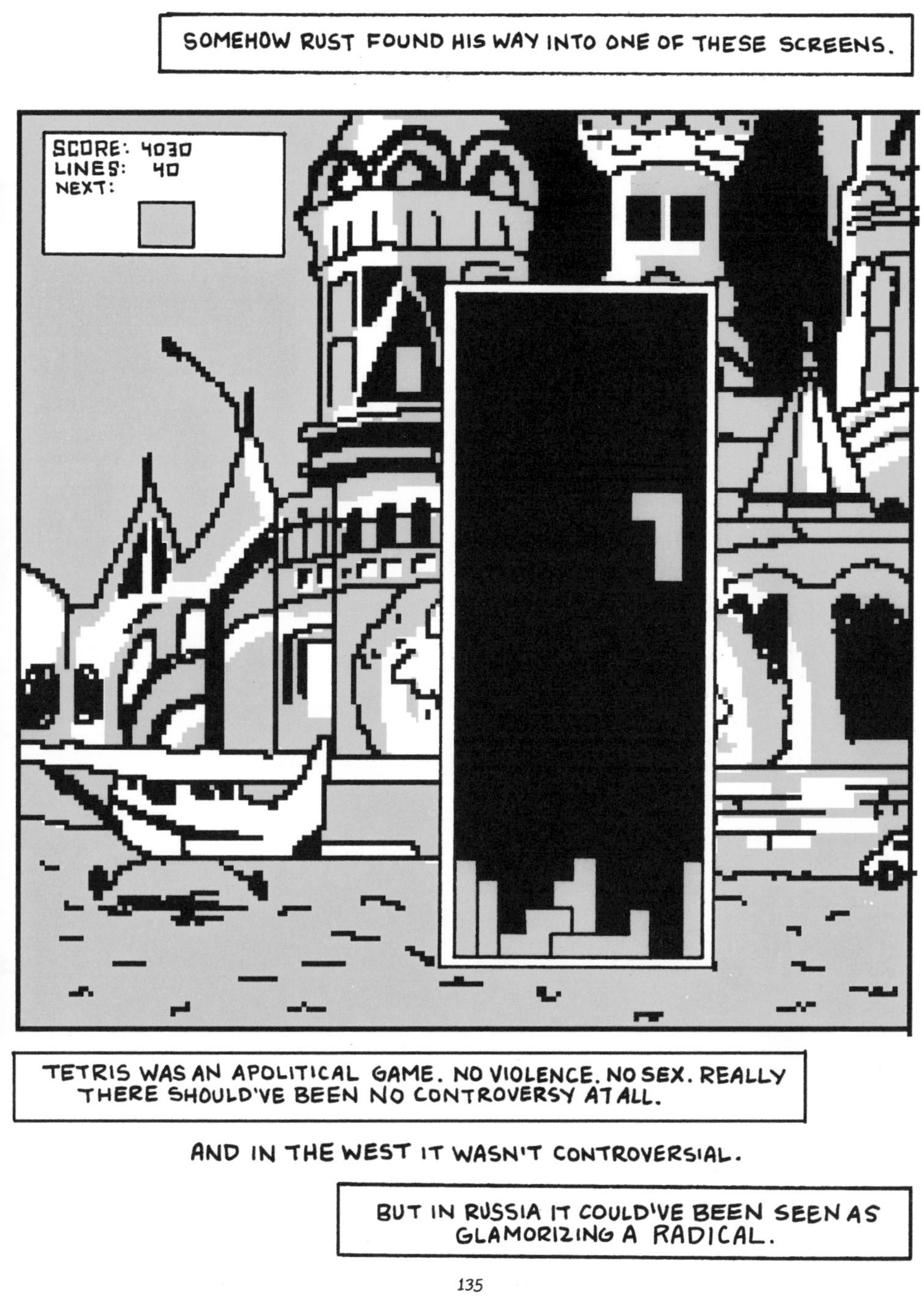
SCORE: 4030
LINES: 40
NEXT:

TETRIS WAS AN APOLITICAL GAME. NO VIOLENCE. NO SEX. REALLY THERE SHOULD'VE BEEN NO CONTROVERSY AT ALL.

AND IN THE WEST IT WASN'T CONTROVERSIAL.

BUT IN RUSSIA IT COULD'VE BEEN SEEN AS GLAMORIZING A RADICAL.

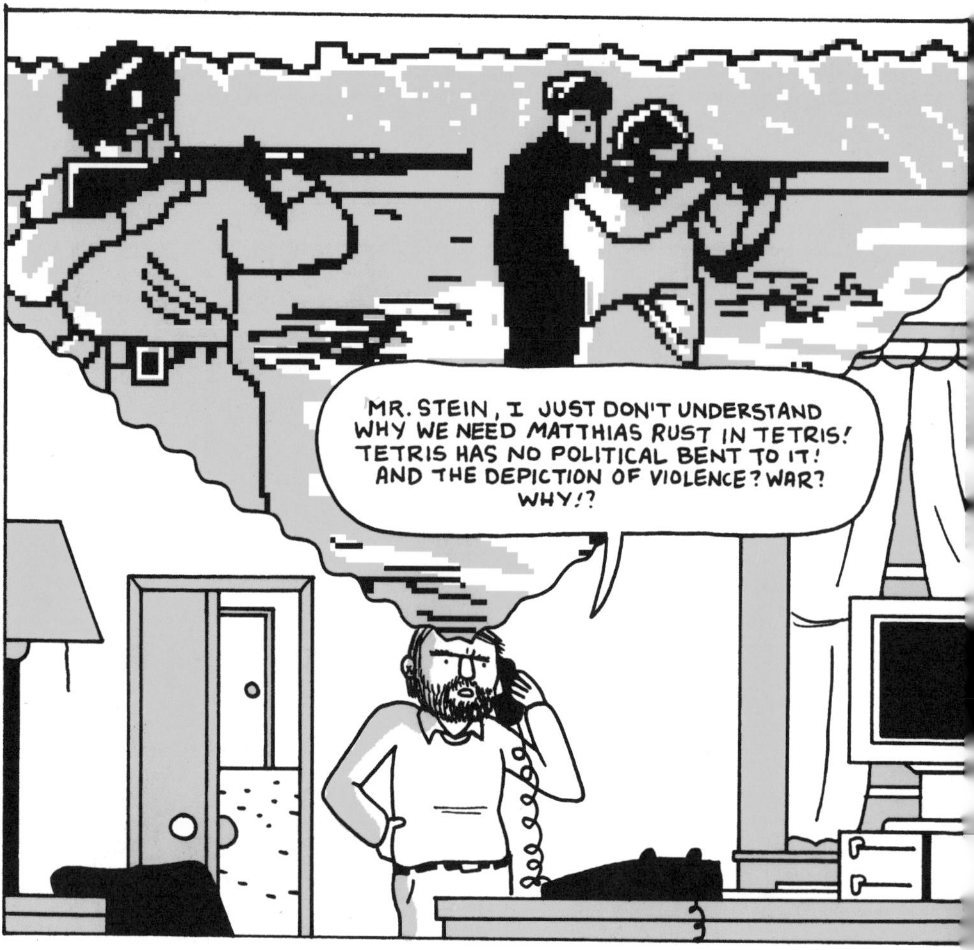
MR. STEIN, I JUST DON'T UNDERSTAND WHY WE NEED MATTHIAS RUST IN TETRIS! TETRIS HAS NO POLITICAL BENT TO IT! AND THE DEPICTION OF VIOLENCE? WAR? WHY!?

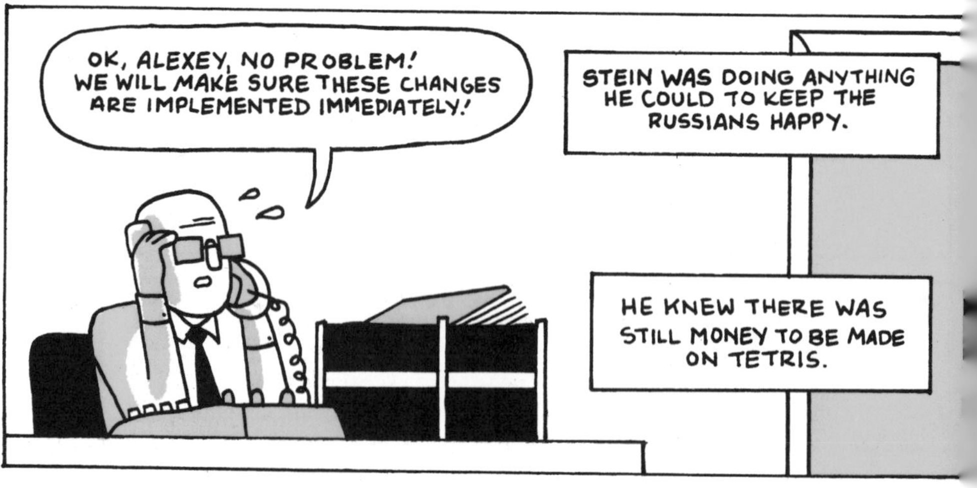
OK, ALEXEY, NO PROBLEM! WE WILL MAKE SURE THESE CHANGES ARE IMPLEMENTED IMMEDIATELY!
STEIN WAS DOING ANYTHING HE COULD TO KEEP THE RUSSIANS HAPPY.
HE KNEW THERE WAS STILL MONEY TO BE MADE ON TETRIS.

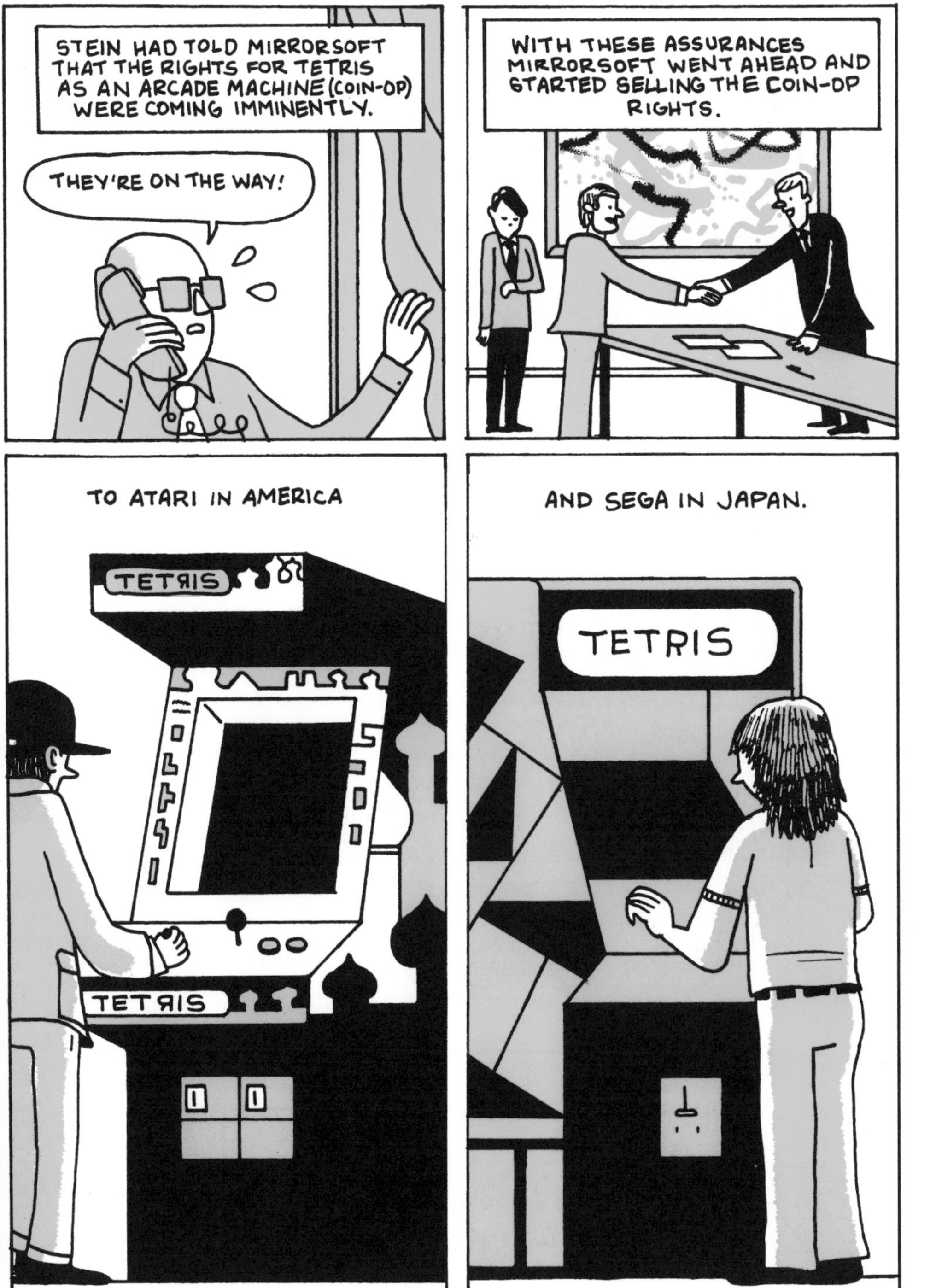
STEIN HAD TOLD MIRRORSOFT THAT THE RIGHTS FOR TETRIS AS AN ARCADE MACHINE (COIN-OP) WERE COMING IMMINENTLY.
THEY'RE ON THE WAY!
WITH THESE ASSURANCES MIRRORSOFT WENT AHEAD AND STARTED SELLING THE COIN-OP RIGHTS.
TO ATARI IN AMERICA
TETRIS
TETRIS
AND SEGA IN JAPAN.
TETRIS

STEIN AND ALEXINKO, HEAD OF ELORG, MET AGAIN IN JULY 1988 IN PARIS.

STEIN SOLELY WANTED TO SHORE UP THE COIN-OP RIGHTS.

ALEXINKO WAS THERE TO GET ON STEIN'S CASE ABOUT WHY ELORG HAD NOT RECEIVED ANY ROYALTIES YET.

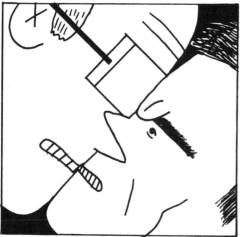

STEIN ENDED UP SIGNING A DEAL WHERE HE WOULD HAVE TO PAY LATE FEES SHOULD HE EVER MISS A ROYALTY PAYMENT IN THE FUTURE.

AND HE STILL DIDN'T GET A DEAL FOR THE COIN-OP RIGHTS.

HENK ROGERS
BULLETPROOF SOFTWARE

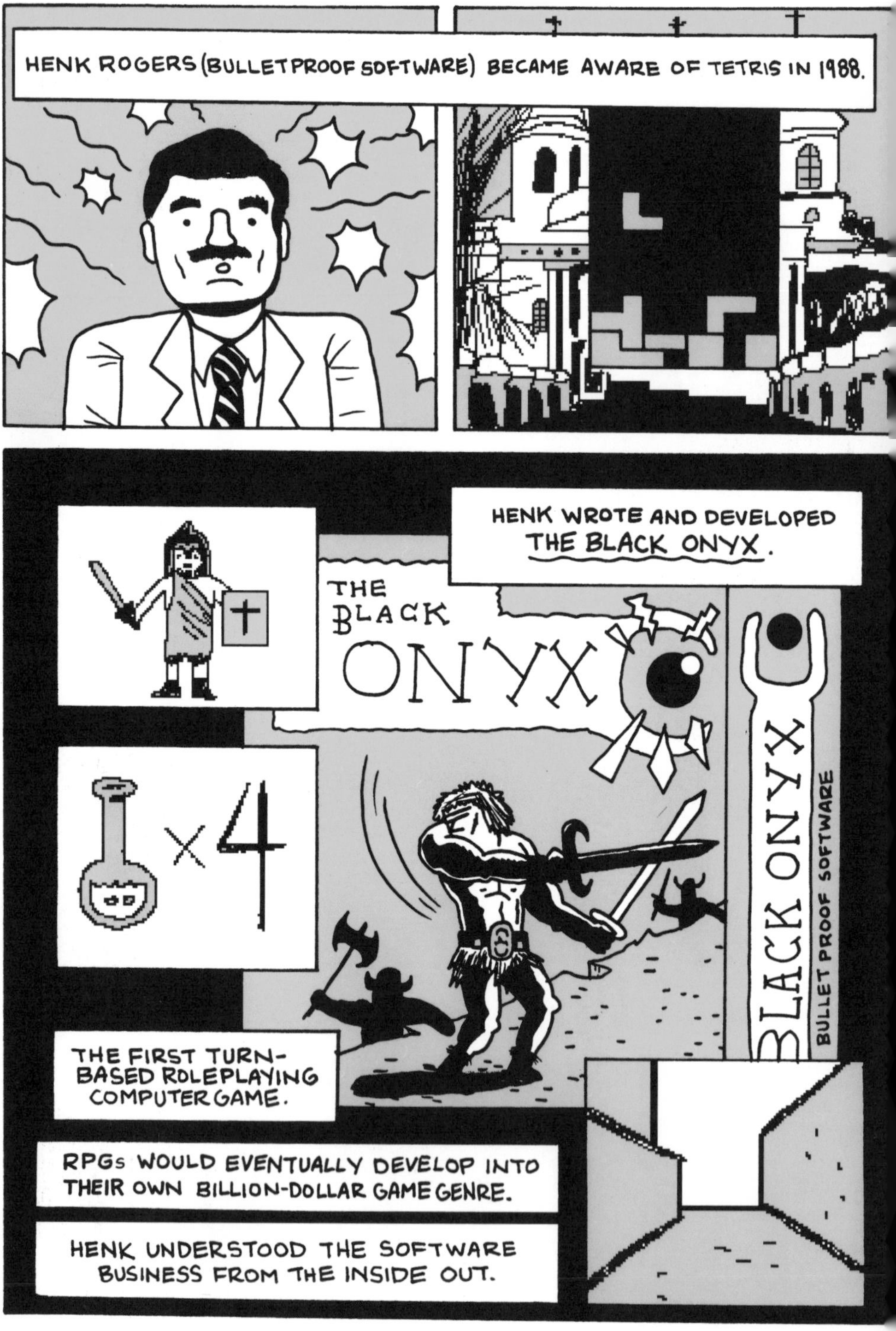
HENK ROGERS (BULLETPROOF SOFTWARE) BECAME AWARE OF TETRIS IN 1988.
HENK WROTE AND DEVELOPED THE BLACK ONYX.
THE BLACK ONYX
BLACK ONYX
BULLET PROOF SOFTWARE
×4
THE FIRST TURN-BASED ROLEPLAYING COMPUTER GAME.
RPGs WOULD EVENTUALLY DEVELOP INTO THEIR OWN BILLION-DOLLAR GAME GENRE.
HENK UNDERSTOOD THE SOFTWARE BUSINESS FROM THE INSIDE OUT.

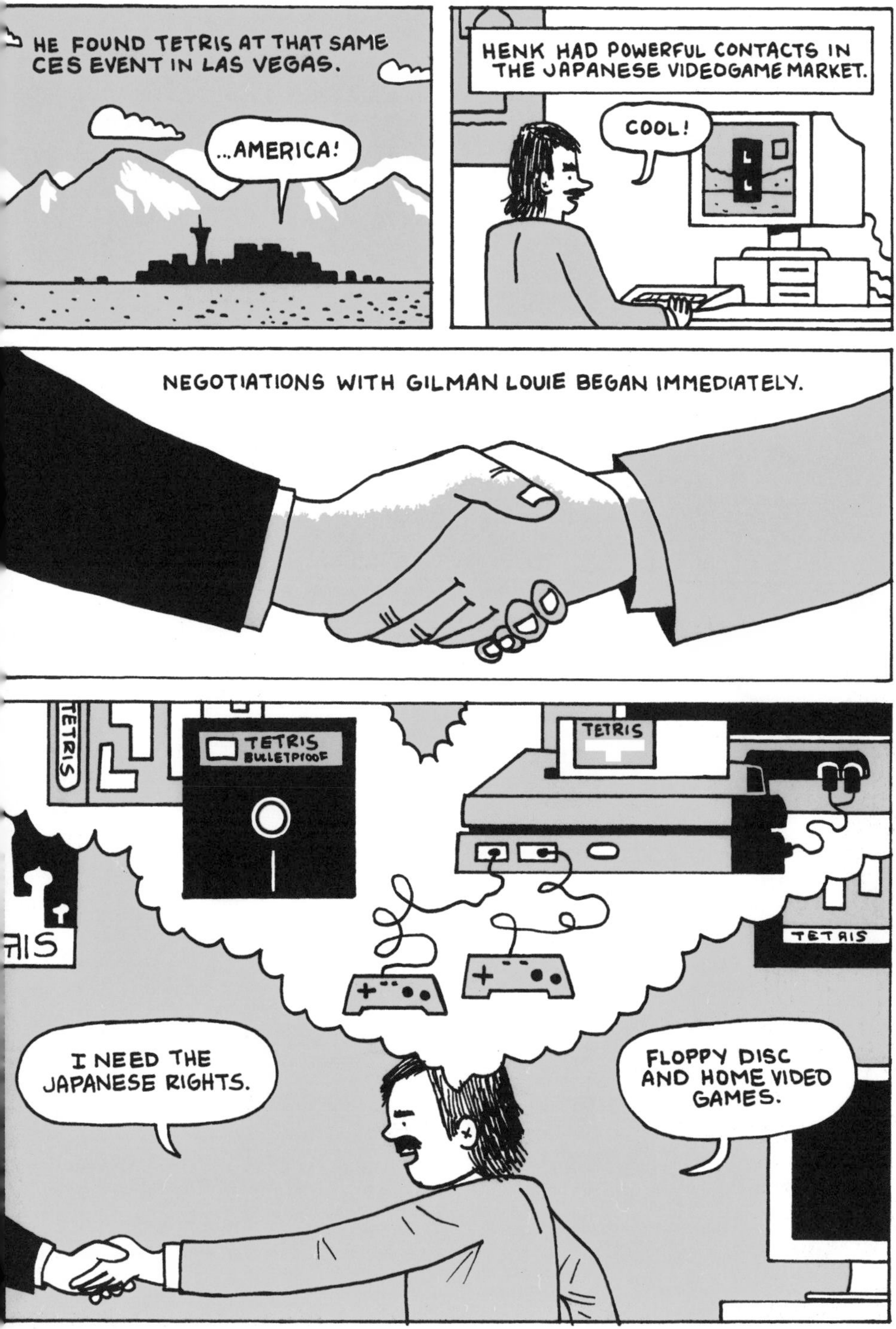
HE FOUND TETRIS AT THAT SAME CES EVENT IN LAS VEGAS.
...AMERICA!
HENK HAD POWERFUL CONTACTS IN THE JAPANESE VIDEOGAME MARKET.
COOL!
NEGOTIATIONS WITH GILMAN LOUIE BEGAN IMMEDIATELY.
TETRIS
TETRIS BULLETPROOF
TETRIS
TETRIS
I NEED THE JAPANESE RIGHTS.
FLOPPY DISC AND HOME VIDEO GAMES.

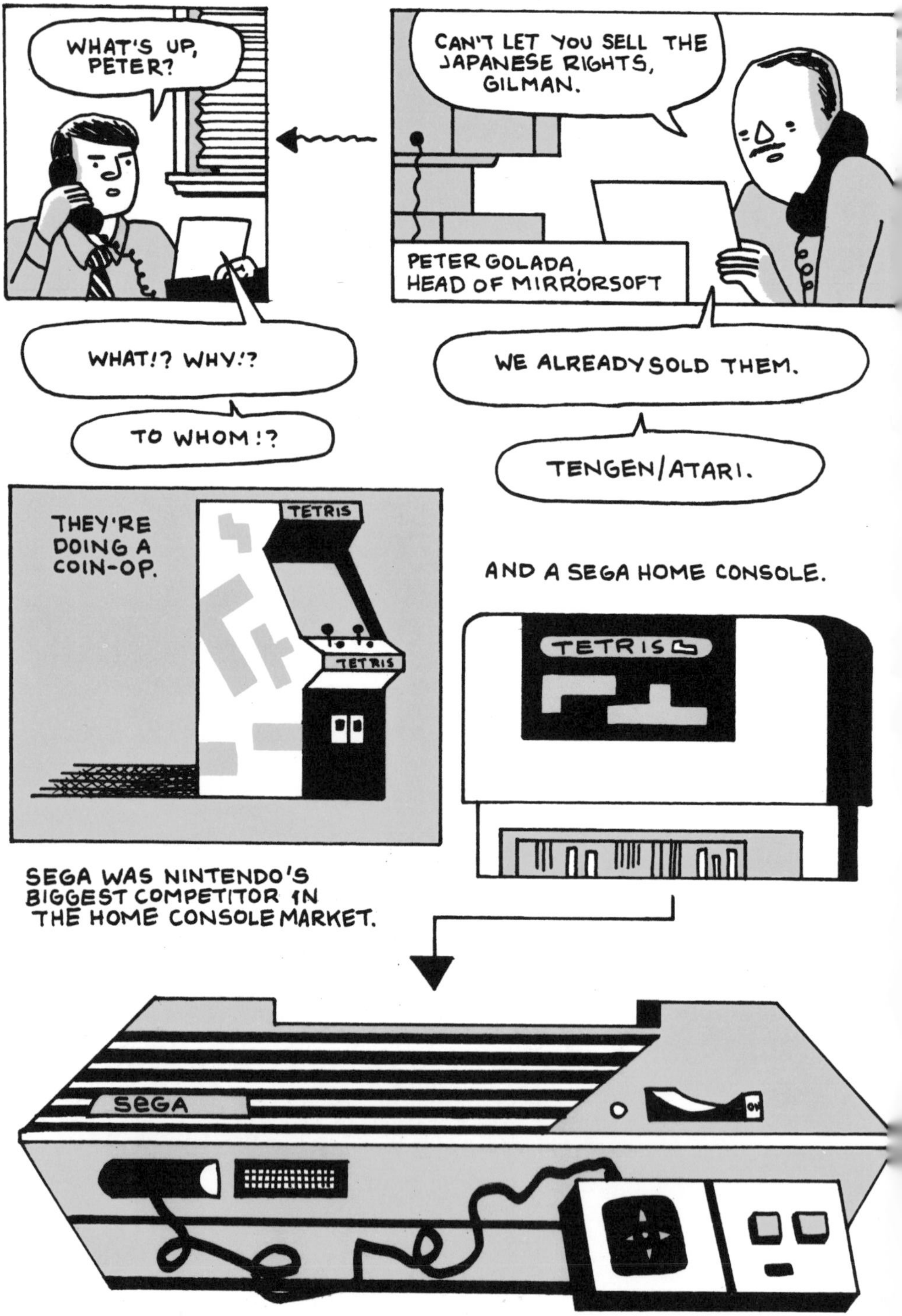

WHAT'S UP, PETER?
CAN'T LET YOU SELL THE JAPANESE RIGHTS, GILMAN.
PETER GOLADA, HEAD OF MIRRORSOFT
WHAT!? WHY!?
TO WHOM!?
WE ALREADY SOLD THEM.
TENGEN/ATARI.
THEY'RE DOING A COIN-OP.
TETRIS
TETRIS
AND A SEGA HOME CONSOLE.
TETRIS
SEGA WAS NINTENDO'S BIGGEST COMPETITOR IN THE HOME CONSOLE MARKET.
SEGA

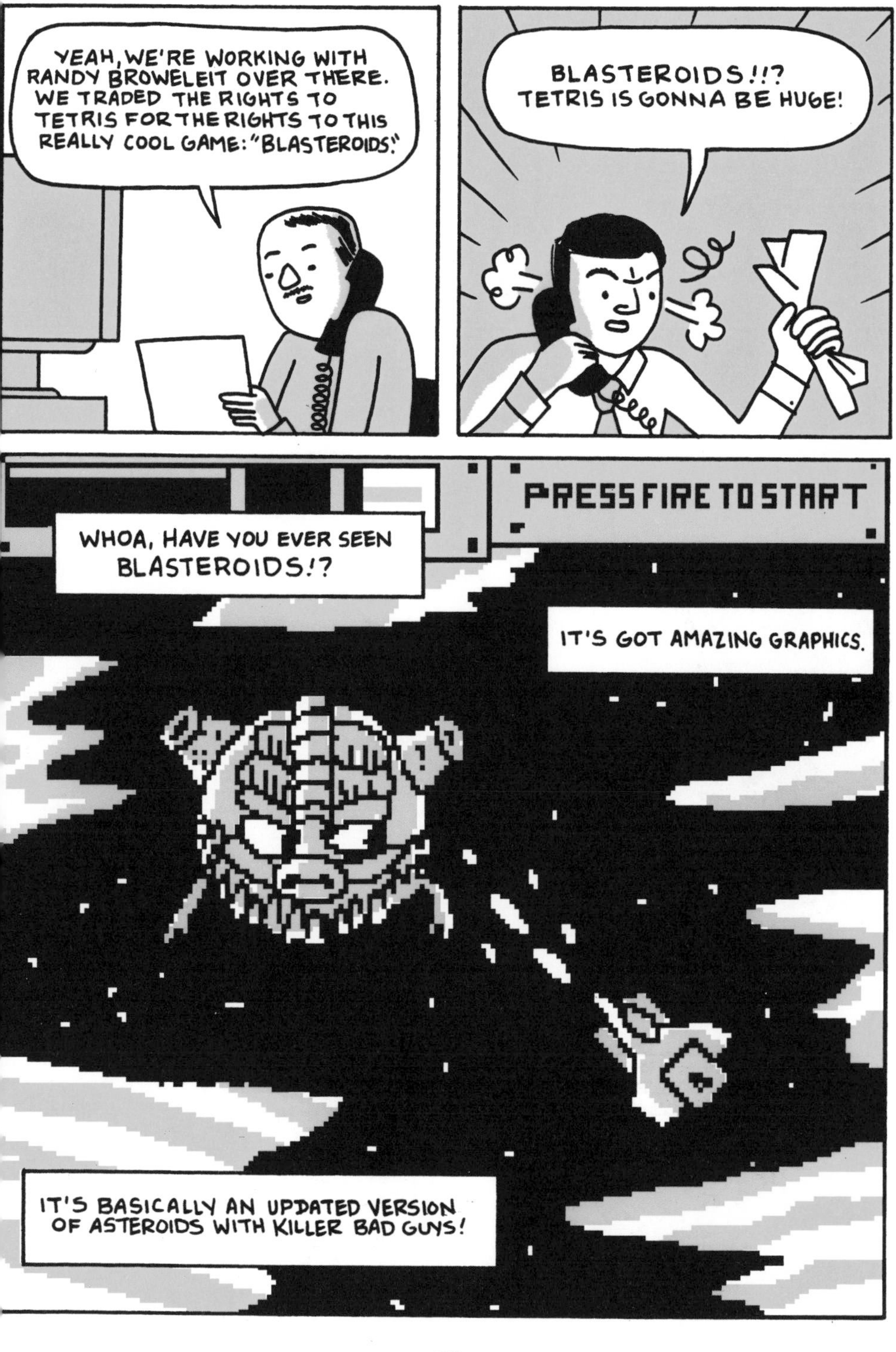
YEAH, WE'RE WORKING WITH RANDY BROWELEIT OVER THERE. WE TRADED THE RIGHTS TO TETRIS FOR THE RIGHTS TO THIS REALLY COOL GAME: "BLASTEROIDS."
BLASTEROIDS!!? TETRIS IS GONNA BE HUGE!
PRESS FIRE TO START
WHOA, HAVE YOU EVER SEEN BLASTEROIDS!?
IT'S GOT AMAZING GRAPHICS.
IT'S BASICALLY AN UPDATED VERSION OF ASTEROIDS WITH KILLER BAD GUYS!

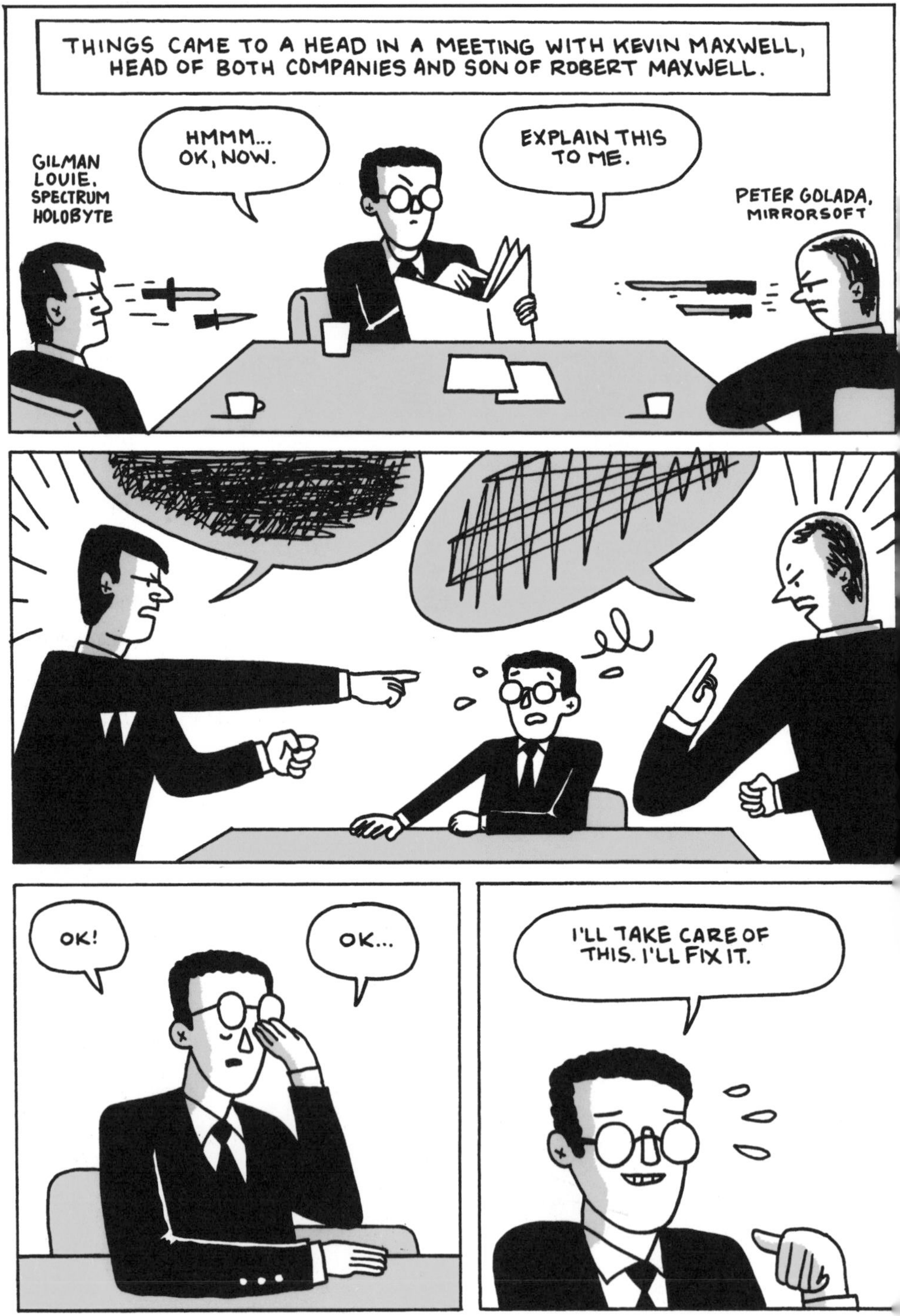
THINGS CAME TO A HEAD IN A MEETING WITH KEVIN MAXWELL, HEAD OF BOTH COMPANIES AND SON OF ROBERT MAXWELL.
GILMAN LOUIE, SPECTRUM HOLOBYTE
HMMM... OK, NOW.
EXPLAIN THIS TO ME.
PETER GOLADA, MIRRORSOFT
OK!
OK...
I'LL TAKE CARE OF THIS. I'LL FIX IT.

GILMAN LOUIE HAD TO MAKE A SAD PHONE CALL TO HENK.

MAXWELL RULED IN FAVOR OF MIRRORSOFT.

BUT I WAS ABLE TO MAKE SURE YOU DIDN'T LEAVE EMPTY HANDED.

HENK ROGERS BULLETPROOF SOFTWARE ←

HIDE NAKAJIMA, ATARI →

ENDED UP WITH

ENDED UP WITH

JAPANESE RIGHTS
TETRIS
FLOPPY DISC
HOME COMPUTER

HE PLANNED TO GET TETRIS TO NINTENDO.

ALL OTHER AVAILABLE RIGHTS:

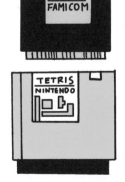
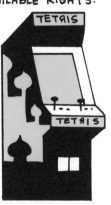

TETRIS FAMICOM

TETRIS NINTENDO

TETRIS

TETRIS

ELORG WAS UNAWARE OF THESE DEALS AND HADN'T GRANTED THESE RIGHTS TO ANYONE. STEIN ONLY ASSUMED HE HAD THEM.

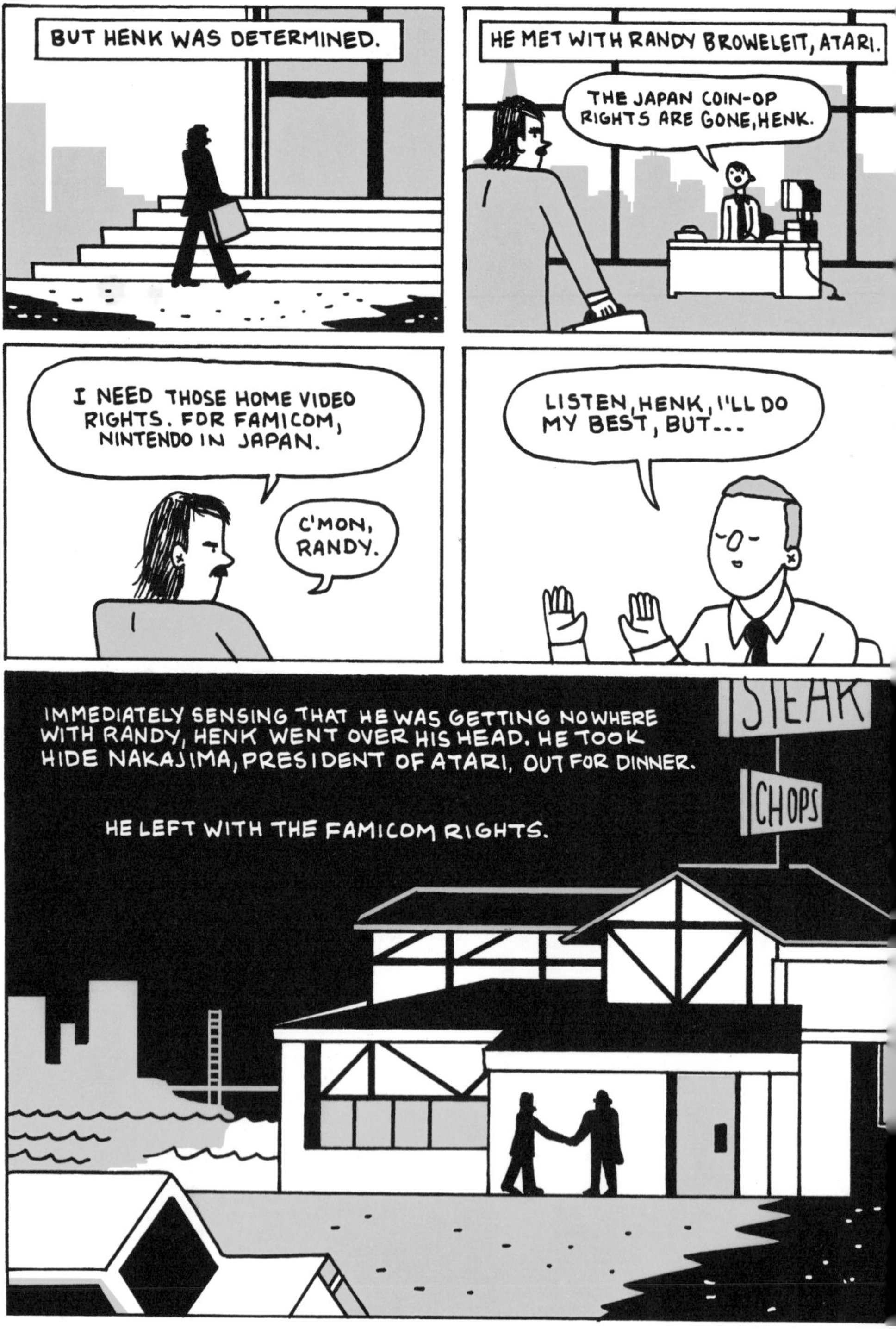
BUT HENK WAS DETERMINED.
HE MET WITH RANDY BROWELEIT, ATARI.
THE JAPAN COIN-OP RIGHTS ARE GONE, HENK.
I NEED THOSE HOME VIDEO RIGHTS. FOR FAMICOM, NINTENDO IN JAPAN.
C'MON, RANDY.
LISTEN, HENK, I'LL DO MY BEST, BUT...
IMMEDIATELY SENSING THAT HE WAS GETTING NOWHERE WITH RANDY, HENK WENT OVER HIS HEAD. HE TOOK HIDE NAKAJIMA, PRESIDENT OF ATARI, OUT FOR DINNER.
HE LEFT WITH THE FAMICOM RIGHTS.
STEAK
CHOPS

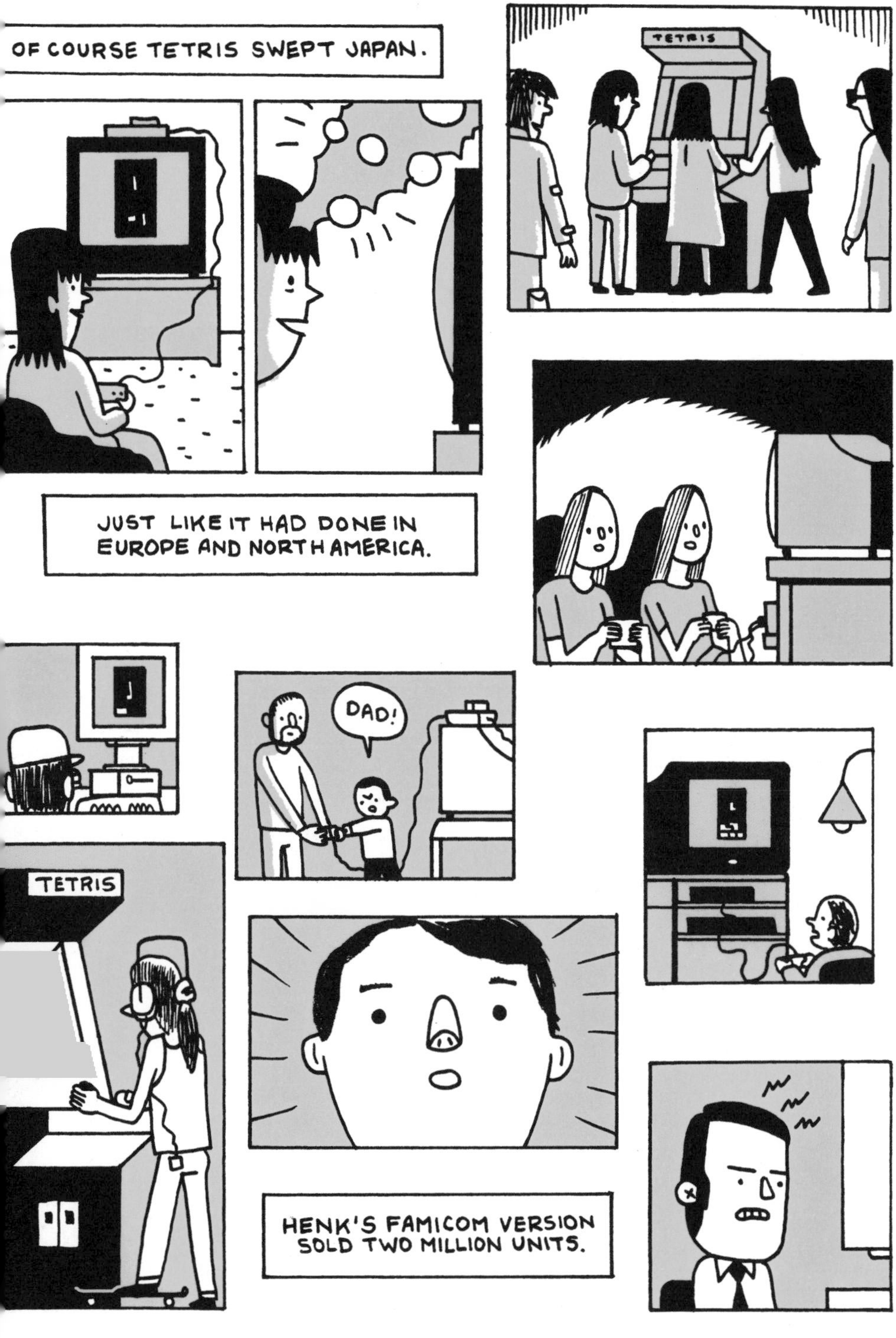
OF COURSE TETRIS SWEPT JAPAN.
TETRIS
JUST LIKE IT HAD DONE IN EUROPE AND NORTH AMERICA.
DAD!
TETRIS
HENK'S FAMICOM VERSION SOLD TWO MILLION UNITS.

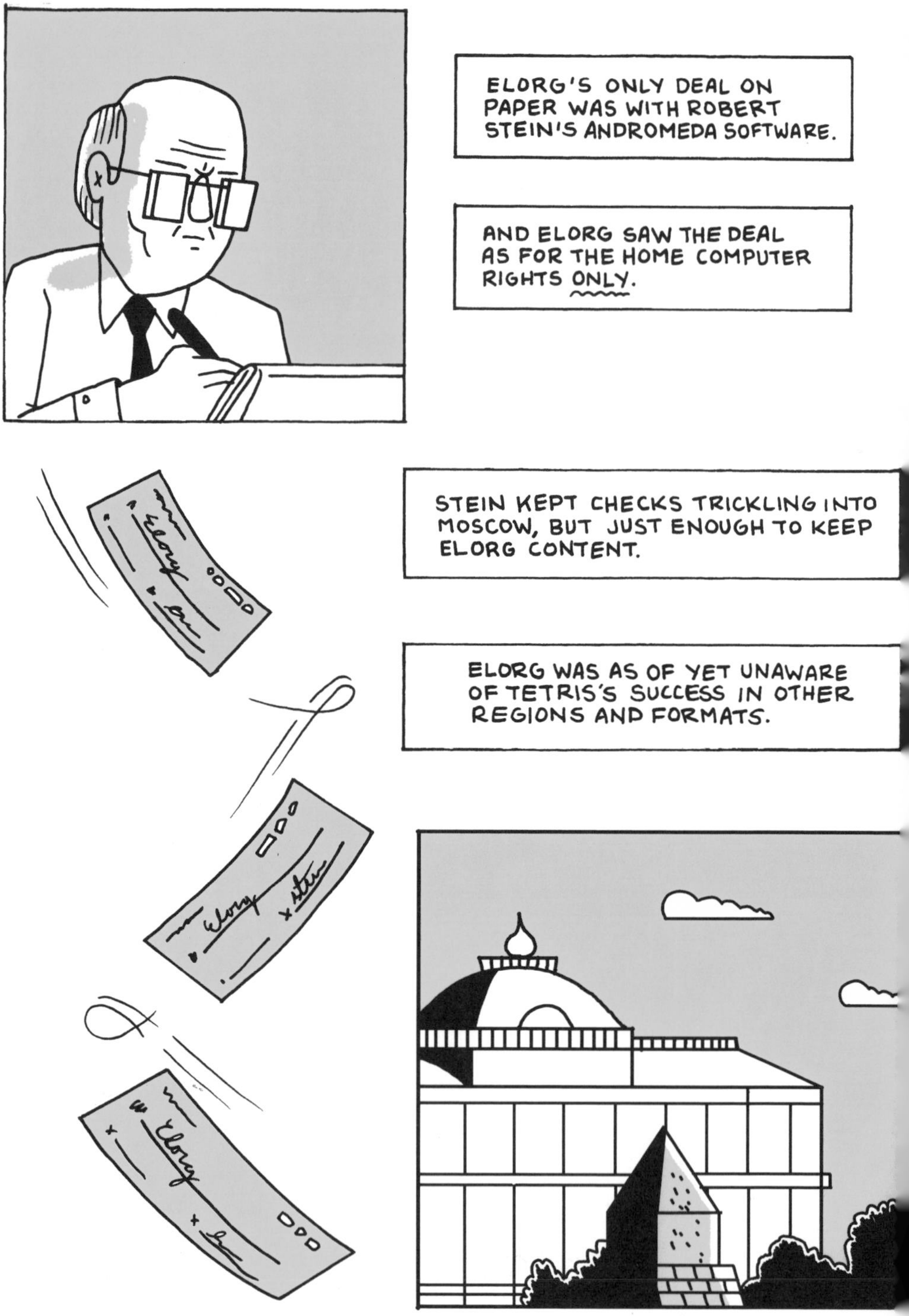
ELORG'S ONLY DEAL ON PAPER WAS WITH ROBERT STEIN'S ANDROMEDA SOFTWARE.
AND ELORG SAW THE DEAL AS FOR THE HOME COMPUTER RIGHTS ONLY.
STEIN KEPT CHECKS TRICKLING INTO MOSCOW, BUT JUST ENOUGH TO KEEP ELORG CONTENT.
ELORG WAS AS OF YET UNAWARE OF TETRIS'S SUCCESS IN OTHER REGIONS AND FORMATS.

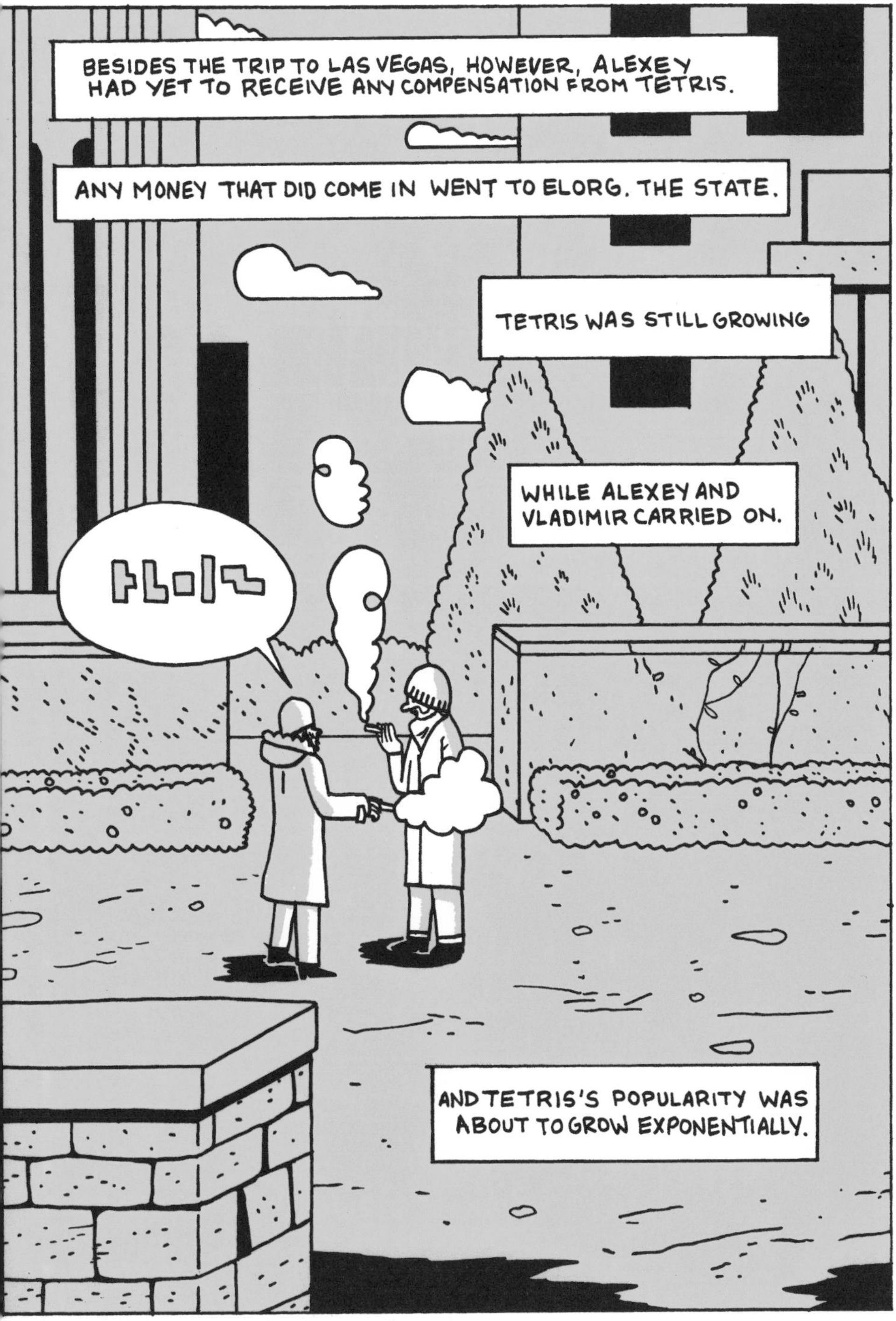
BESIDES THE TRIP TO LAS VEGAS, HOWEVER, ALEXEY HAD YET TO RECEIVE ANY COMPENSATION FROM TETRIS.
ANY MONEY THAT DID COME IN WENT TO ELORG. THE STATE.
TETRIS WAS STILL GROWING
WHILE ALEXEY AND VLADIMIR CARRIED ON.
AND TETRIS'S POPULARITY WAS ABOUT TO GROW EXPONENTIALLY.

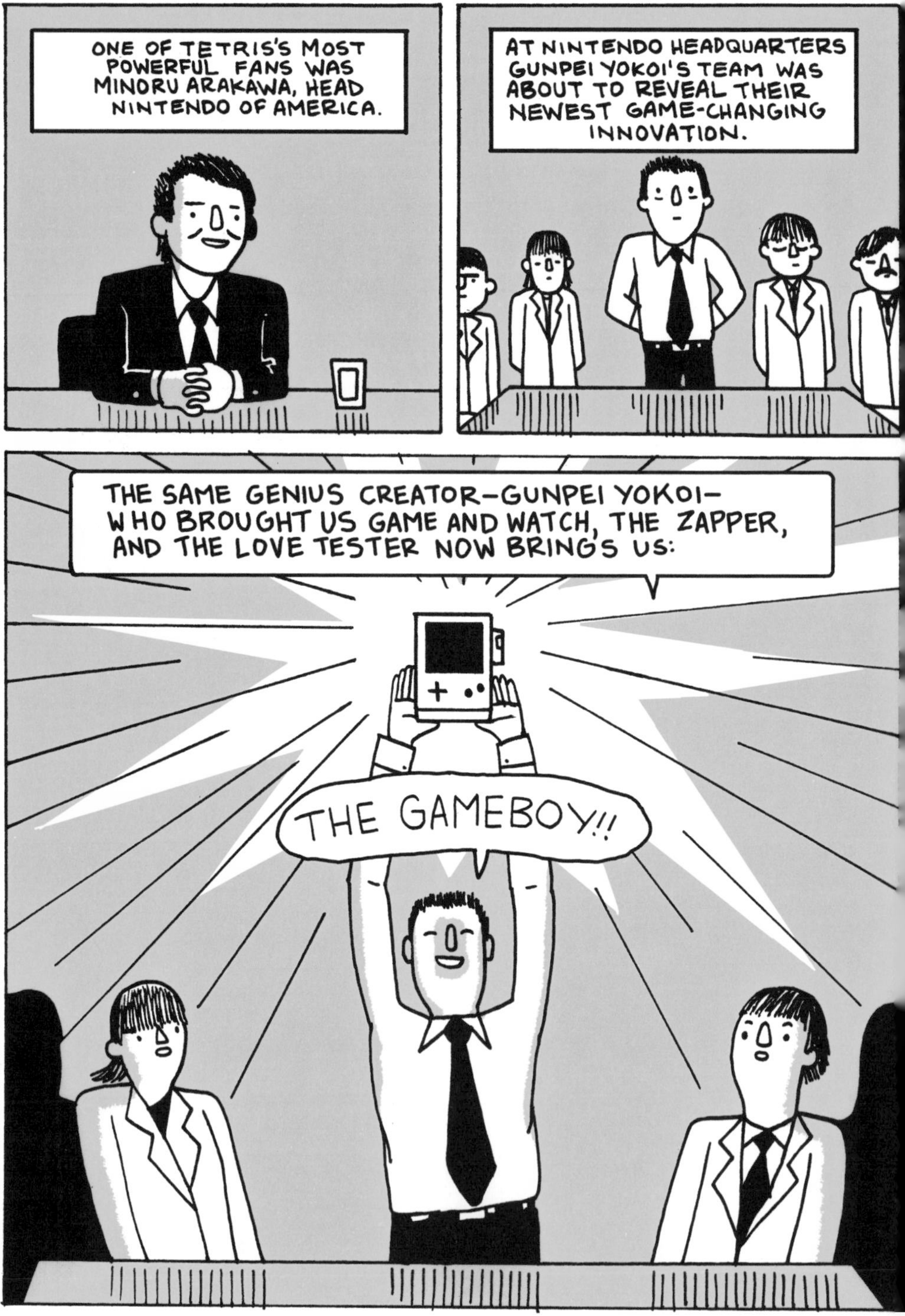
ONE OF TETRIS'S MOST POWERFUL FANS WAS MINORU ARAKAWA, HEAD NINTENDO OF AMERICA.
AT NINTENDO HEADQUARTERS GUNPEI YOKOI'S TEAM WAS ABOUT TO REVEAL THEIR NEWEST GAME-CHANGING INNOVATION.
THE SAME GENIUS CREATOR—GUNPEI YOKOI—WHO BROUGHT US GAME AND WATCH, THE ZAPPER, AND THE LOVE TESTER NOW BRINGS US:
THE GAMEBOY!!

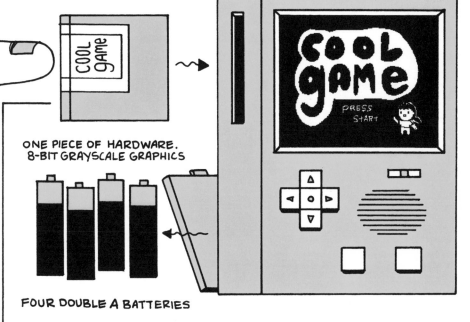

THE GAMEBOY ALLOWS THE PLAYER TO BRING ALL THE FUN OF NINTENDO WITH THEM.
THIS IS LIGHT YEARS BEYOND WHAT WE STARTED WITH GAME AND WATCH.
COOL GAME
COOL GAME
PRESS START
ONE PIECE OF HARDWARE. 8-BIT GRAYSCALE GRAPHICS
FOUR DOUBLE A BATTERIES
COOL GAME
COOL GAME
COOL GAME
MANUAL
HUNDREDS OF GAMES
THIS IS TRULY NES IN YOUR POCKET.
SHOVE

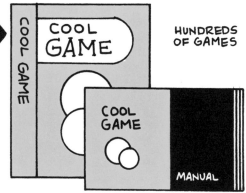

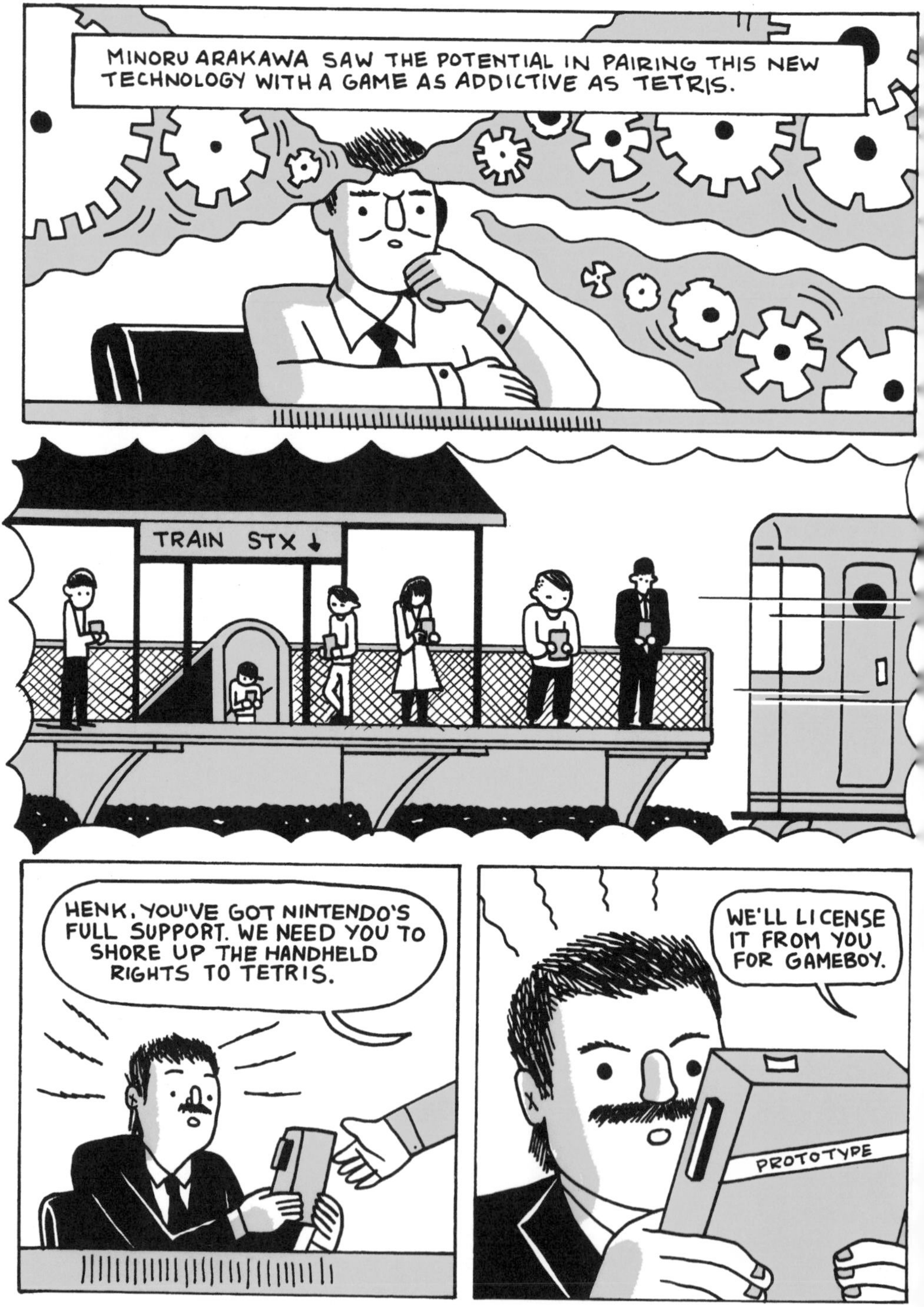
MINORU ARAKAWA SAW THE POTENTIAL IN PAIRING THIS NEW TECHNOLOGY WITH A GAME AS ADDICTIVE AS TETRIS.
TRAIN STX
HENK, YOU'VE GOT NINTENDO'S FULL SUPPORT. WE NEED YOU TO SHORE UP THE HANDHELD RIGHTS TO TETRIS.
WE'LL LICENSE IT FROM YOU FOR GAMEBOY.
PROTOTYPE

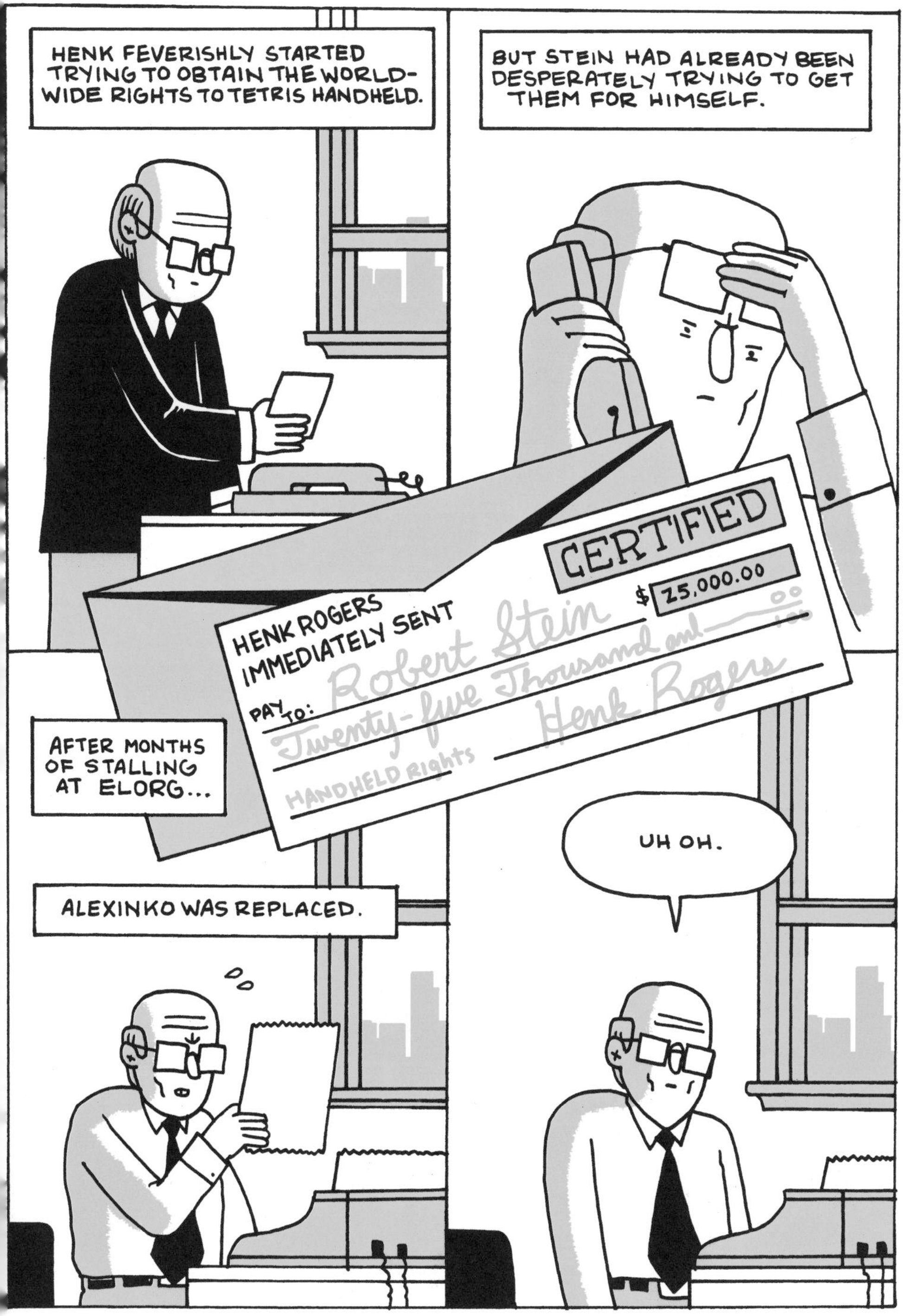
HENK FEVERISHLY STARTED TRYING TO OBTAIN THE WORLD-WIDE RIGHTS TO TETRIS HANDHELD.
BUT STEIN HAD ALREADY BEEN DESPERATELY TRYING TO GET THEM FOR HIMSELF.
HENK ROGERS IMMEDIATELY SENT
CERTIFIED
$ 25,000.00
PAY TO: Robert Stein
Twenty-five Thousand and 00/100
Henk Rogers
HANDHELD Rights
AFTER MONTHS OF STALLING AT ELORG...
ALEXINKO WAS REPLACED.
UH OH.

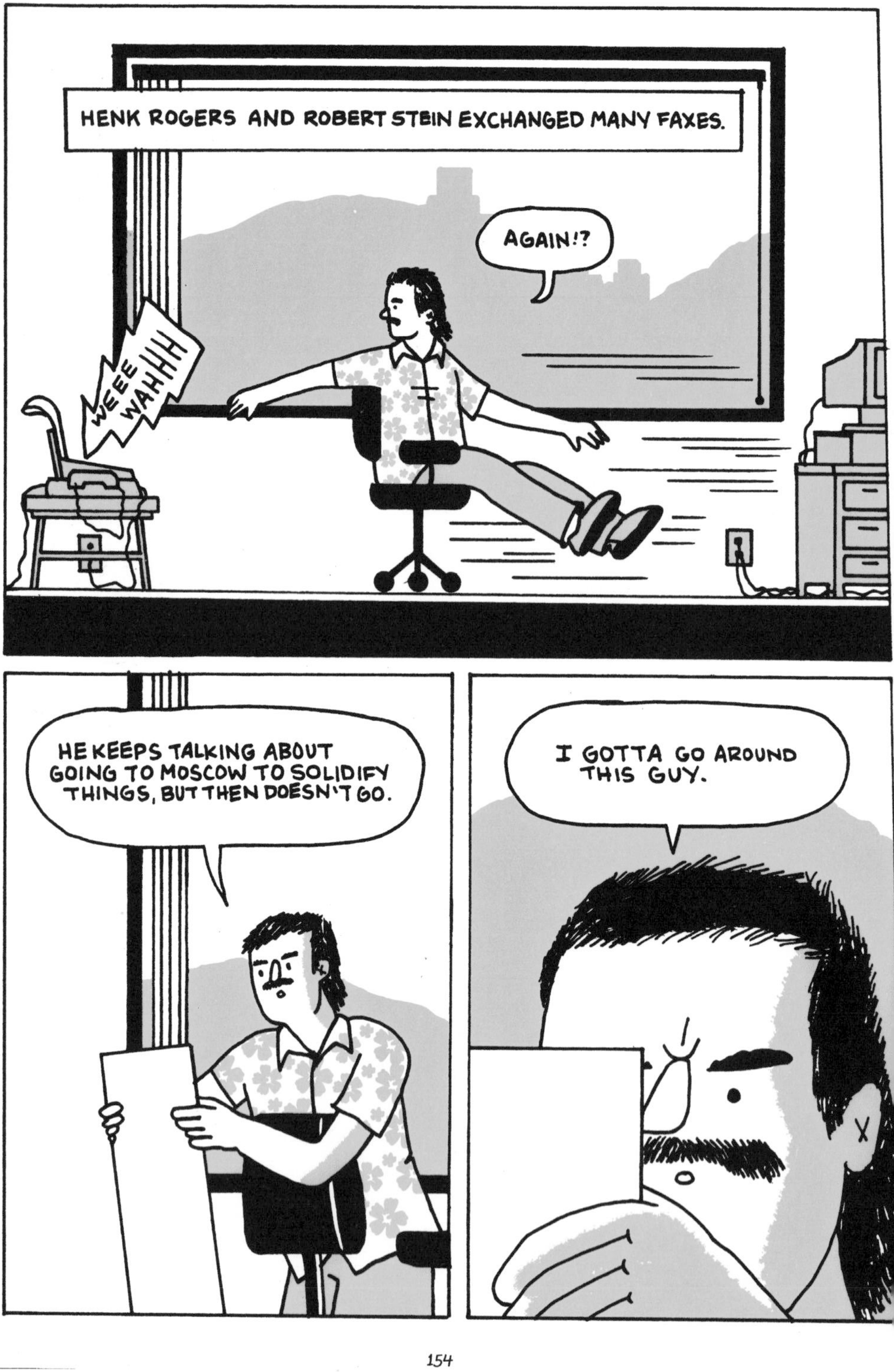
HENK ROGERS AND ROBERT STEIN EXCHANGED MANY FAXES.
AGAIN!?
WEEE WAHHHH
HE KEEPS TALKING ABOUT GOING TO MOSCOW TO SOLIDIFY THINGS, BUT THEN DOESN'T GO.
I GOTTA GO AROUND THIS GUY.

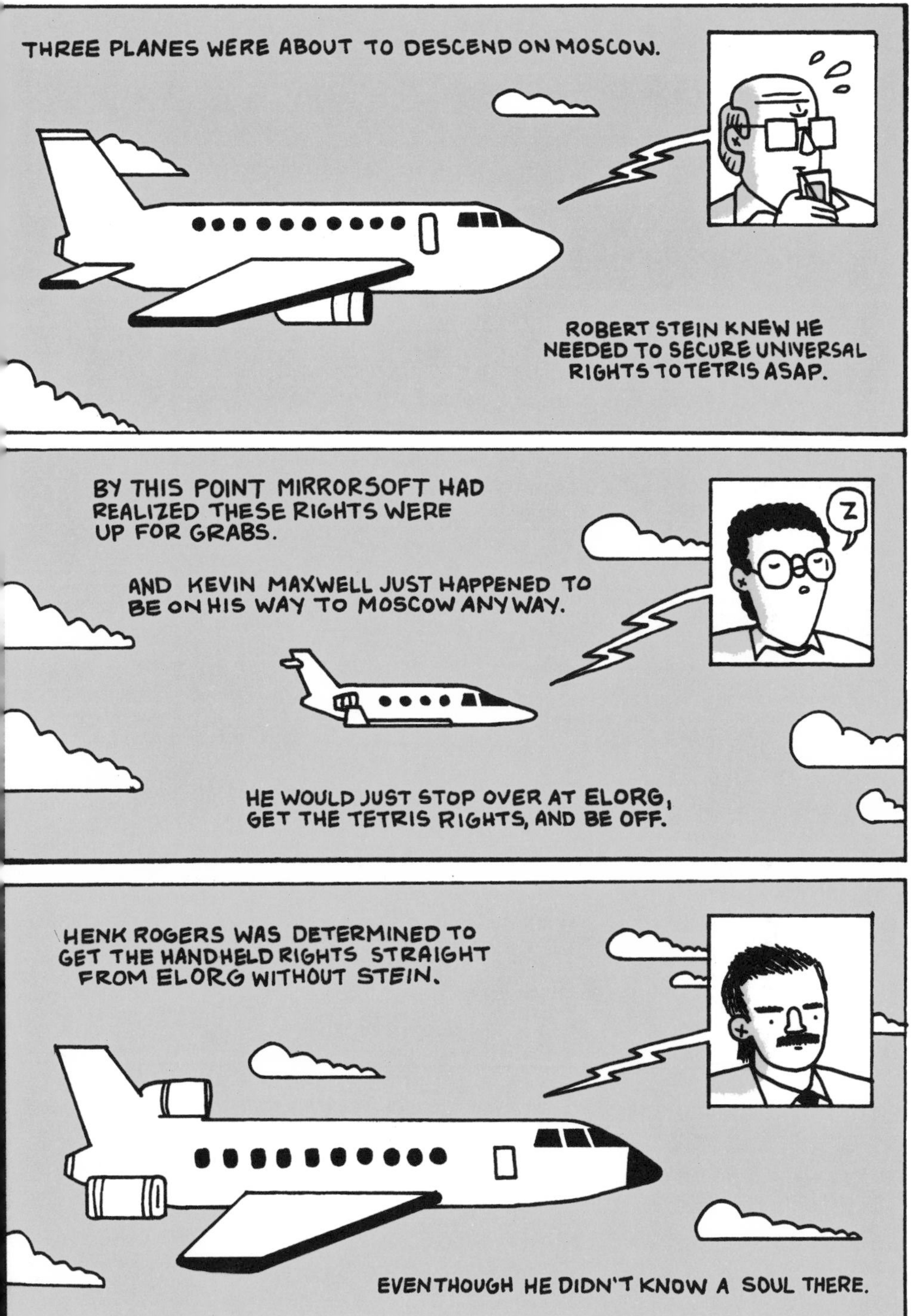
THREE PLANES WERE ABOUT TO DESCEND ON MOSCOW.
ROBERT STEIN KNEW HE NEEDED TO SECURE UNIVERSAL RIGHTS TO TETRIS ASAP.
BY THIS POINT MIRRORSOFT HAD REALIZED THESE RIGHTS WERE UP FOR GRABS.
Z
AND KEVIN MAXWELL JUST HAPPENED TO BE ON HIS WAY TO MOSCOW ANYWAY.
HE WOULD JUST STOP OVER AT ELORG, GET THE TETRIS RIGHTS, AND BE OFF.
HENK ROGERS WAS DETERMINED TO GET THE HANDHELD RIGHTS STRAIGHT FROM ELORG WITHOUT STEIN.
EVEN THOUGH HE DIDN'T KNOW A SOUL THERE.

EVGENI NIKOLAEVICH BELIKOV
ELORG (ELEKTRONORGTECHNICA)

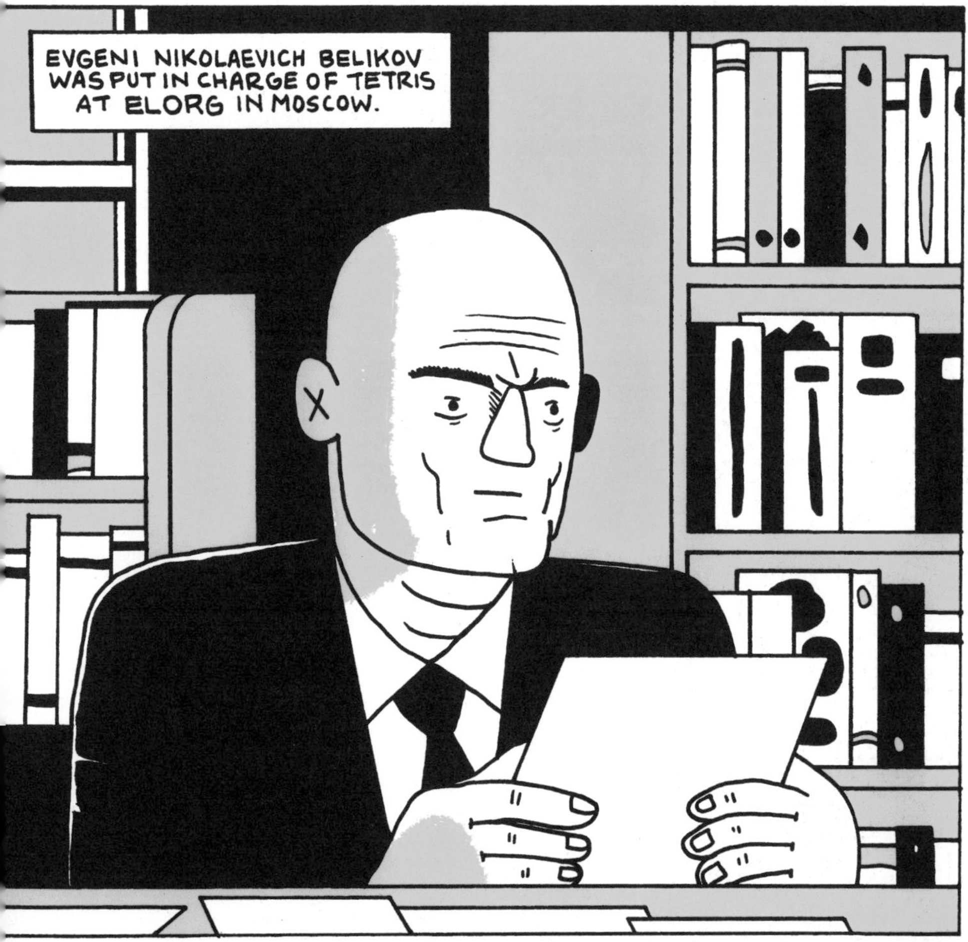
EVGENI NIKOLAEVICH BELIKOV WAS PUT IN CHARGE OF TETRIS AT ELORG IN MOSCOW.

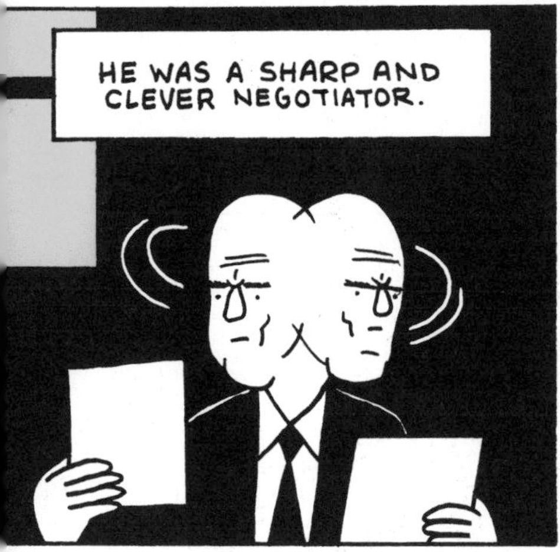
HE WAS A SHARP AND CLEVER NEGOTIATOR.

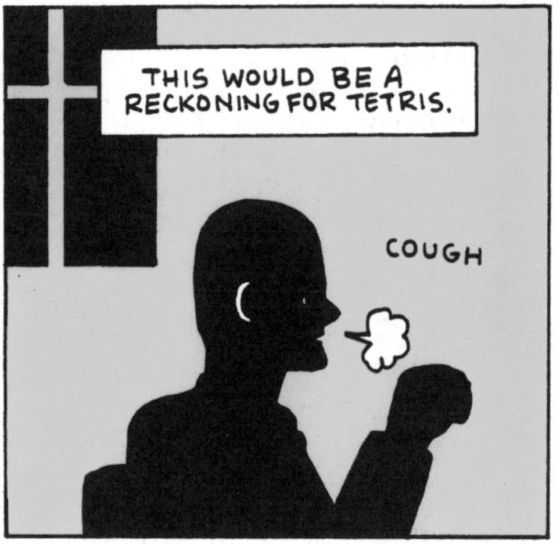
THIS WOULD BE A RECKONING FOR TETRIS.
COUGH

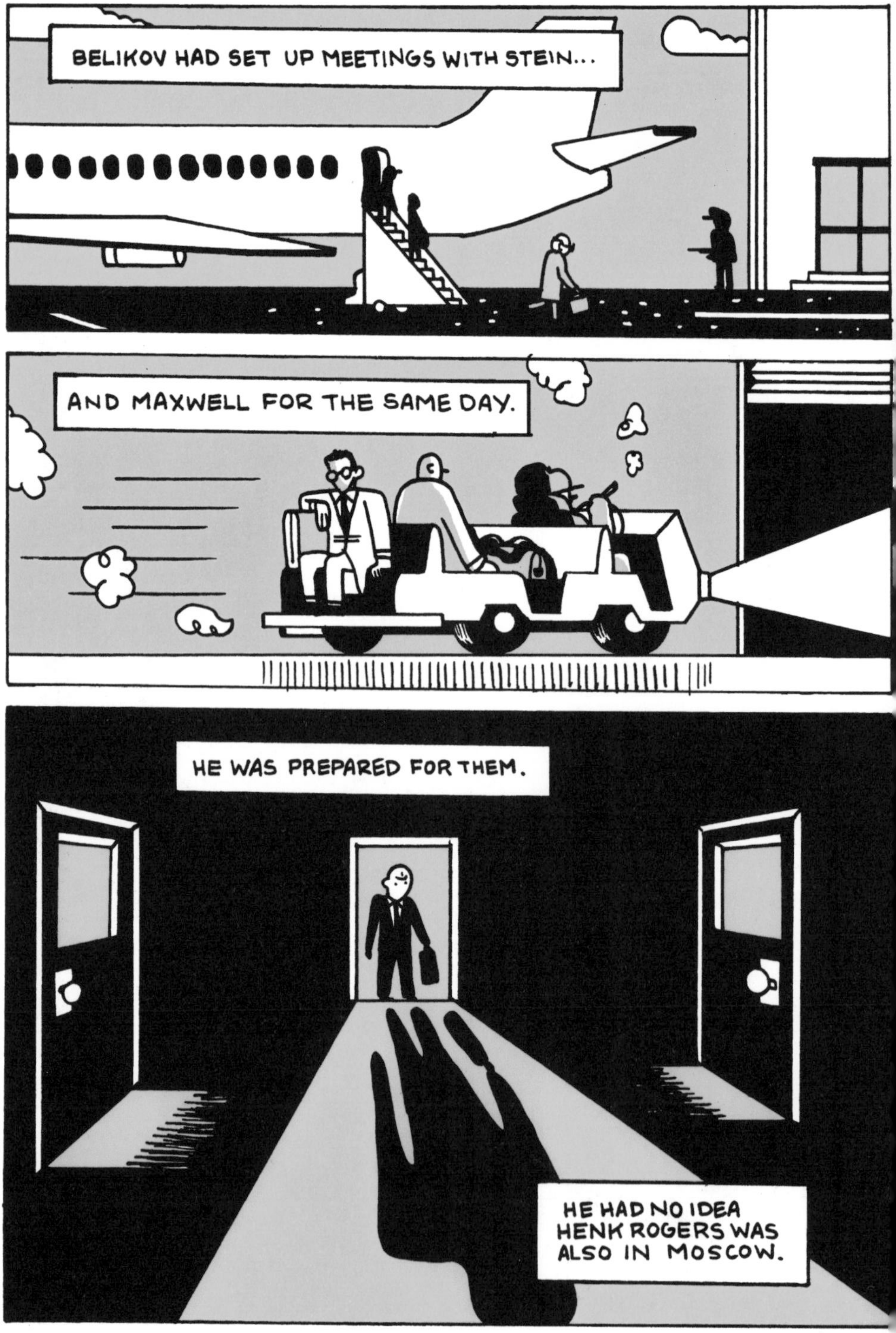
BELIKOV HAD SET UP MEETINGS WITH STEIN...
AND MAXWELL FOR THE SAME DAY.
HE WAS PREPARED FOR THEM.
HE HAD NO IDEA HENK ROGERS WAS ALSO IN MOSCOW.

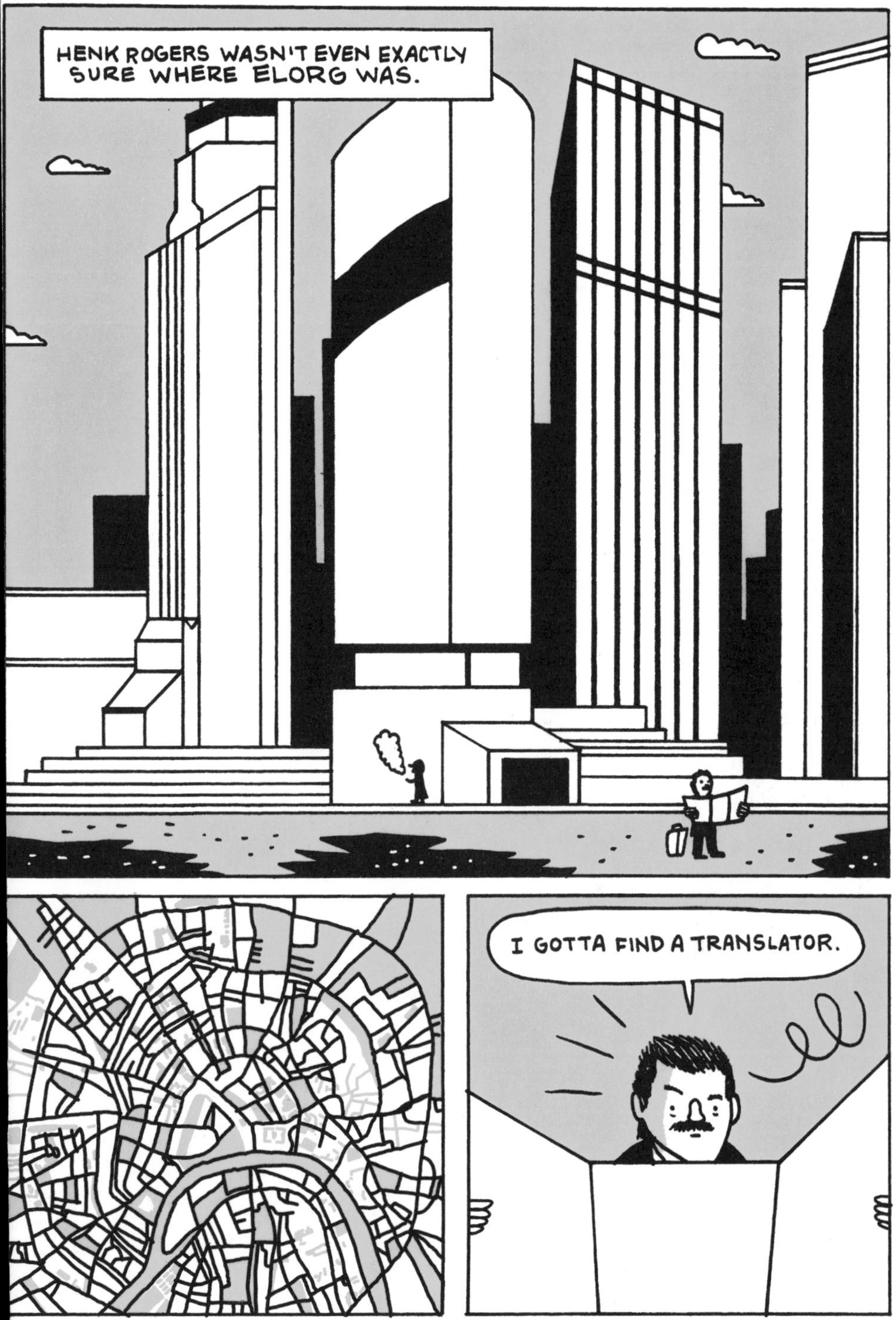
HENK ROGERS WASN'T EVEN EXACTLY SURE WHERE ELORG WAS.
I GOTTA FIND A TRANSLATOR.

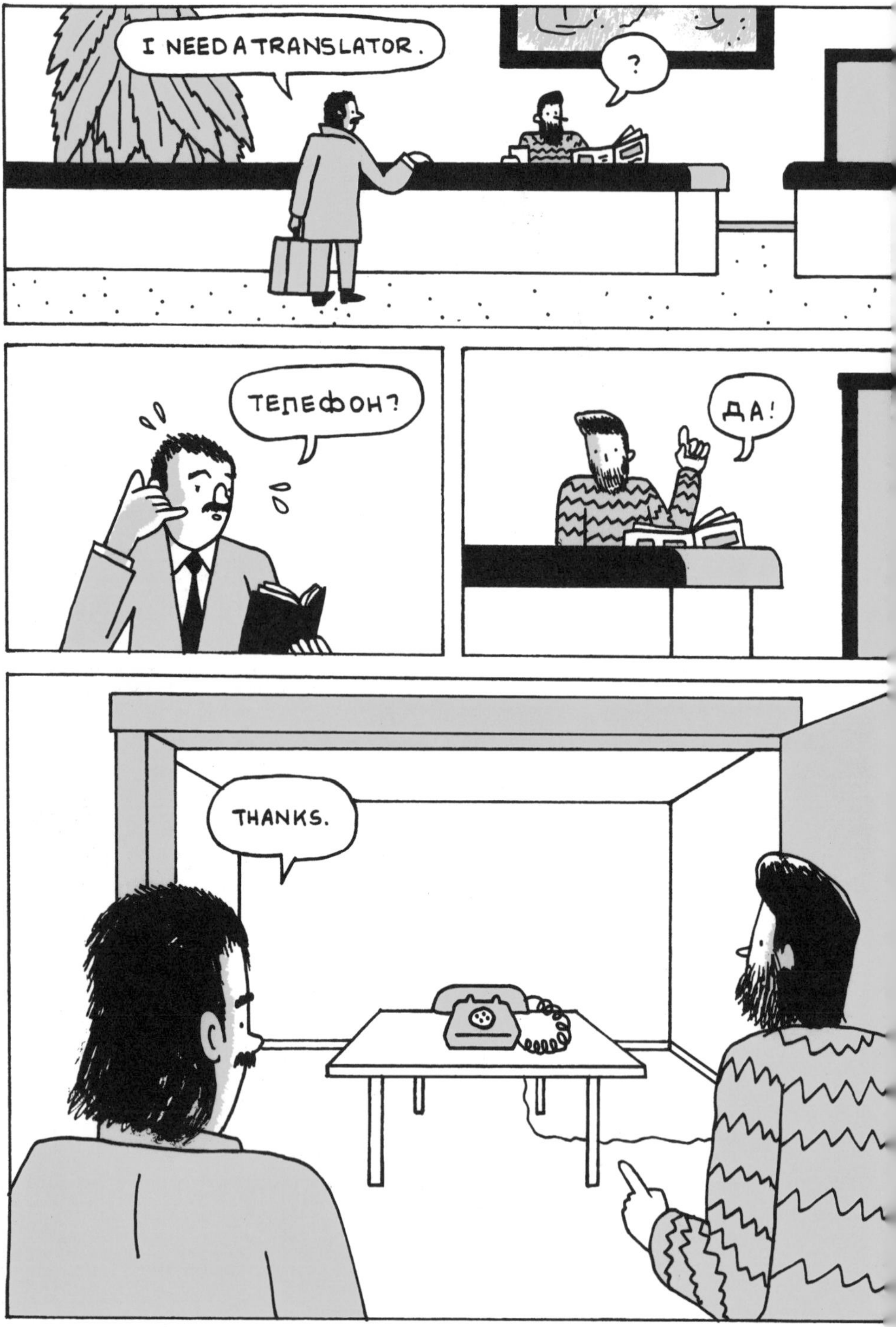
I NEED A TRANSLATOR.
?
ТЕЛЕФОН?
ДА!
THANKS.

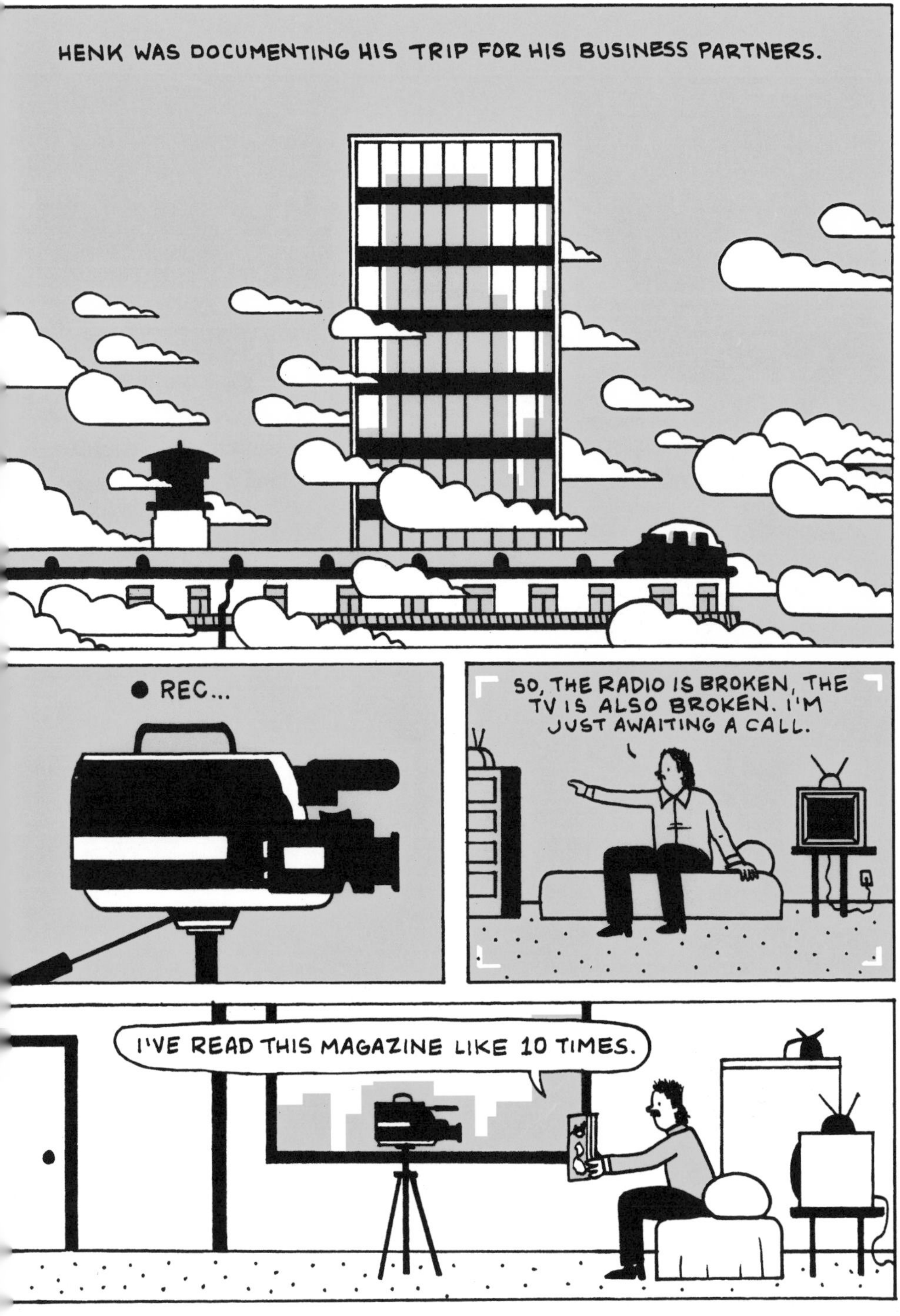
HENK WAS DOCUMENTING HIS TRIP FOR HIS BUSINESS PARTNERS.
● REC...
SO, THE RADIO IS BROKEN, THE TV IS ALSO BROKEN. I'M JUST AWAITING A CALL.
I'VE READ THIS MAGAZINE LIKE 10 TIMES.

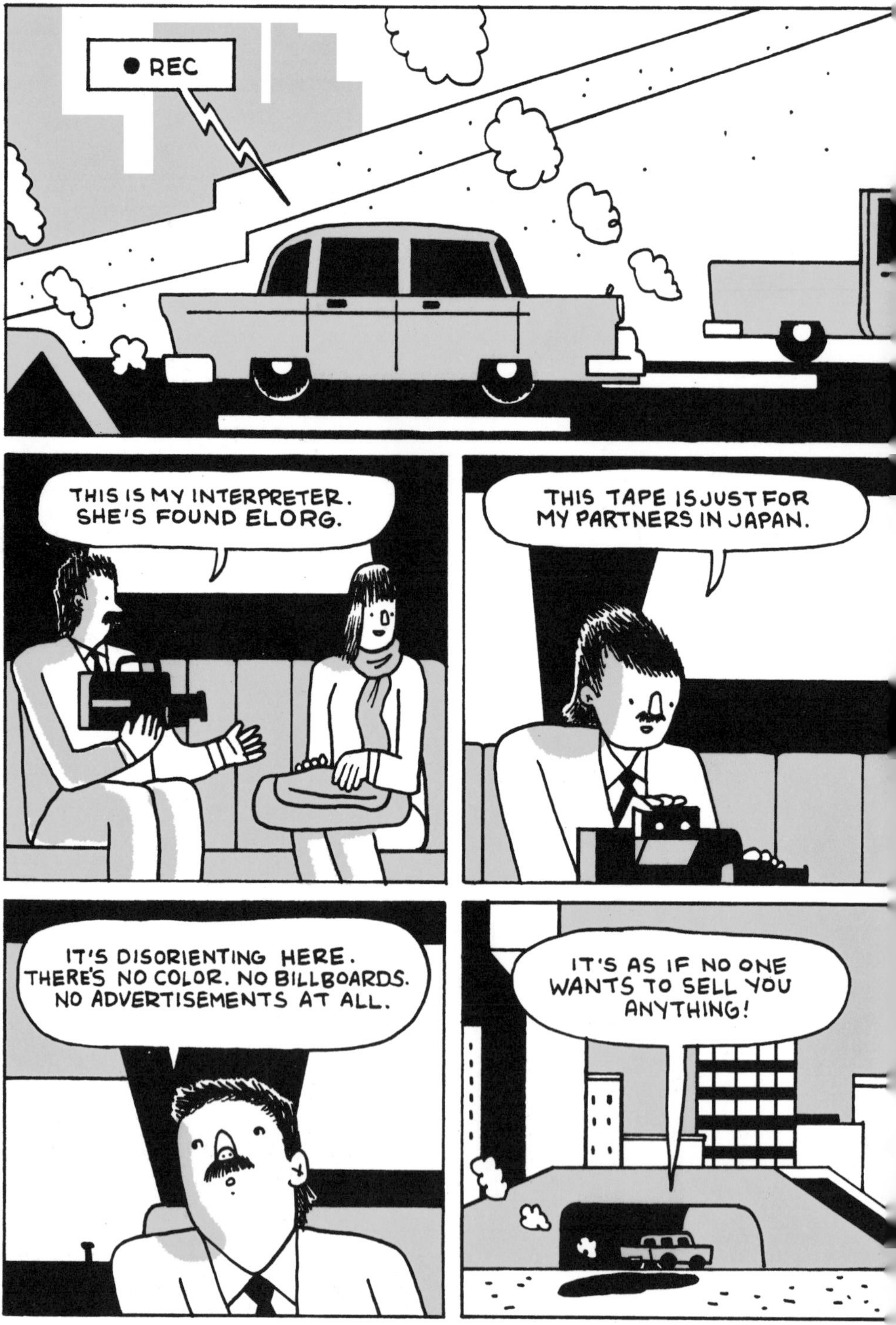
● REC
THIS IS MY INTERPRETER. SHE'S FOUND ELORG.
THIS TAPE IS JUST FOR MY PARTNERS IN JAPAN.
IT'S DISORIENTING HERE. THERE'S NO COLOR. NO BILLBOARDS. NO ADVERTISEMENTS AT ALL.
IT'S AS IF NO ONE WANTS TO SELL YOU ANYTHING!

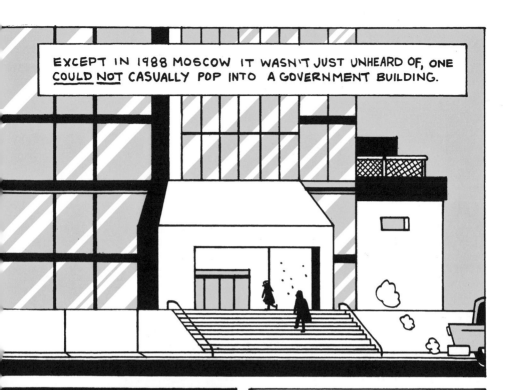

EXCEPT IN 1988 MOSCOW IT WASN'T JUST UNHEARD OF, ONE COULD NOT CASUALLY POP INTO A GOVERNMENT BUILDING.

THIS IS HENK ROGERS, OF BULLETPROOF SOFTWARE, TO TALK ABOUT TETRIS.

WHAT!?

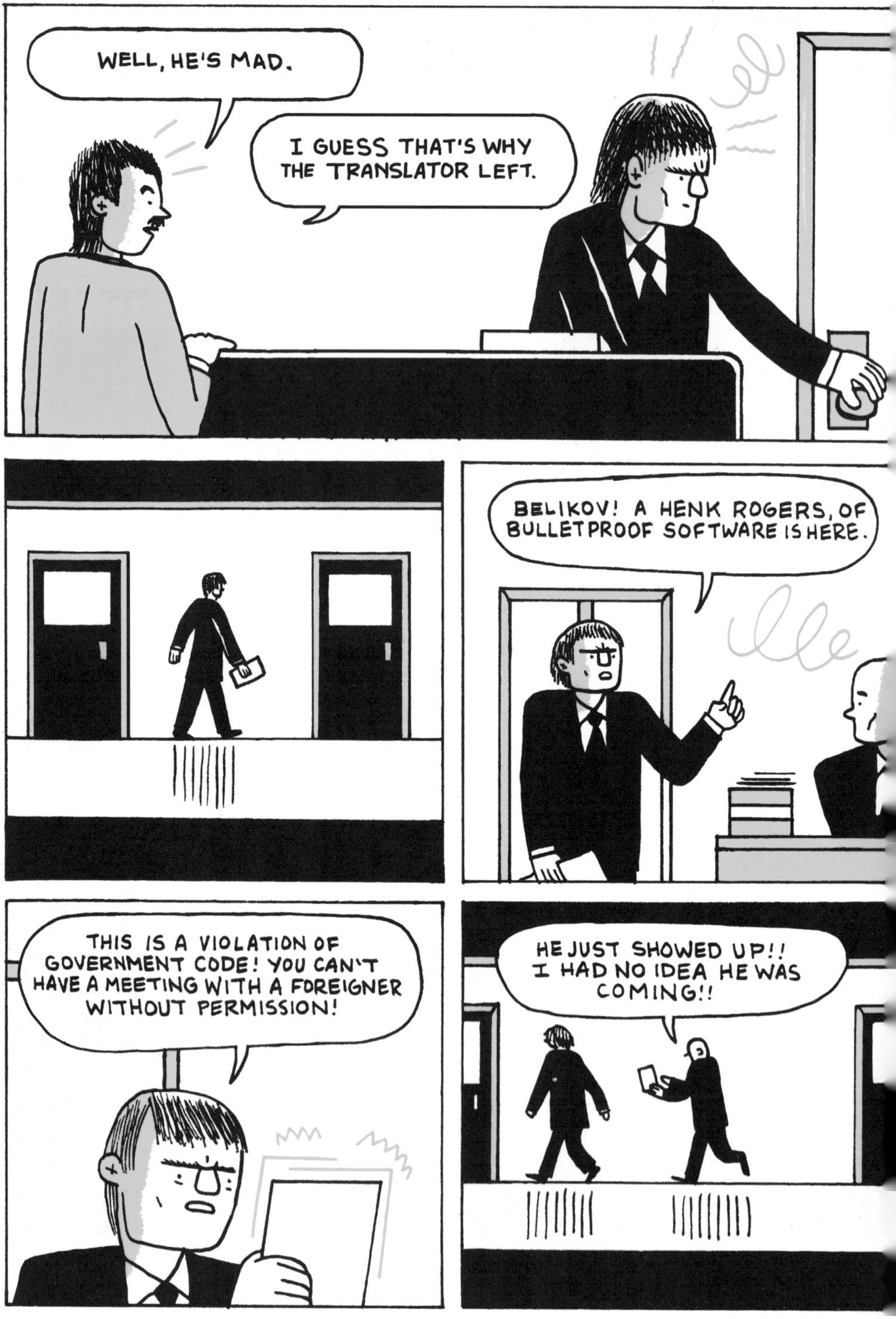
WELL, HE'S MAD.
I GUESS THAT'S WHY THE TRANSLATOR LEFT.
BELIKOV! A HENK ROGERS, OF BULLETPROOF SOFTWARE IS HERE.
THIS IS A VIOLATION OF GOVERNMENT CODE! YOU CAN'T HAVE A MEETING WITH A FOREIGNER WITHOUT PERMISSION!
HE JUST SHOWED UP!! I HAD NO IDEA HE WAS COMING!!

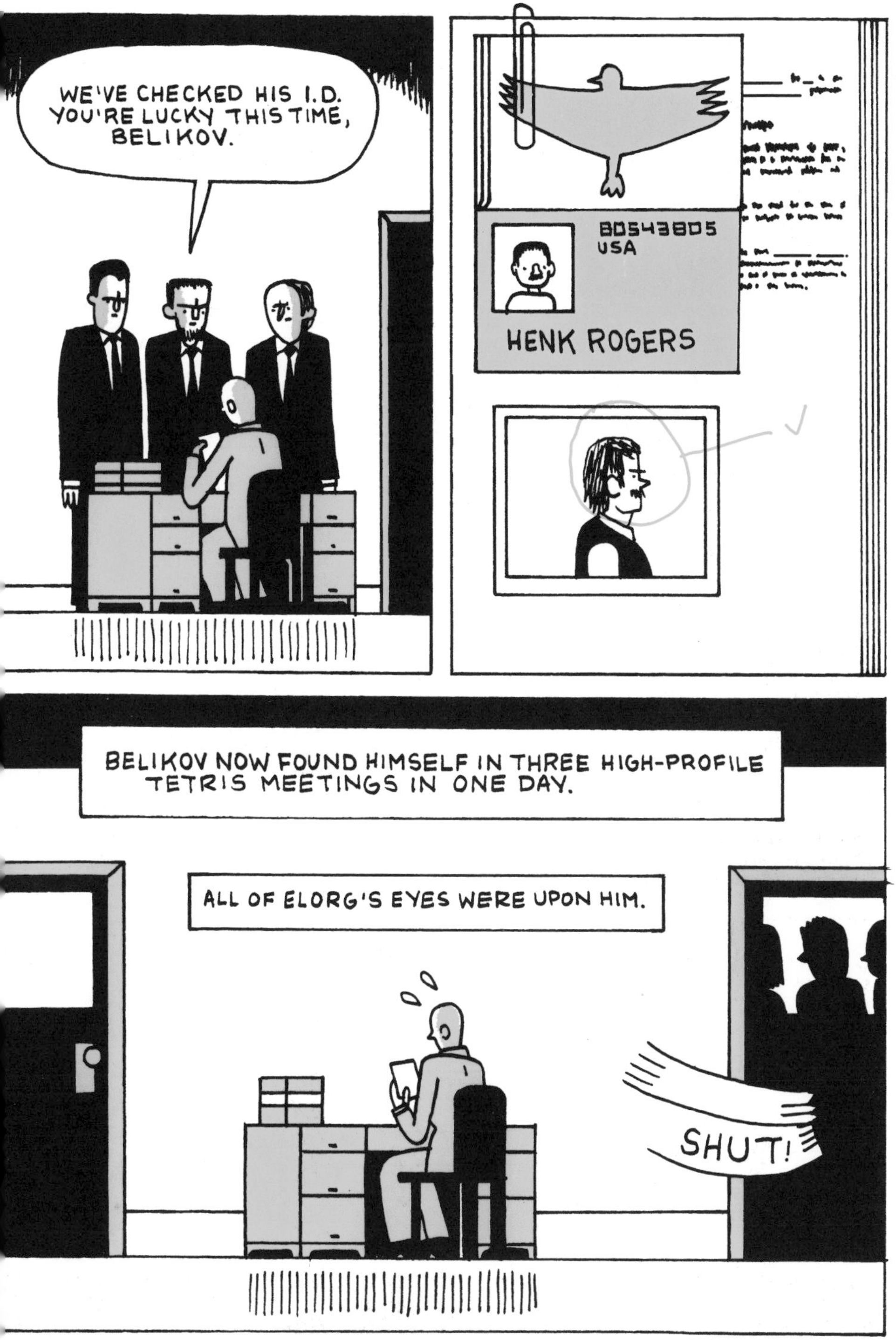
WE'VE CHECKED HIS I.D. YOU'RE LUCKY THIS TIME, BELIKOV.
B0543805
USA
HENK ROGERS
BELIKOV NOW FOUND HIMSELF IN THREE HIGH-PROFILE TETRIS MEETINGS IN ONE DAY.
ALL OF ELORG'S EYES WERE UPON HIM.
SHUT!

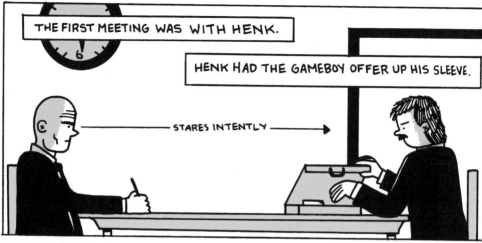

THE FIRST MEETING WAS WITH HENK.

HENK HAD THE GAMEBOY OFFER UP HIS SLEEVE.

STARES INTENTLY

OK.

AHEM.

HELLO MR. BELIKOV. FIRST LET ME SHOW OFF OUR FAMICOM VERSION OF TETRIS. THIS SOLD TWO MILLION UNITS.

TETRIS

?

WHAT IS THIS?

YOU DON'T HAVE THE RIGHTS TO THIS!!

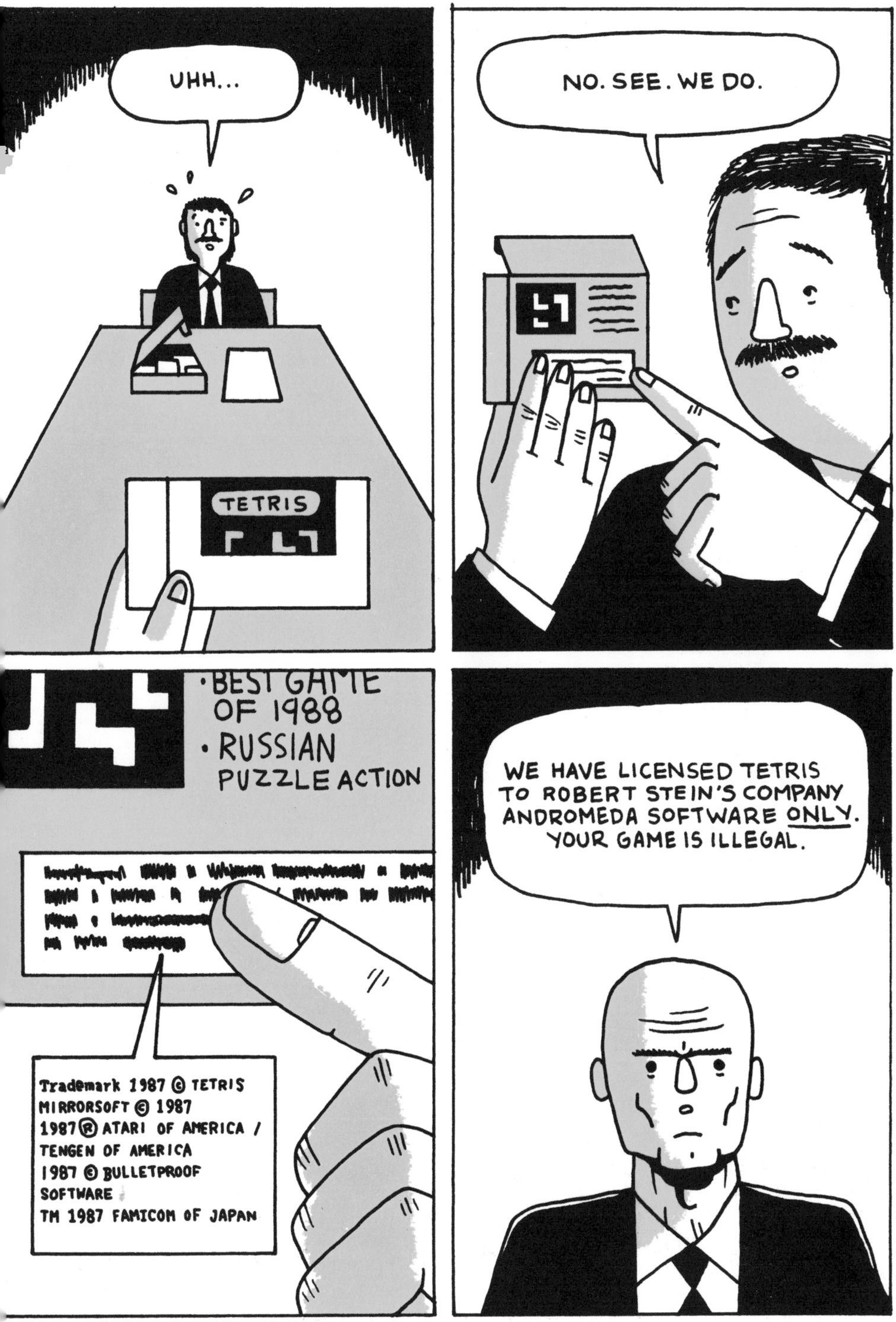

UHH...
TETRIS
NO. SEE. WE DO.
·BEST GAME OF 1988
·RUSSIAN PUZZLE ACTION
Trademark 1987 © TETRIS
MIRRORSOFT © 1987
1987 ® ATARI OF AMERICA / TENGEN OF AMERICA
1987 © BULLETPROOF SOFTWARE
TM 1987 FAMICOM OF JAPAN
WE HAVE LICENSED TETRIS TO ROBERT STEIN'S COMPANY ANDROMEDA SOFTWARE ONLY. YOUR GAME IS ILLEGAL.

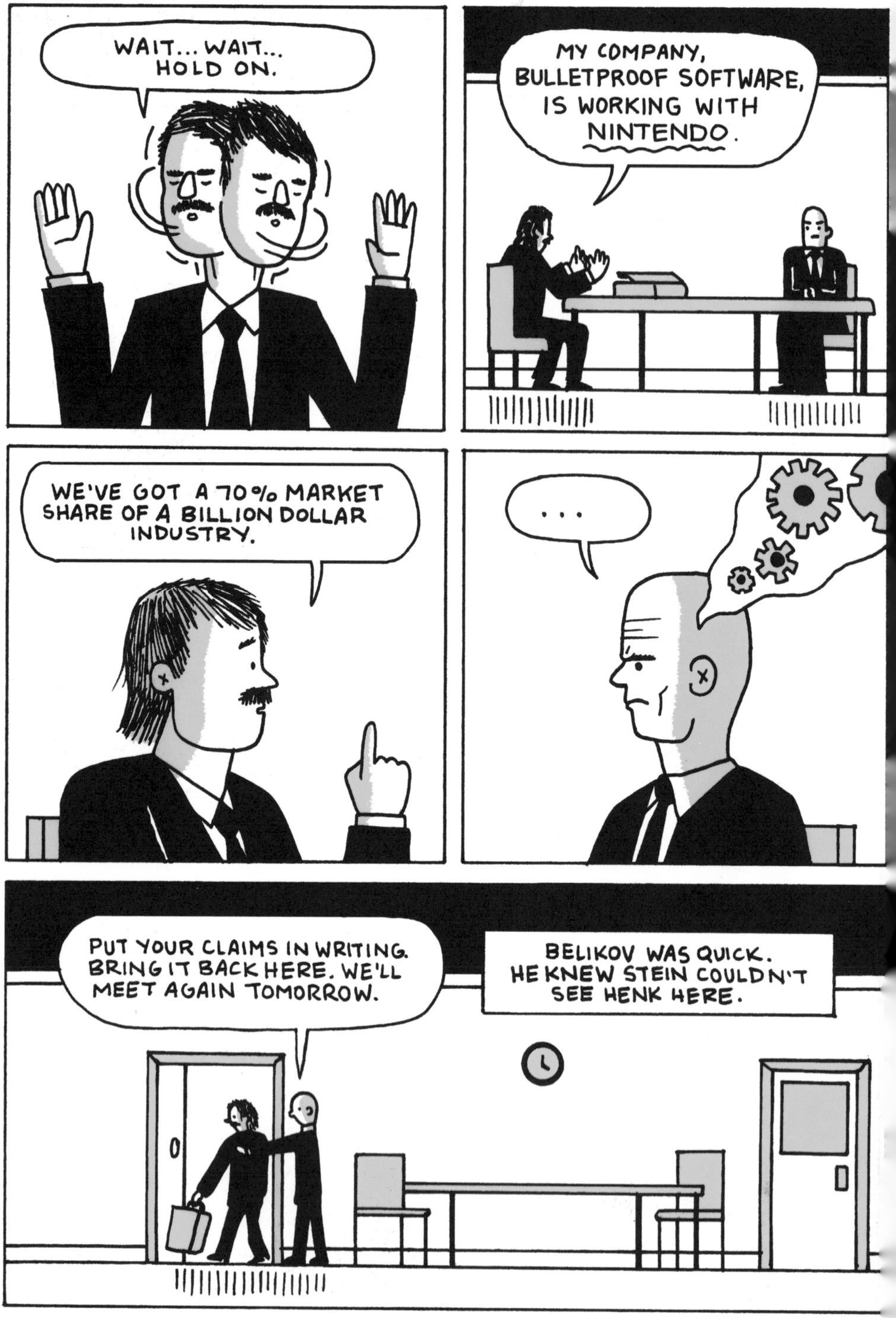
WAIT... WAIT... HOLD ON.
MY COMPANY, BULLETPROOF SOFTWARE, IS WORKING WITH NINTENDO.
WE'VE GOT A 70% MARKET SHARE OF A BILLION DOLLAR INDUSTRY.
...
PUT YOUR CLAIMS IN WRITING. BRING IT BACK HERE. WE'LL MEET AGAIN TOMORROW.
BELIKOV WAS QUICK. HE KNEW STEIN COULDN'T SEE HENK HERE.

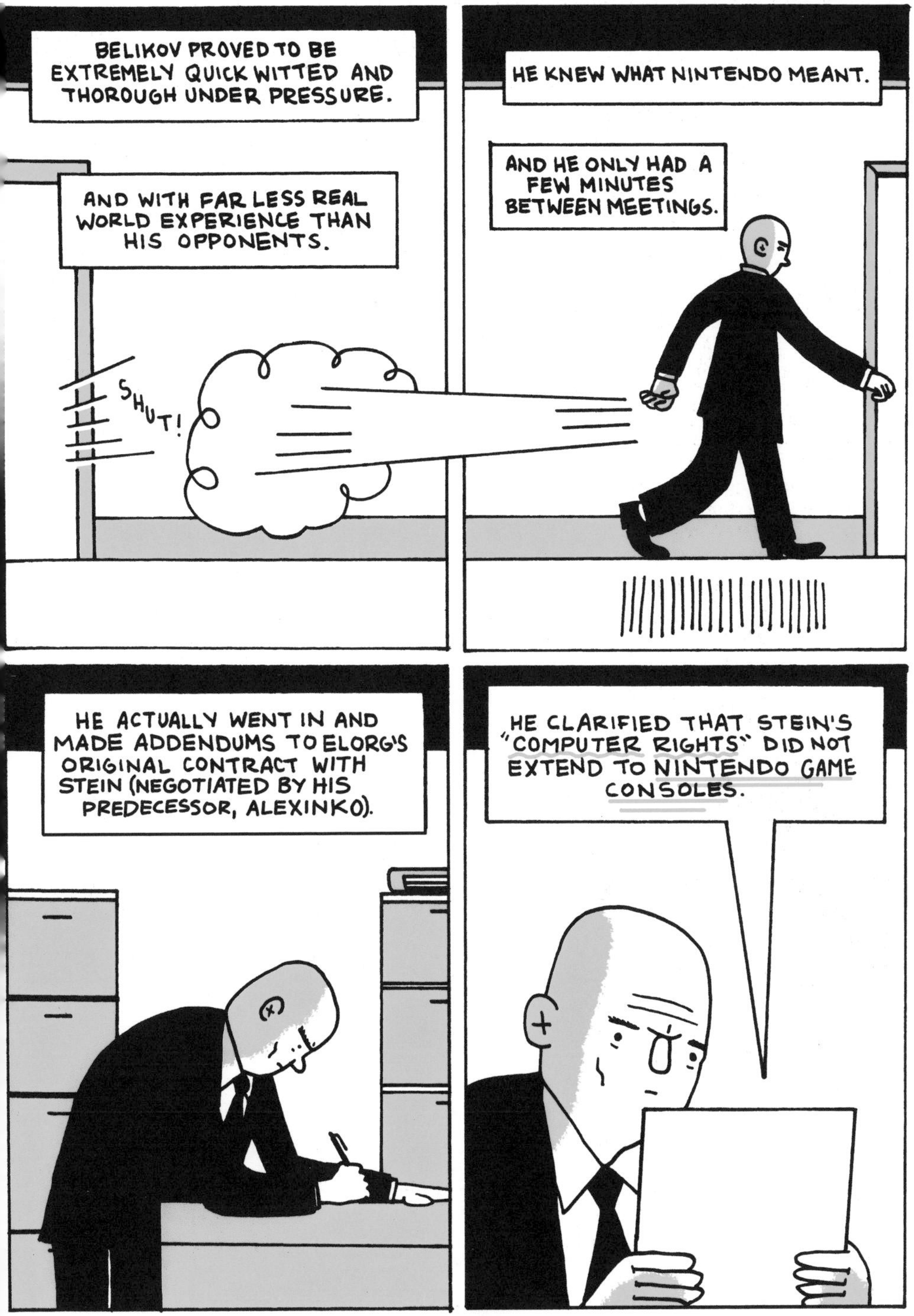
BELIKOV PROVED TO BE EXTREMELY QUICK WITTED AND THOROUGH UNDER PRESSURE.
AND WITH FAR LESS REAL WORLD EXPERIENCE THAN HIS OPPONENTS.
SHUT!
HE KNEW WHAT NINTENDO MEANT.
AND HE ONLY HAD A FEW MINUTES BETWEEN MEETINGS.
HE ACTUALLY WENT IN AND MADE ADDENDUMS TO ELORG'S ORIGINAL CONTRACT WITH STEIN (NEGOTIATED BY HIS PREDECESSOR, ALEXINKO).
HE CLARIFIED THAT STEIN'S "COMPUTER RIGHTS" DID NOT EXTEND TO NINTENDO GAME CONSOLES.

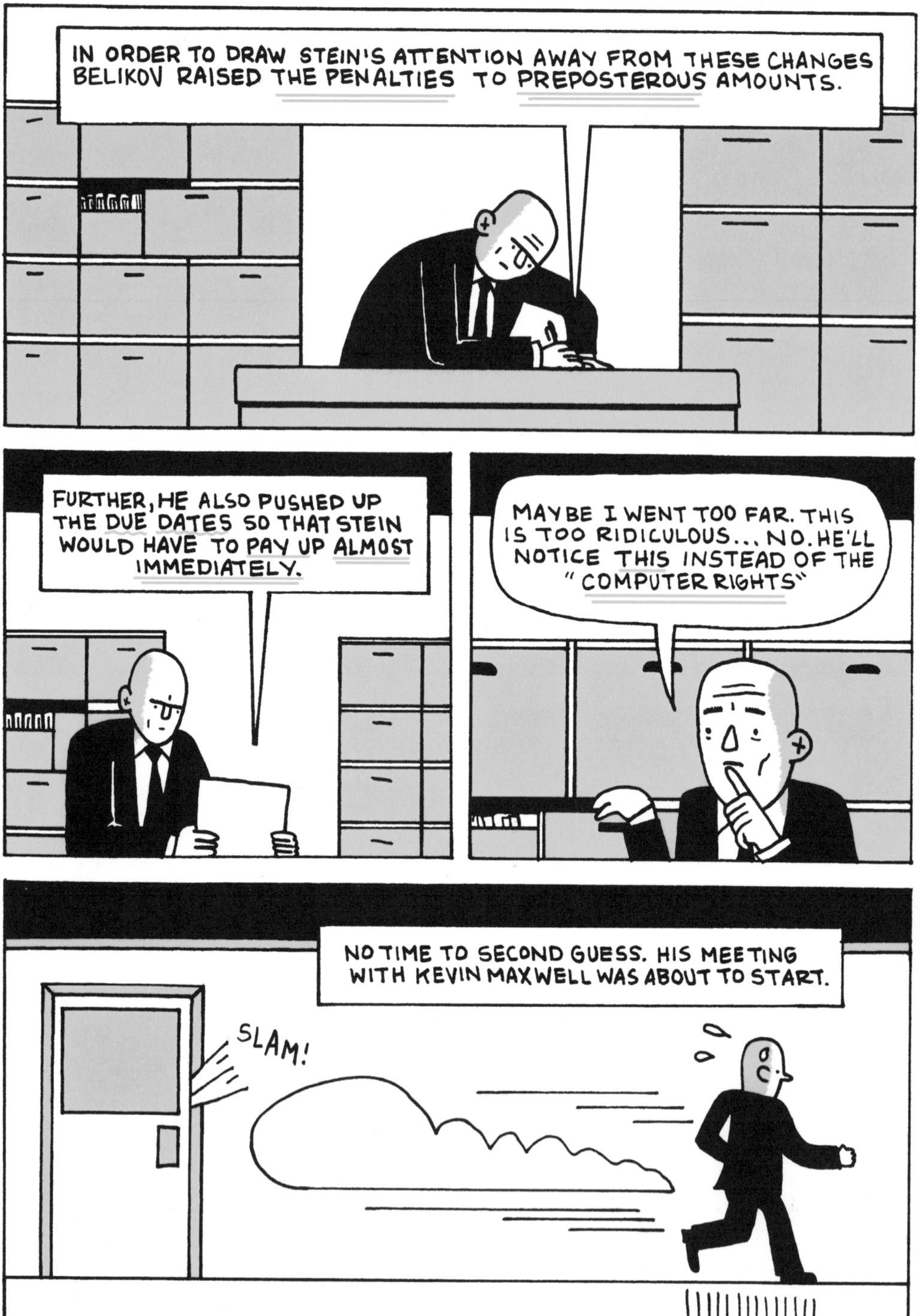
IN ORDER TO DRAW STEIN'S ATTENTION AWAY FROM THESE CHANGES BELIKOV RAISED THE PENALTIES TO PREPOSTEROUS AMOUNTS.
FURTHER, HE ALSO PUSHED UP THE DUE DATES SO THAT STEIN WOULD HAVE TO PAY UP ALMOST IMMEDIATELY.
MAYBE I WENT TOO FAR. THIS IS TOO RIDICULOUS... NO. HE'LL NOTICE THIS INSTEAD OF THE "COMPUTER RIGHTS"
NO TIME TO SECOND GUESS. HIS MEETING WITH KEVIN MAXWELL WAS ABOUT TO START.
SLAM!

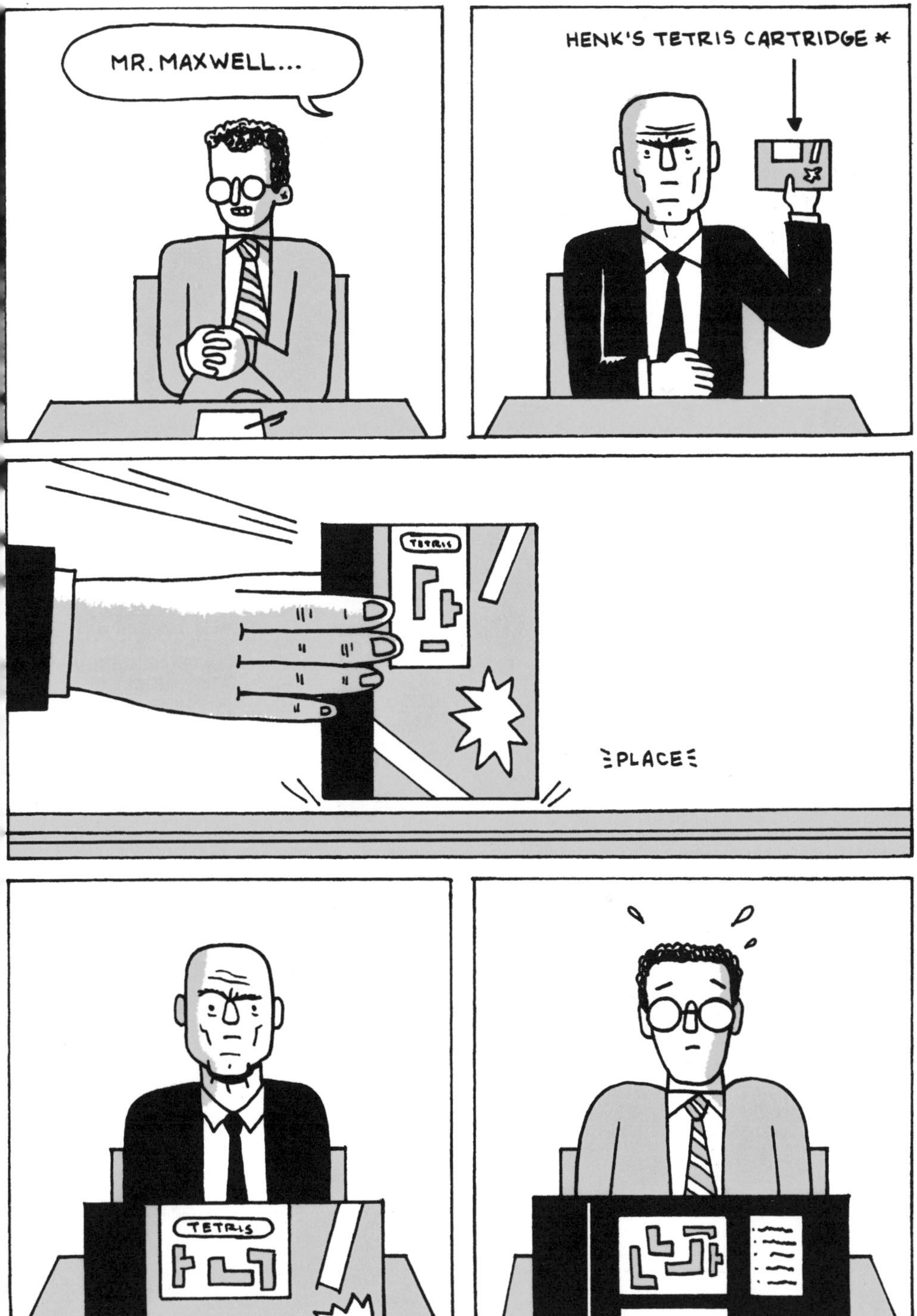
MR. MAXWELL...
HENK'S TETRIS CARTRIDGE *
TETRIS
PLACE
TETRIS

* WHICH BELIKOV DIDN'T KNOW EXISTED UNTIL THIS MORNING.

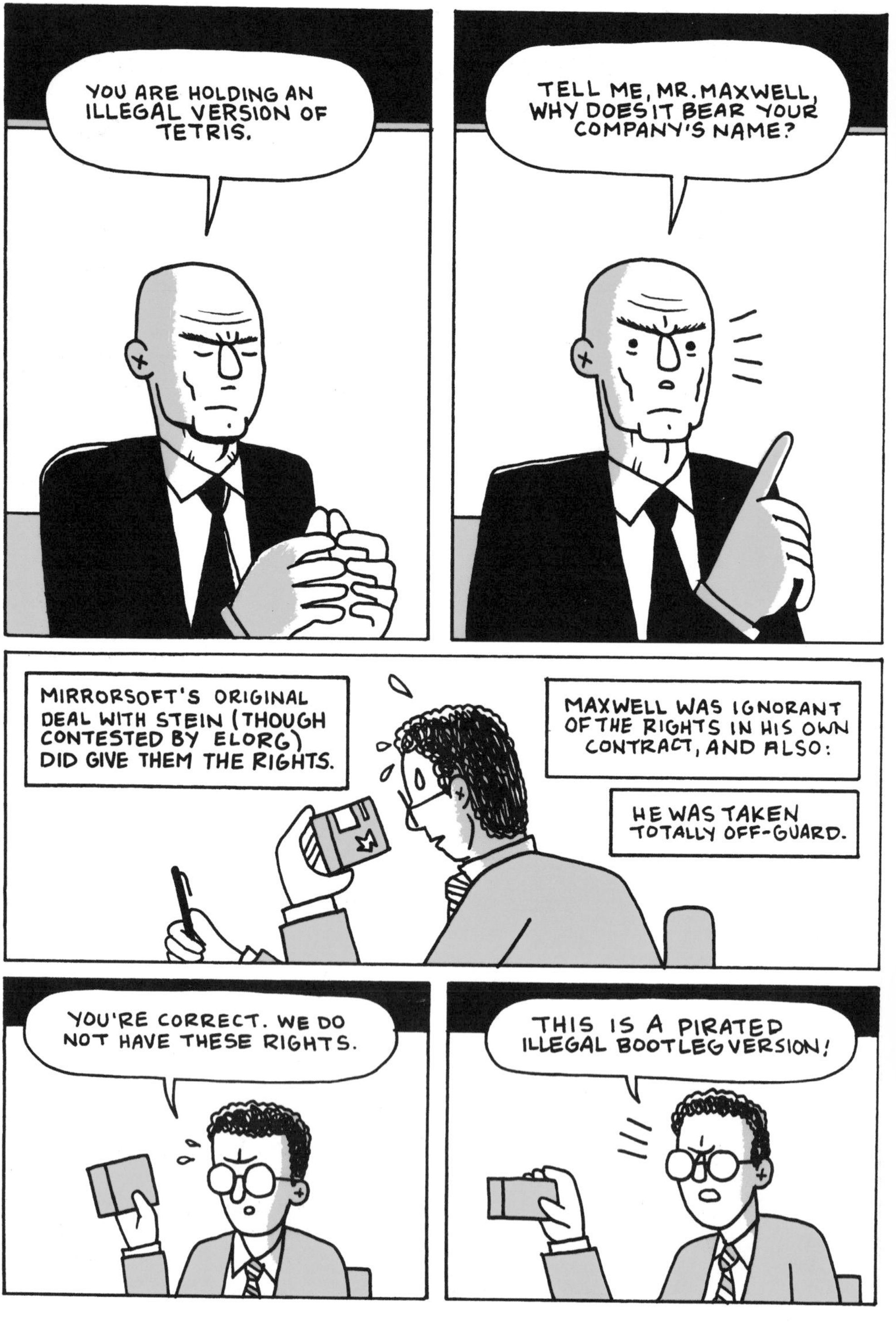
YOU ARE HOLDING AN ILLEGAL VERSION OF TETRIS.
TELL ME, MR. MAXWELL, WHY DOES IT BEAR YOUR COMPANY'S NAME?
MIRRORSOFT'S ORIGINAL DEAL WITH STEIN (THOUGH CONTESTED BY ELORG) DID GIVE THEM THE RIGHTS.
MAXWELL WAS IGNORANT OF THE RIGHTS IN HIS OWN CONTRACT, AND ALSO:
HE WAS TAKEN TOTALLY OFF-GUARD.
YOU'RE CORRECT. WE DO NOT HAVE THESE RIGHTS.
THIS IS A PIRATED ILLEGAL BOOTLEG VERSION!

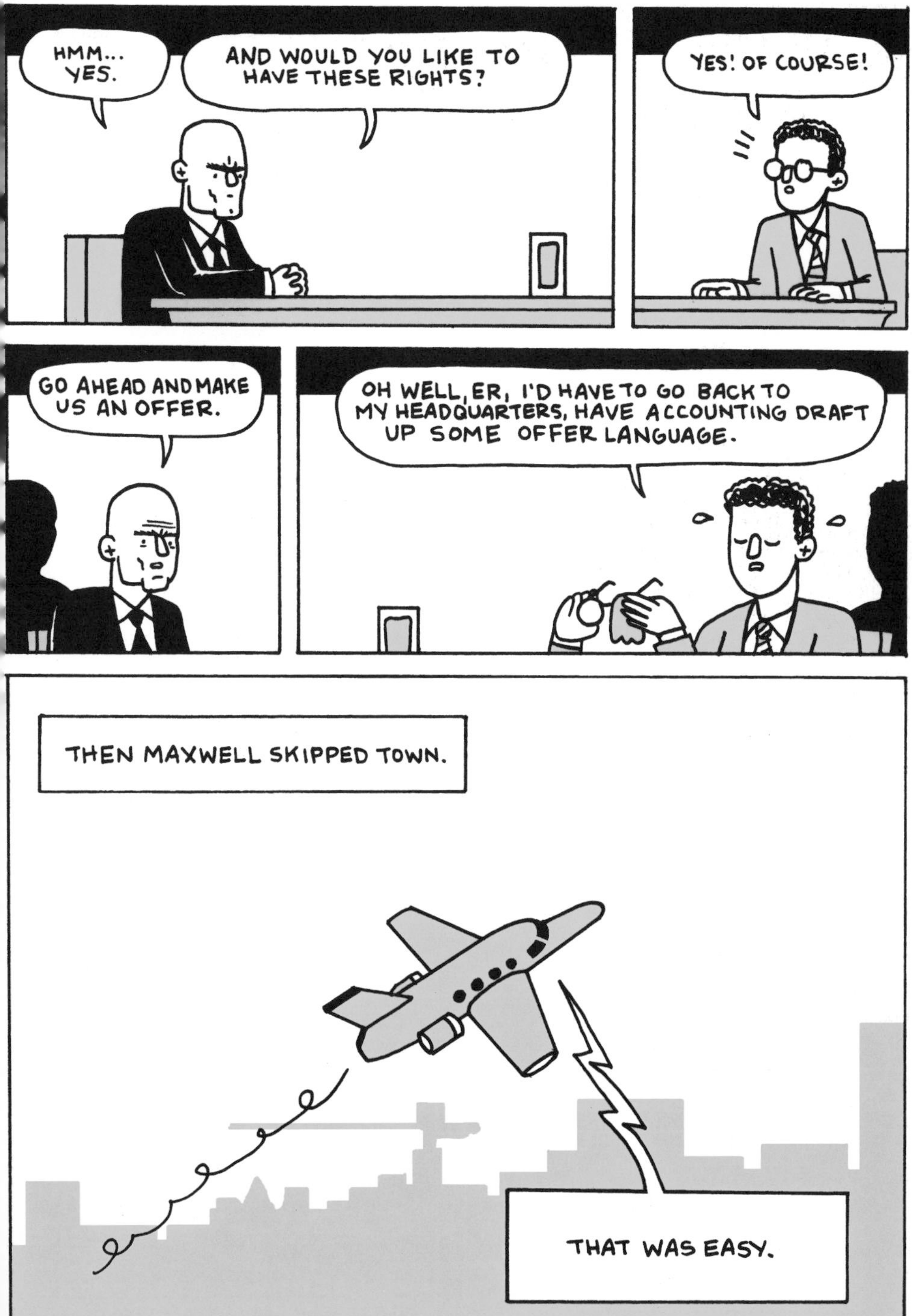
HMM... YES.
AND WOULD YOU LIKE TO HAVE THESE RIGHTS?
YES! OF COURSE!
GO AHEAD AND MAKE US AN OFFER.
OH WELL, ER, I'D HAVE TO GO BACK TO MY HEADQUARTERS, HAVE ACCOUNTING DRAFT UP SOME OFFER LANGUAGE.
THEN MAXWELL SKIPPED TOWN.
THAT WAS EASY.

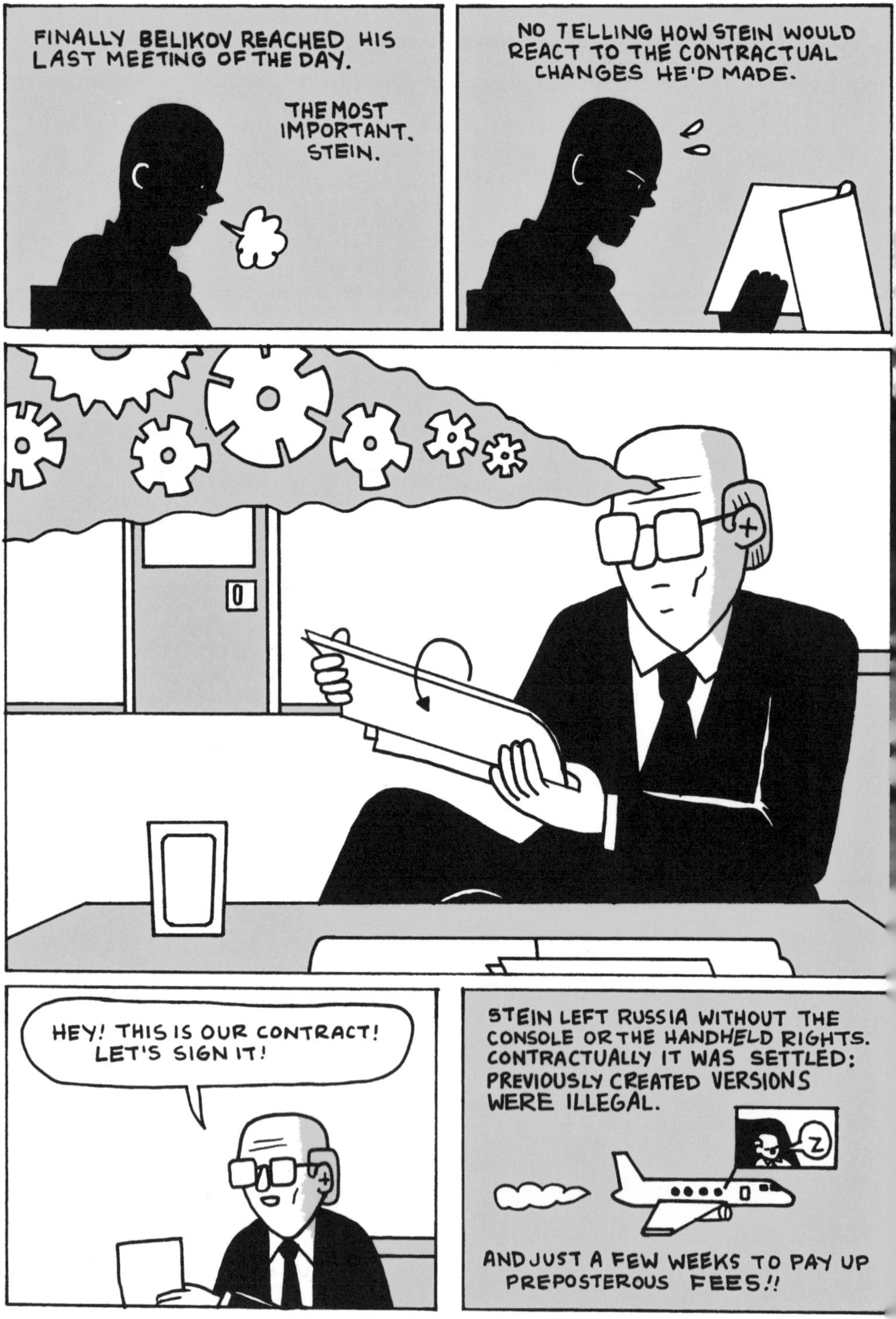
FINALLY BELIKOV REACHED HIS LAST MEETING OF THE DAY.
THE MOST IMPORTANT. STEIN.
NO TELLING HOW STEIN WOULD REACT TO THE CONTRACTUAL CHANGES HE'D MADE.
HEY! THIS IS OUR CONTRACT! LET'S SIGN IT!
STEIN LEFT RUSSIA WITHOUT THE CONSOLE OR THE HANDHELD RIGHTS. CONTRACTUALLY IT WAS SETTLED: PREVIOUSLY CREATED VERSIONS WERE ILLEGAL.
Z
AND JUST A FEW WEEKS TO PAY UP PREPOSTEROUS FEES!!

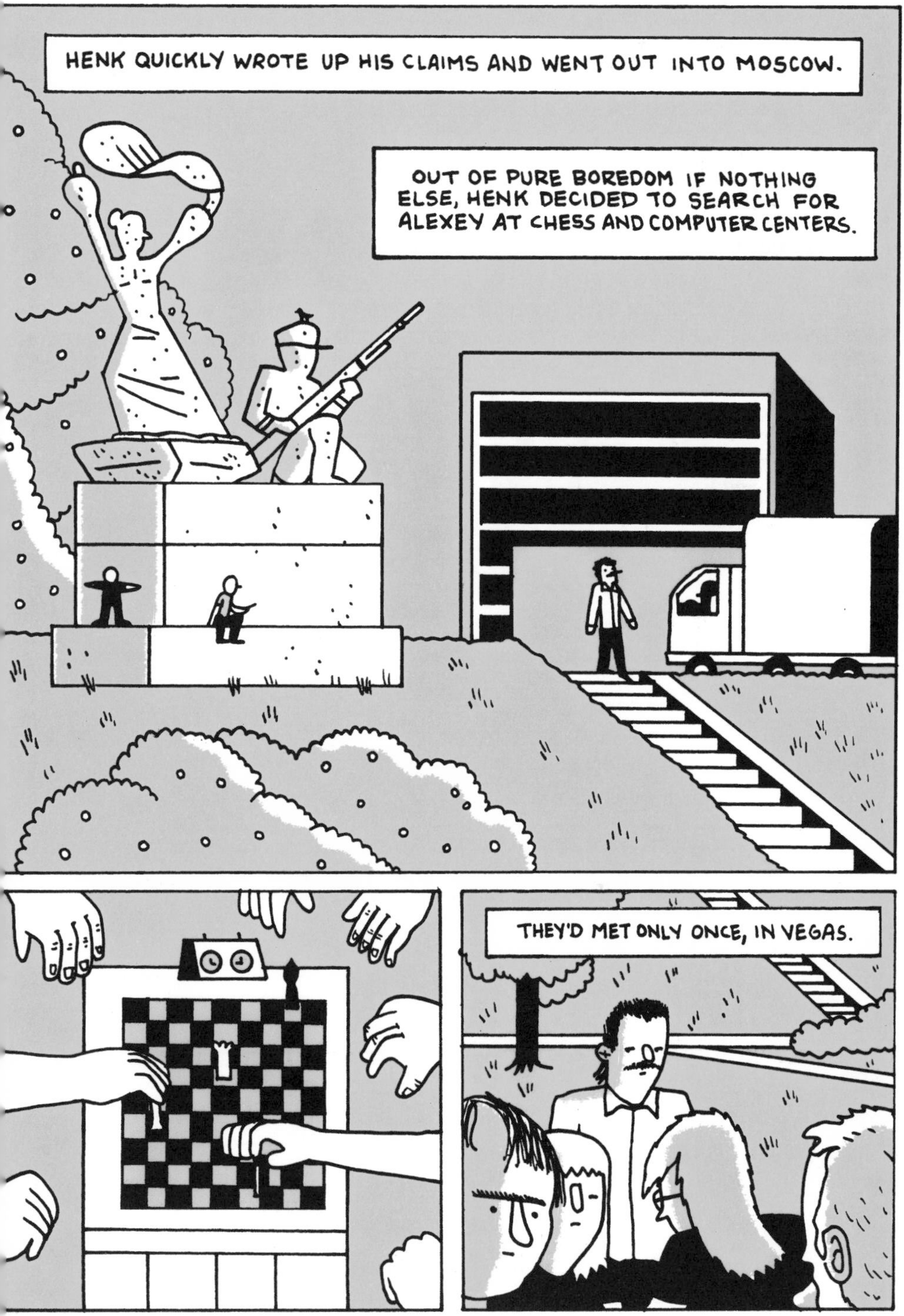
HENK QUICKLY WROTE UP HIS CLAIMS AND WENT OUT INTO MOSCOW.
OUT OF PURE BOREDOM IF NOTHING ELSE, HENK DECIDED TO SEARCH FOR ALEXEY AT CHESS AND COMPUTER CENTERS.
THEY'D MET ONLY ONCE, IN VEGAS.

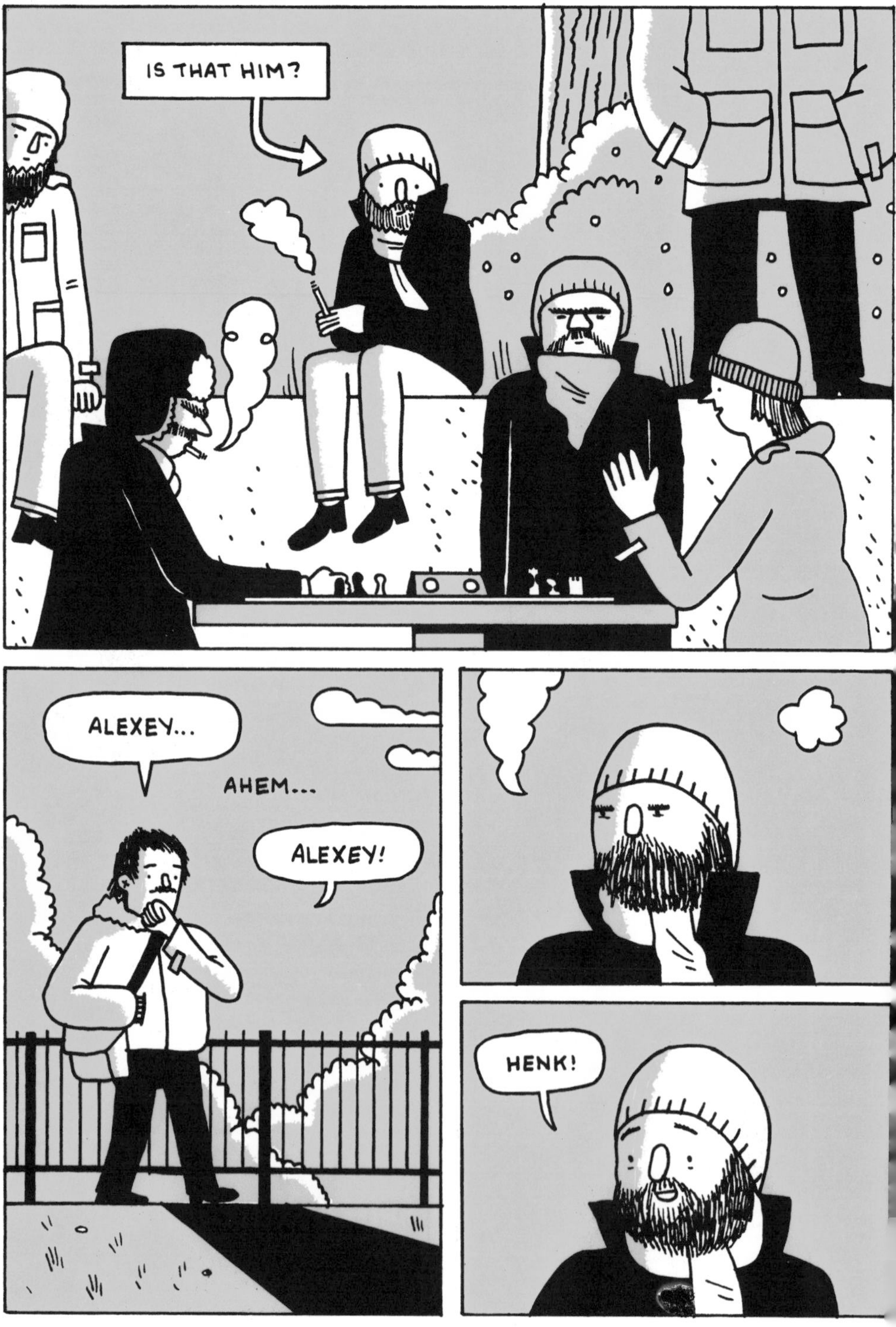
IS THAT HIM?
ALEXEY...
AHEM...
ALEXEY!
HENK!

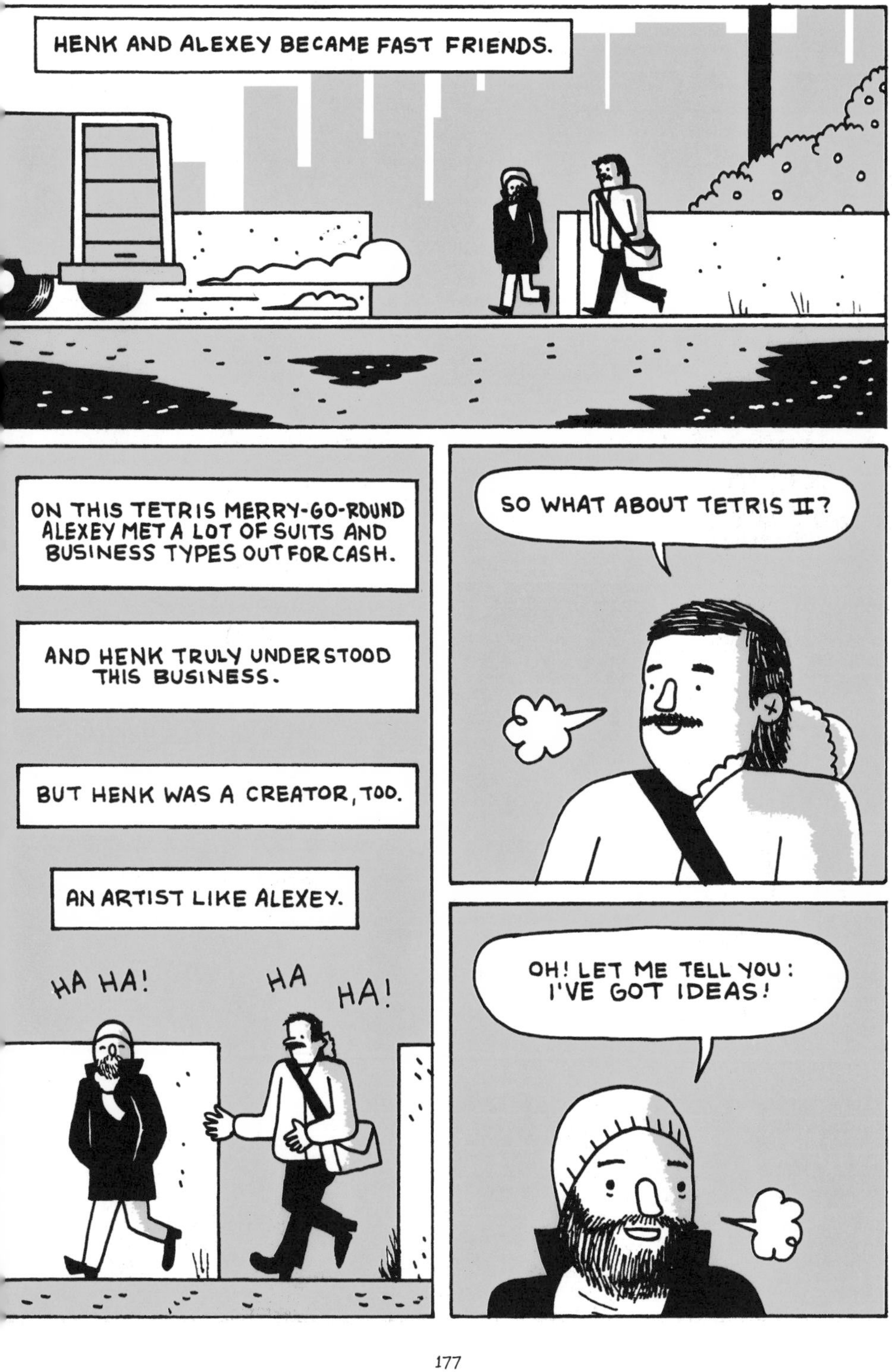
HENK AND ALEXEY BECAME FAST FRIENDS.
ON THIS TETRIS MERRY-GO-ROUND ALEXEY MET A LOT OF SUITS AND BUSINESS TYPES OUT FOR CASH.
AND HENK TRULY UNDERSTOOD THIS BUSINESS.
BUT HENK WAS A CREATOR, TOO.
AN ARTIST LIKE ALEXEY.
HA HA!
HA HA!
SO WHAT ABOUT TETRIS II?
OH! LET ME TELL YOU: I'VE GOT IDEAS!

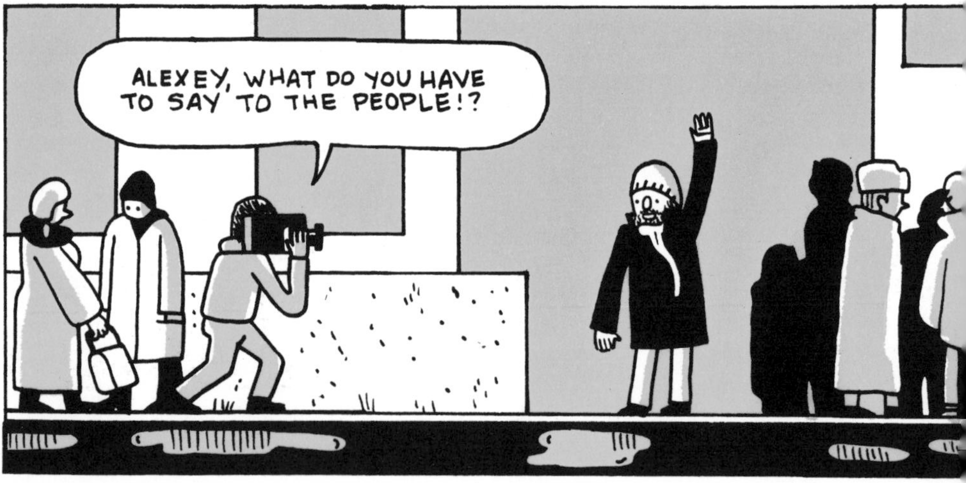
ALEXEY, WHAT DO YOU HAVE TO SAY TO THE PEOPLE!?

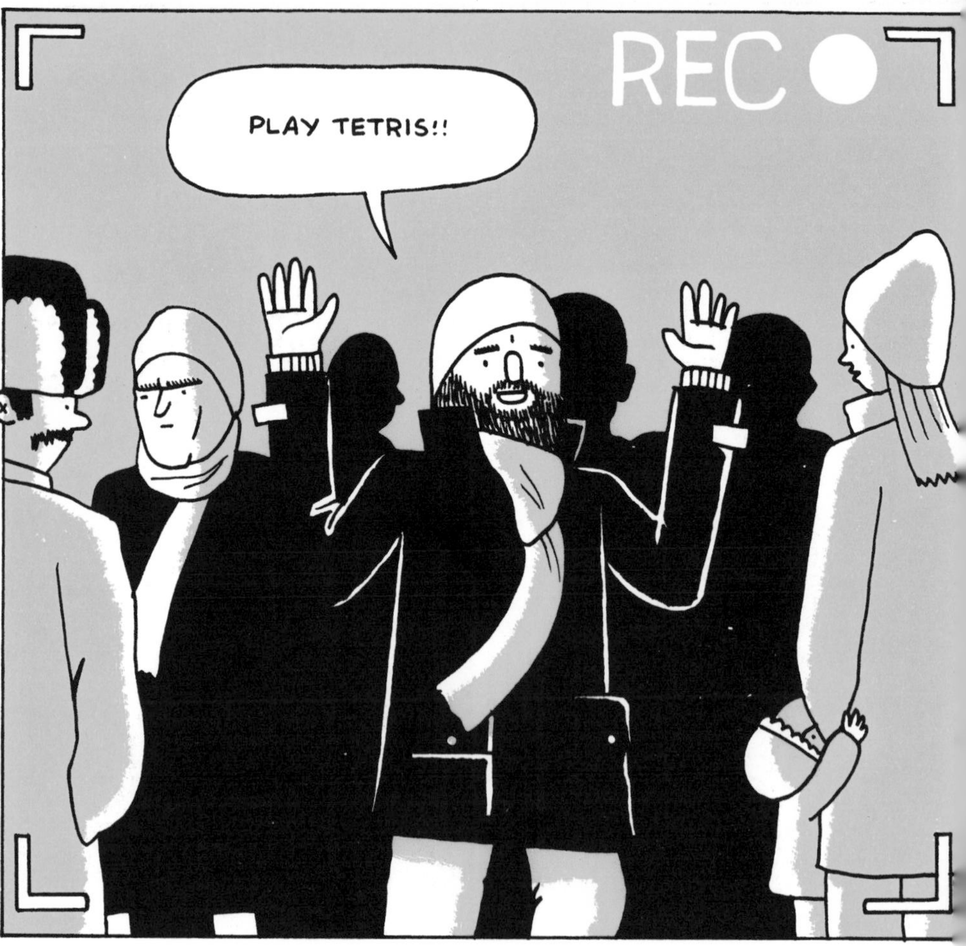
REC
PLAY TETRIS!!

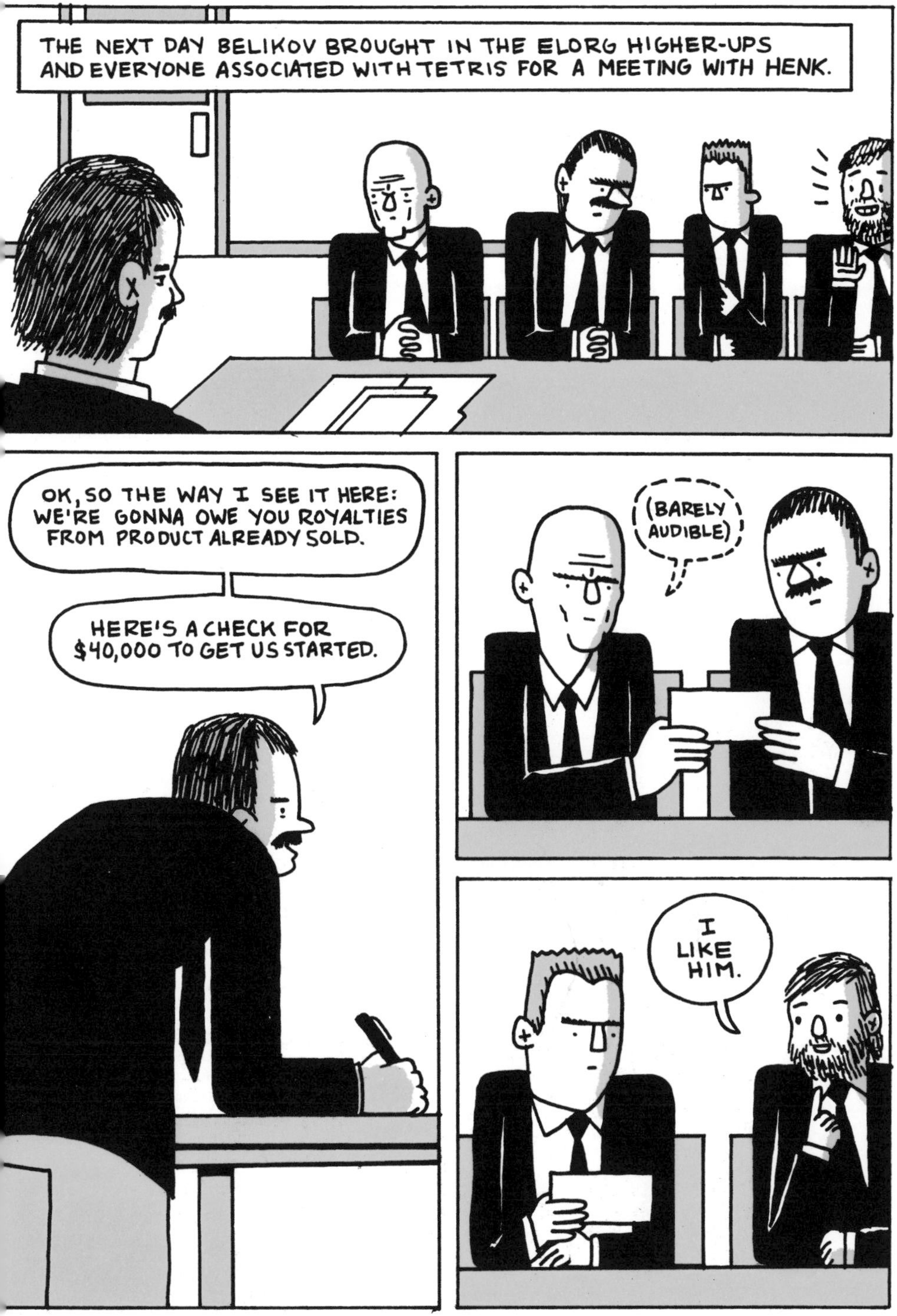
THE NEXT DAY BELIKOV BROUGHT IN THE ELORG HIGHER-UPS AND EVERYONE ASSOCIATED WITH TETRIS FOR A MEETING WITH HENK.
OK, SO THE WAY I SEE IT HERE: WE'RE GONNA OWE YOU ROYALTIES FROM PRODUCT ALREADY SOLD.
HERE'S A CHECK FOR $40,000 TO GET US STARTED.
(BARELY AUDIBLE)
I LIKE HIM.

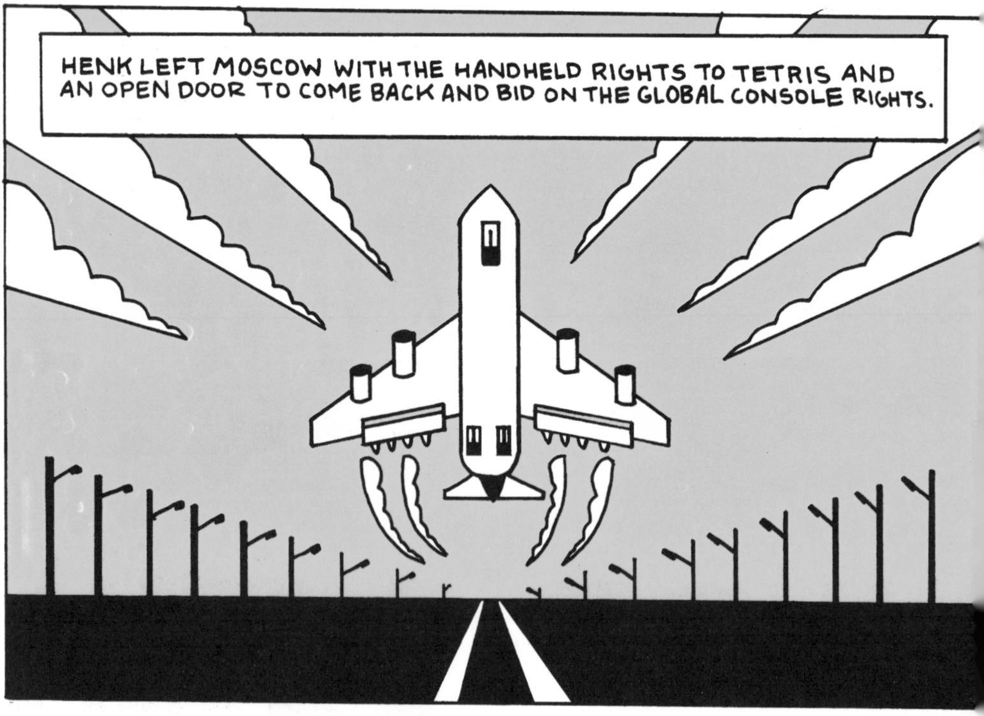
HENK LEFT MOSCOW WITH THE HANDHELD RIGHTS TO TETRIS AND AN OPEN DOOR TO COME BACK AND BID ON THE GLOBAL CONSOLE RIGHTS.

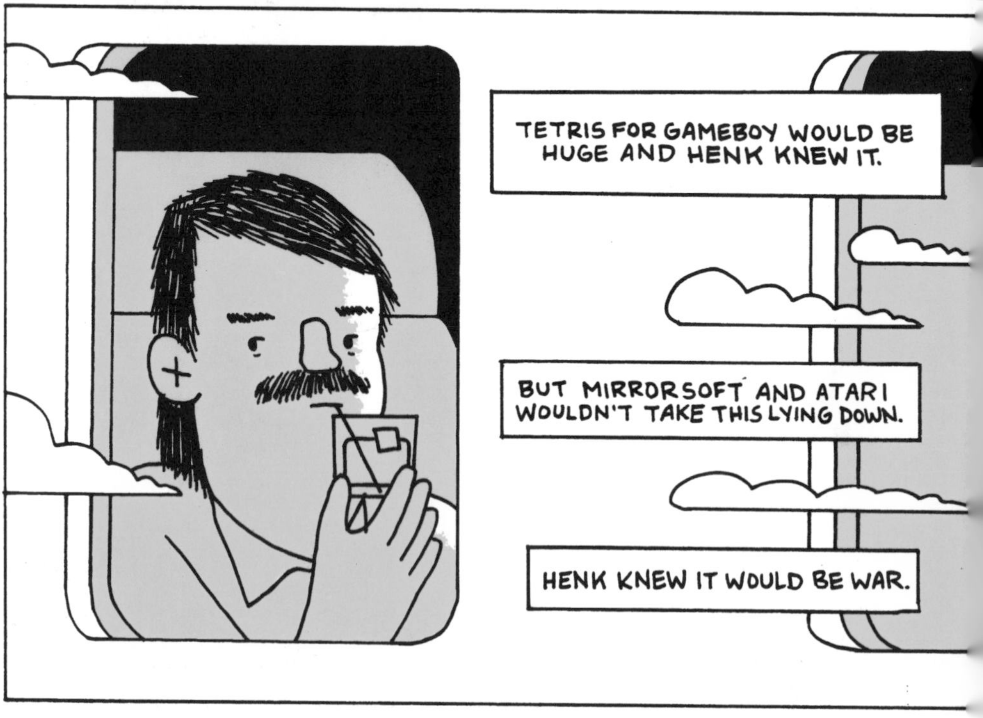
TETRIS FOR GAMEBOY WOULD BE HUGE AND HENK KNEW IT.
BUT MIRRORSOFT AND ATARI WOULDN'T TAKE THIS LYING DOWN.
HENK KNEW IT WOULD BE WAR.

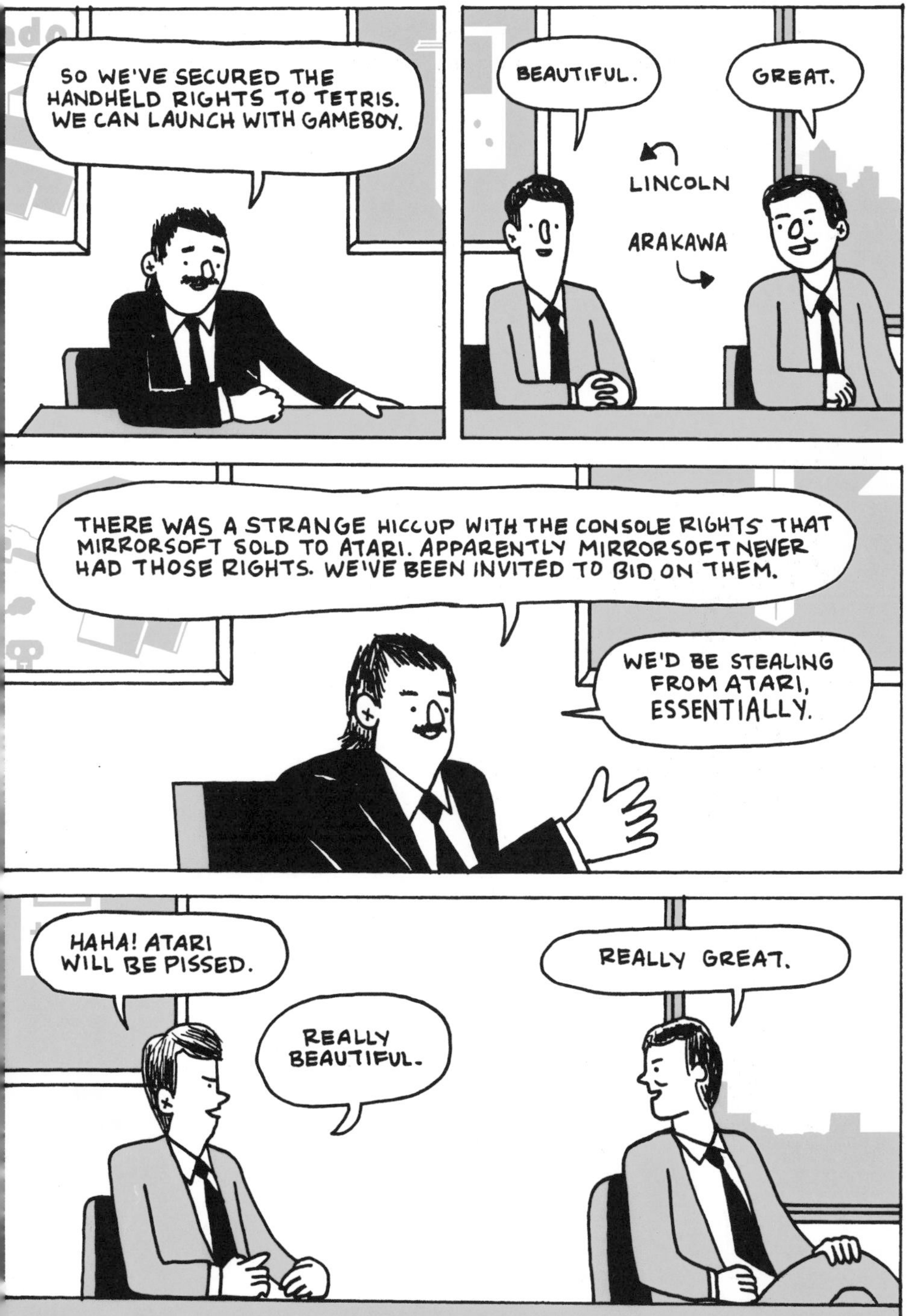
SO WE'VE SECURED THE HANDHELD RIGHTS TO TETRIS. WE CAN LAUNCH WITH GAMEBOY.
BEAUTIFUL.
GREAT.
LINCOLN
ARAKAWA
THERE WAS A STRANGE HICCUP WITH THE CONSOLE RIGHTS THAT MIRRORSOFT SOLD TO ATARI. APPARENTLY MIRRORSOFT NEVER HAD THOSE RIGHTS. WE'VE BEEN INVITED TO BID ON THEM.
WE'D BE STEALING FROM ATARI, ESSENTIALLY.
HAHA! ATARI WILL BE PISSED.
REALLY BEAUTIFUL.
REALLY GREAT.

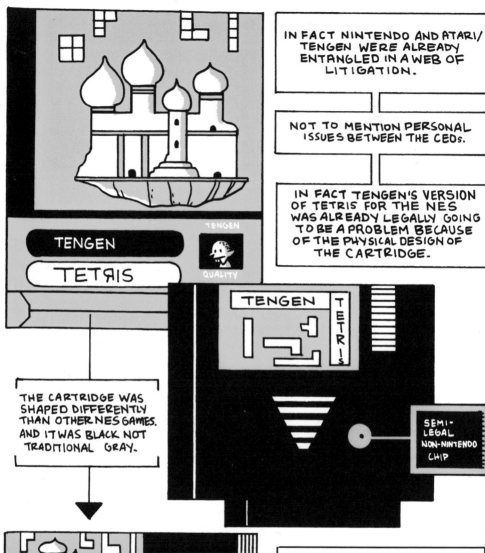

IN FACT NINTENDO AND ATARI/ TENGEN WERE ALREADY ENTANGLED IN A WEB OF LITIGATION.

NOT TO MENTION PERSONAL ISSUES BETWEEN THE CEOs.

IN FACT TENGEN'S VERSION OF TETRIS FOR THE NES WAS ALREADY LEGALLY GOING TO BE A PROBLEM BECAUSE OF THE PHYSICAL DESIGN OF THE CARTRIDGE.

TENGEN

TETЯIS

TENGEN
QUALITY

TENGEN

TETRIS

THE CARTRIDGE WAS SHAPED DIFFERENTLY THAN OTHER NES GAMES. AND IT WAS BLACK NOT TRADITIONAL GRAY.

SEMI- LEGAL NON-NINTENDO CHIP

TENGEN
TETRIS
PLAYER MANUAL

THEIR VERSION (ALONG WITH ALL TENGEN GAMES) USED ALTERNATIVE NON-NINTENDO COMPUTER CHIPS.

ATARI SAID THEIR CHIPS WERE CREATED ON THEIR OWN IN A LEGAL FASHION.

NINTENDO DISAGREED.

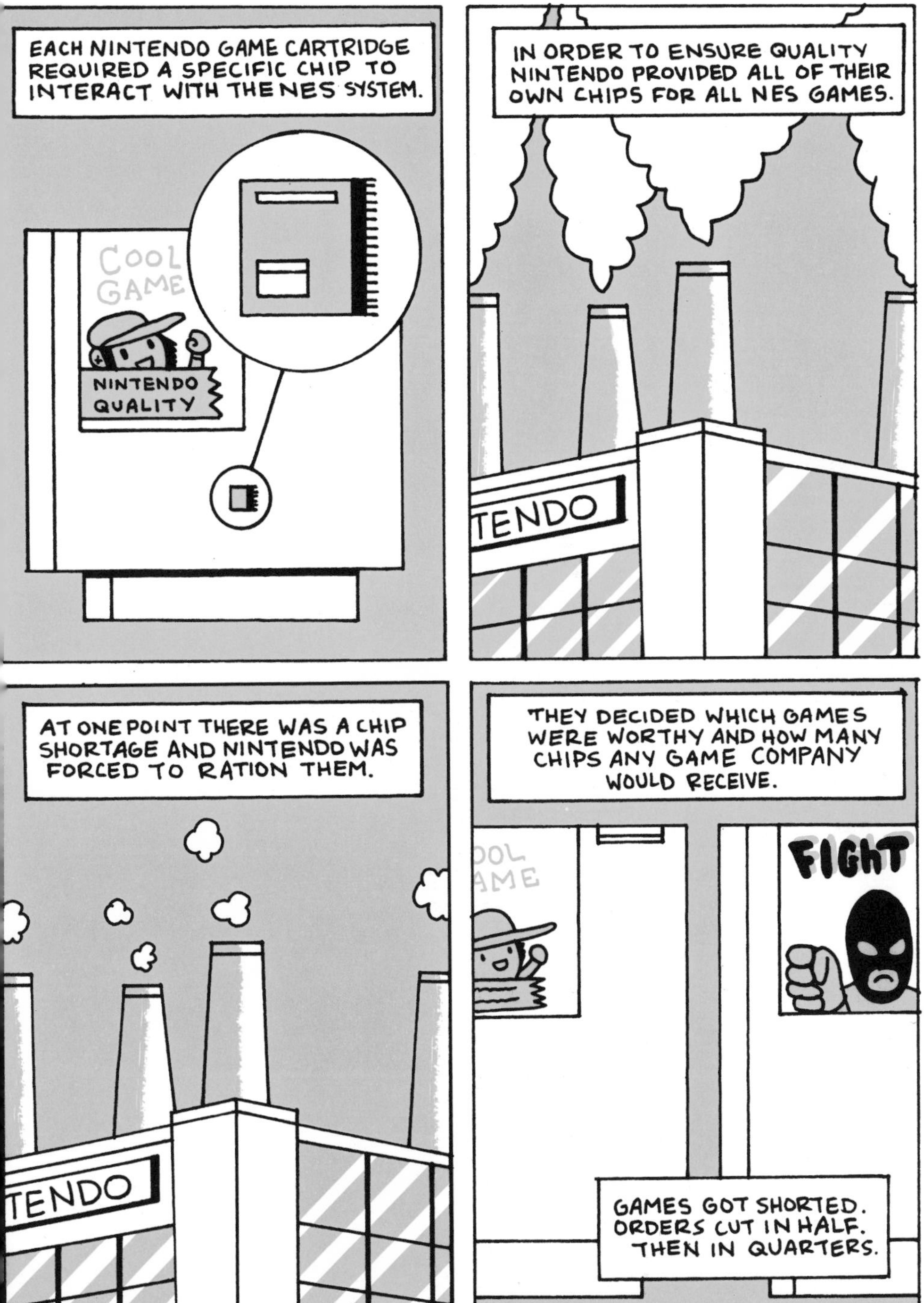
EACH NINTENDO GAME CARTRIDGE REQUIRED A SPECIFIC CHIP TO INTERACT WITH THE NES SYSTEM.
COOL GAME
NINTENDO QUALITY
IN ORDER TO ENSURE QUALITY NINTENDO PROVIDED ALL OF THEIR OWN CHIPS FOR ALL NES GAMES.
TENDO
AT ONE POINT THERE WAS A CHIP SHORTAGE AND NINTENDO WAS FORCED TO RATION THEM.
TENDO
THEY DECIDED WHICH GAMES WERE WORTHY AND HOW MANY CHIPS ANY GAME COMPANY WOULD RECEIVE.
FIGHT
GAMES GOT SHORTED. ORDERS CUT IN HALF. THEN IN QUARTERS.

HIDE NAKAJIMA
NAMCO / SEGA / ATARI JAPAN

DAN VAN ELDEREN
ATARI

RANDY BROWELEIT
ATARI/TENGEN

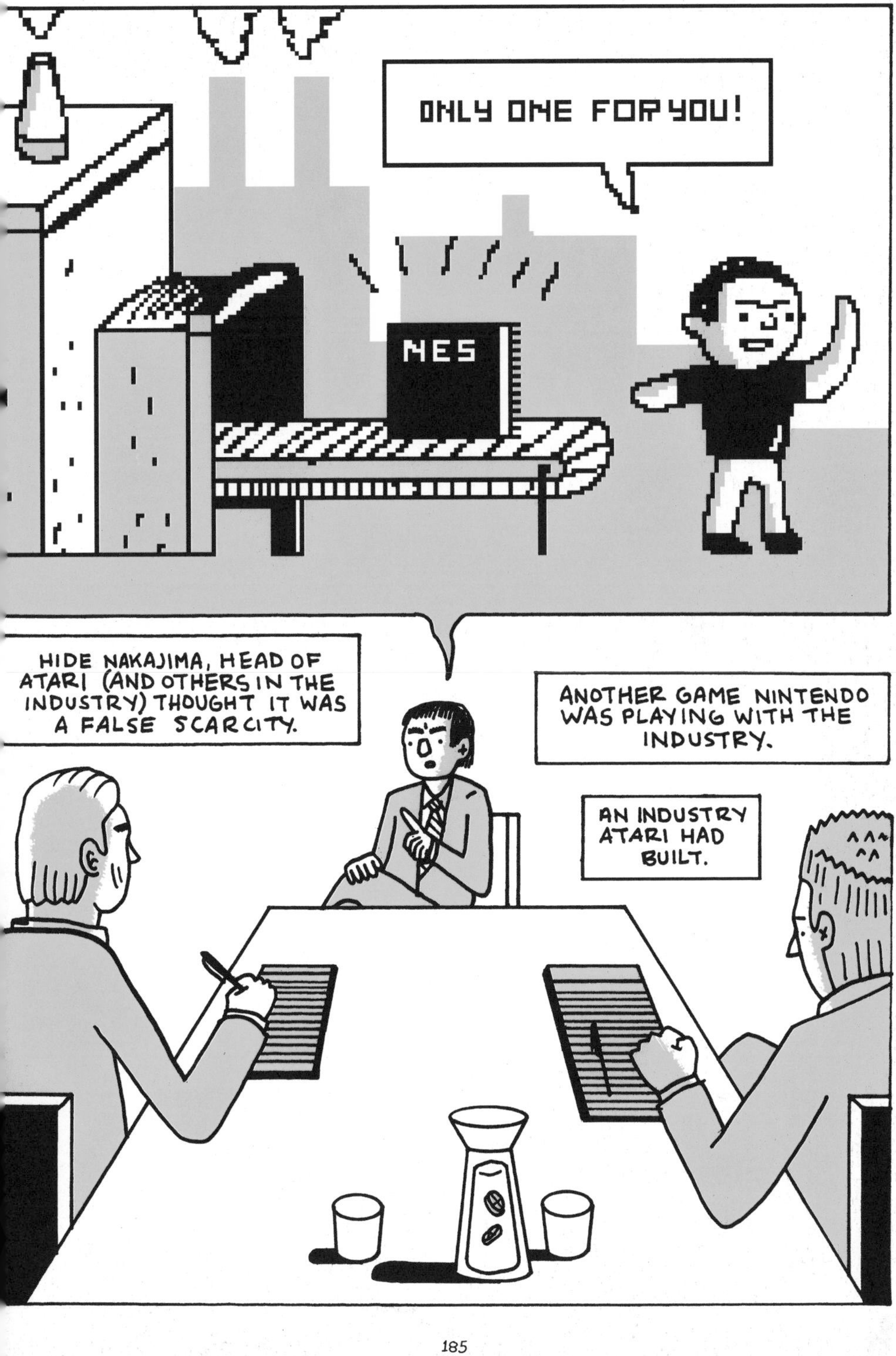
ONLY ONE FOR YOU!
NES
HIDE NAKAJIMA, HEAD OF ATARI (AND OTHERS IN THE INDUSTRY) THOUGHT IT WAS A FALSE SCARCITY.
ANOTHER GAME NINTENDO WAS PLAYING WITH THE INDUSTRY.
AN INDUSTRY ATARI HAD BUILT.

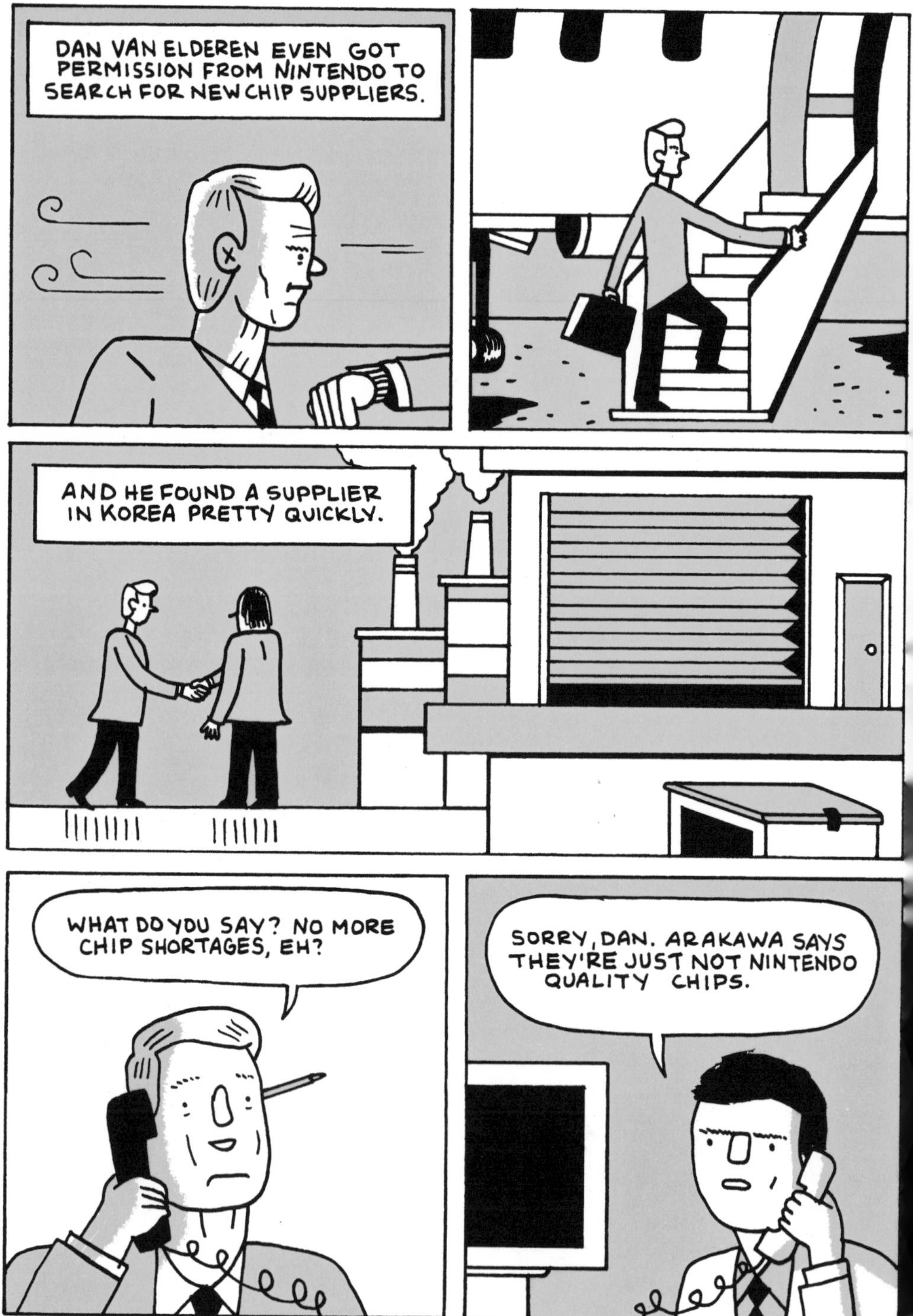
DAN VAN ELDEREN EVEN GOT PERMISSION FROM NINTENDO TO SEARCH FOR NEW CHIP SUPPLIERS.
AND HE FOUND A SUPPLIER IN KOREA PRETTY QUICKLY.
WHAT DO YOU SAY? NO MORE CHIP SHORTAGES, EH?
SORRY, DAN. ARAKAWA SAYS THEY'RE JUST NOT NINTENDO QUALITY CHIPS.

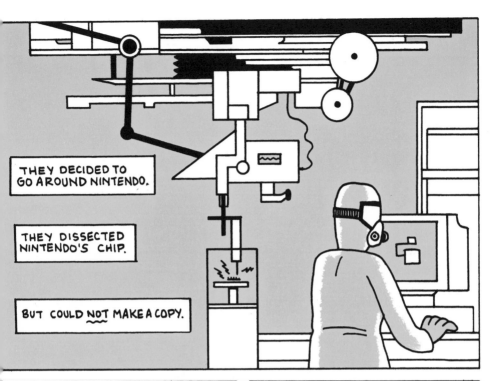

THEY DECIDED TO GO AROUND NINTENDO.

THEY DISSECTED NINTENDO'S CHIP.

BUT COULD NOT MAKE A COPY.

ATARI WAS ABLE TO OBTAIN THE COPYRIGHTED CODE VIA SUBPOENA IN THE END.

LEGALLY ATARI COULD ONLY USE THIS COPY OF NINTENDO'S CODE TO DEFEND THEMSELVES AGAINST INFRINGEMENT.

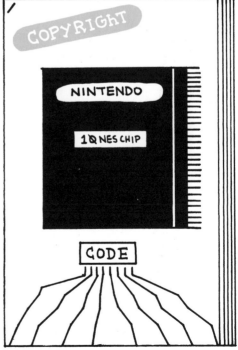

COPYRIGHT

NINTENDO

10 NES CHIP

CODE

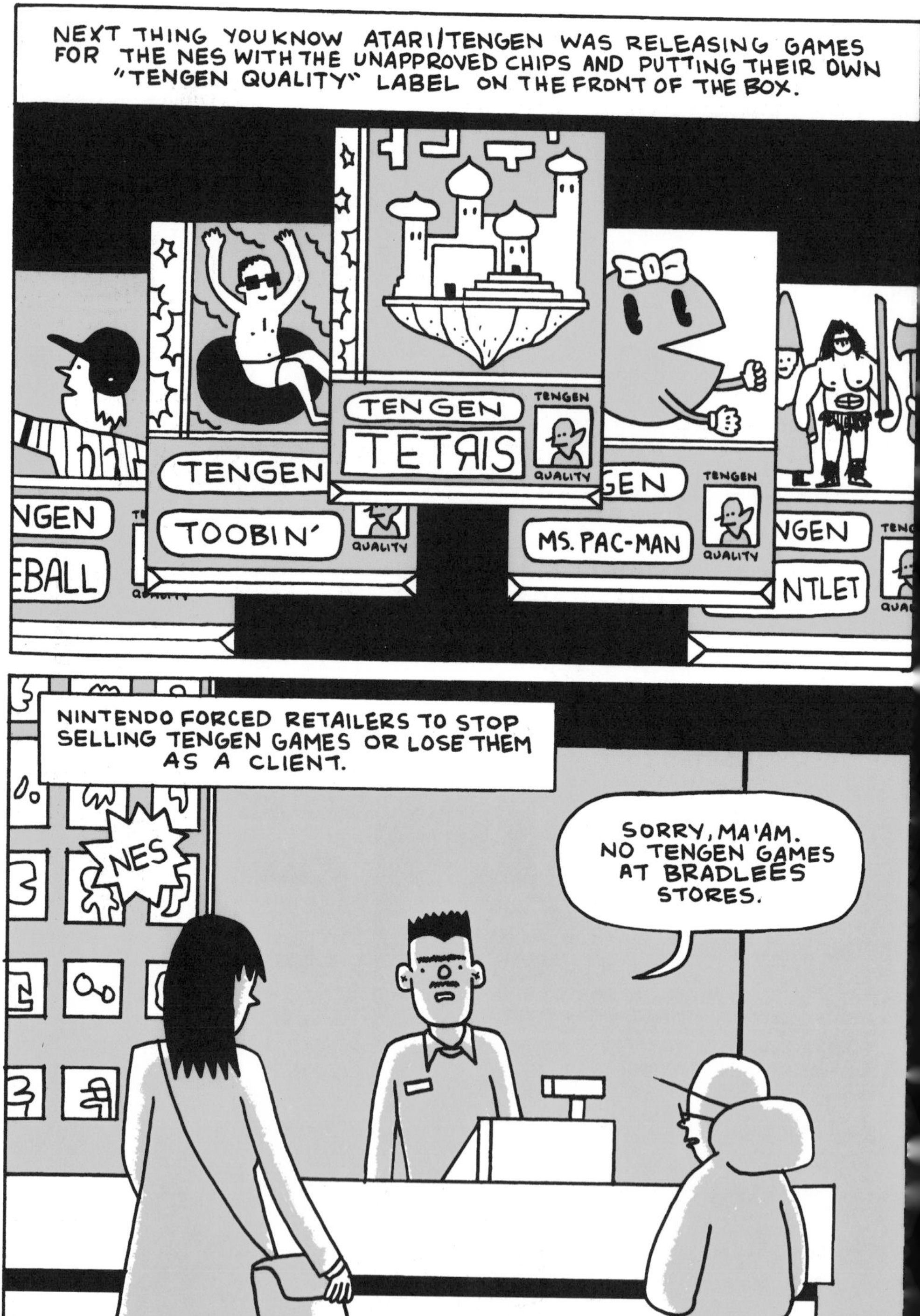
NEXT THING YOU KNOW ATARI/TENGEN WAS RELEASING GAMES FOR THE NES WITH THE UNAPPROVED CHIPS AND PUTTING THEIR OWN "TENGEN QUALITY" LABEL ON THE FRONT OF THE BOX.
TENGEN TOOBIN'
TENGEN TETRIS
TENGEN QUALITY
MS. PAC-MAN
NINTENDO FORCED RETAILERS TO STOP SELLING TENGEN GAMES OR LOSE THEM AS A CLIENT.
NES
SORRY, MA'AM. NO TENGEN GAMES AT BRADLEES STORES.

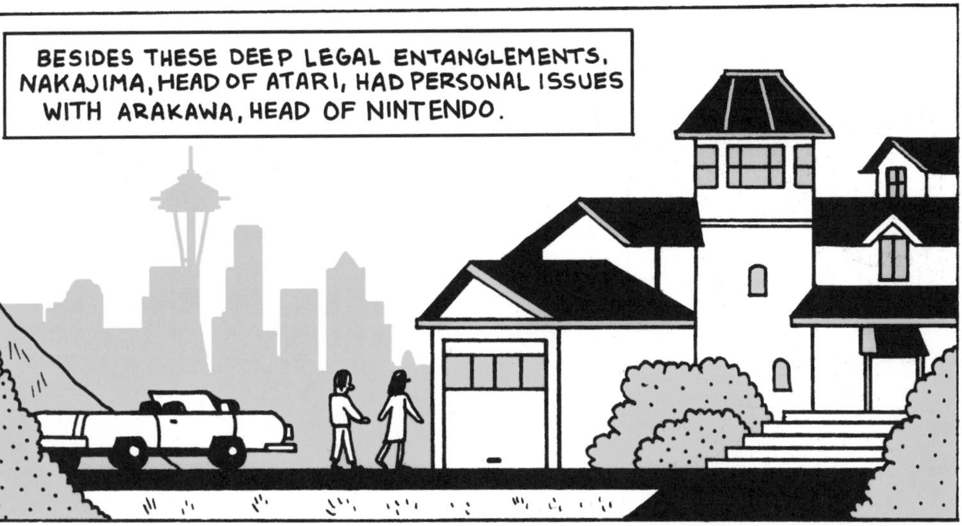
BESIDES THESE DEEP LEGAL ENTANGLEMENTS, NAKAJIMA, HEAD OF ATARI, HAD PERSONAL ISSUES WITH ARAKAWA, HEAD OF NINTENDO.

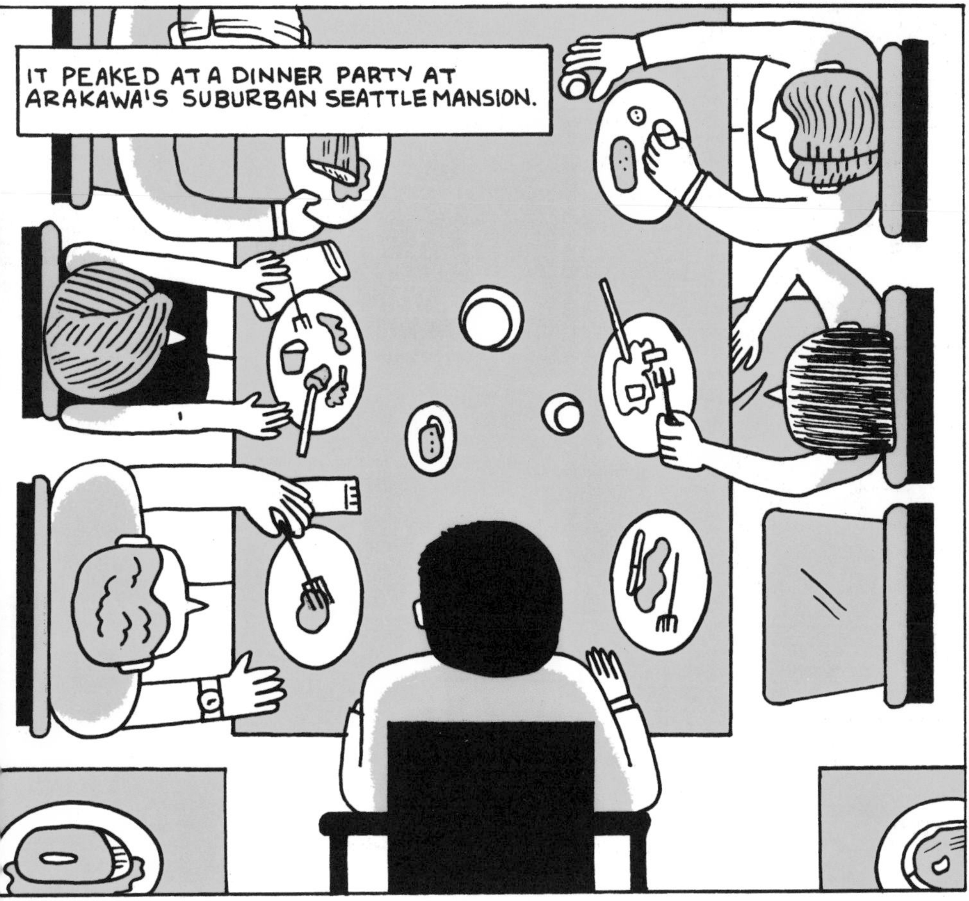
IT PEAKED AT A DINNER PARTY AT ARAKAWA'S SUBURBAN SEATTLE MANSION.

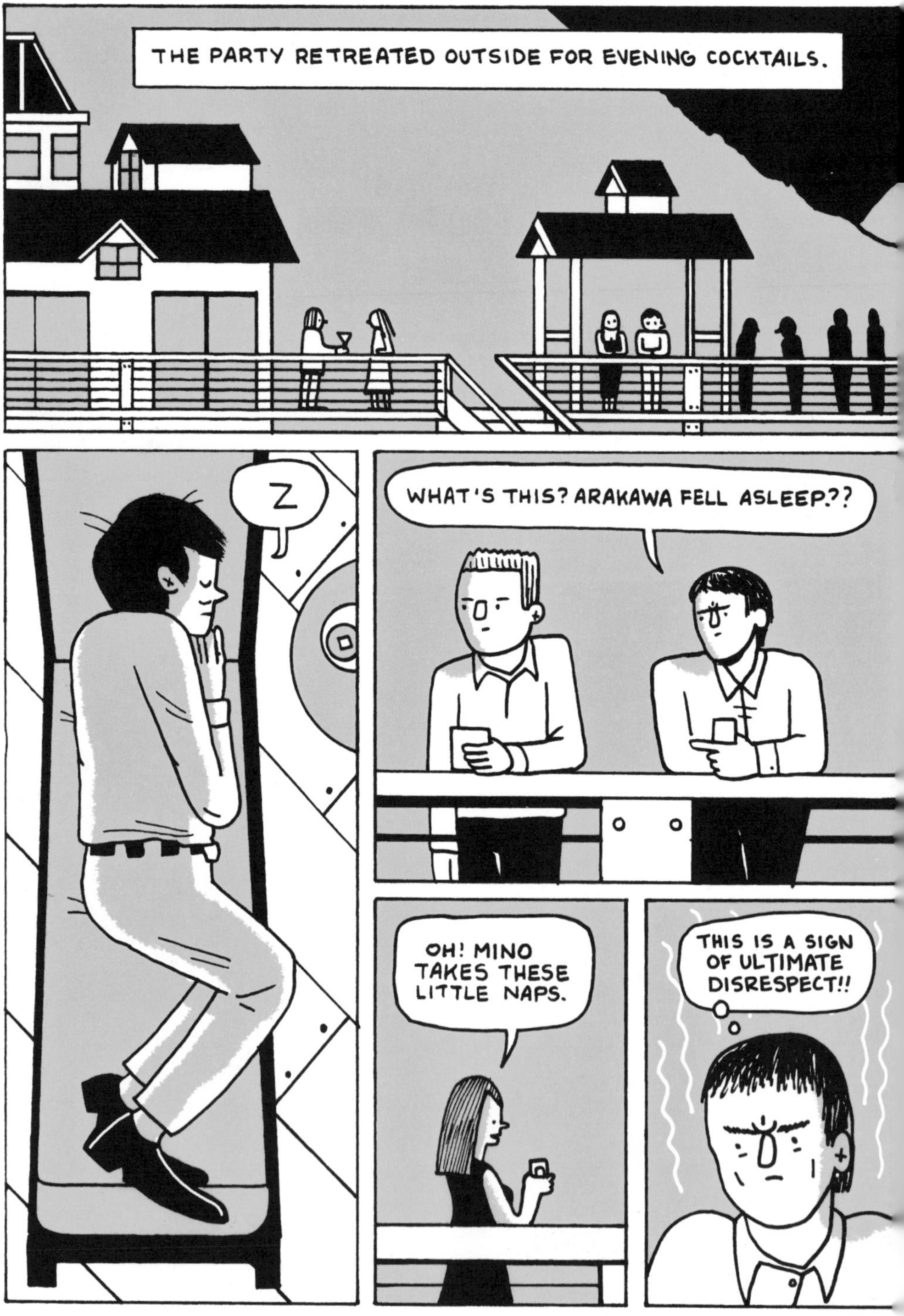
THE PARTY RETREATED OUTSIDE FOR EVENING COCKTAILS.
Z
WHAT'S THIS? ARAKAWA FELL ASLEEP.??
OH! MINO TAKES THESE LITTLE NAPS.
THIS IS A SIGN OF ULTIMATE DISRESPECT!!

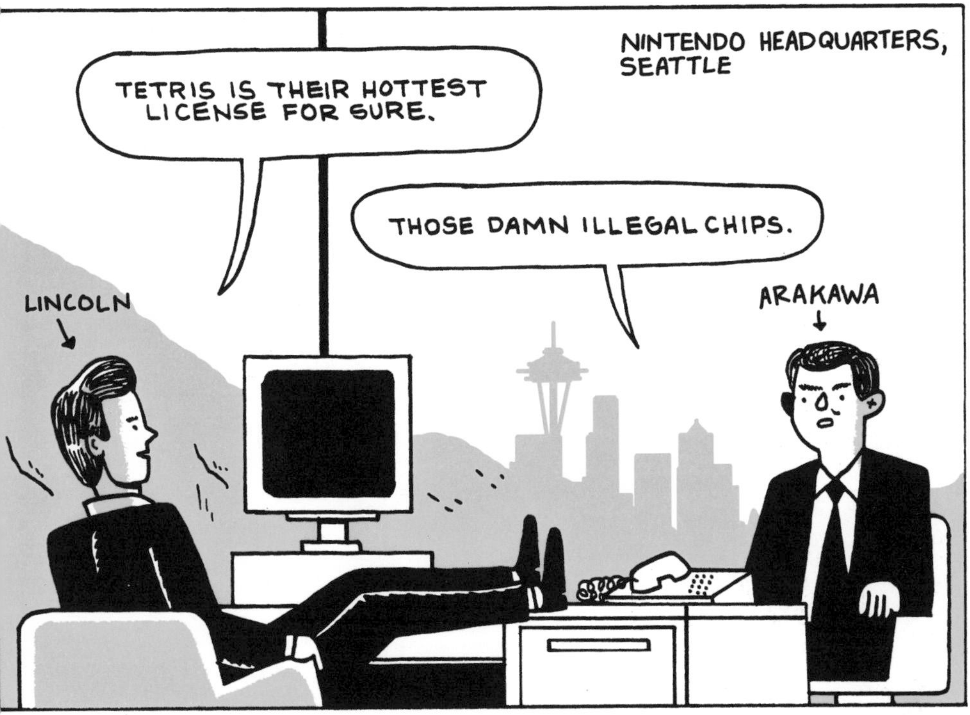
NINTENDO HEADQUARTERS, SEATTLE
TETRIS IS THEIR HOTTEST LICENSE FOR SURE.
THOSE DAMN ILLEGAL CHIPS.
LINCOLN
ARAKAWA

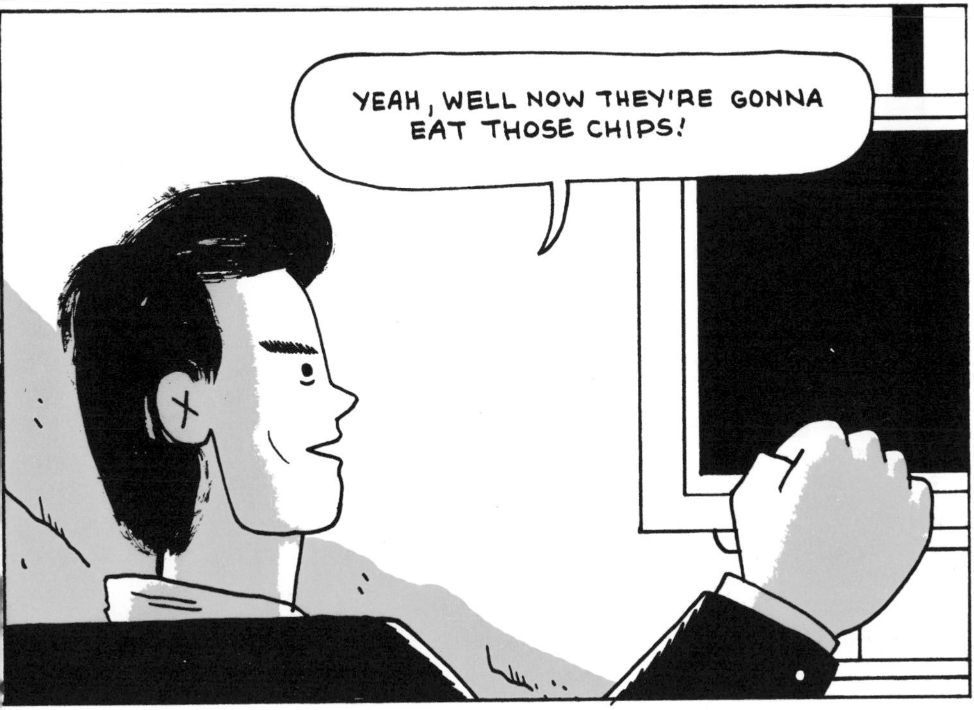
YEAH, WELL NOW THEY'RE GONNA EAT THOSE CHIPS!

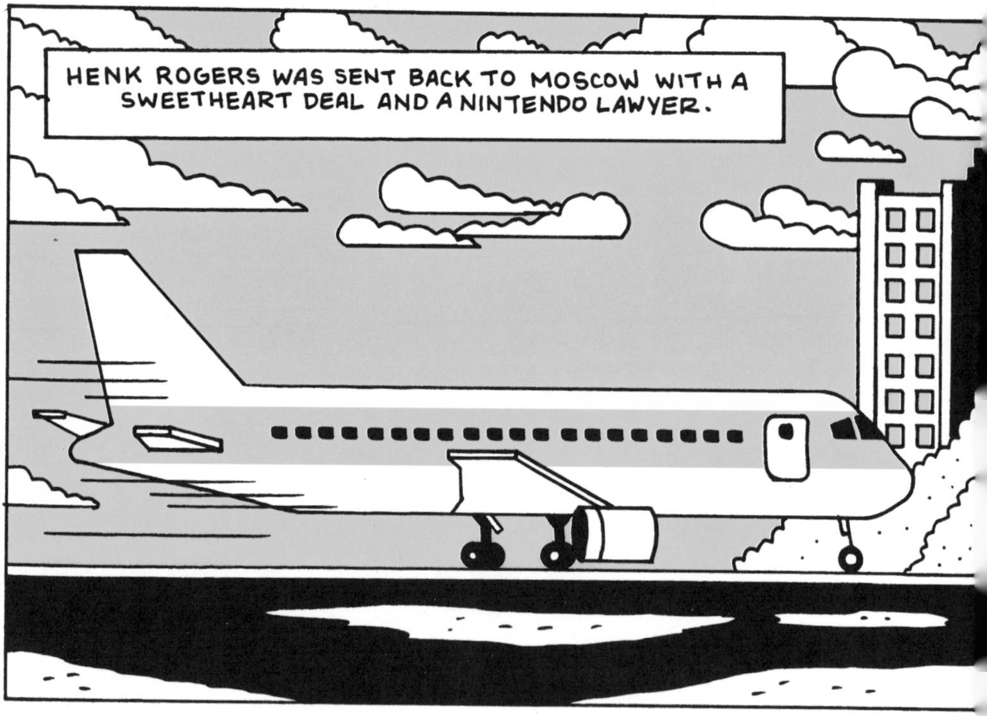
HENK ROGERS WAS SENT BACK TO MOSCOW WITH A SWEETHEART DEAL AND A NINTENDO LAWYER.

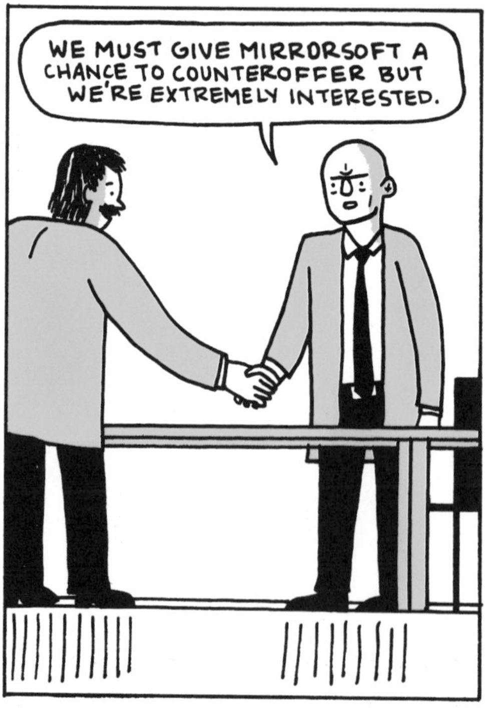
WE MUST GIVE MIRRORSOFT A CHANCE TO COUNTEROFFER BUT WE'RE EXTREMELY INTERESTED.

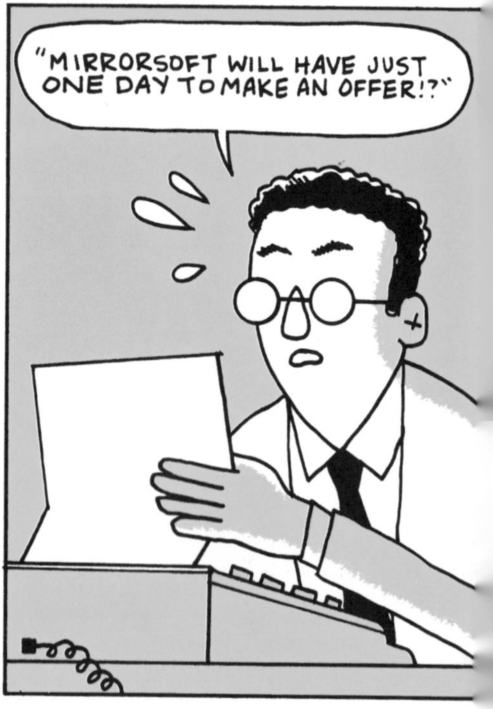
"MIRRORSOFT WILL HAVE JUST ONE DAY TO MAKE AN OFFER!?"

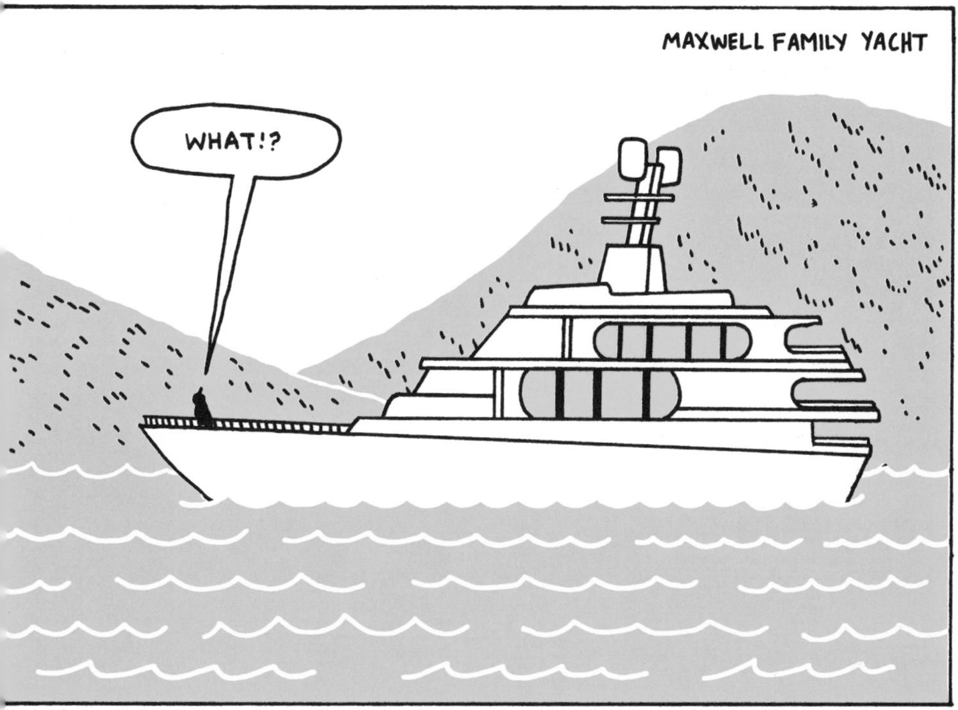
MAXWELL FAMILY YACHT
WHAT!?

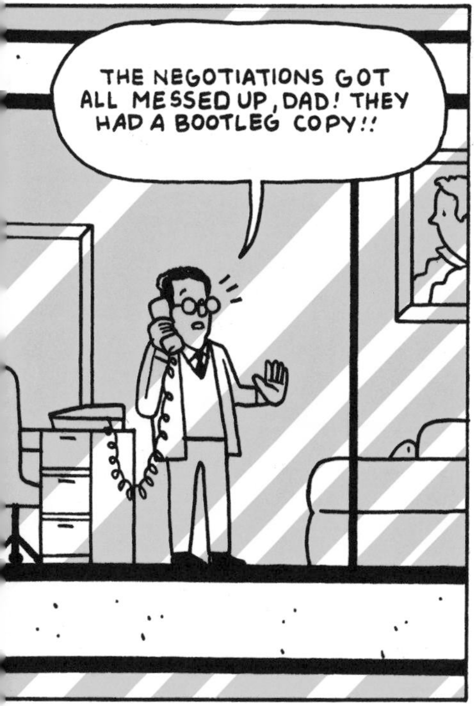
THE NEGOTIATIONS GOT ALL MESSED UP, DAD! THEY HAD A BOOTLEG COPY!!

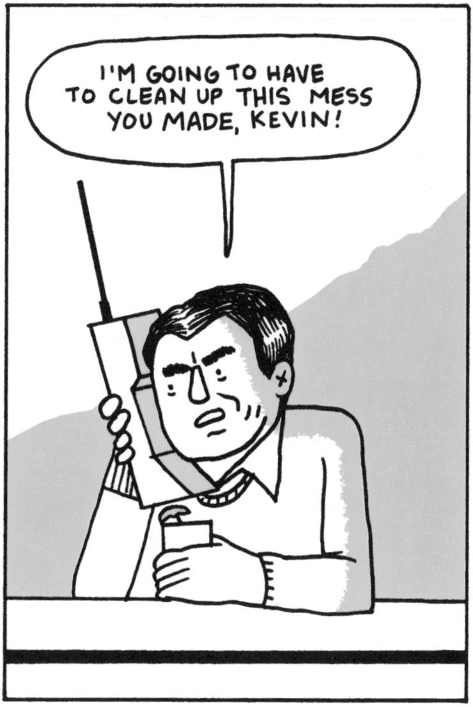
I'M GOING TO HAVE TO CLEAN UP THIS MESS YOU MADE, KEVIN!

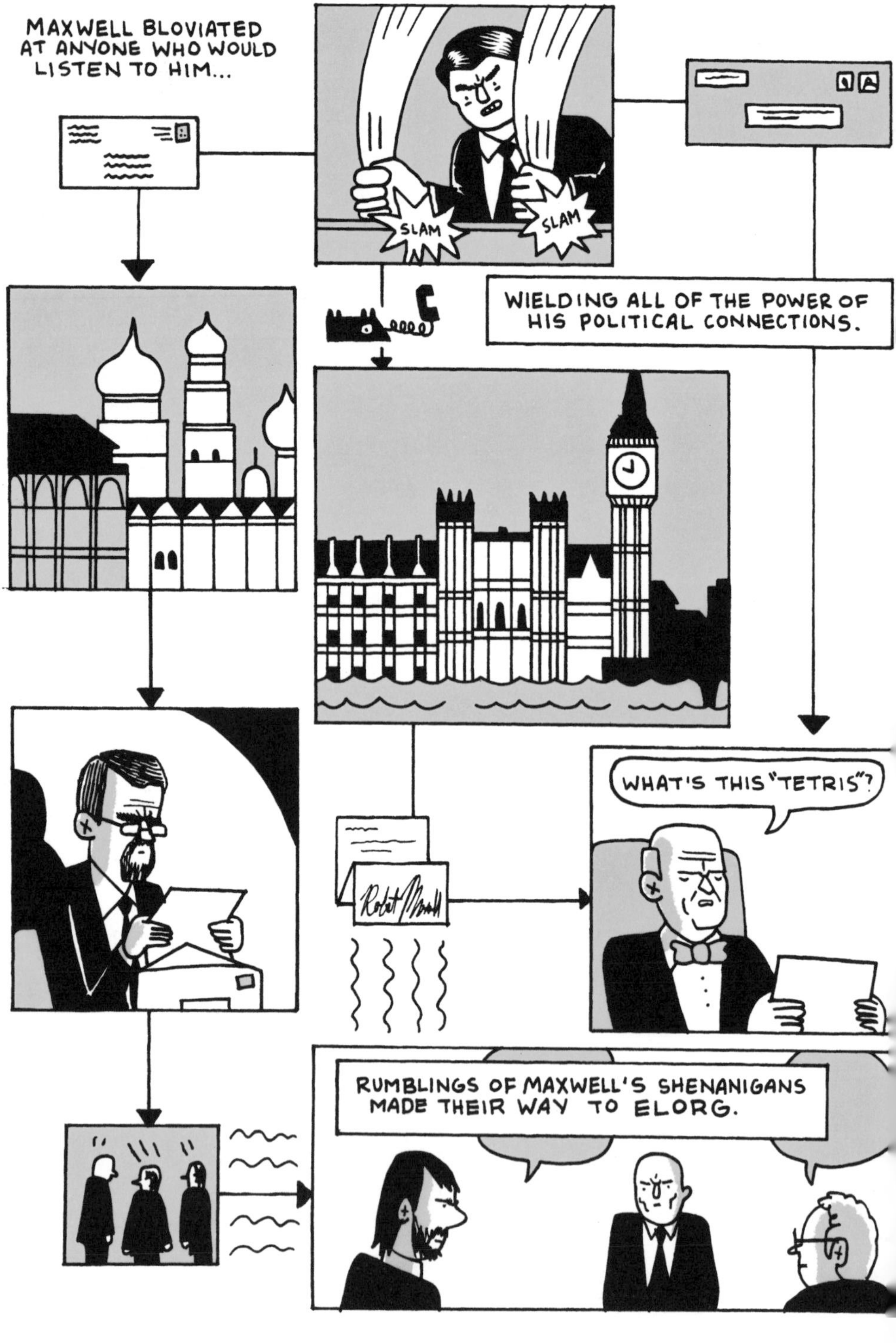
MAXWELL BLOVIATED AT ANYONE WHO WOULD LISTEN TO HIM...
SLAM
SLAM
WIELDING ALL OF THE POWER OF HIS POLITICAL CONNECTIONS.
WHAT'S THIS "TETRIS"?
RUMBLINGS OF MAXWELL'S SHENANIGANS MADE THEIR WAY TO ELORG.

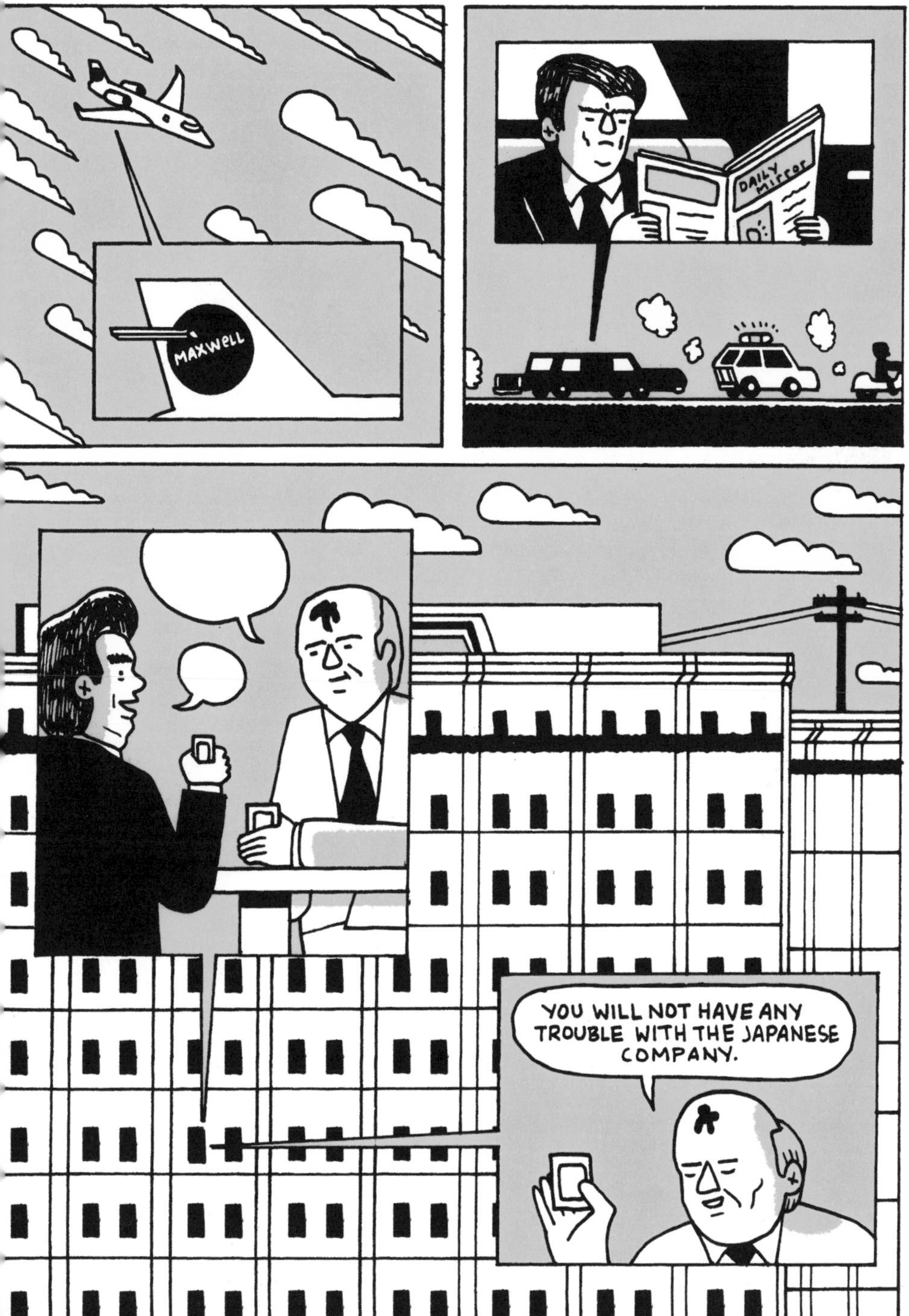
MAXWELL
DAILY MIRROR
YOU WILL NOT HAVE ANY TROUBLE WITH THE JAPANESE COMPANY.

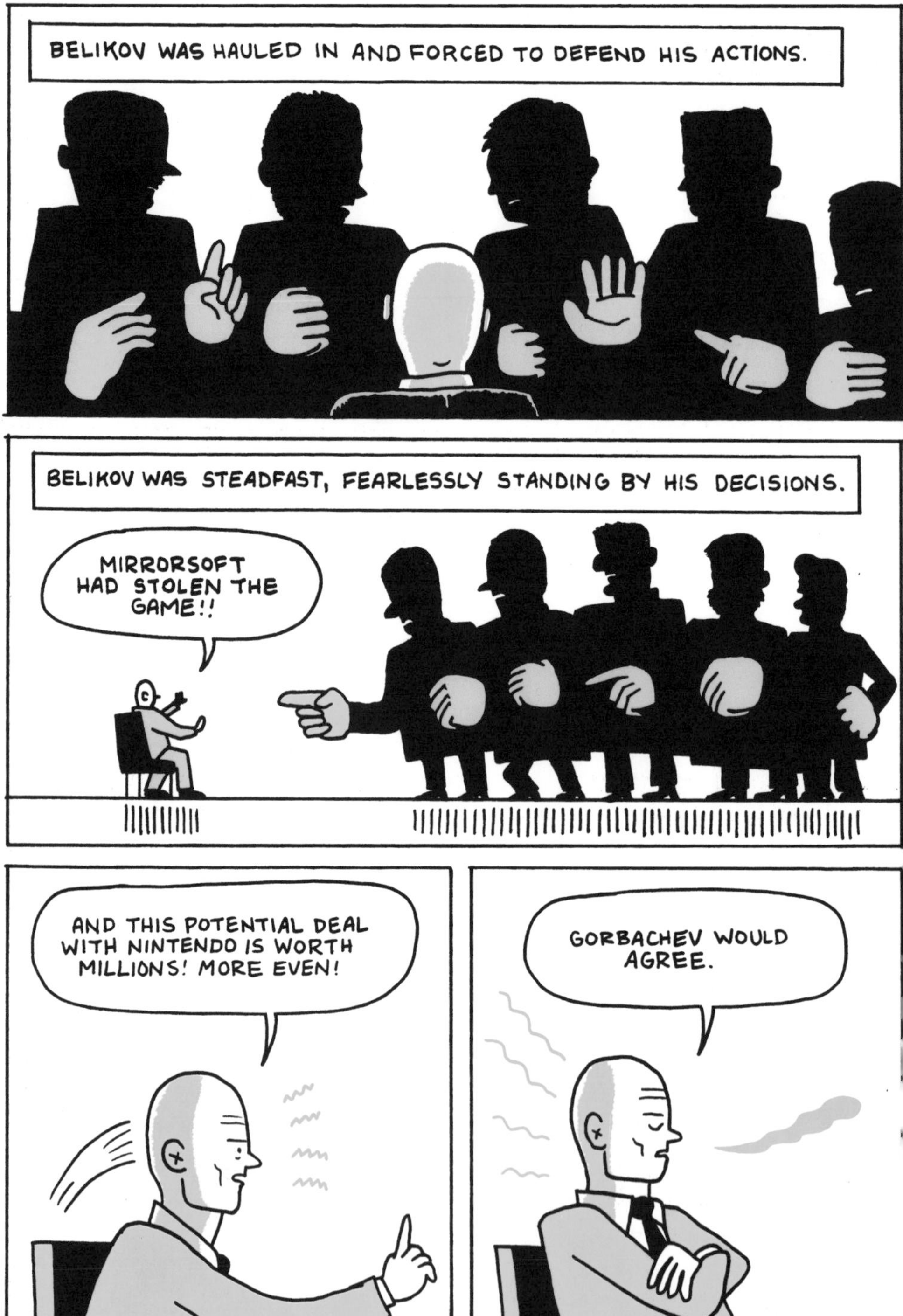
BELIKOV WAS HAULED IN AND FORCED TO DEFEND HIS ACTIONS.
BELIKOV WAS STEADFAST, FEARLESSLY STANDING BY HIS DECISIONS.
MIRRORSOFT HAD STOLEN THE GAME!!
AND THIS POTENTIAL DEAL WITH NINTENDO IS WORTH MILLIONS! MORE EVEN!
GORBACHEV WOULD AGREE.

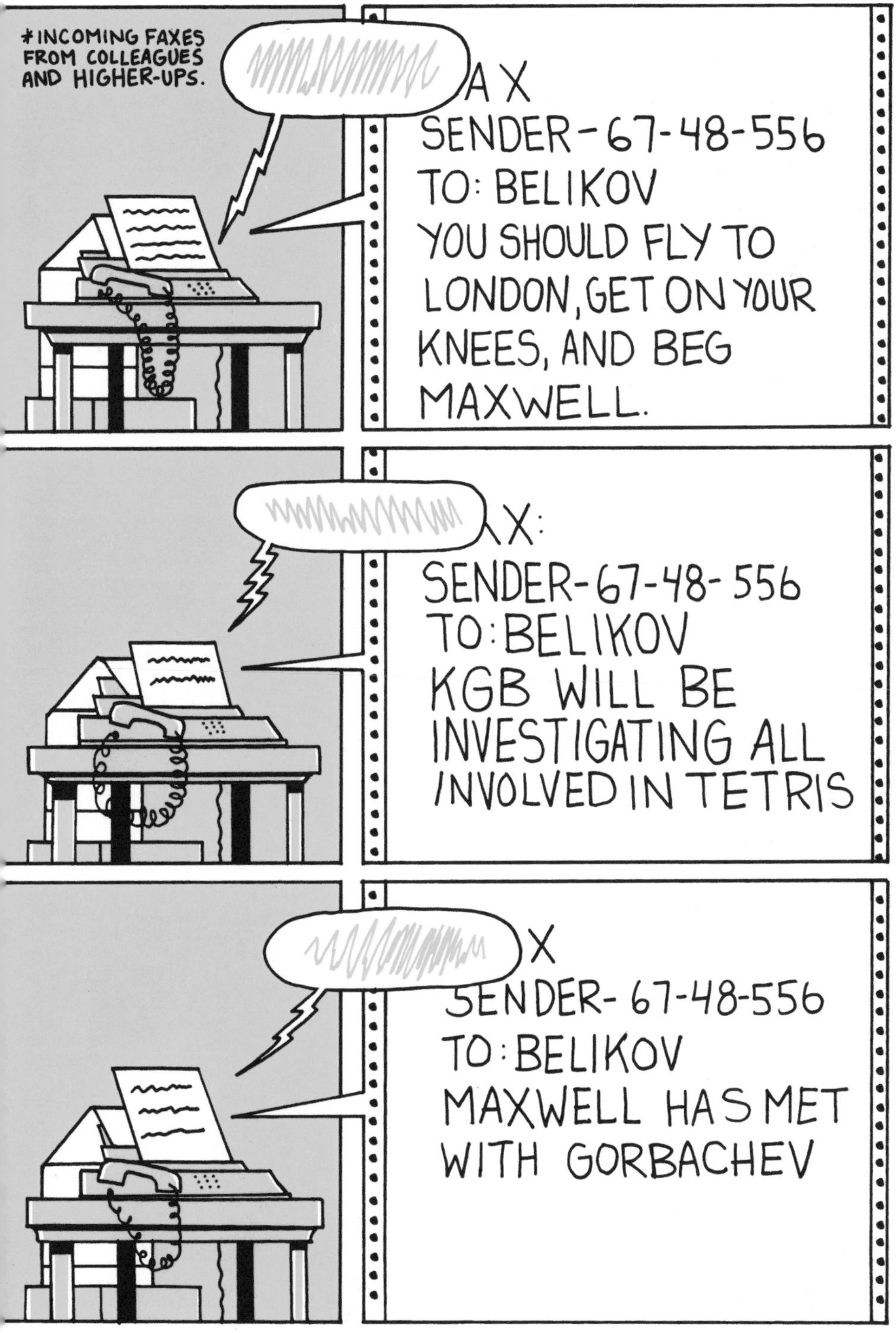
*INCOMING FAXES FROM COLLEAGUES AND HIGHER-UPS.
AX
SENDER-67-48-556
TO: BELIKOV
YOU SHOULD FLY TO LONDON, GET ON YOUR KNEES, AND BEG MAXWELL.
X:
SENDER-67-48-556
TO: BELIKOV
KGB WILL BE INVESTIGATING ALL INVOLVED IN TETRIS
X
SENDER-67-48-556
TO: BELIKOV
MAXWELL HAS MET WITH GORBACHEV

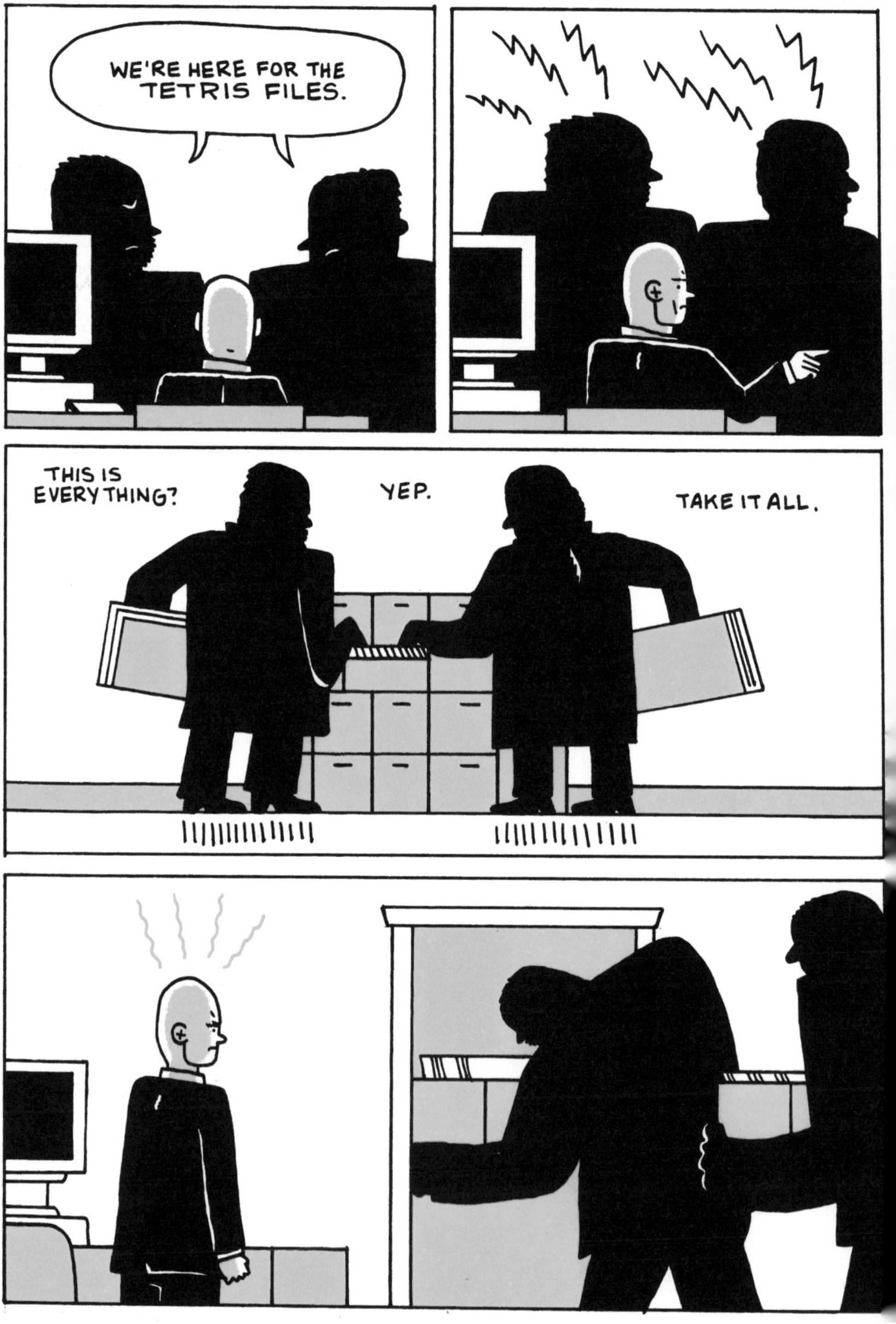
WE'RE HERE FOR THE TETRIS FILES.
THIS IS EVERYTHING?
YEP.
TAKE IT ALL.

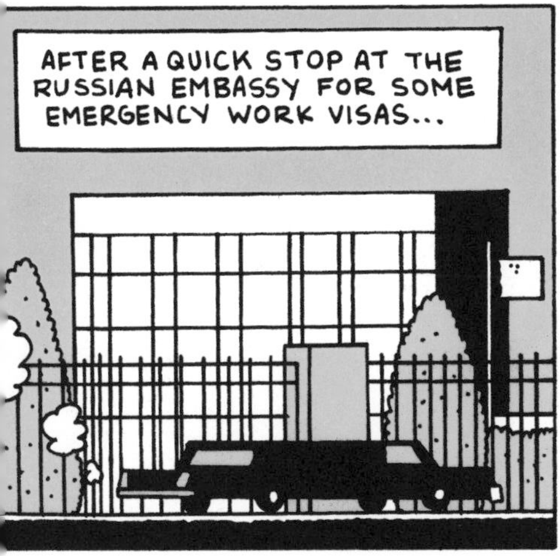
AFTER A QUICK STOP AT THE RUSSIAN EMBASSY FOR SOME EMERGENCY WORK VISAS...

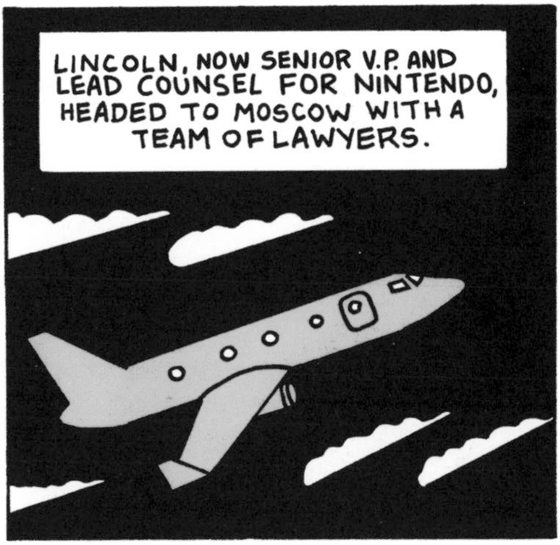
LINCOLN, NOW SENIOR V.P. AND LEAD COUNSEL FOR NINTENDO, HEADED TO MOSCOW WITH A TEAM OF LAWYERS.

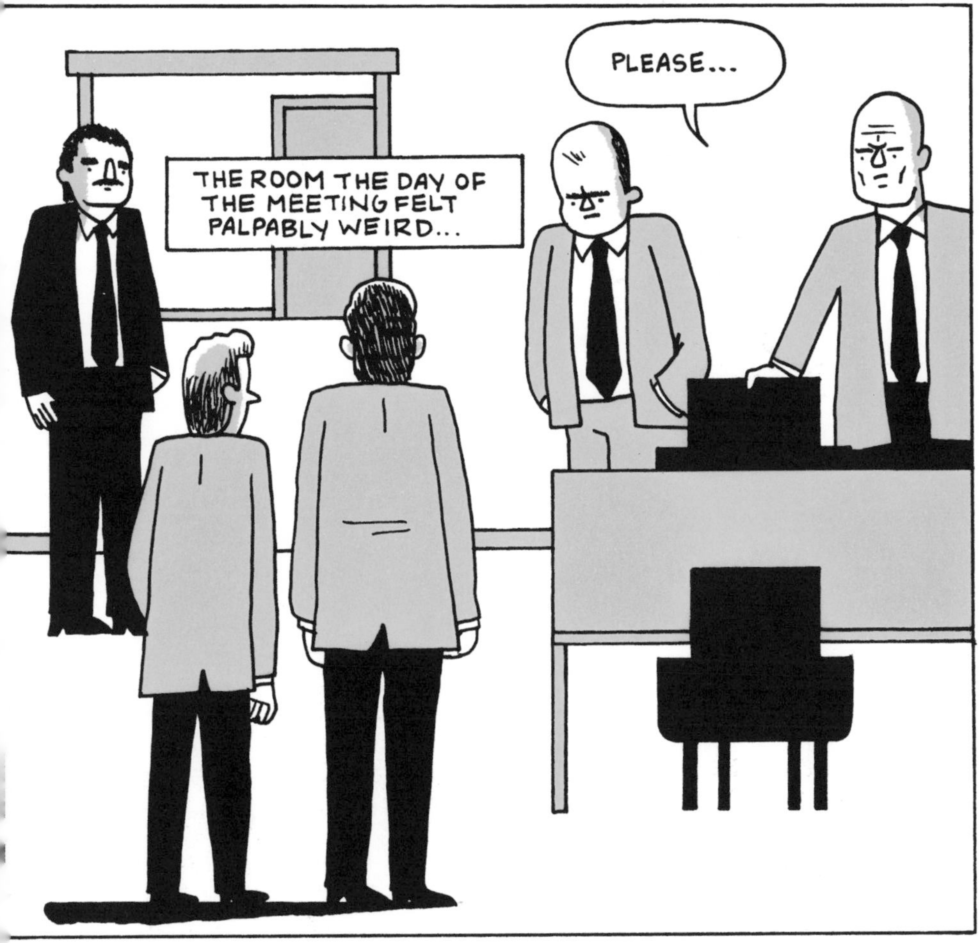
THE ROOM THE DAY OF THE MEETING FELT PALPABLY WEIRD...
PLEASE...

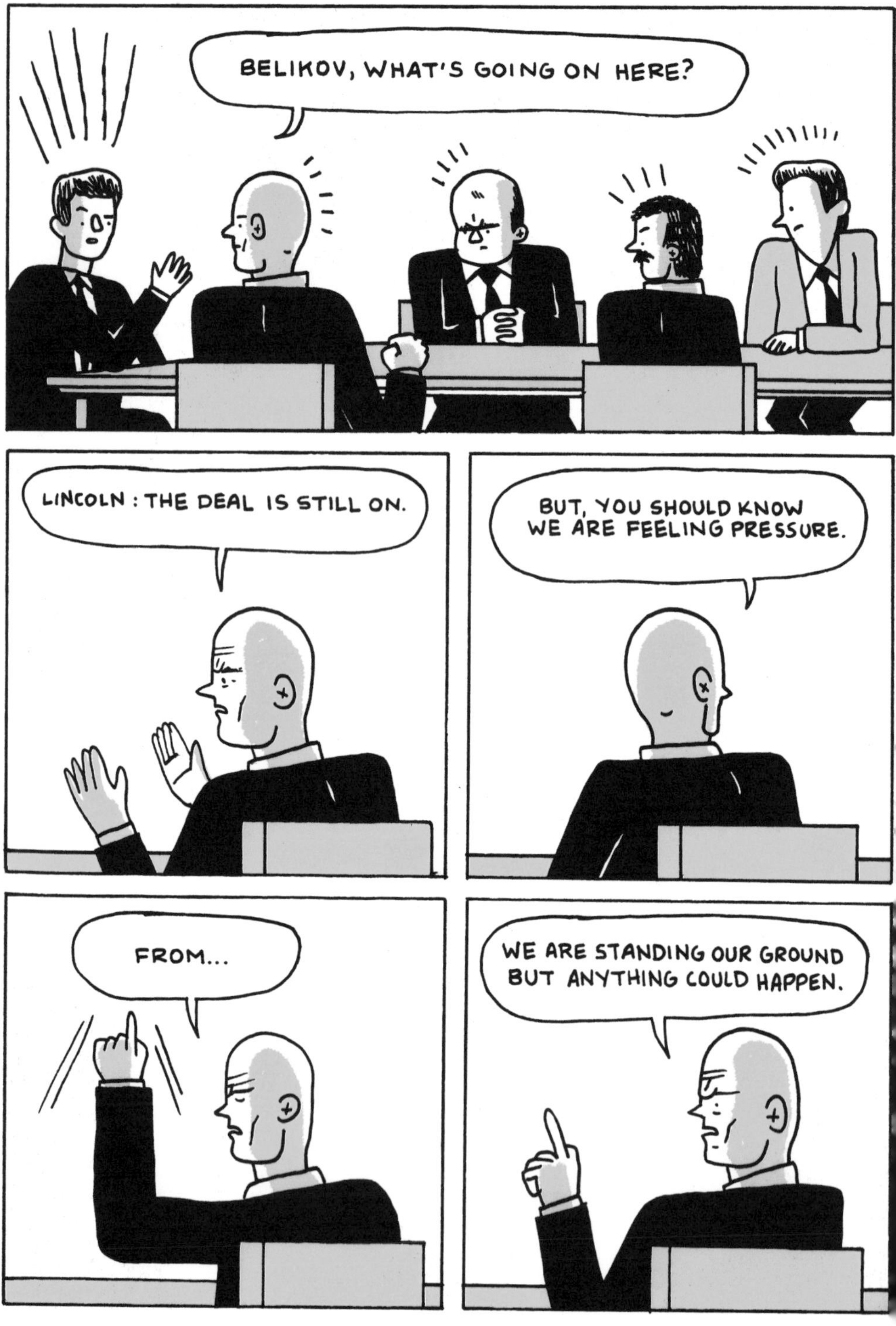
BELIKOV, WHAT'S GOING ON HERE?
LINCOLN : THE DEAL IS STILL ON.
BUT, YOU SHOULD KNOW WE ARE FEELING PRESSURE.
FROM...
WE ARE STANDING OUR GROUND BUT ANYTHING COULD HAPPEN.

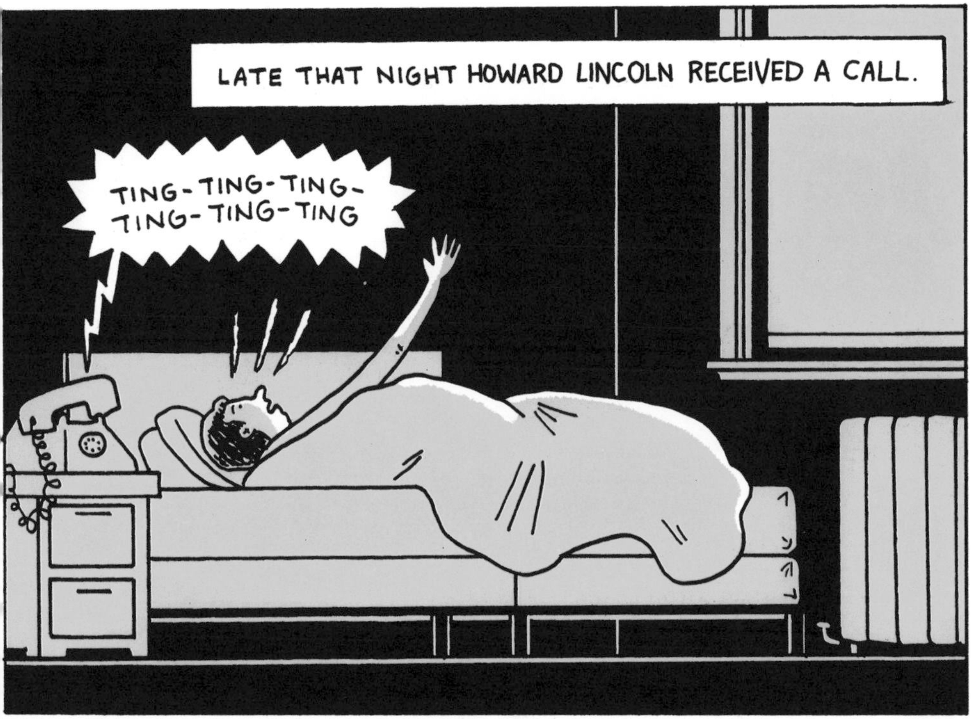
LATE THAT NIGHT HOWARD LINCOLN RECEIVED A CALL.
TING-TING-TING-TING-TING-TING

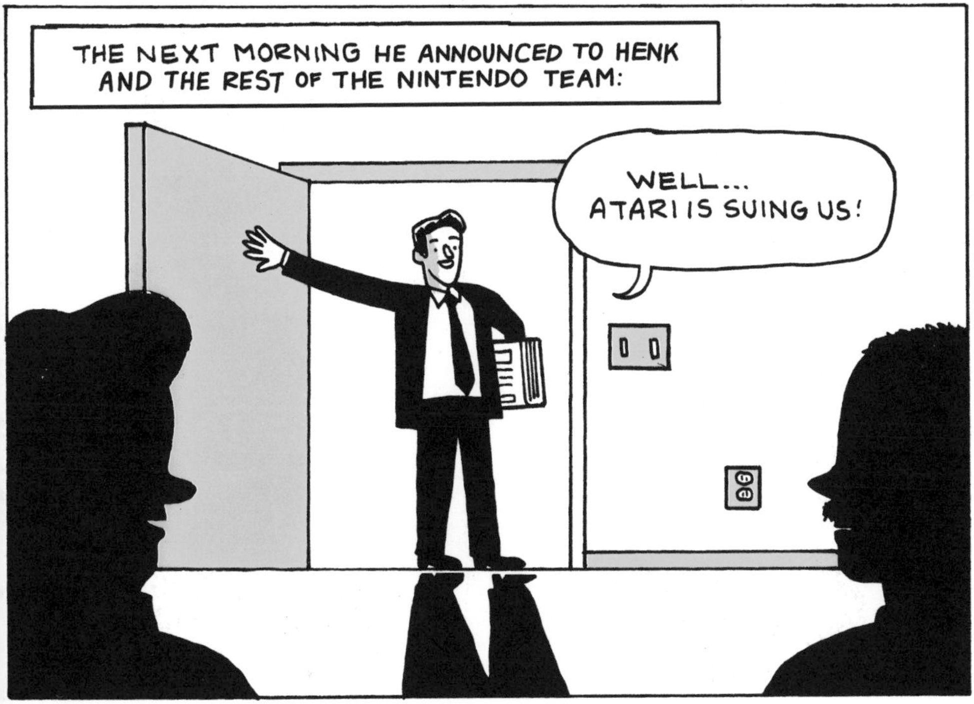
THE NEXT MORNING HE ANNOUNCED TO HENK AND THE REST OF THE NINTENDO TEAM:
WELL... ATARI IS SUING US!

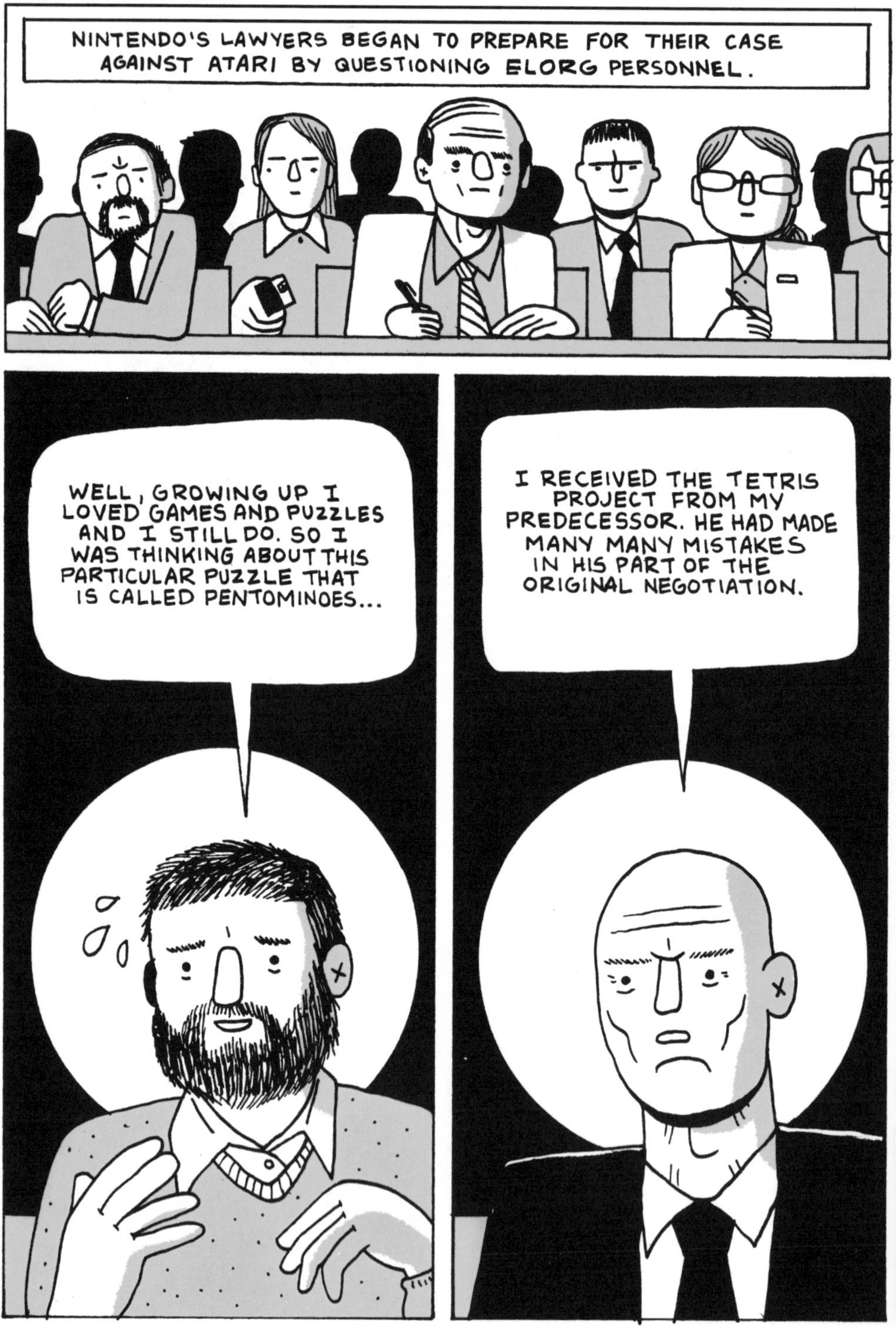
NINTENDO'S LAWYERS BEGAN TO PREPARE FOR THEIR CASE AGAINST ATARI BY QUESTIONING ELORG PERSONNEL.
WELL, GROWING UP I LOVED GAMES AND PUZZLES AND I STILL DO. SO I WAS THINKING ABOUT THIS PARTICULAR PUZZLE THAT IS CALLED PENTOMINOES...
I RECEIVED THE TETRIS PROJECT FROM MY PREDECESSOR. HE HAD MADE MANY MANY MISTAKES IN HIS PART OF THE ORIGINAL NEGOTIATION.

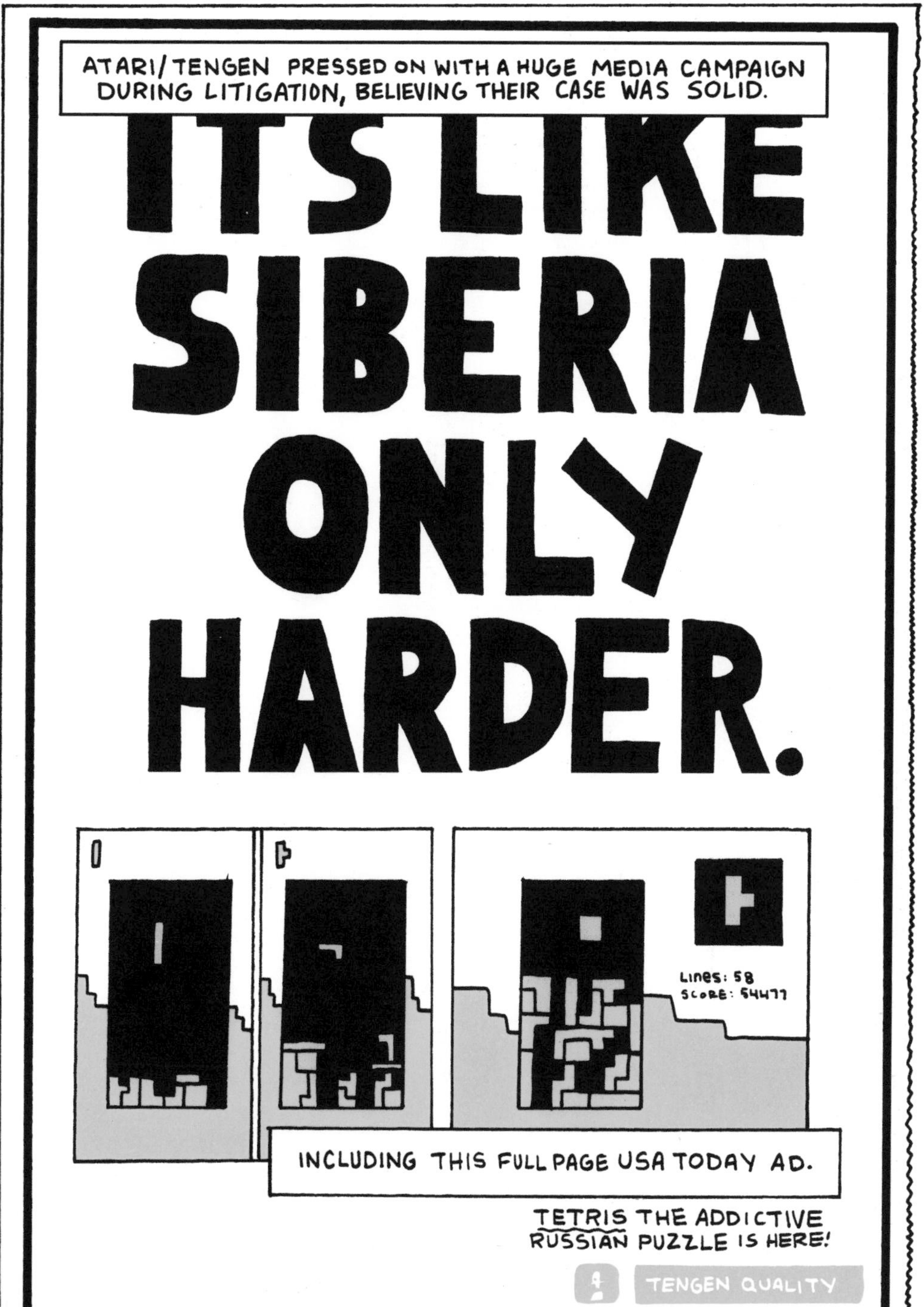
ATARI/TENGEN PRESSED ON WITH A HUGE MEDIA CAMPAIGN DURING LITIGATION, BELIEVING THEIR CASE WAS SOLID.
ITS LIKE SIBERIA ONLY HARDER.
Lines: 58
SCORE: 54477
INCLUDING THIS FULL PAGE USA TODAY AD.
TETRIS THE ADDICTIVE RUSSIAN PUZZLE IS HERE!
TENGEN QUALITY

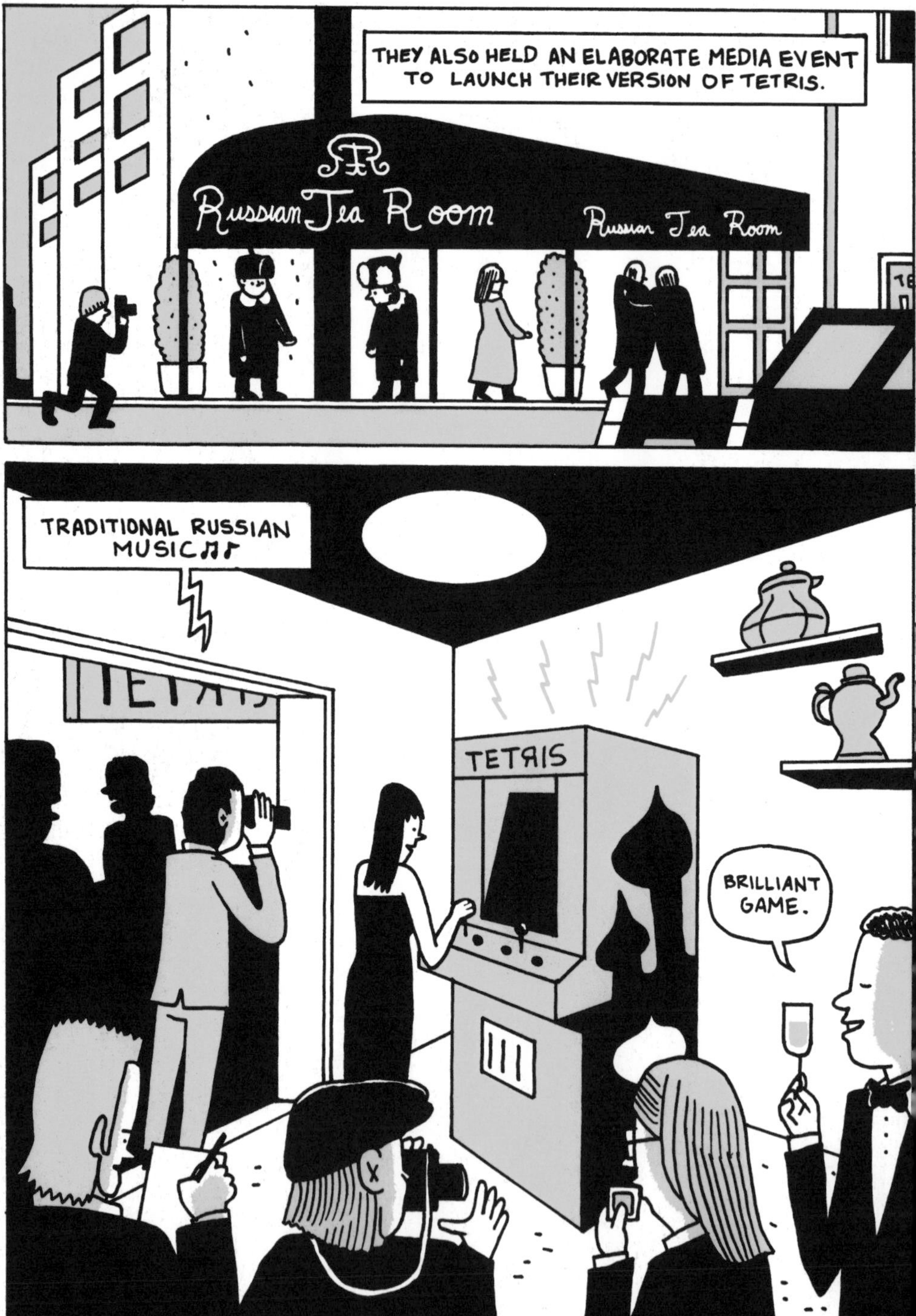
THEY ALSO HELD AN ELABORATE MEDIA EVENT TO LAUNCH THEIR VERSION OF TETRIS.
Russian Tea Room
Russian Tea Room
TRADITIONAL RUSSIAN MUSIC♫♪
TETRIS
BRILLIANT GAME.

HON. FERN M. SMITH
U.S. DISTRICT COURT JUDGE
NORTHERN CALIFORNIA
WOULD DECIDE THE FATE OF
ELORG, NINTENDO, AND
ATARI'S CLAIMS TO
TETRIS

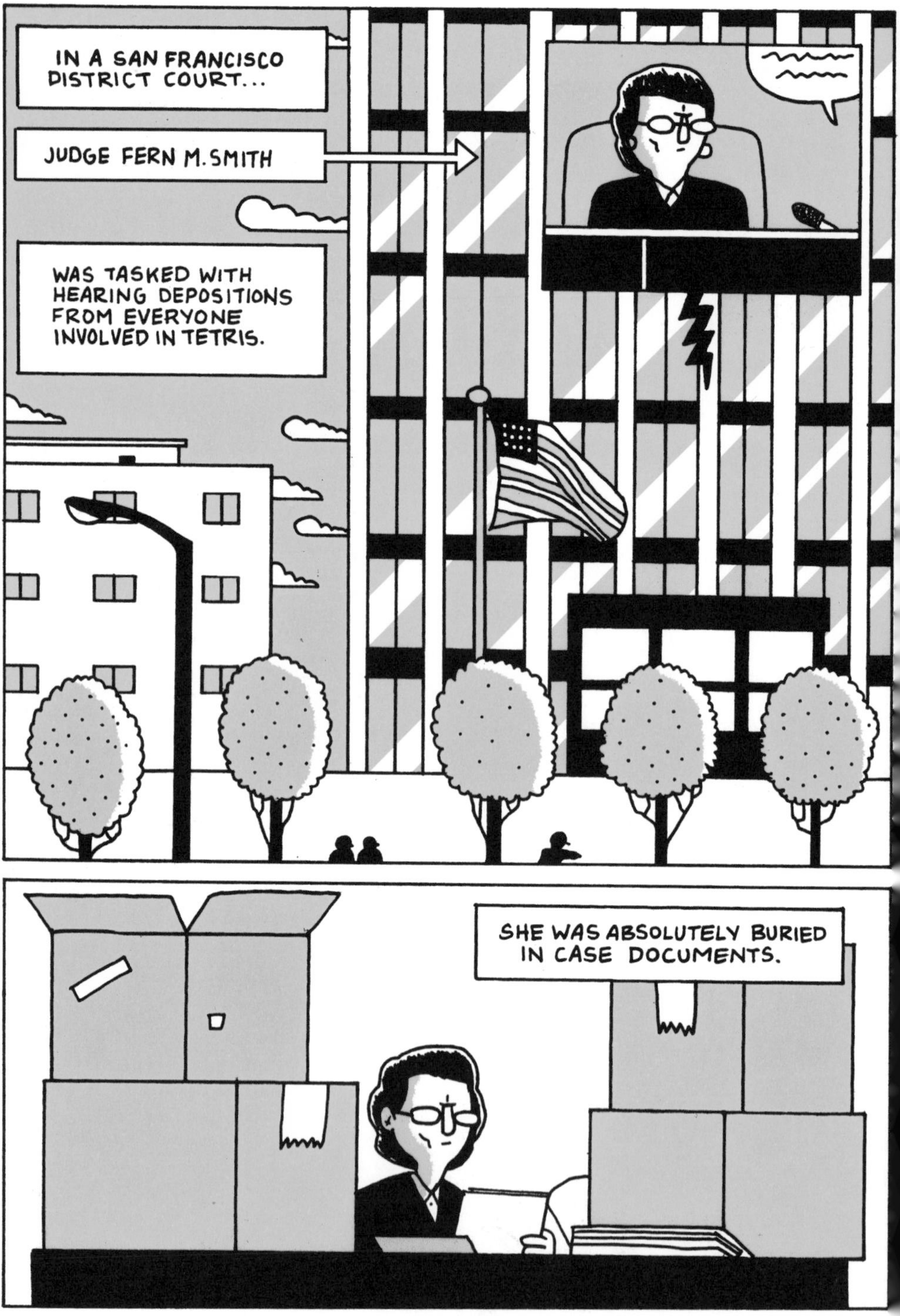
IN A SAN FRANCISCO DISTRICT COURT...
JUDGE FERN M. SMITH
WAS TASKED WITH HEARING DEPOSITIONS FROM EVERYONE INVOLVED IN TETRIS.
SHE WAS ABSOLUTELY BURIED IN CASE DOCUMENTS.

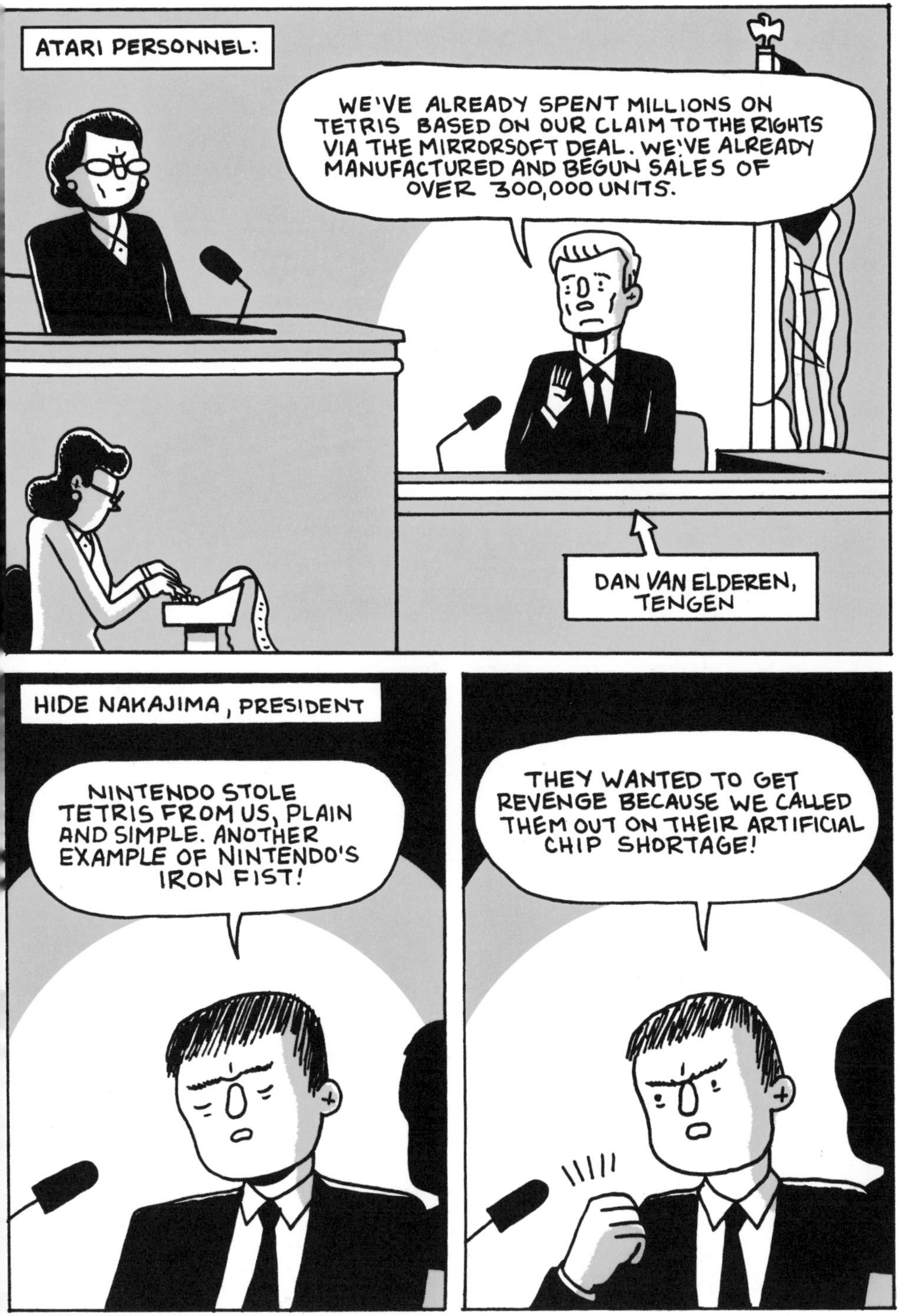
ATARI PERSONNEL:
WE'VE ALREADY SPENT MILLIONS ON TETRIS BASED ON OUR CLAIM TO THE RIGHTS VIA THE MIRRORSOFT DEAL. WE'VE ALREADY MANUFACTURED AND BEGUN SALES OF OVER 300,000 UNITS.
DAN VAN ELDEREN, TENGEN
HIDE NAKAJIMA, PRESIDENT
NINTENDO STOLE TETRIS FROM US, PLAIN AND SIMPLE. ANOTHER EXAMPLE OF NINTENDO'S IRON FIST!
THEY WANTED TO GET REVENGE BECAUSE WE CALLED THEM OUT ON THEIR ARTIFICIAL CHIP SHORTAGE!

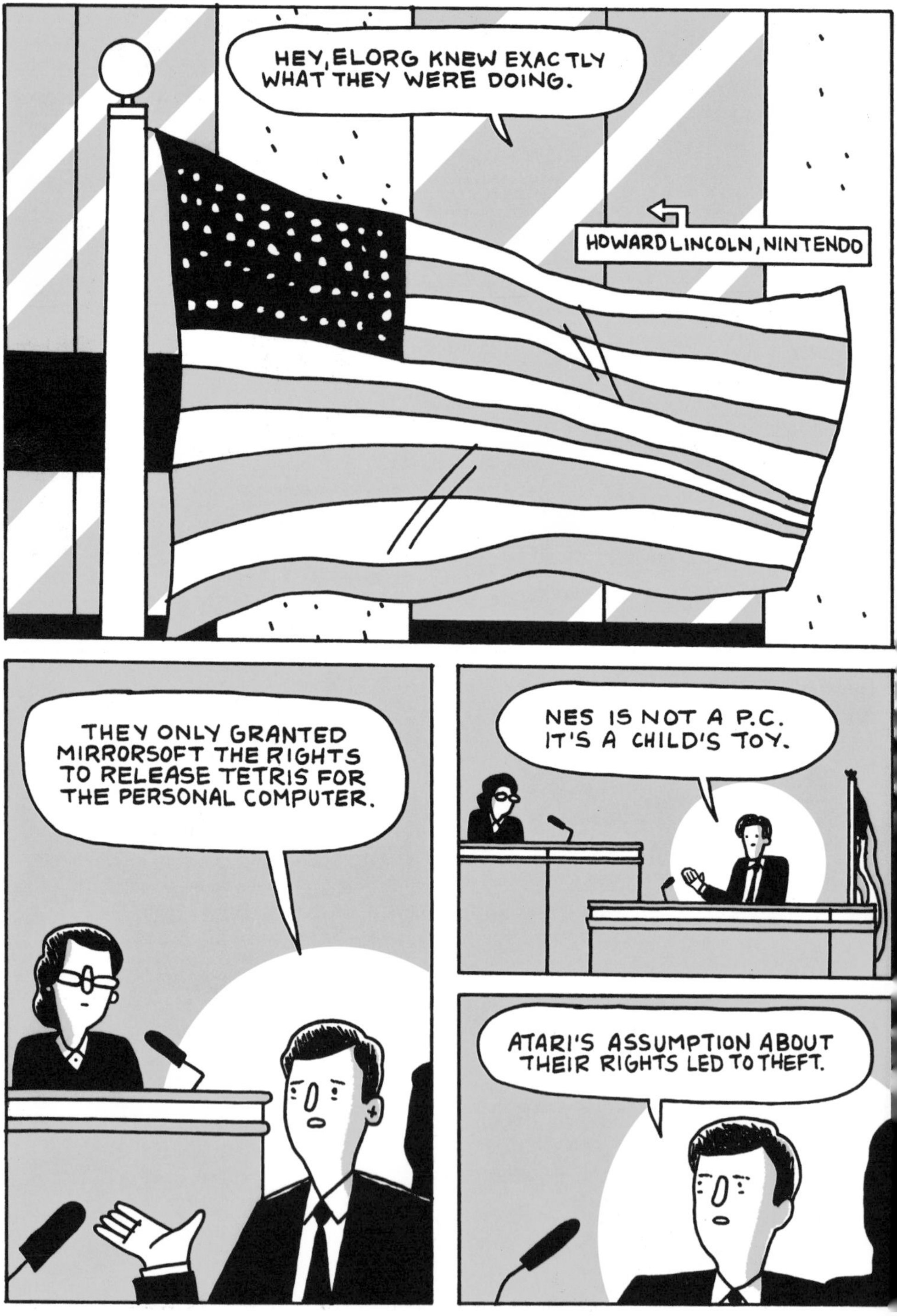
HEY, ELORG KNEW EXACTLY WHAT THEY WERE DOING.
HOWARD LINCOLN, NINTENDO
THEY ONLY GRANTED MIRRORSOFT THE RIGHTS TO RELEASE TETRIS FOR THE PERSONAL COMPUTER.
NES IS NOT A P.C. IT'S A CHILD'S TOY.
ATARI'S ASSUMPTION ABOUT THEIR RIGHTS LED TO THEFT.

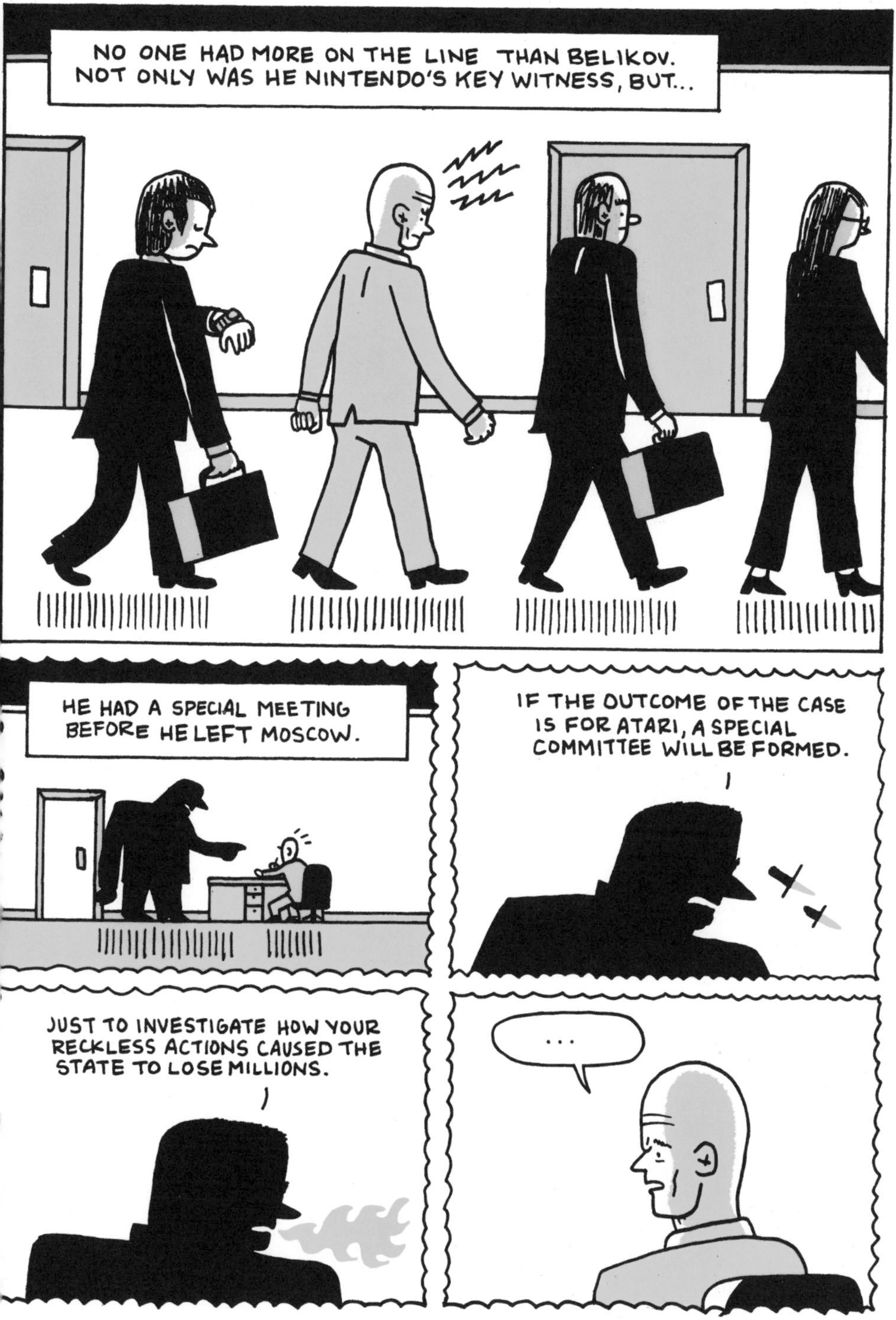
NO ONE HAD MORE ON THE LINE THAN BELIKOV. NOT ONLY WAS HE NINTENDO'S KEY WITNESS, BUT...
HE HAD A SPECIAL MEETING BEFORE HE LEFT MOSCOW.
IF THE OUTCOME OF THE CASE IS FOR ATARI, A SPECIAL COMMITTEE WILL BE FORMED.
JUST TO INVESTIGATE HOW YOUR RECKLESS ACTIONS CAUSED THE STATE TO LOSE MILLIONS.
...

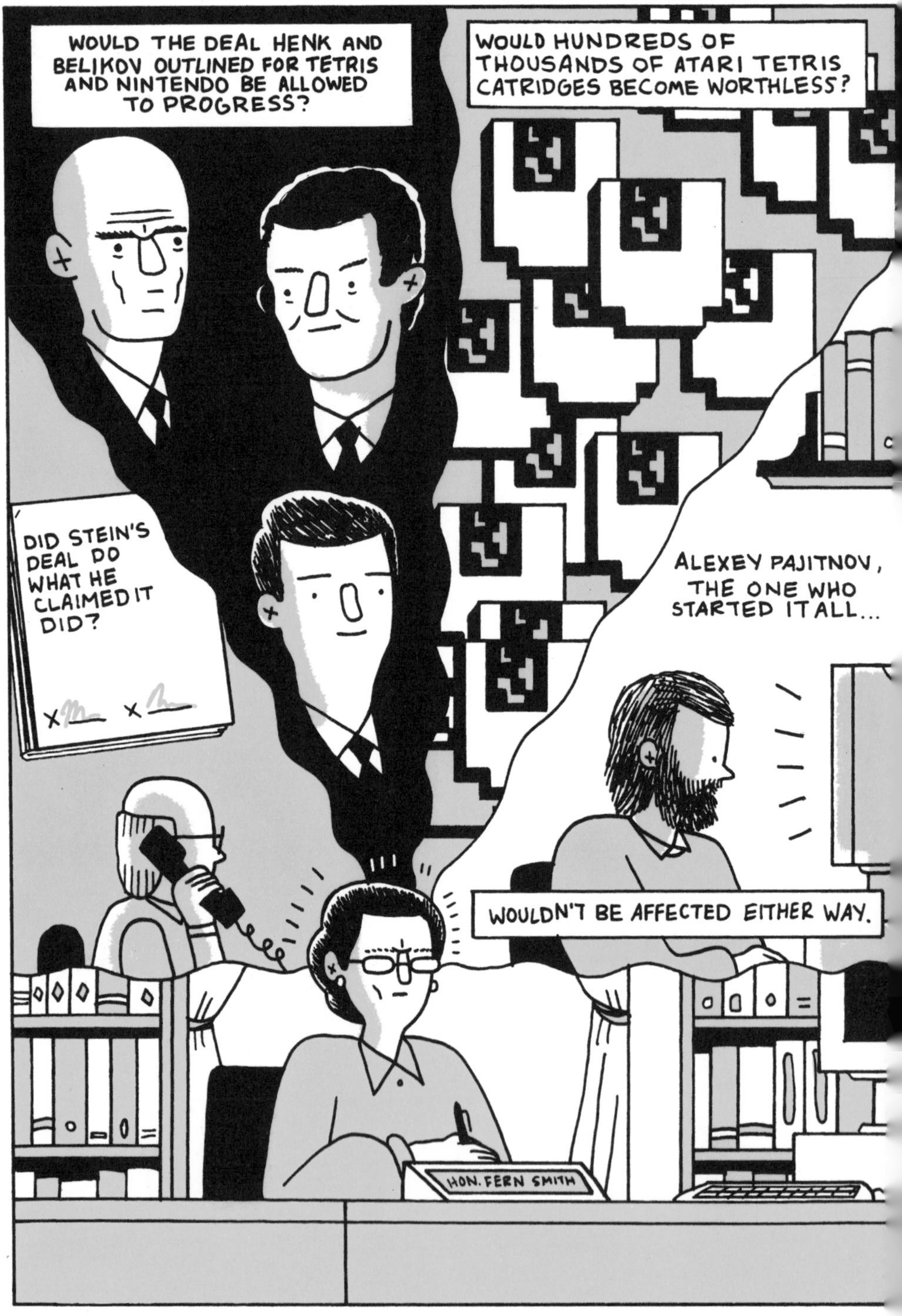
WOULD THE DEAL HENK AND BELIKOV OUTLINED FOR TETRIS AND NINTENDO BE ALLOWED TO PROGRESS?
WOULD HUNDREDS OF THOUSANDS OF ATARI TETRIS CATRIDGES BECOME WORTHLESS?
DID STEIN'S DEAL DO WHAT HE CLAIMED IT DID?
ALEXEY PAJITNOV, THE ONE WHO STARTED IT ALL...
WOULDN'T BE AFFECTED EITHER WAY.
HON. FERN SMITH

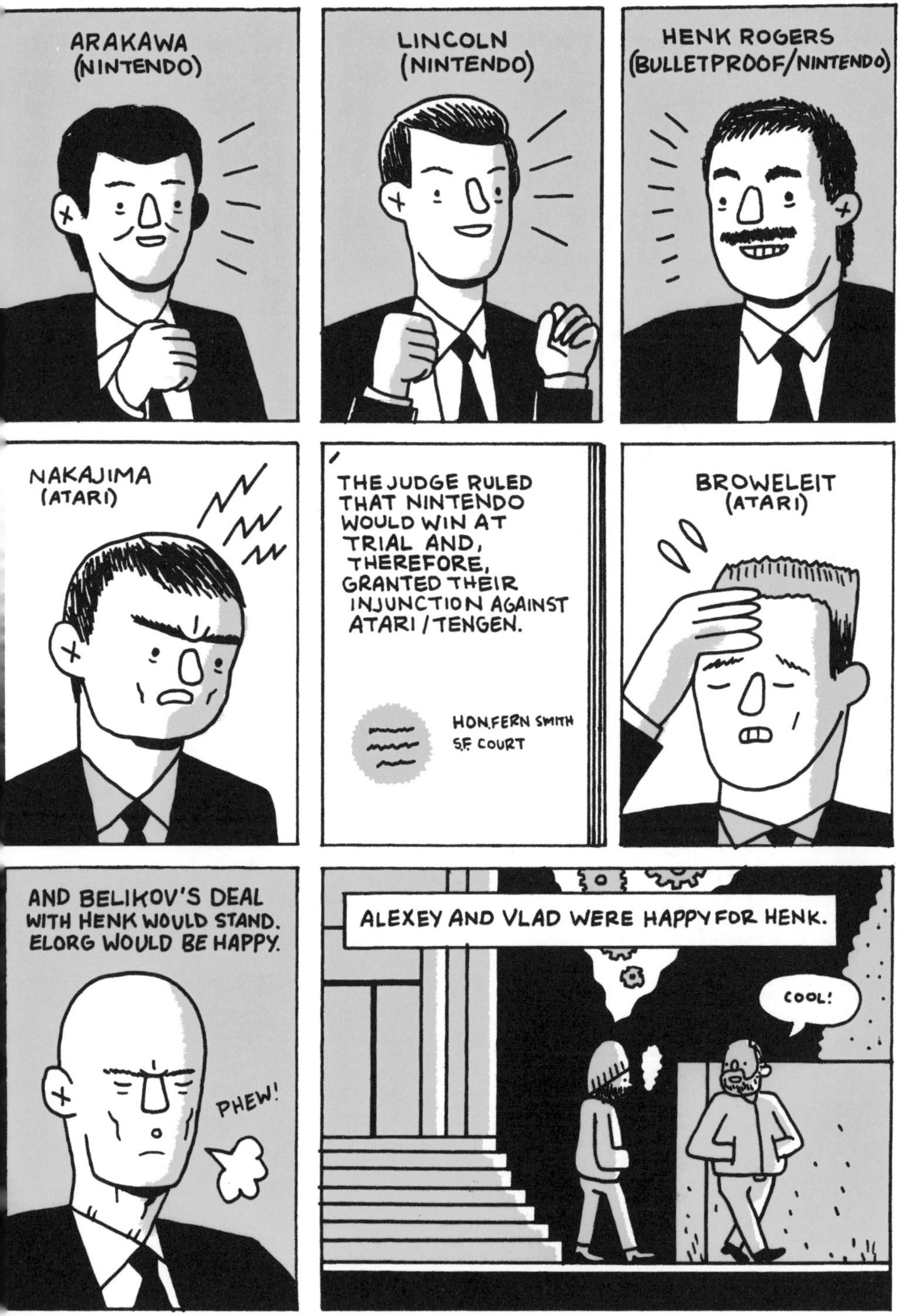
ARAKAWA (NINTENDO)
LINCOLN (NINTENDO)
HENK ROGERS (BULLETPROOF/NINTENDO)
NAKAJIMA (ATARI)
THE JUDGE RULED THAT NINTENDO WOULD WIN AT TRIAL AND, THEREFORE, GRANTED THEIR INJUNCTION AGAINST ATARI / TENGEN.
HON. FERN SMITH
S.F. COURT
BROWELEIT (ATARI)
AND BELIKOV'S DEAL WITH HENK WOULD STAND. ELORG WOULD BE HAPPY.
PHEW!
ALEXEY AND VLAD WERE HAPPY FOR HENK.
COOL!

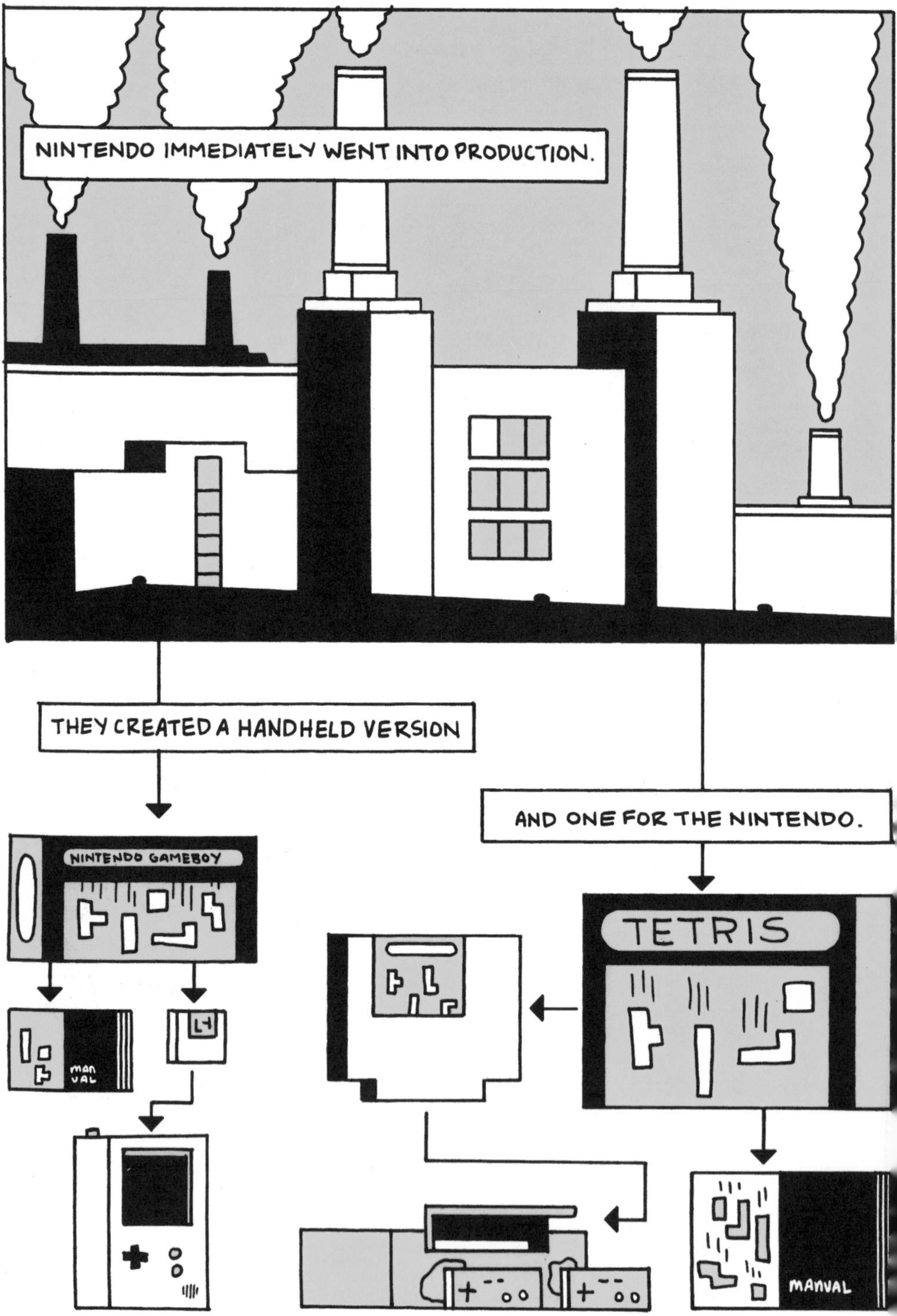
NINTENDO IMMEDIATELY WENT INTO PRODUCTION.
THEY CREATED A HANDHELD VERSION
AND ONE FOR THE NINTENDO.
NINTENDO GAMEBOY
MAN
UAL
TETRIS
MANUAL

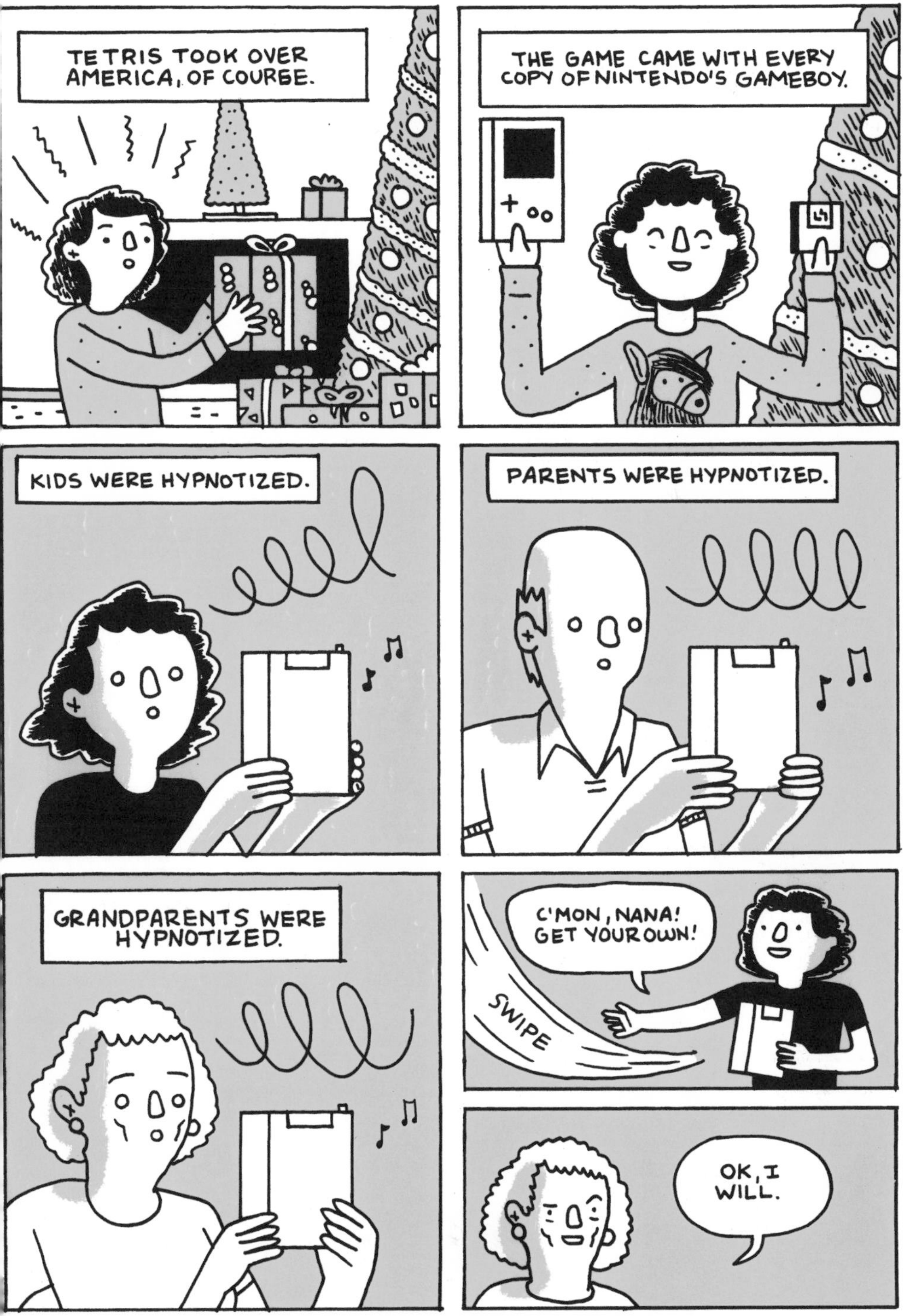
TETRIS TOOK OVER AMERICA, OF COURSE.
THE GAME CAME WITH EVERY COPY OF NINTENDO'S GAMEBOY.
KIDS WERE HYPNOTIZED.
PARENTS WERE HYPNOTIZED.
GRANDPARENTS WERE HYPNOTIZED.
C'MON, NANA! GET YOUR OWN!
SWIPE
OK, I WILL.

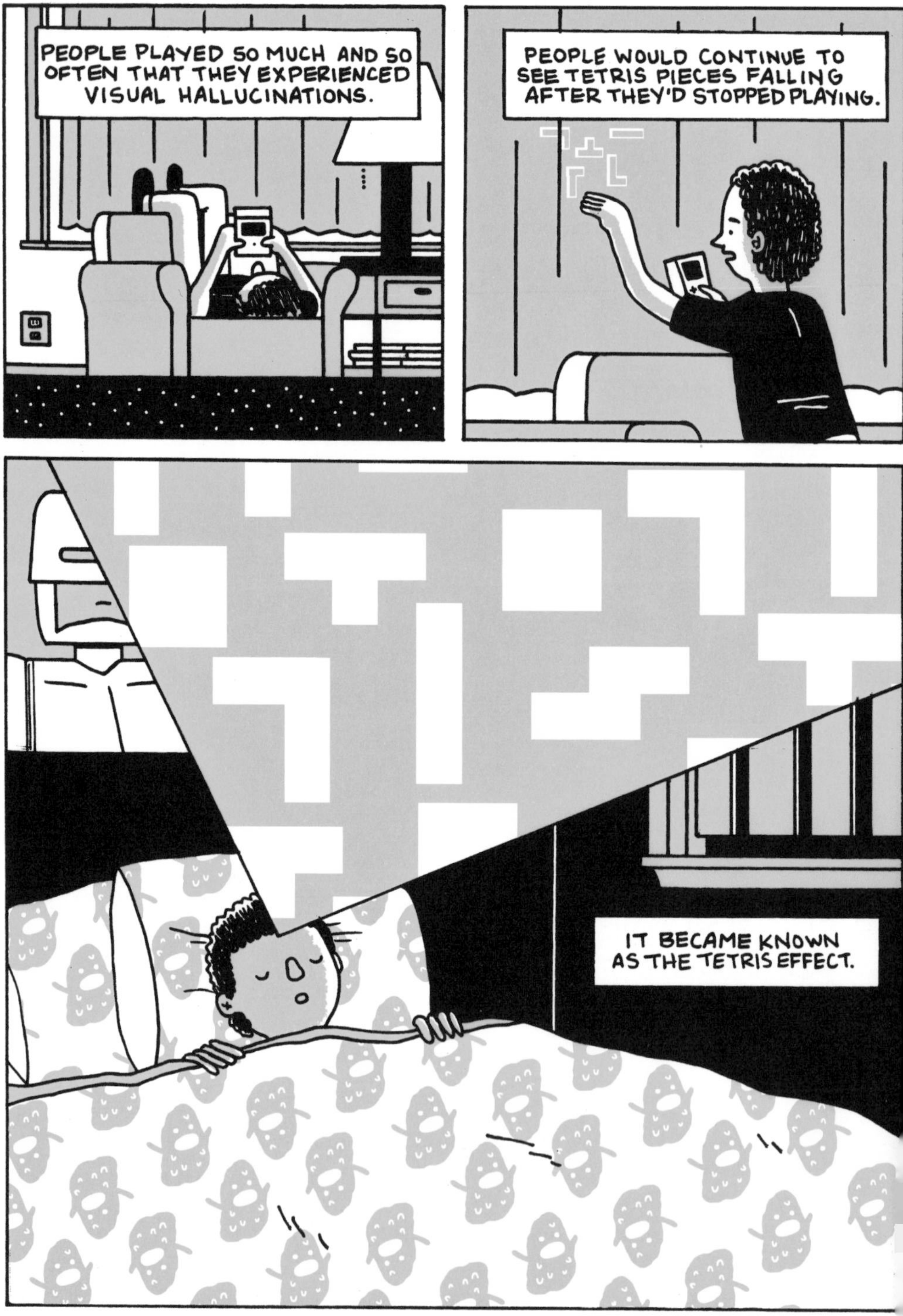
PEOPLE PLAYED SO MUCH AND SO OFTEN THAT THEY EXPERIENCED VISUAL HALLUCINATIONS.
PEOPLE WOULD CONTINUE TO SEE TETRIS PIECES FALLING AFTER THEY'D STOPPED PLAYING.
IT BECAME KNOWN AS THE TETRIS EFFECT.

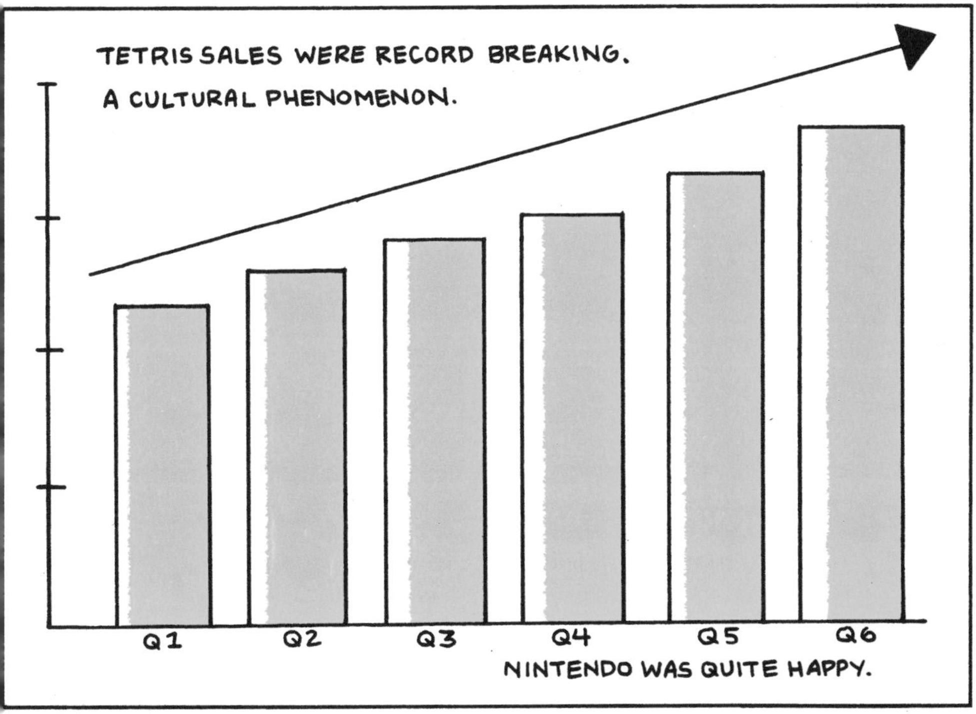
TETRIS SALES WERE RECORD BREAKING.
A CULTURAL PHENOMENON.
Q1
Q2
Q3
Q4
Q5
Q6
NINTENDO WAS QUITE HAPPY.

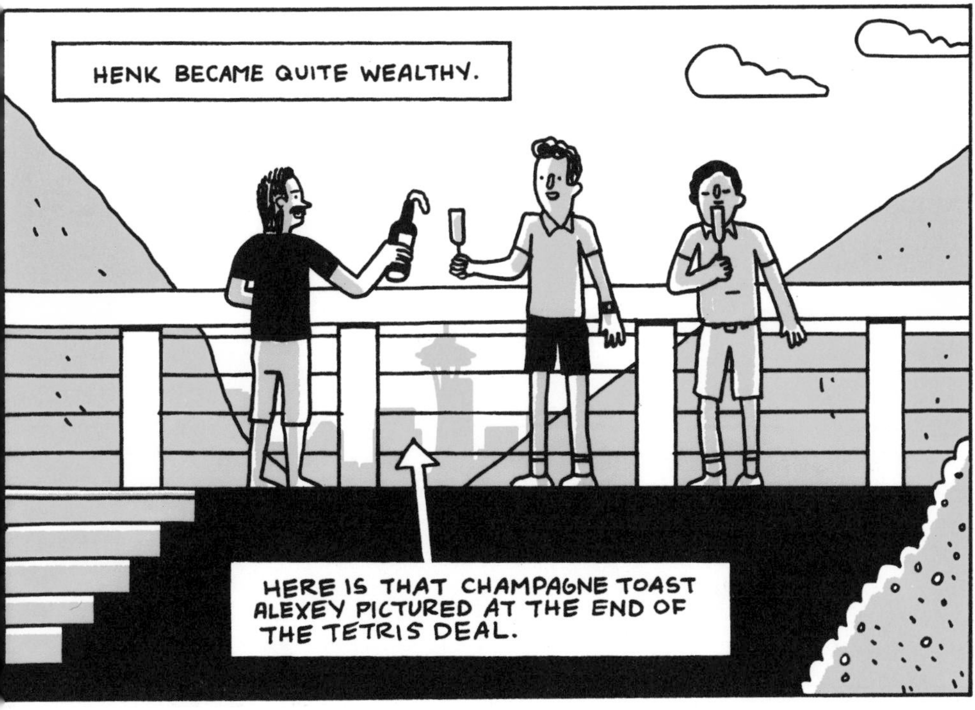
HENK BECAME QUITE WEALTHY.
HERE IS THAT CHAMPAGNE TOAST ALEXEY PICTURED AT THE END OF THE TETRIS DEAL.

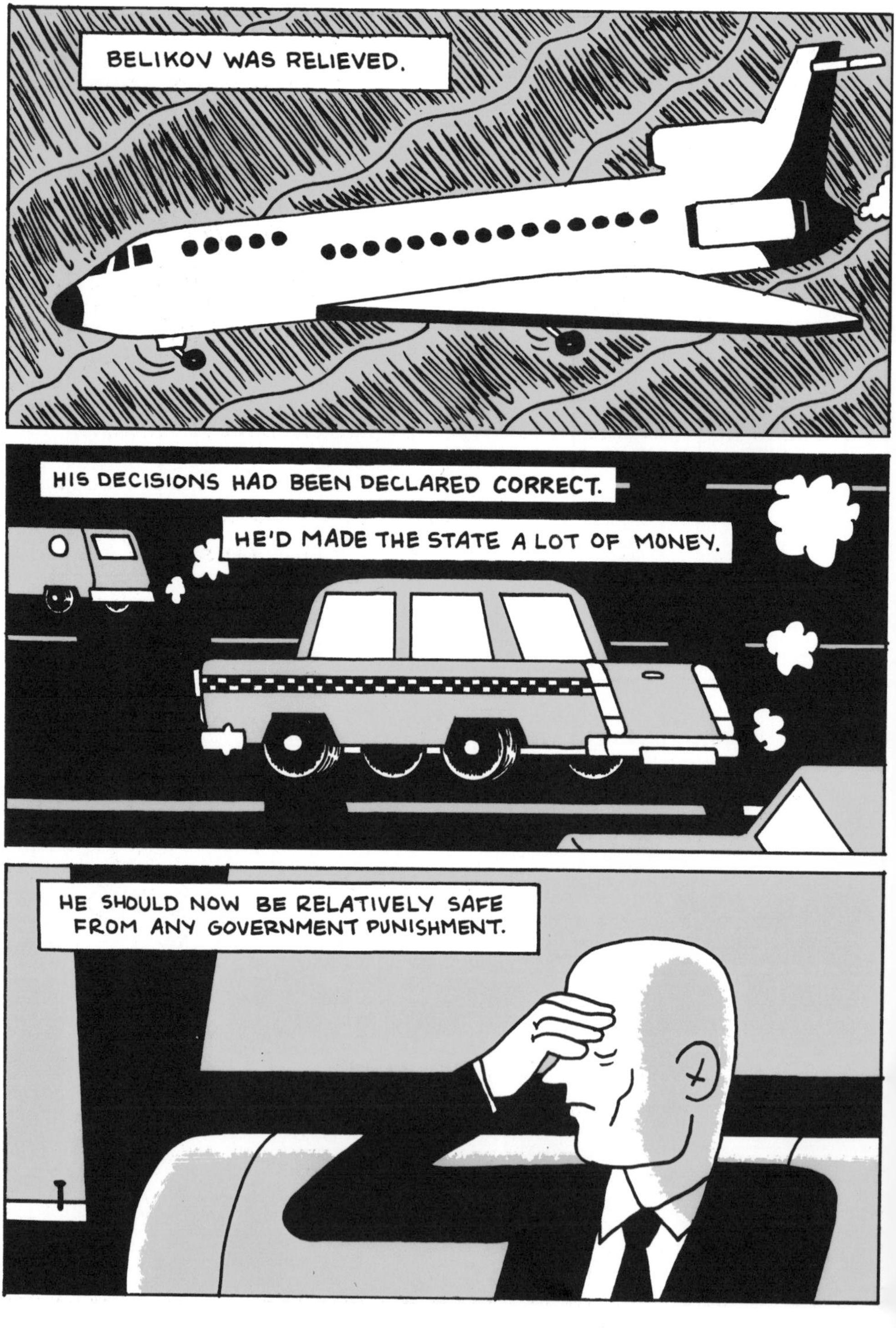
BELIKOV WAS RELIEVED.
HIS DECISIONS HAD BEEN DECLARED CORRECT.
HE'D MADE THE STATE A LOT OF MONEY.
HE SHOULD NOW BE RELATIVELY SAFE FROM ANY GOVERNMENT PUNISHMENT.

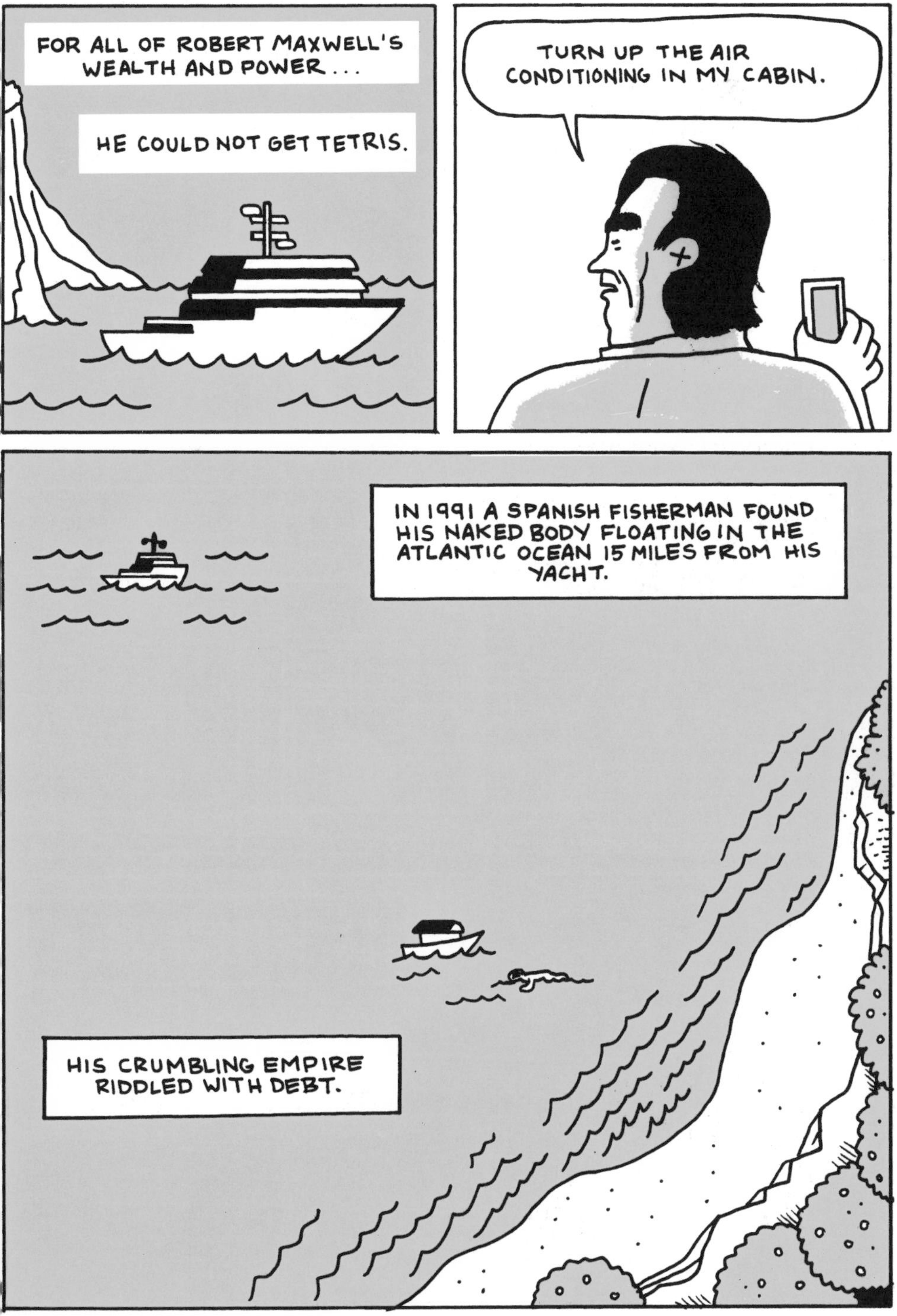
FOR ALL OF ROBERT MAXWELL'S WEALTH AND POWER...
HE COULD NOT GET TETRIS.
TURN UP THE AIR CONDITIONING IN MY CABIN.
IN 1991 A SPANISH FISHERMAN FOUND HIS NAKED BODY FLOATING IN THE ATLANTIC OCEAN 15 MILES FROM HIS YACHT.
HIS CRUMBLING EMPIRE RIDDLED WITH DEBT.

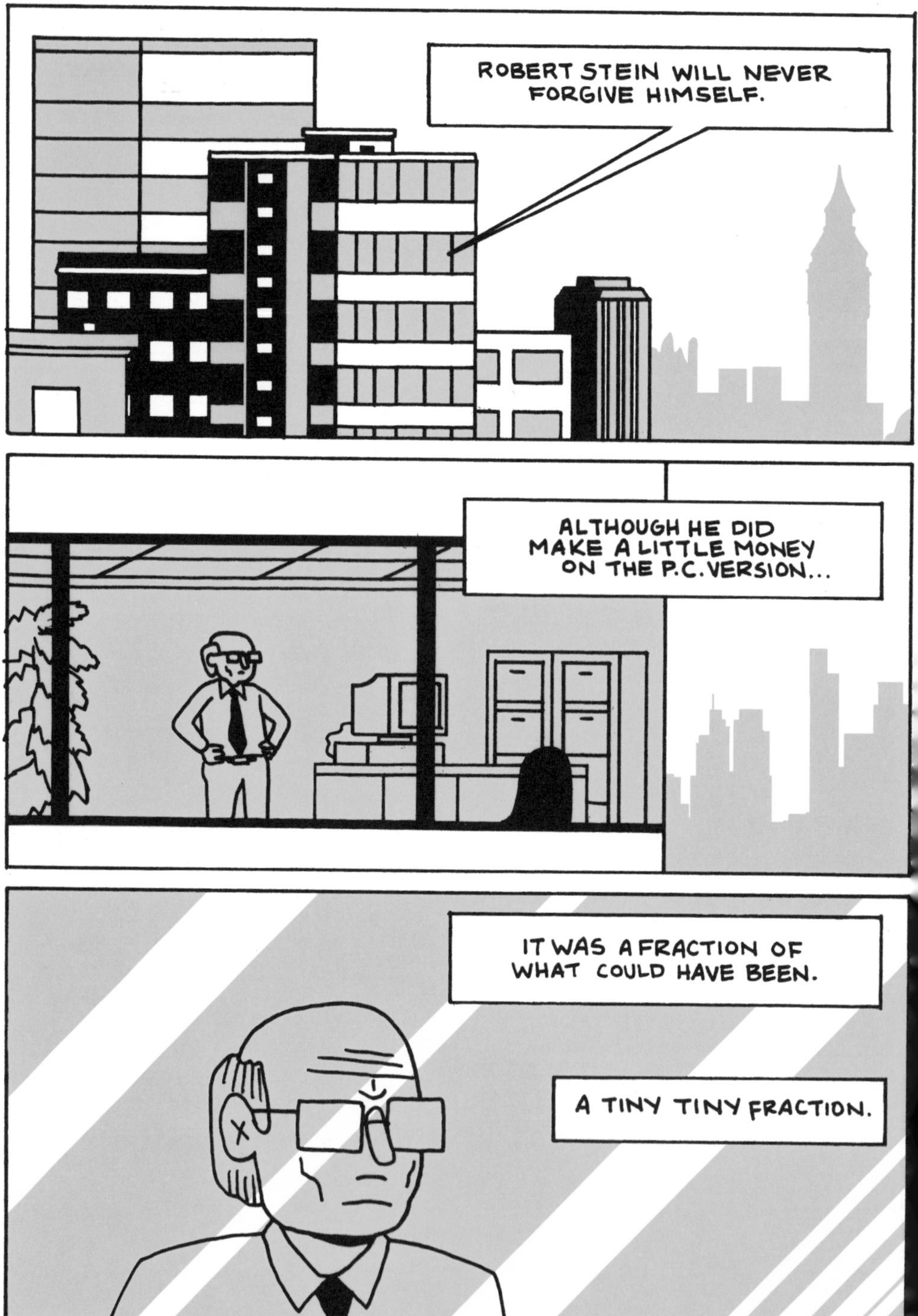
ROBERT STEIN WILL NEVER FORGIVE HIMSELF.
ALTHOUGH HE DID MAKE A LITTLE MONEY ON THE P.C. VERSION...
IT WAS A FRACTION OF WHAT COULD HAVE BEEN.
A TINY TINY FRACTION.

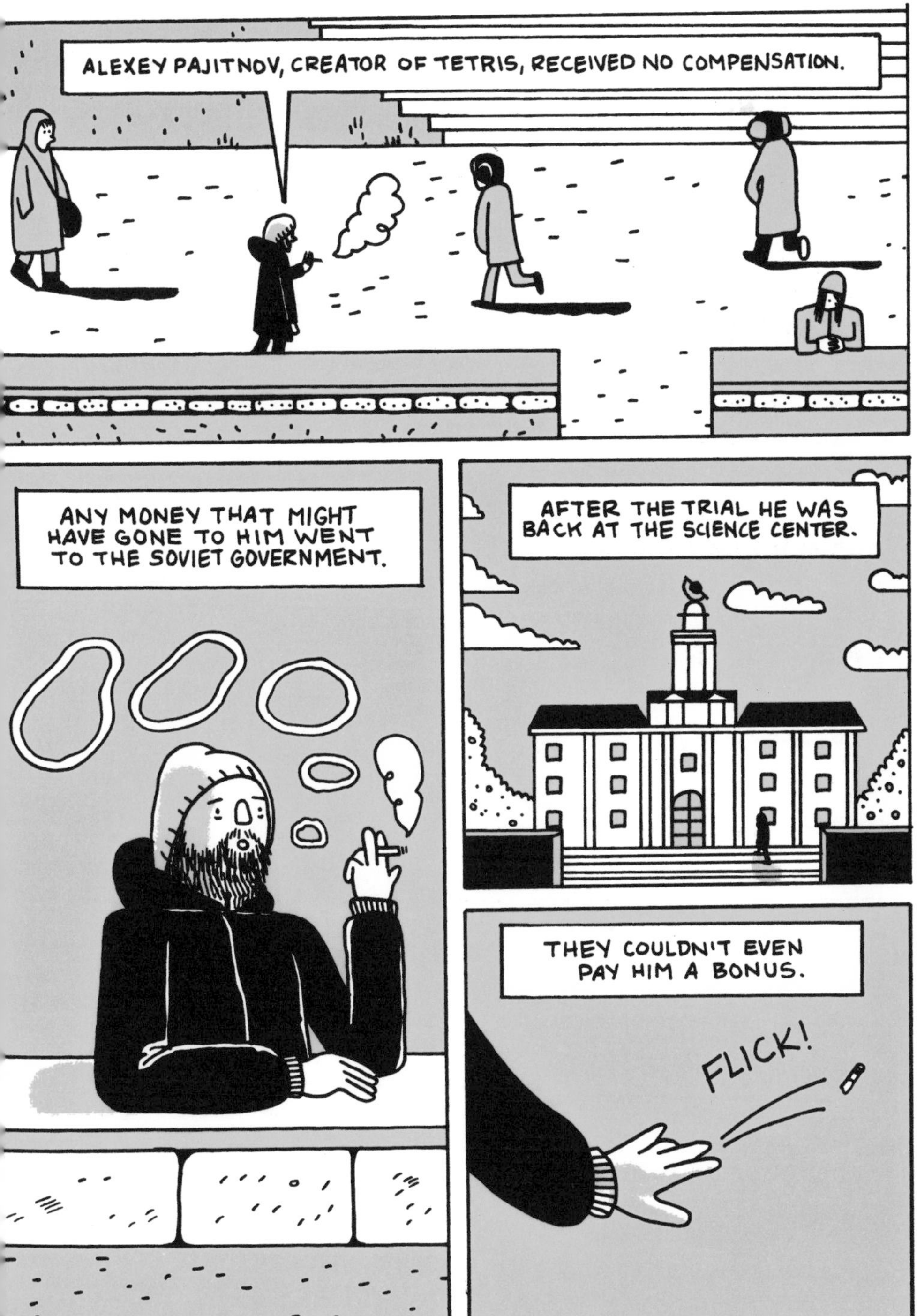
ALEXEY PAJITNOV, CREATOR OF TETRIS, RECEIVED NO COMPENSATION.
ANY MONEY THAT MIGHT HAVE GONE TO HIM WENT TO THE SOVIET GOVERNMENT.
AFTER THE TRIAL HE WAS BACK AT THE SCIENCE CENTER.
THEY COULDN'T EVEN PAY HIM A BONUS.
FLICK!

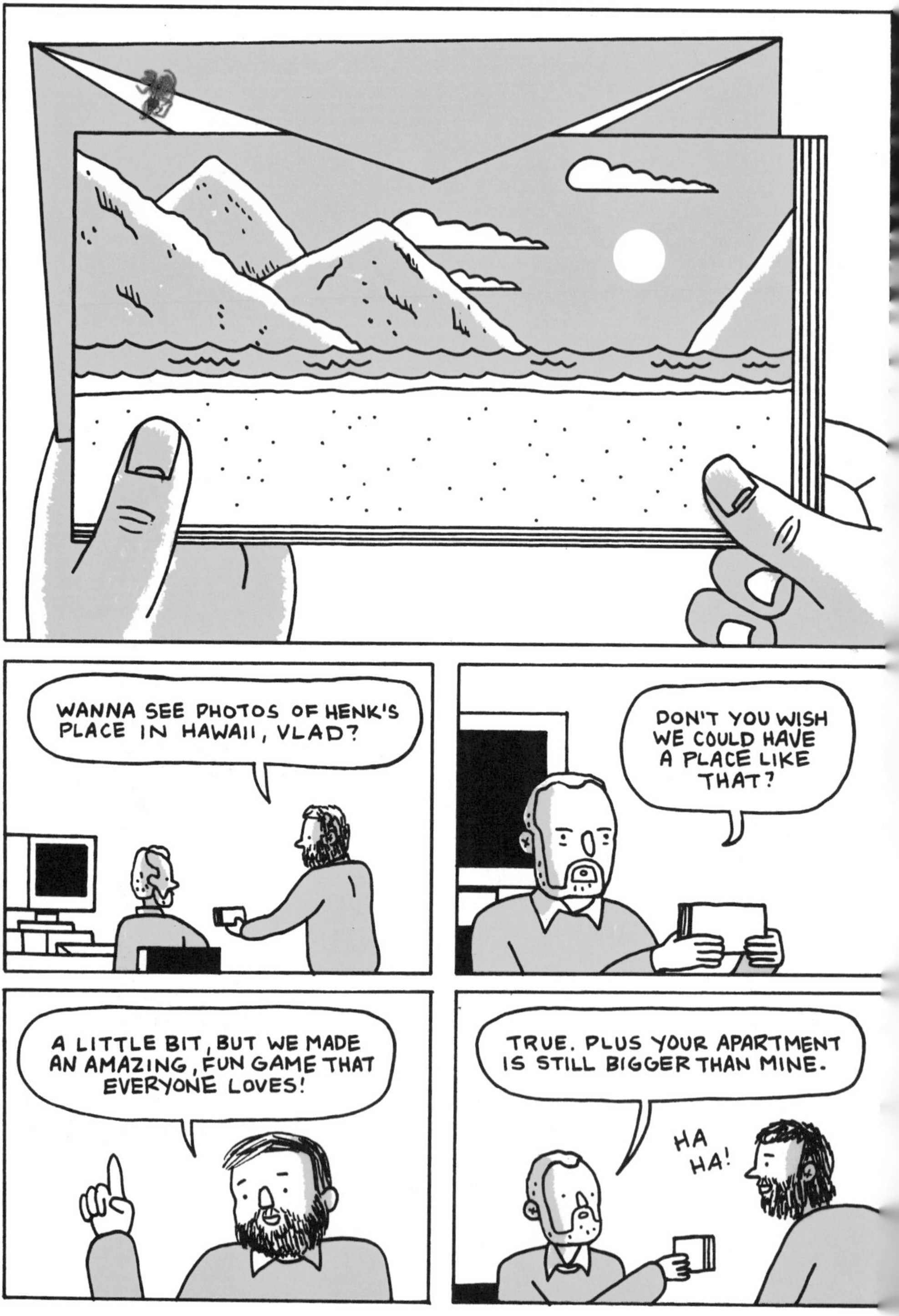
WANNA SEE PHOTOS OF HENK'S PLACE IN HAWAII, VLAD?
DON'T YOU WISH WE COULD HAVE A PLACE LIKE THAT?
A LITTLE BIT, BUT WE MADE AN AMAZING, FUN GAME THAT EVERYONE LOVES!
TRUE. PLUS YOUR APARTMENT IS STILL BIGGER THAN MINE.
HA HA!

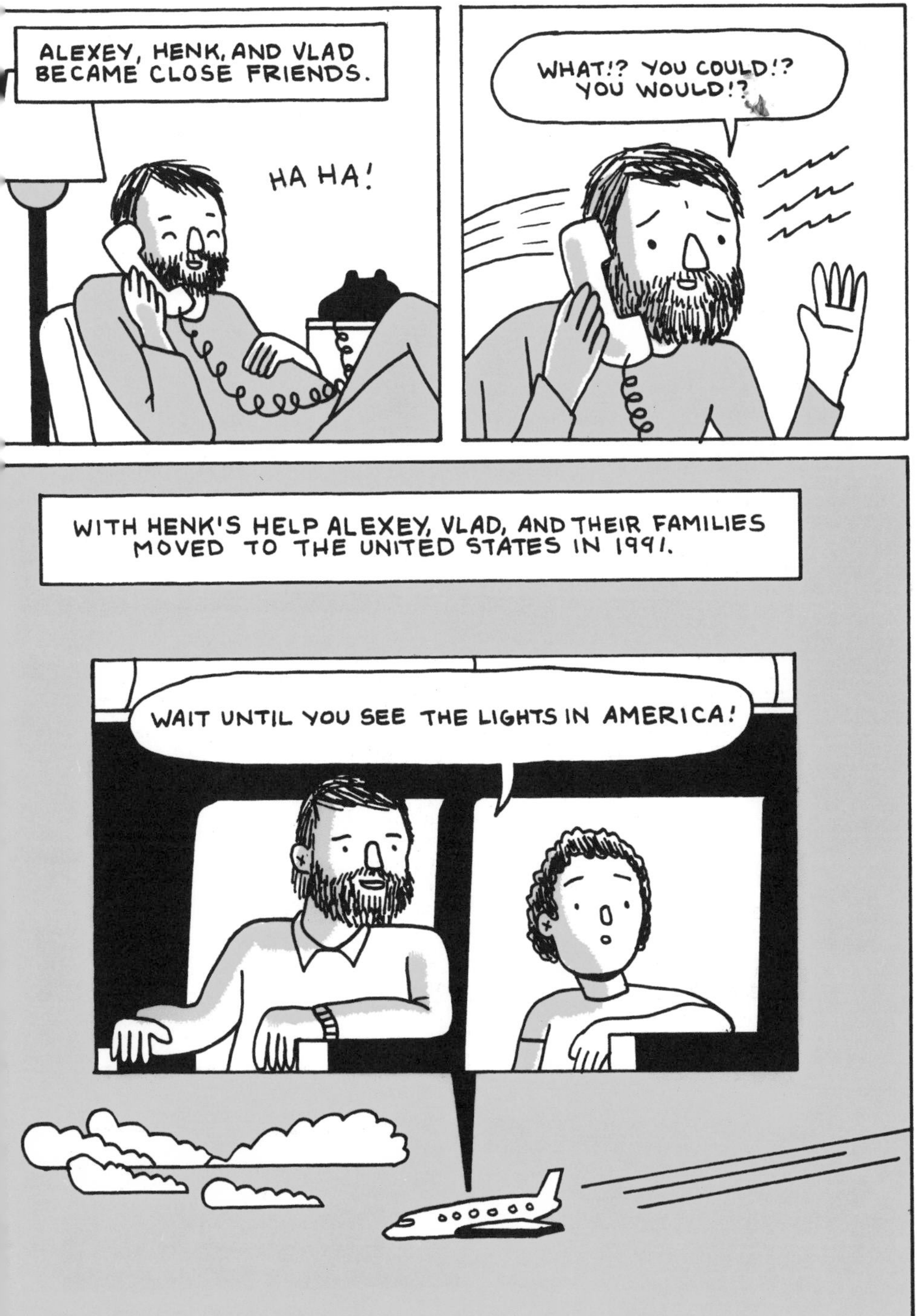
ALEXEY, HENK, AND VLAD BECAME CLOSE FRIENDS.
HA HA!
WHAT!? YOU COULD!? YOU WOULD!?
WITH HENK'S HELP ALEXEY, VLAD, AND THEIR FAMILIES MOVED TO THE UNITED STATES IN 1991.
WAIT UNTIL YOU SEE THE LIGHTS IN AMERICA!

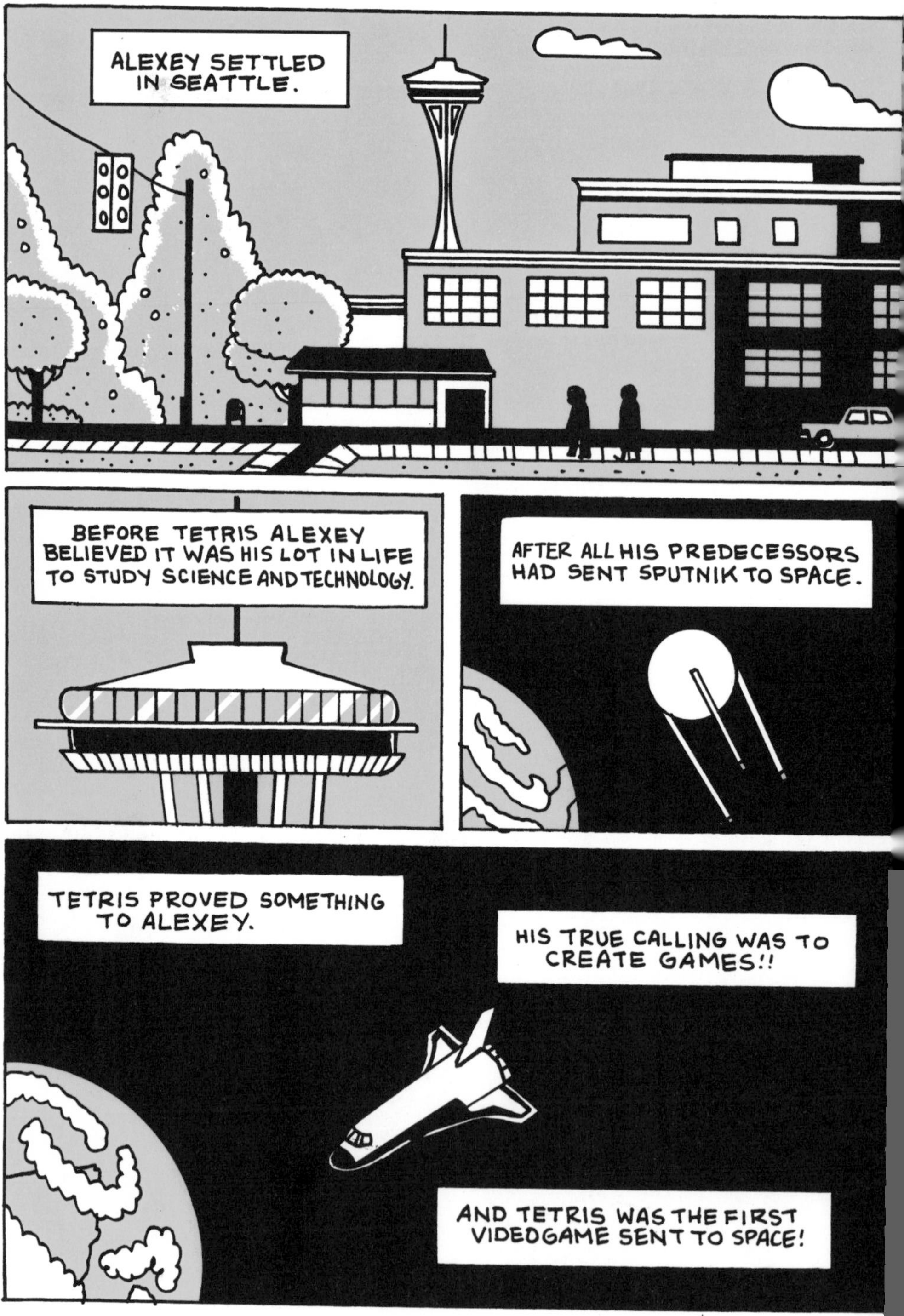
ALEXEY SETTLED IN SEATTLE.
BEFORE TETRIS ALEXEY BELIEVED IT WAS HIS LOT IN LIFE TO STUDY SCIENCE AND TECHNOLOGY.
AFTER ALL HIS PREDECESSORS HAD SENT SPUTNIK TO SPACE.
TETRIS PROVED SOMETHING TO ALEXEY.
HIS TRUE CALLING WAS TO CREATE GAMES!!
AND TETRIS WAS THE FIRST VIDEOGAME SENT TO SPACE!

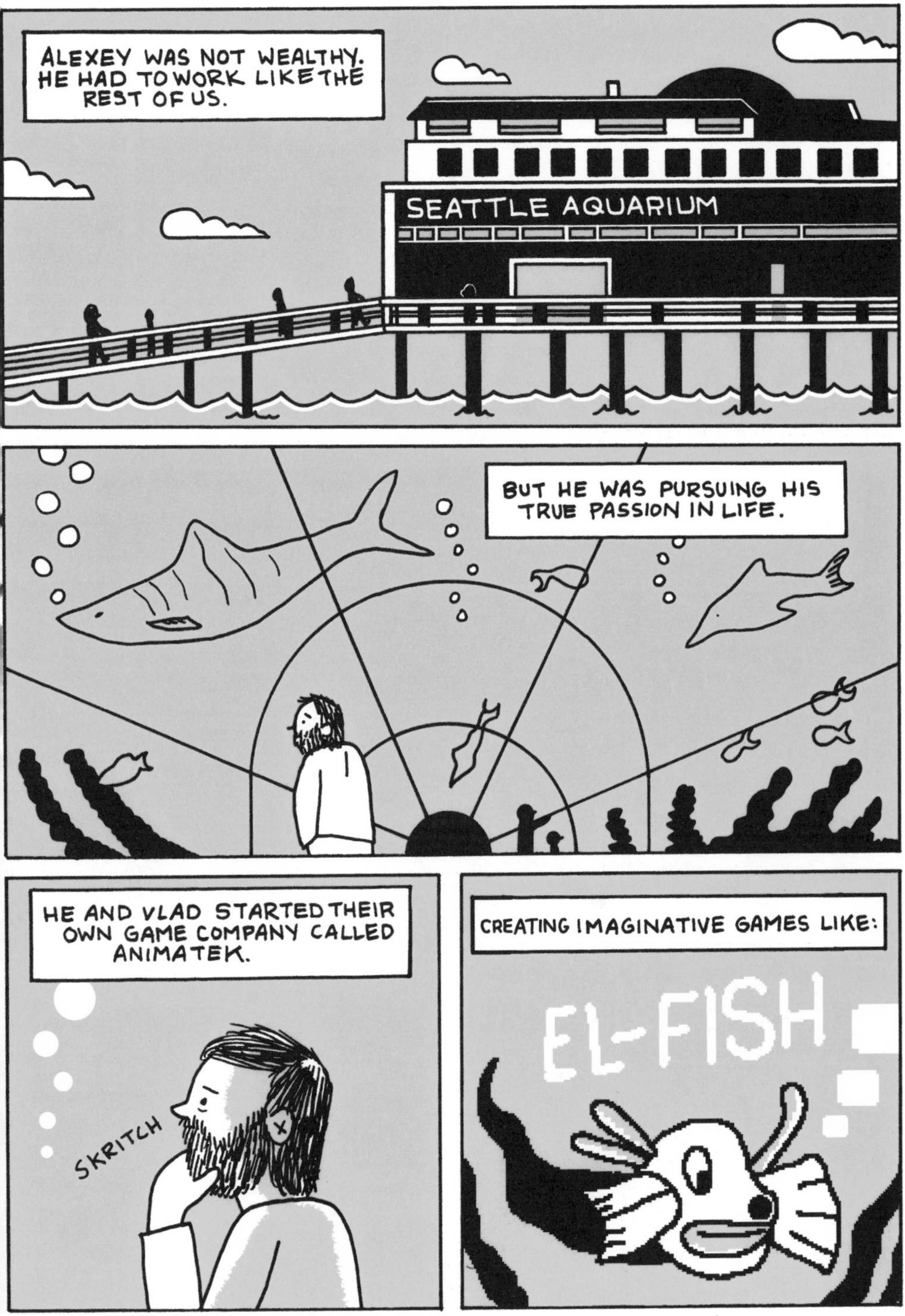
ALEXEY WAS NOT WEALTHY. HE HAD TO WORK LIKE THE REST OF US.
SEATTLE AQUARIUM
BUT HE WAS PURSUING HIS TRUE PASSION IN LIFE.
HE AND VLAD STARTED THEIR OWN GAME COMPANY CALLED ANIMATEK.
SKRITCH
CREATING IMAGINATIVE GAMES LIKE:
EL-FISH

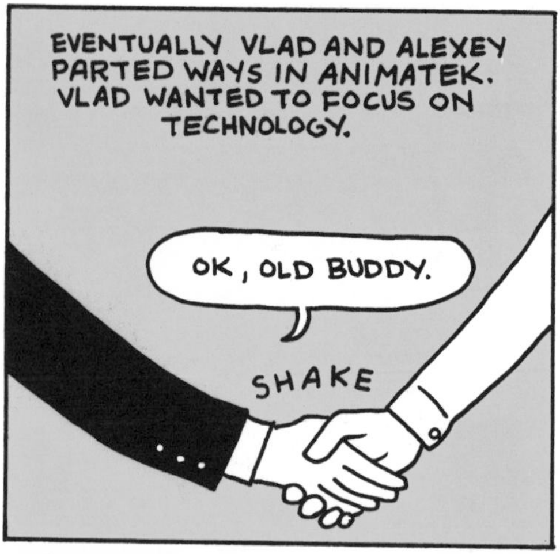
EVENTUALLY VLAD AND ALEXEY PARTED WAYS IN ANIMATEK. VLAD WANTED TO FOCUS ON TECHNOLOGY.
OK, OLD BUDDY.
SHAKE

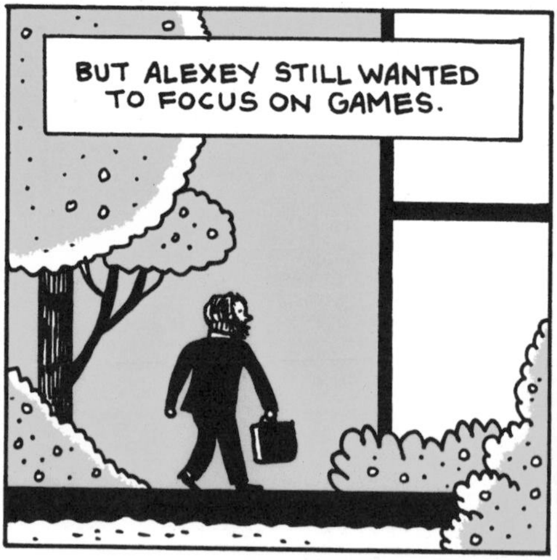
BUT ALEXEY STILL WANTED TO FOCUS ON GAMES.

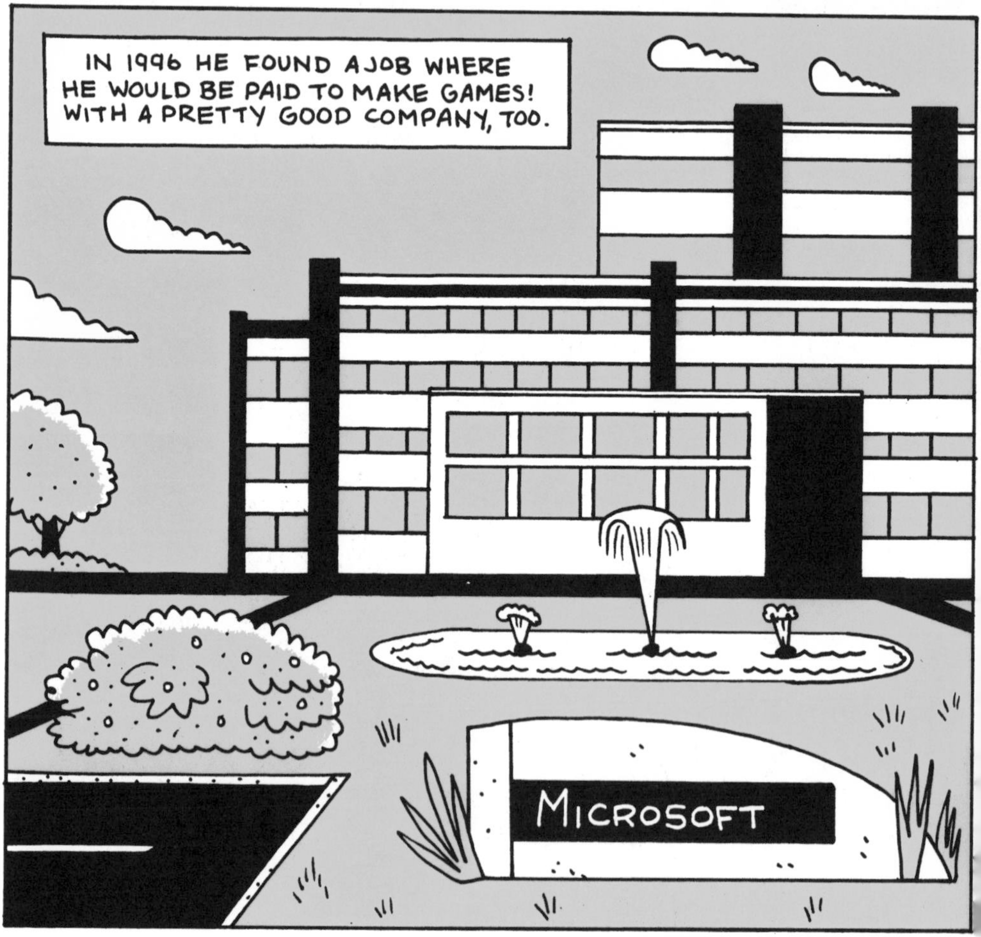
IN 1996 HE FOUND A JOB WHERE HE WOULD BE PAID TO MAKE GAMES! WITH A PRETTY GOOD COMPANY, TOO.
MICROSOFT

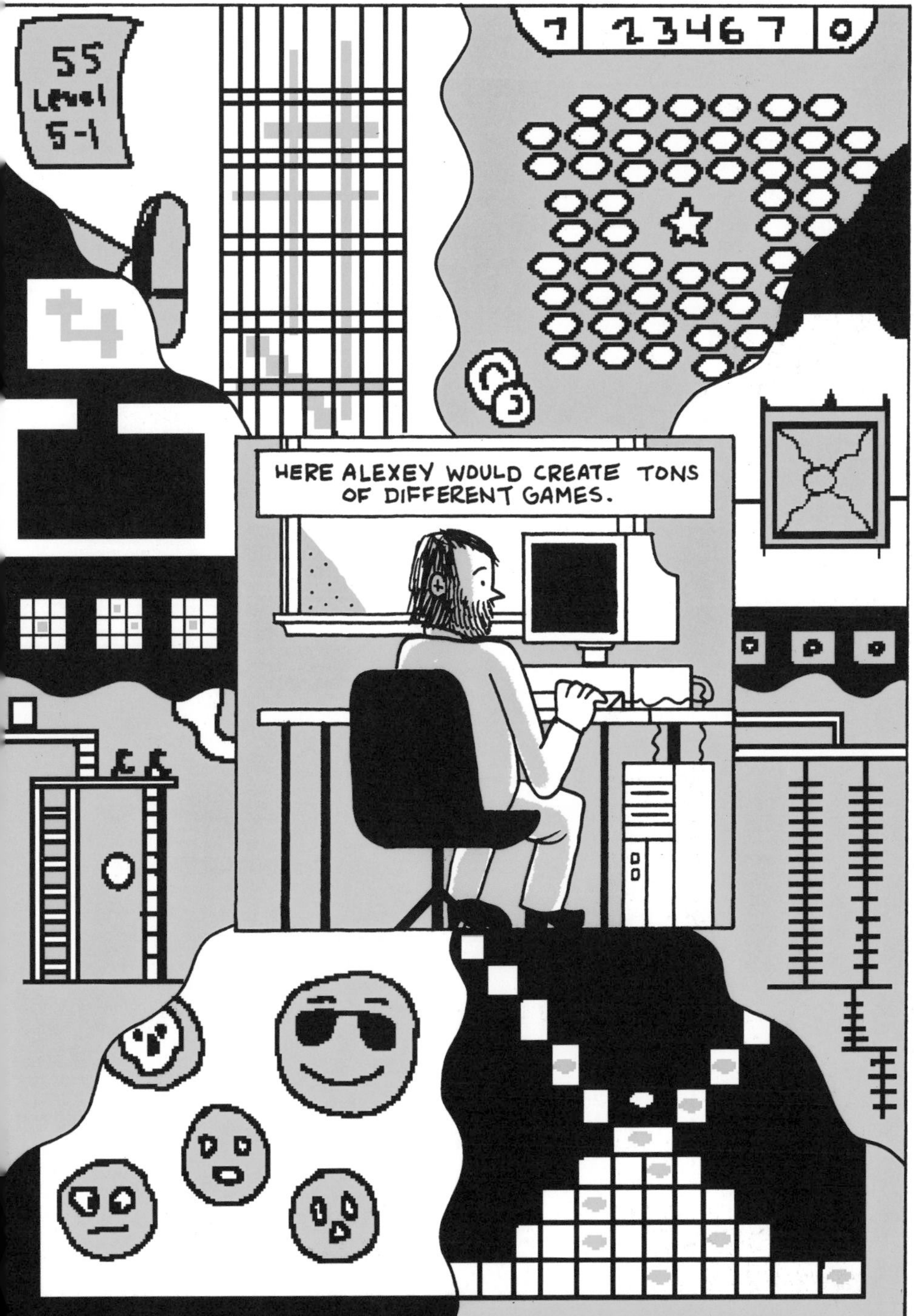
55
Level
5-1
7
23467
0
HERE ALEXEY WOULD CREATE TONS OF DIFFERENT GAMES.

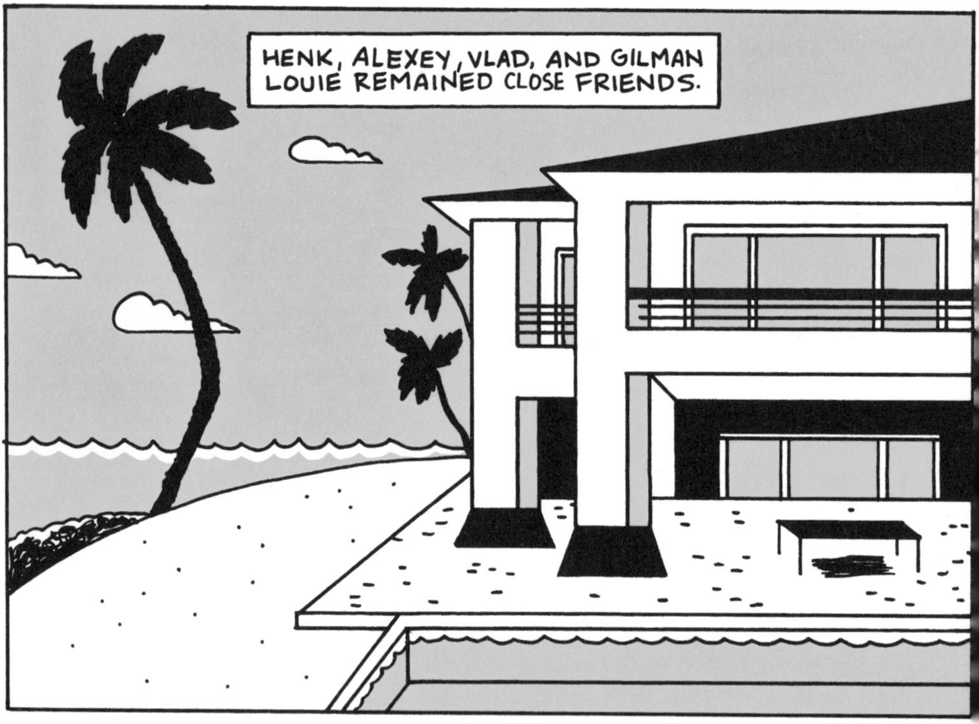
HENK, ALEXEY, VLAD, AND GILMAN LOUIE REMAINED CLOSE FRIENDS.

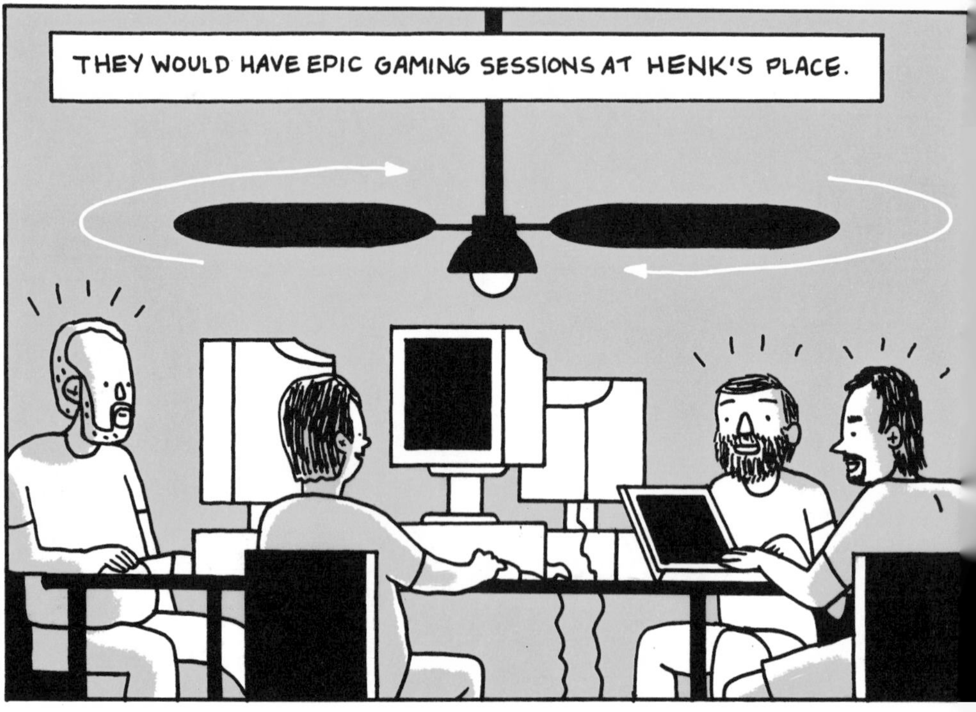
THEY WOULD HAVE EPIC GAMING SESSIONS AT HENK'S PLACE.

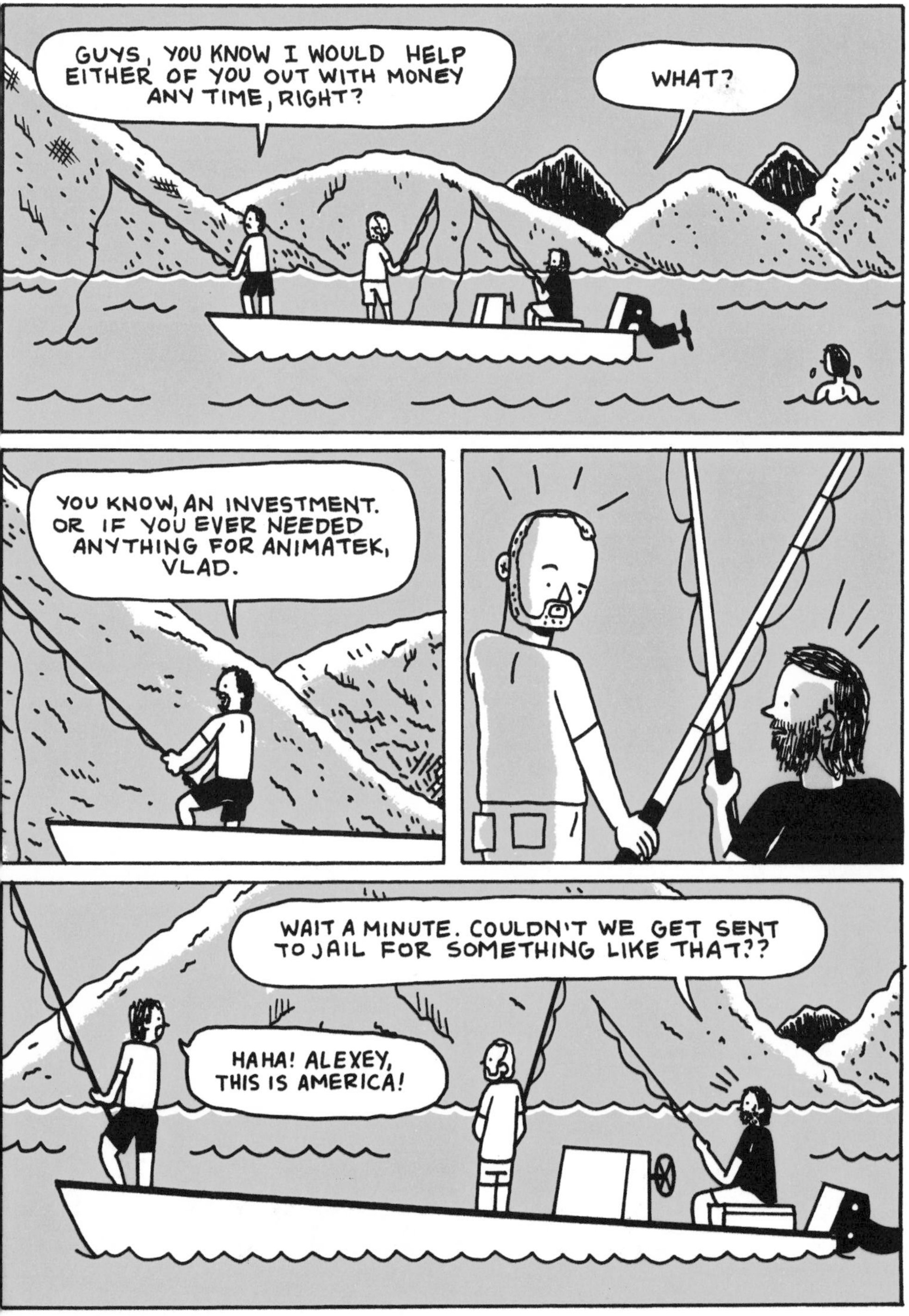
GUYS, YOU KNOW I WOULD HELP EITHER OF YOU OUT WITH MONEY ANY TIME, RIGHT?
WHAT?
YOU KNOW, AN INVESTMENT. OR IF YOU EVER NEEDED ANYTHING FOR ANIMATEK, VLAD.
WAIT A MINUTE. COULDN'T WE GET SENT TO JAIL FOR SOMETHING LIKE THAT??
HAHA! ALEXEY, THIS IS AMERICA!

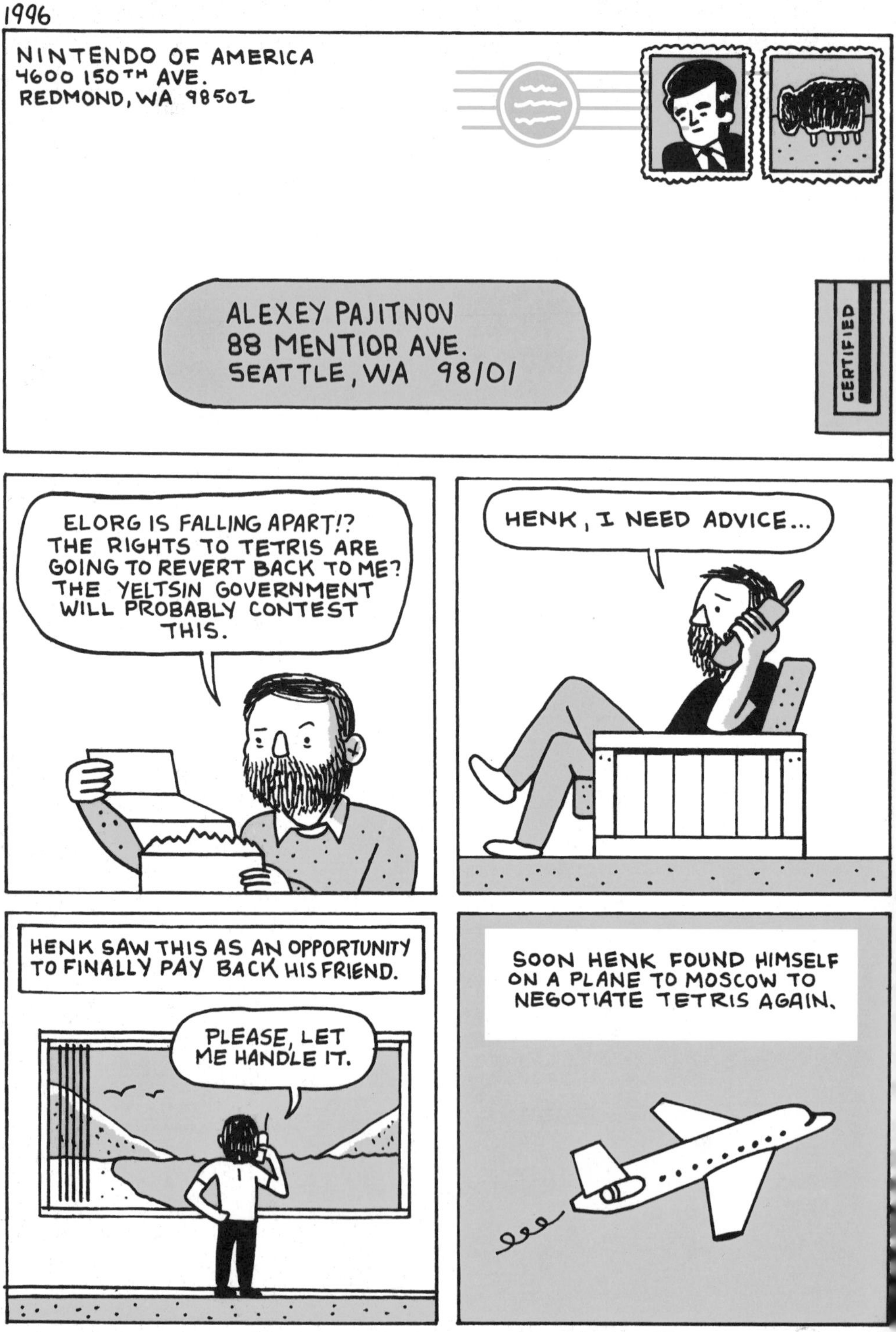
1996
NINTENDO OF AMERICA
4600 150TH AVE.
REDMOND, WA 98502
ALEXEY PAJITNOV
88 MENTIOR AVE.
SEATTLE, WA 98101
CERTIFIED
ELORG IS FALLING APART!? THE RIGHTS TO TETRIS ARE GOING TO REVERT BACK TO ME? THE YELTSIN GOVERNMENT WILL PROBABLY CONTEST THIS.
HENK, I NEED ADVICE...
HENK SAW THIS AS AN OPPORTUNITY TO FINALLY PAY BACK HIS FRIEND.
PLEASE, LET ME HANDLE IT.
SOON HENK FOUND HIMSELF ON A PLANE TO MOSCOW TO NEGOTIATE TETRIS AGAIN.

HENK ROGERS
BLUE PLANET SOFTWARE
THE TETRIS COMPANY

ALEXEY PAJITNOV
THE TETRIS COMPANY

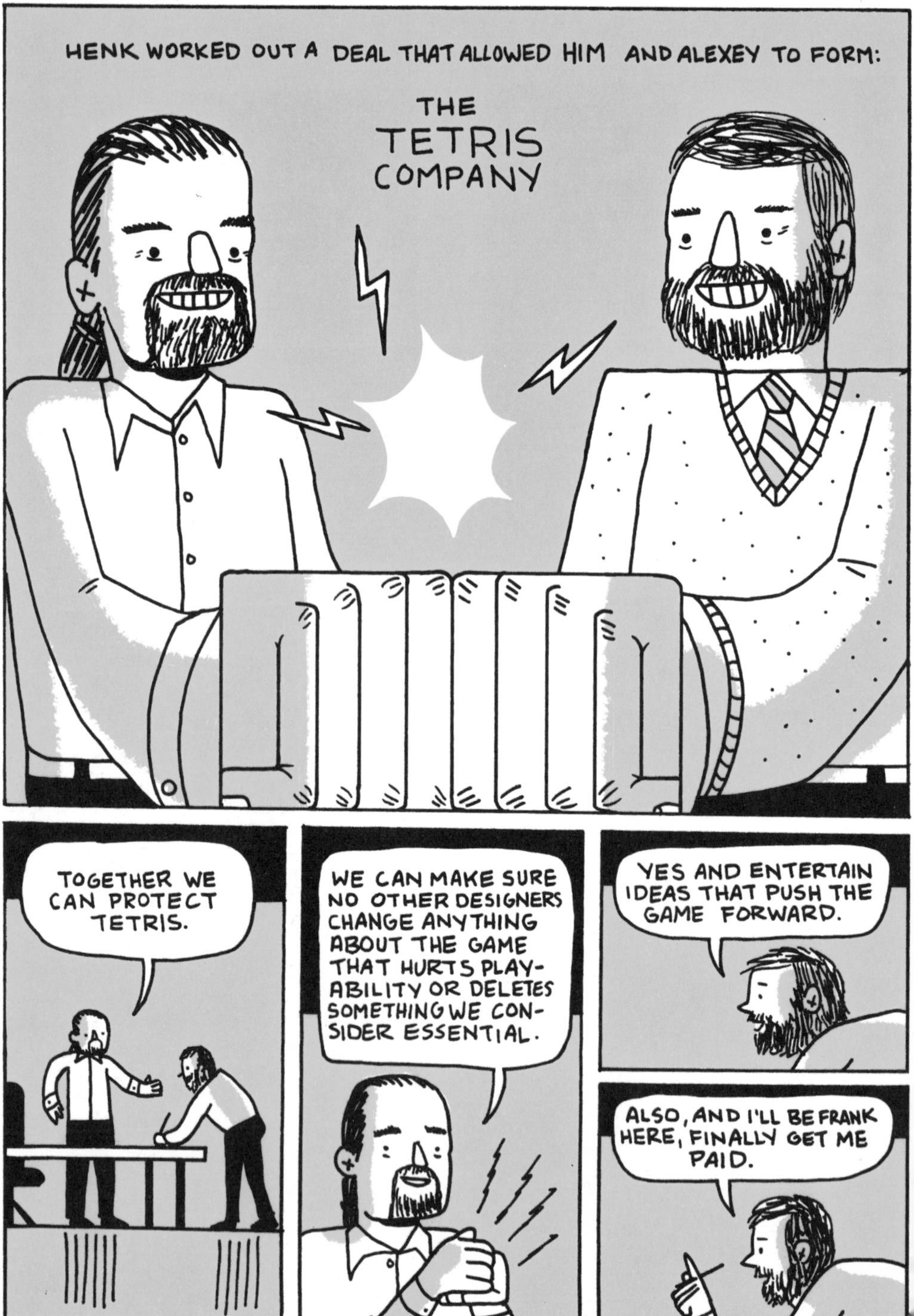
HENK WORKED OUT A DEAL THAT ALLOWED HIM AND ALEXEY TO FORM:
THE TETRIS COMPANY
TOGETHER WE CAN PROTECT TETRIS.
WE CAN MAKE SURE NO OTHER DESIGNERS CHANGE ANYTHING ABOUT THE GAME THAT HURTS PLAY-ABILITY OR DELETES SOMETHING WE CON-SIDER ESSENTIAL.
YES AND ENTERTAIN IDEAS THAT PUSH THE GAME FORWARD.
ALSO, AND I'LL BE FRANK HERE, FINALLY GET ME PAID.

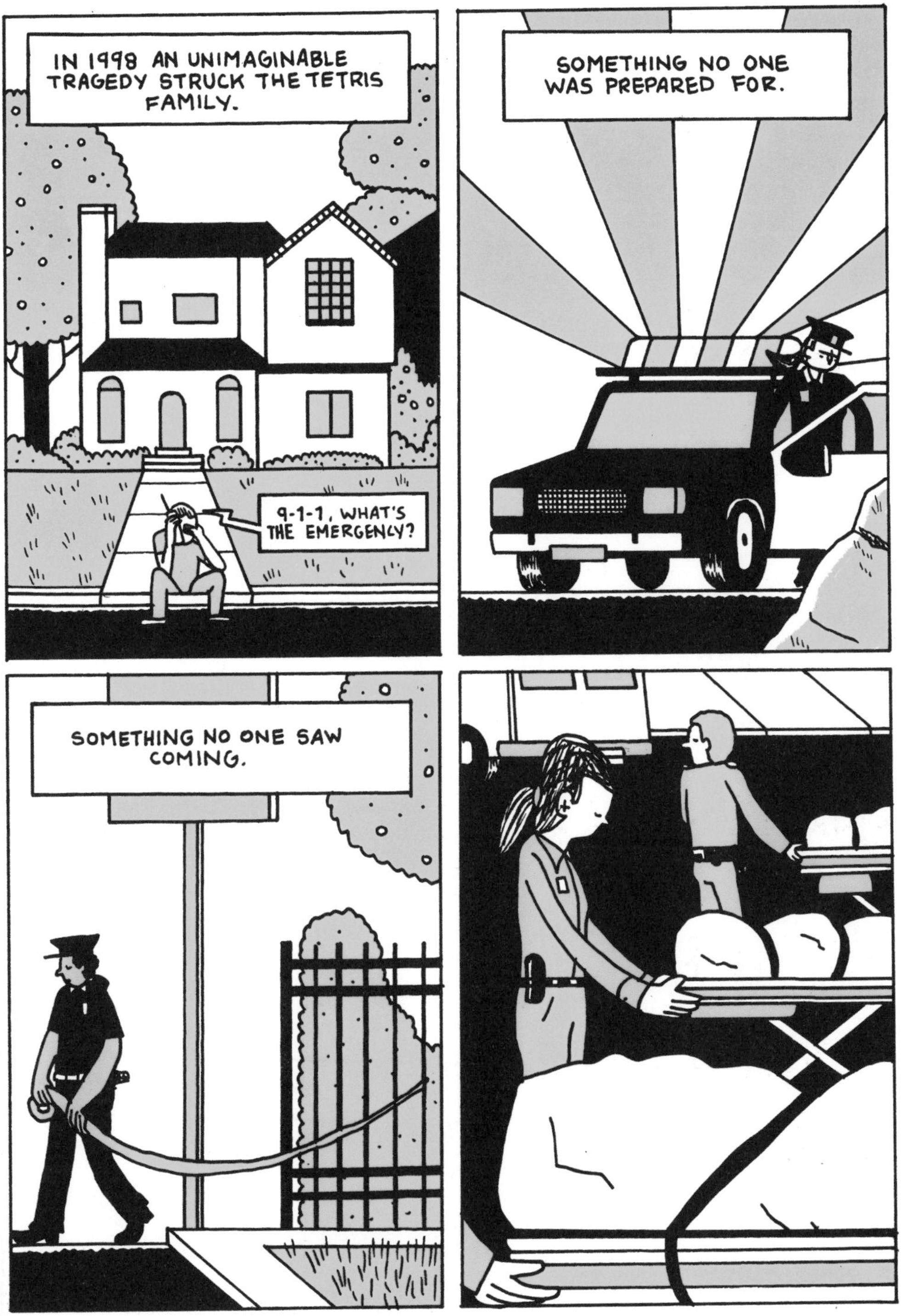
IN 1998 AN UNIMAGINABLE TRAGEDY STRUCK THE TETRIS FAMILY.
9-1-1, WHAT'S THE EMERGENCY?
SOMETHING NO ONE WAS PREPARED FOR.
SOMETHING NO ONE SAW COMING.

TETRIS GAME CO-CREATOR PUSHED PAST THE BRINK

PALO ALTO- XXXXXX XXXXX
XXX XXXXX XXXXX XXXX XXX
XXX XXXXX XXXXX XXXX XXX
TETRIS CREATOR XXX XXX XX
XXX MURDER/SUICIDE XXXXX.
XXX XXXXX XXXXX WIFE XX
XXXXX XXX XXXX 12 YEAR
OLD SON XXX XXXXX XXXXX
 WITH A HAMMER. XX XX

XXX XXXXX XXXXX
 XXX XXXXX XXXXX XXXX XXX
WITH A HUNTING KNIFE. XXX
XXX XXXXX XXXXX XXXX XXX

XXX XX
XXX XX
XXX XX
XXX XX

XXX XXXXX XXXXX XXXX XXX
XXX XXXXX XXXXX XXXX XXX

XXX XXXXX XXXXX XXXX XXX
XXX XXXXX XXXXX XXXX XXX
XXX XXXXX XXXXX XXXX XXX
XXX XXXXX XXXXX XXXX XXX
XXX XXXXX XXXXX XXXX XXX

XXX XXXXX XXXXX XXXX XXX
XXX XXXXX XXXXX XXXX XXX

XXX XXXXX XXXXX XXXX XXX
XXX XXXXX XXXXX XXXX XXX
XXX XXXXX XXXXX XXXX XXX
XXX XXXXX XXXXX XXXX XXX
XXX XXXXX XXXXX XXXX XXX
XXX XXXXX XXXXX XXXX XXX
XXX XXXXX XXXXX XXXX XXX
XXX XXXXX XXXXX XXXX XXX
XXX XXXXX XXXXX XXXX XXX
XXX XXXXX XXXXX XXXX XXX
XXX XXXXX XXXXX XXXX XXX

THE STORY WAS OBVIOUS TO THE MEDIA. VLAD HAD FINANCIAL TROUBLES WITH ANIMATEK AND WAS DRIVEN TO MADNESS...

TETRIS FOR NINTENDO GAMEBOY (BELOW)

IT'S UNKNOWABLE WHY VLAD AND OTHERS LIKE HIM DO WHAT HE DID.

HENK ROGERS (STOCK)

232

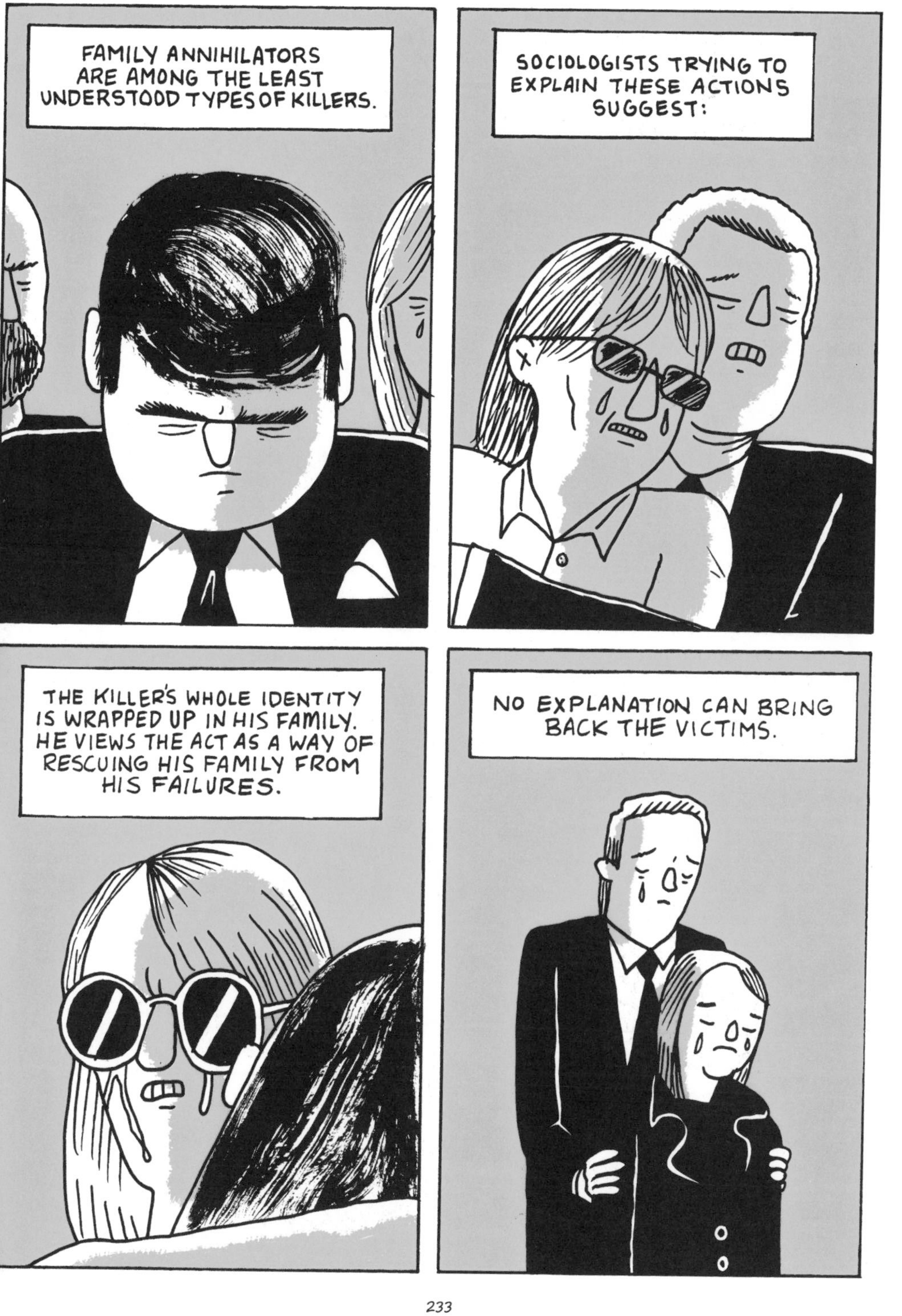
FAMILY ANNIHILATORS ARE AMONG THE LEAST UNDERSTOOD TYPES OF KILLERS.
SOCIOLOGISTS TRYING TO EXPLAIN THESE ACTIONS SUGGEST:
THE KILLER'S WHOLE IDENTITY IS WRAPPED UP IN HIS FAMILY. HE VIEWS THE ACT AS A WAY OF RESCUING HIS FAMILY FROM HIS FAILURES.
NO EXPLANATION CAN BRING BACK THE VICTIMS.

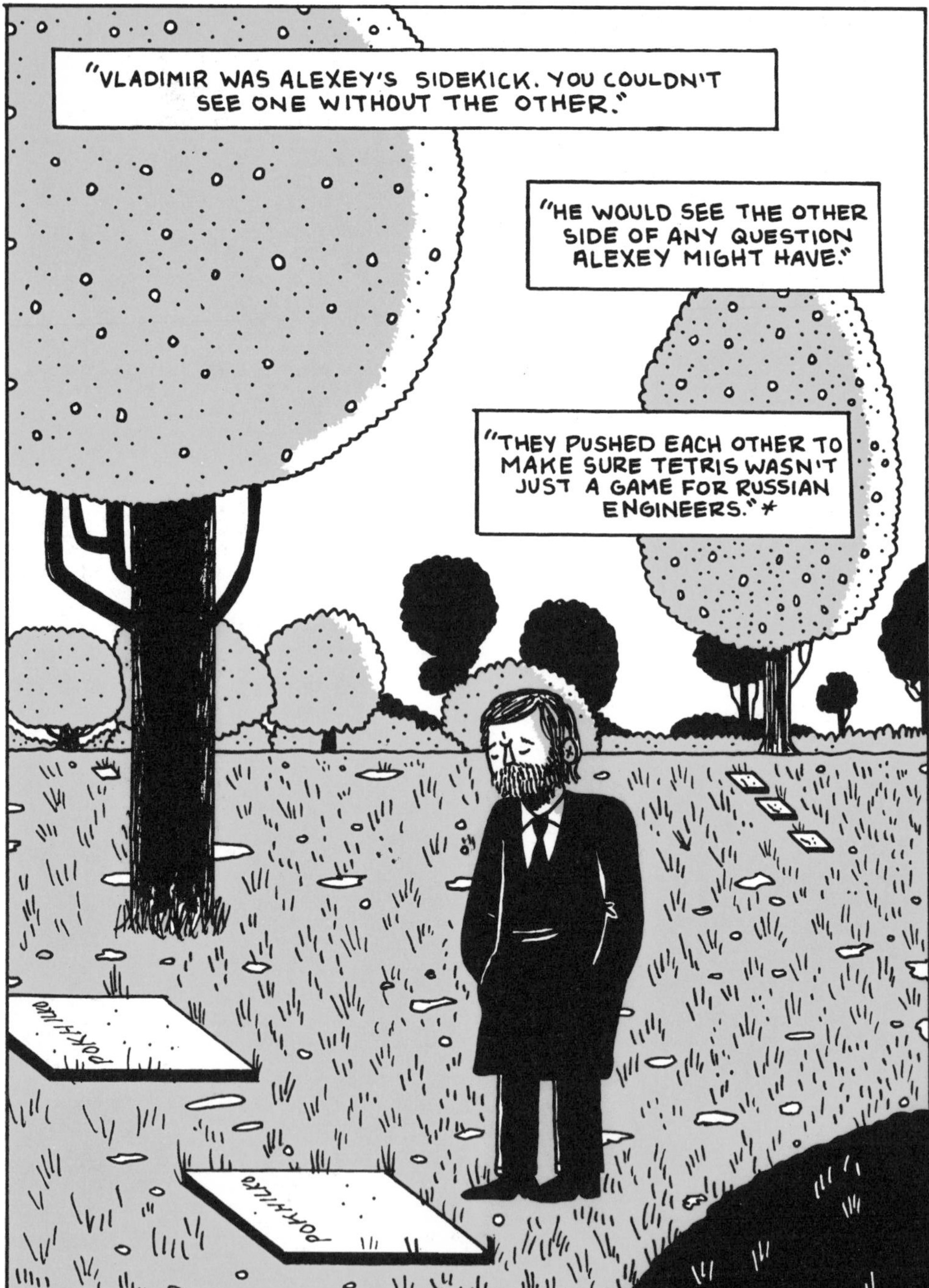
"VLADIMIR WAS ALEXEY'S SIDEKICK. YOU COULDN'T SEE ONE WITHOUT THE OTHER."
"HE WOULD SEE THE OTHER SIDE OF ANY QUESTION ALEXEY MIGHT HAVE."
"THEY PUSHED EACH OTHER TO MAKE SURE TETRIS WASN'T JUST A GAME FOR RUSSIAN ENGINEERS."*

*GILMAN LOUIE

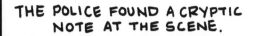

THE POLICE FOUND A CRYPTIC
NOTE AT THE SCENE.

I've been eaten alive.
Vladimir just remember
that I am exist.

The DAVIL.

TETRIS AND THE TETRIS COMPANY ENDURED.

THEY BROUGHT TETRIS TO NEW AUDIENCES.

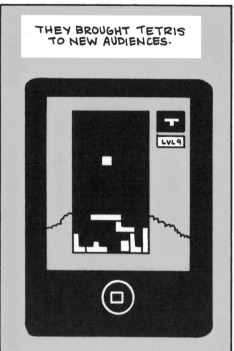

THEY DESTROYED INFERIOR TETRIS CLONES.

IN 1989 COLIN FAHEY WAS A FAN OF TETRIS LIKE EVERYONE ELSE.

BUT HE CAME UP WITH A PROFOUND CONCEPT.

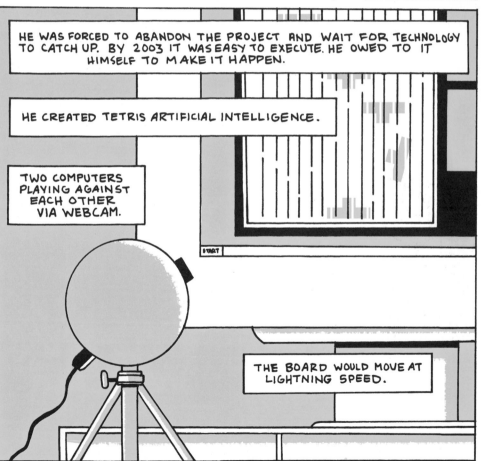

HE WAS FORCED TO ABANDON THE PROJECT AND WAIT FOR TECHNOLOGY TO CATCH UP. BY 2003 IT WAS EASY TO EXECUTE. HE OWED TO IT HIMSELF TO MAKE IT HAPPEN.

HE CREATED TETRIS ARTIFICIAL INTELLIGENCE.

TWO COMPUTERS PLAYING AGAINST EACH OTHER VIA WEBCAM.

START

THE BOARD WOULD MOVE AT LIGHTNING SPEED.

TETRIS'S SIMPLE DESIGN ALLOWED IT TO BE ADAPTED TO ALL KINDS OF MEDIA.

TO GRAPHIC CALCULATORS

TO REGULAR CALCULATORS

TO OSCILLOSCOPES

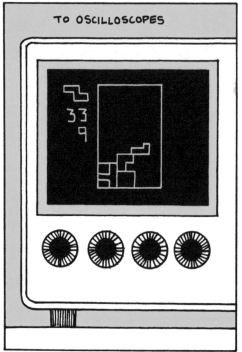

TO T-SHIRTS

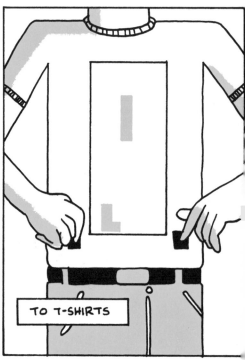

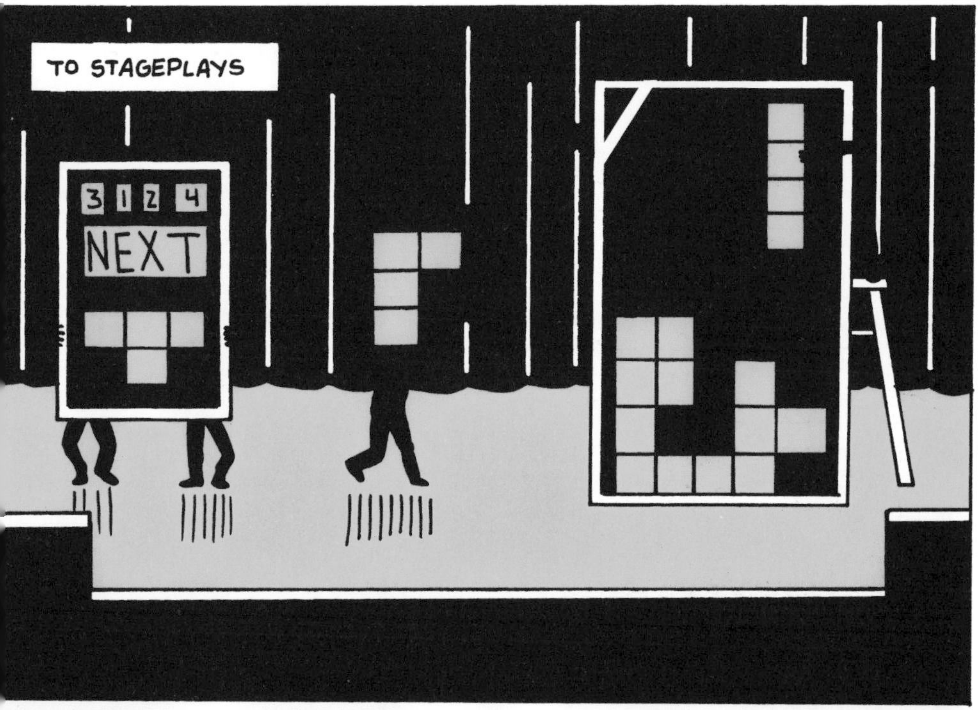
TO STAGEPLAYS
3 1 2 4
NEXT

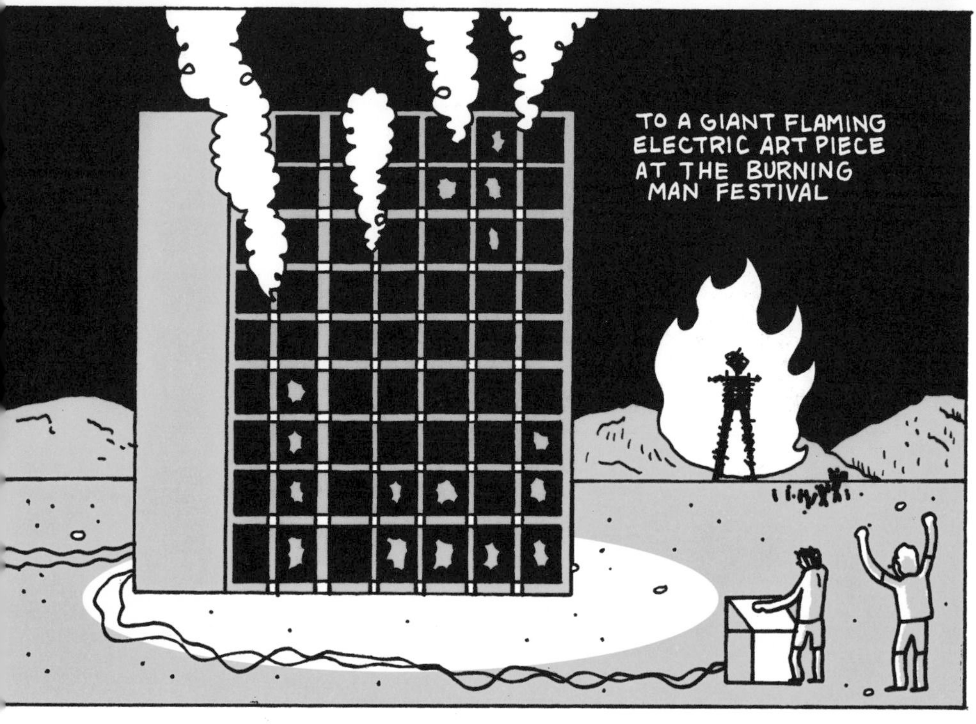
TO A GIANT FLAMING ELECTRIC ART PIECE AT THE BURNING MAN FESTIVAL

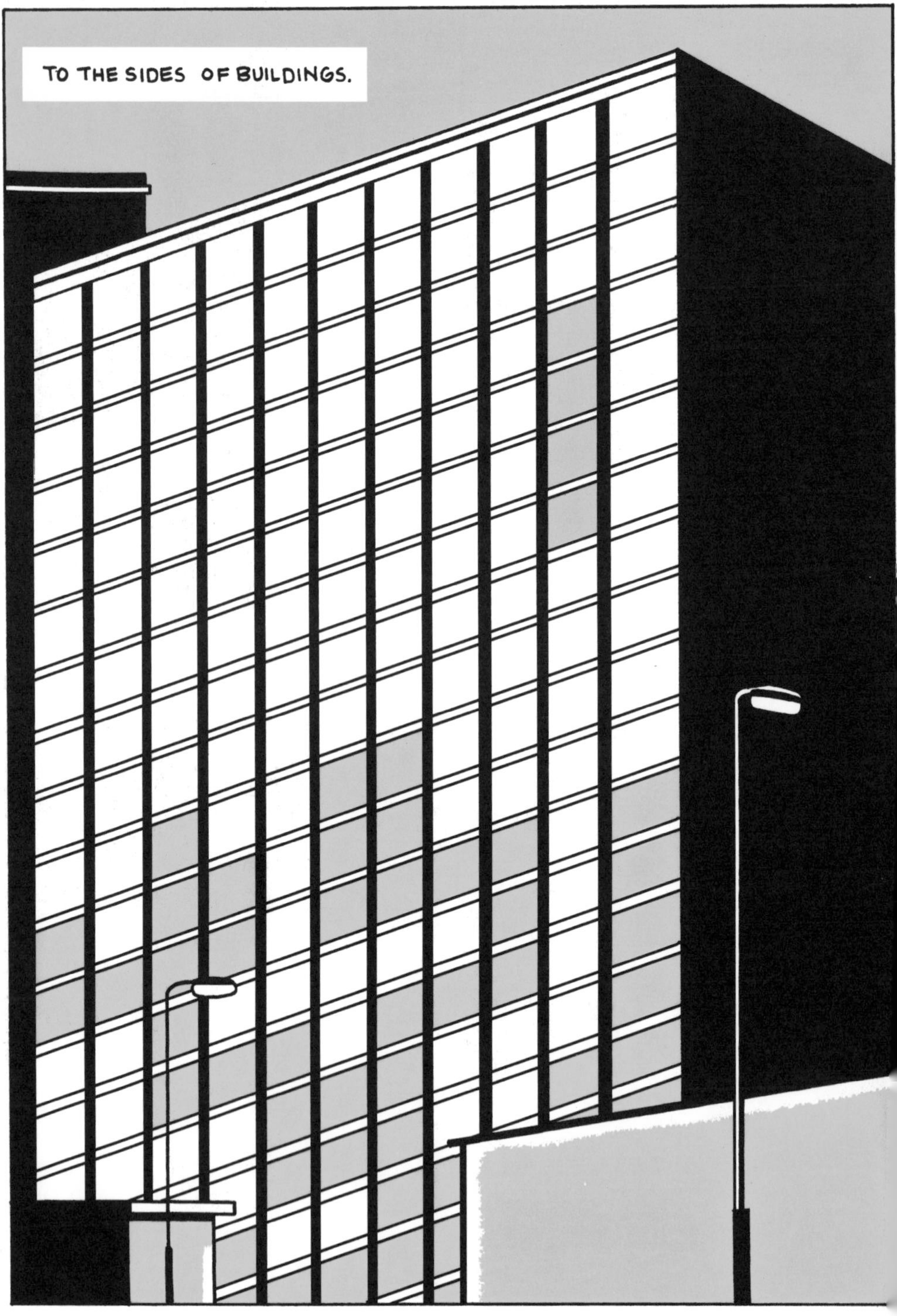
TO THE SIDES OF BUILDINGS.

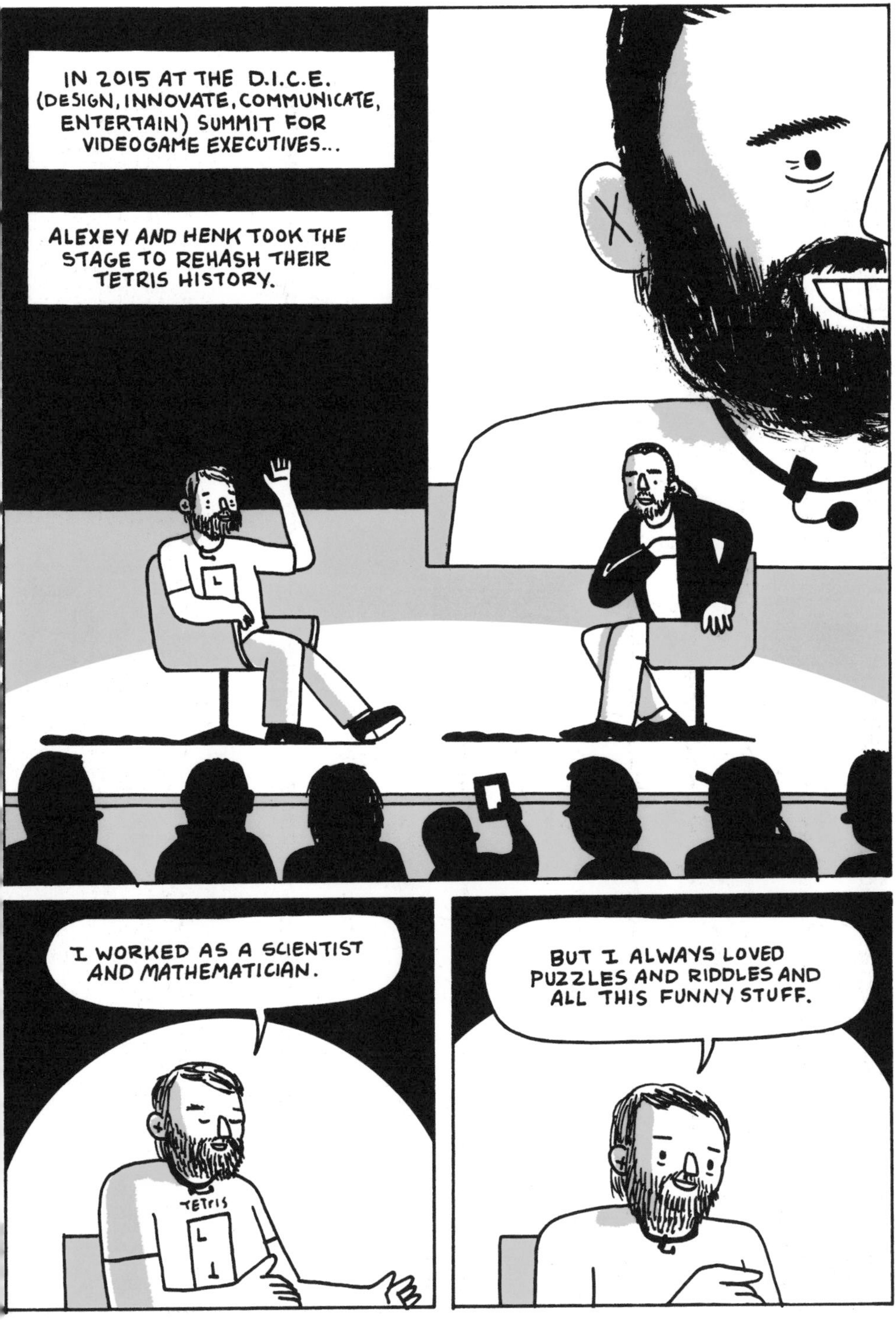
IN 2015 AT THE D.I.C.E. (DESIGN, INNOVATE, COMMUNICATE, ENTERTAIN) SUMMIT FOR VIDEOGAME EXECUTIVES...
ALEXEY AND HENK TOOK THE STAGE TO REHASH THEIR TETRIS HISTORY.
I WORKED AS A SCIENTIST AND MATHEMATICIAN.
TETRIS
BUT I ALWAYS LOVED PUZZLES AND RIDDLES AND ALL THIS FUNNY STUFF.

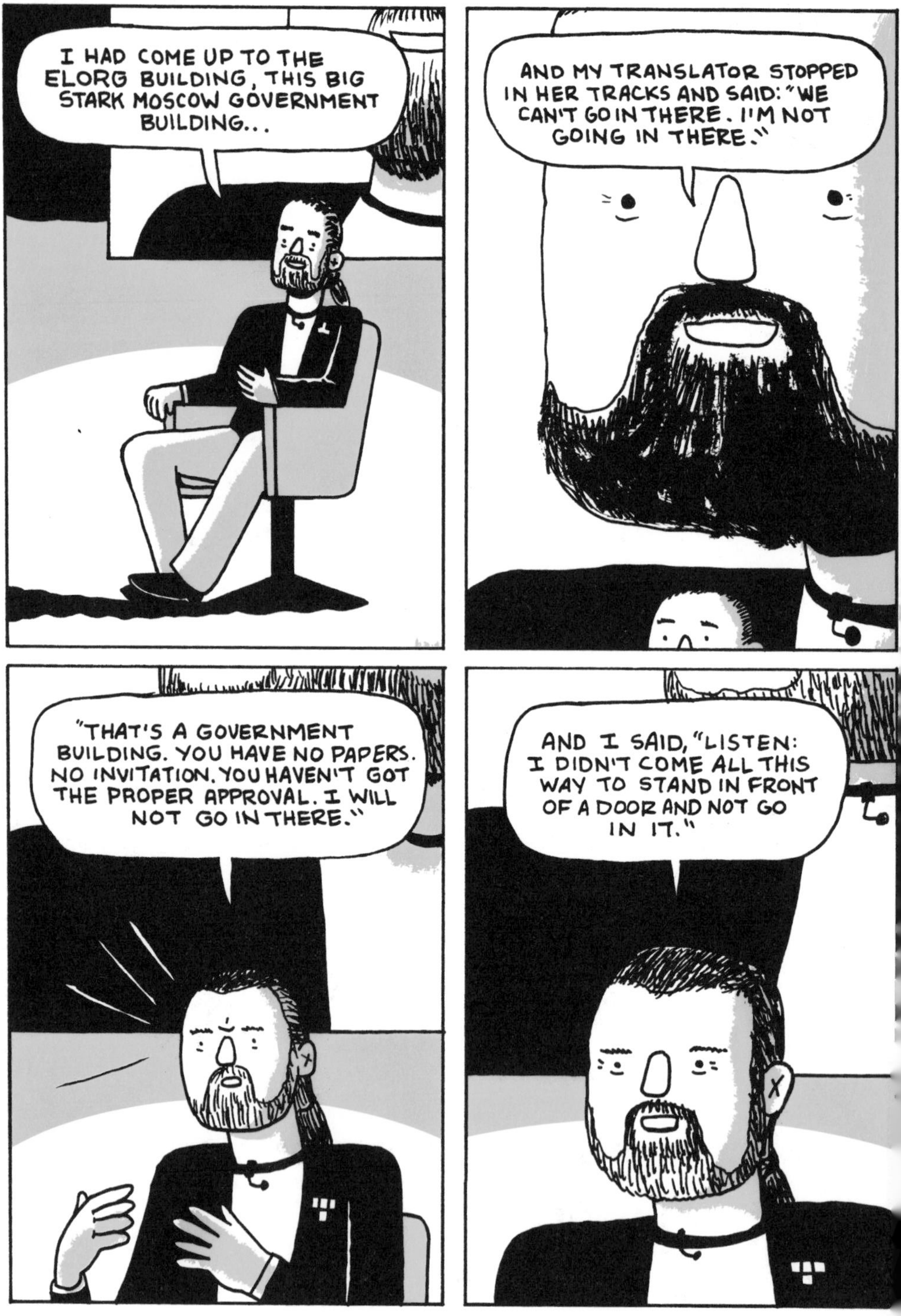
I HAD COME UP TO THE ELORG BUILDING, THIS BIG STARK MOSCOW GOVERNMENT BUILDING...
AND MY TRANSLATOR STOPPED IN HER TRACKS AND SAID: "WE CAN'T GO IN THERE. I'M NOT GOING IN THERE."
"THAT'S A GOVERNMENT BUILDING. YOU HAVE NO PAPERS. NO INVITATION. YOU HAVEN'T GOT THE PROPER APPROVAL. I WILL NOT GO IN THERE."
AND I SAID, "LISTEN: I DIDN'T COME ALL THIS WAY TO STAND IN FRONT OF A DOOR AND NOT GO IN IT."

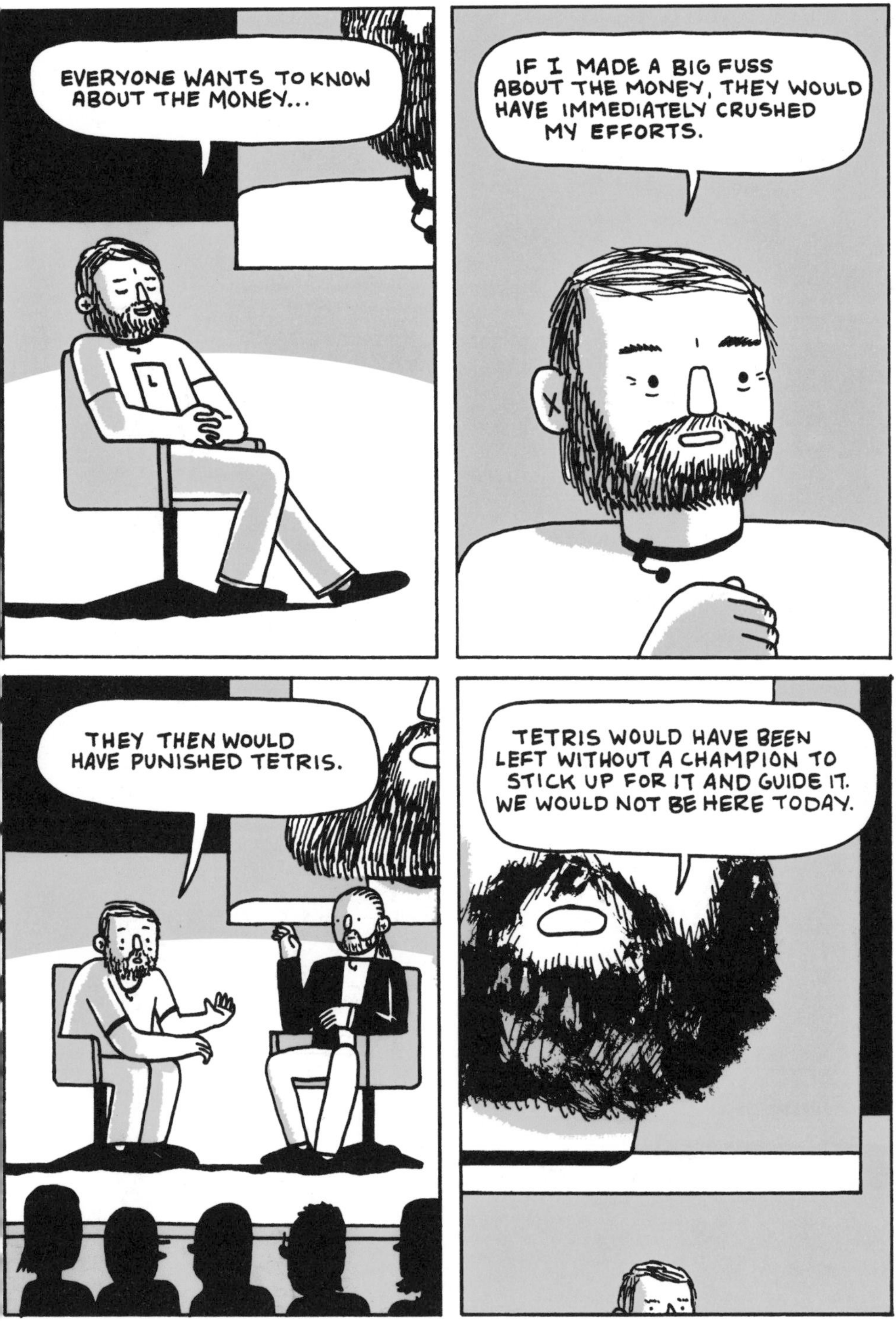
EVERYONE WANTS TO KNOW ABOUT THE MONEY...
IF I MADE A BIG FUSS ABOUT THE MONEY, THEY WOULD HAVE IMMEDIATELY CRUSHED MY EFFORTS.
THEY THEN WOULD HAVE PUNISHED TETRIS.
TETRIS WOULD HAVE BEEN LEFT WITHOUT A CHAMPION TO STICK UP FOR IT AND GUIDE IT. WE WOULD NOT BE HERE TODAY.

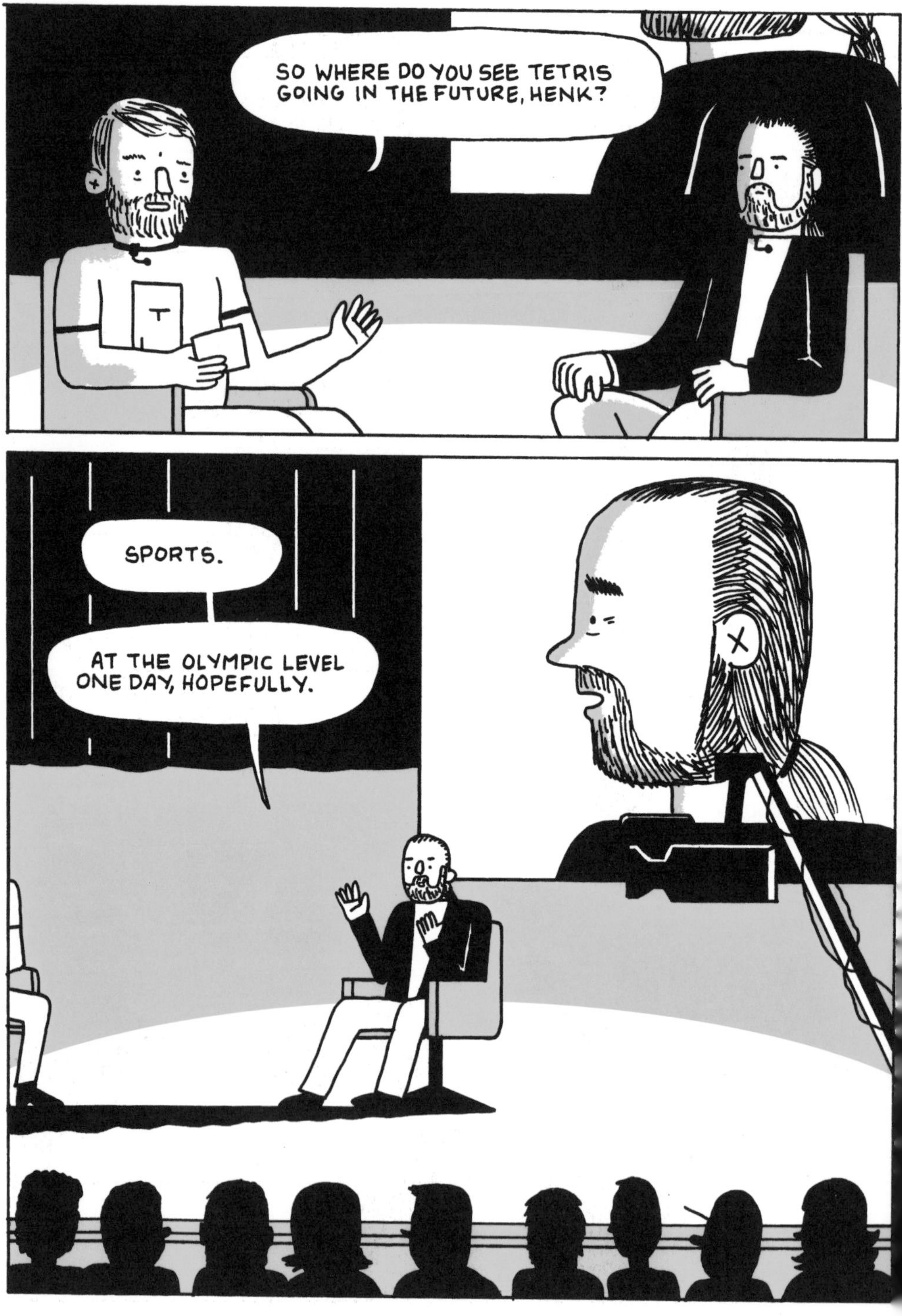
SO WHERE DO YOU SEE TETRIS GOING IN THE FUTURE, HENK?
SPORTS.
AT THE OLYMPIC LEVEL ONE DAY, HOPEFULLY.

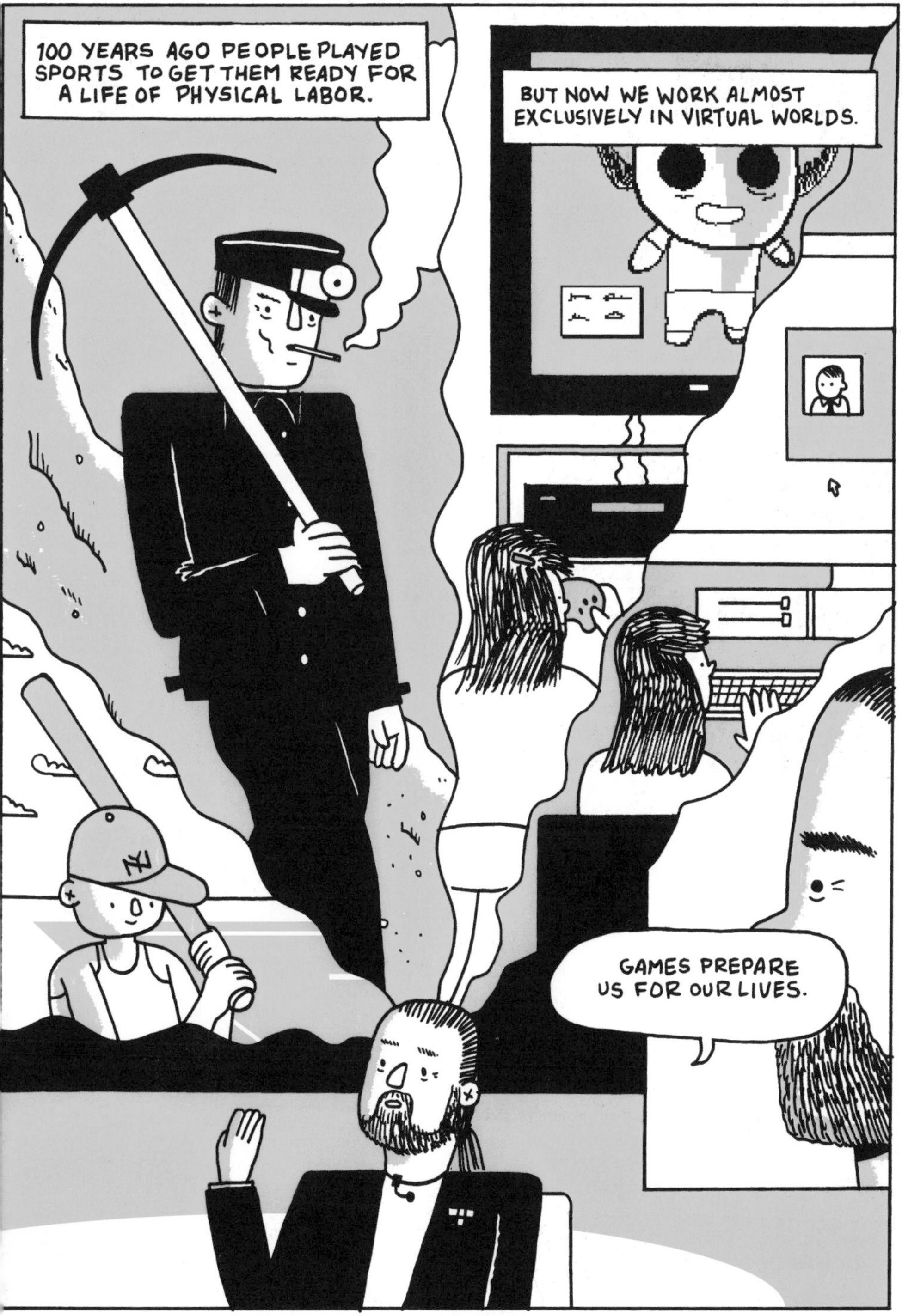
100 YEARS AGO PEOPLE PLAYED SPORTS TO GET THEM READY FOR A LIFE OF PHYSICAL LABOR.
BUT NOW WE WORK ALMOST EXCLUSIVELY IN VIRTUAL WORLDS.
GAMES PREPARE US FOR OUR LIVES.

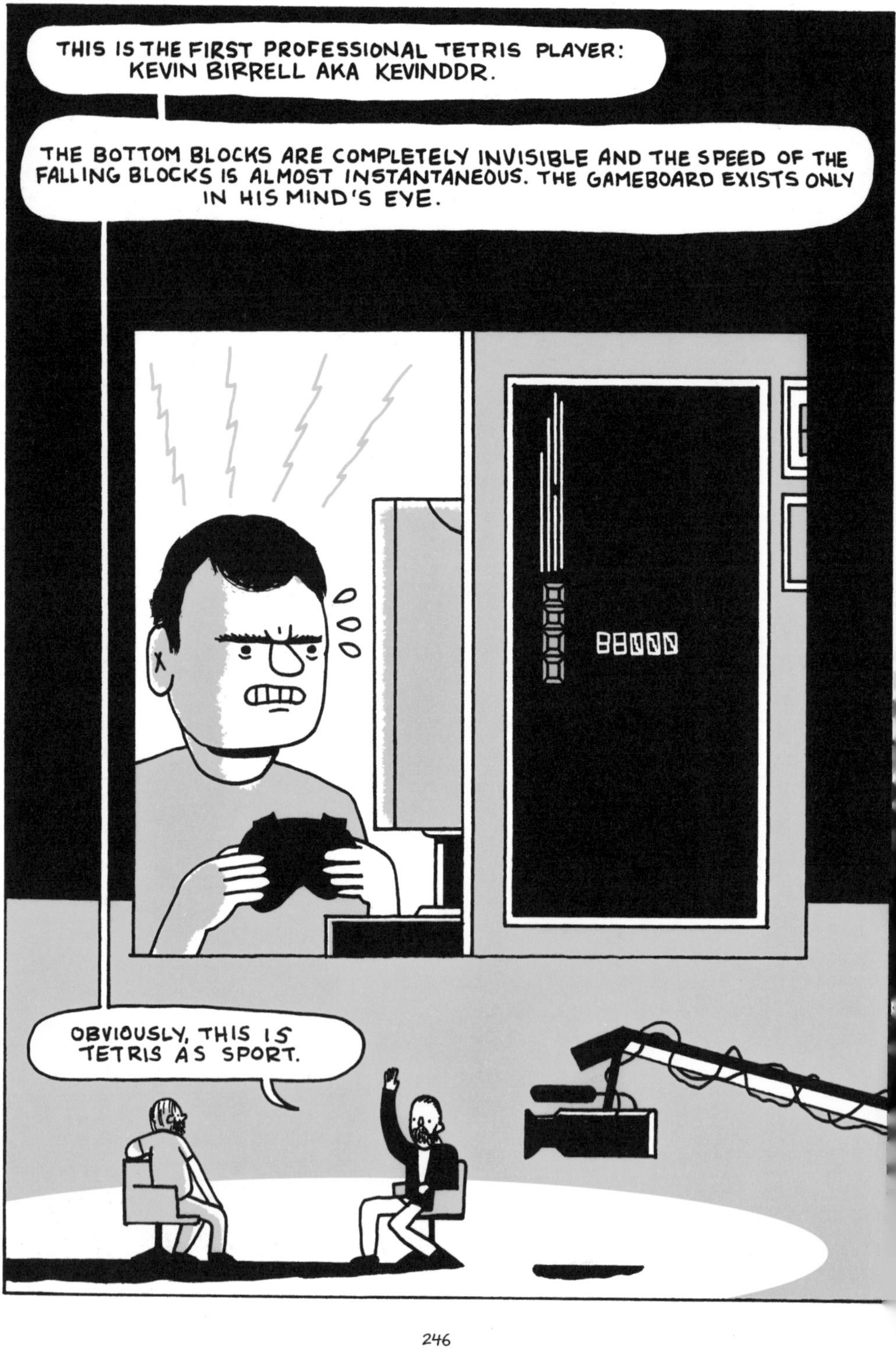
THIS IS THE FIRST PROFESSIONAL TETRIS PLAYER: KEVIN BIRRELL AKA KEVINDDR.
THE BOTTOM BLOCKS ARE COMPLETELY INVISIBLE AND THE SPEED OF THE FALLING BLOCKS IS ALMOST INSTANTANEOUS. THE GAMEBOARD EXISTS ONLY IN HIS MIND'S EYE.
OBVIOUSLY, THIS IS TETRIS AS SPORT.

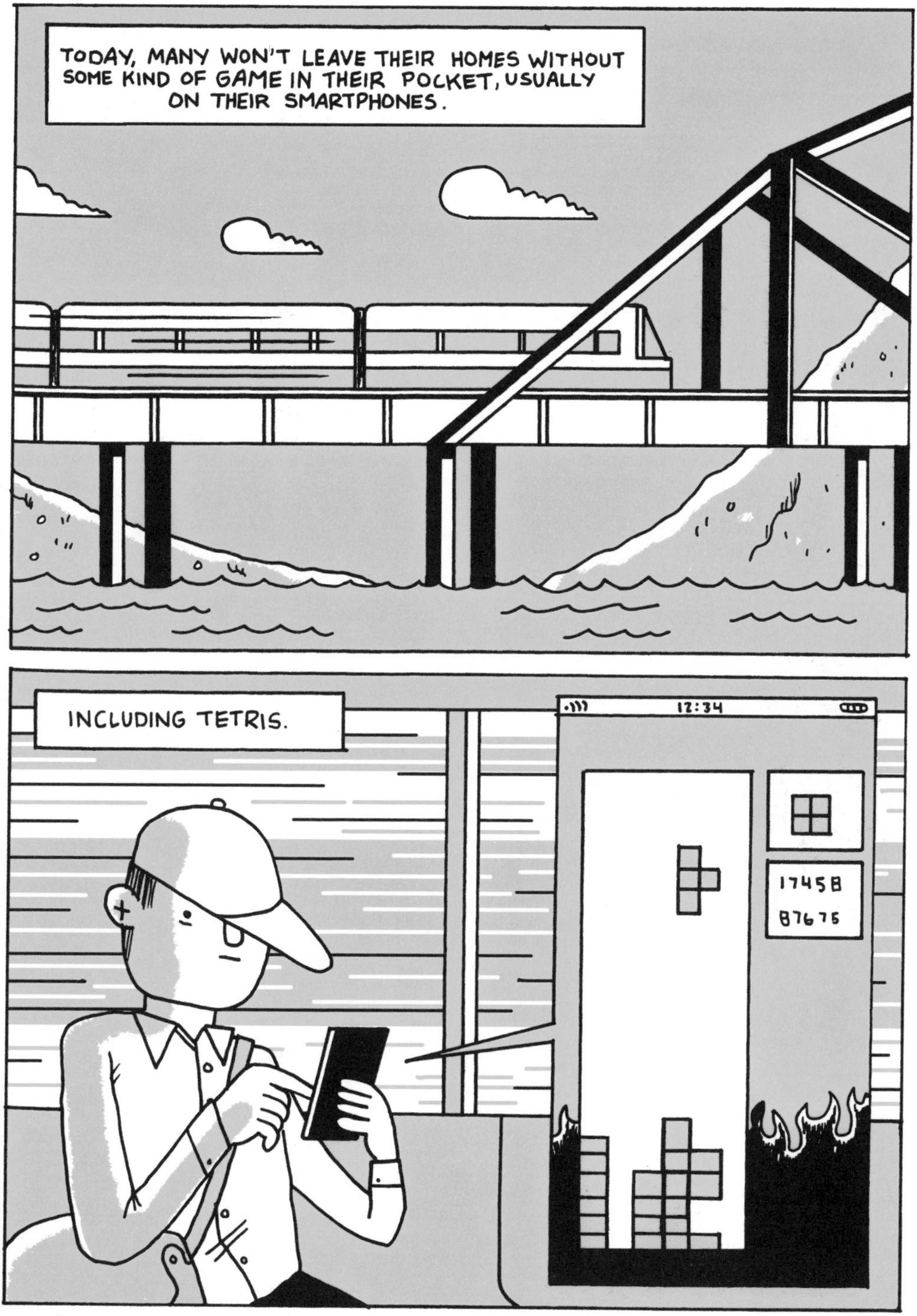
TODAY, MANY WON'T LEAVE THEIR HOMES WITHOUT SOME KIND OF GAME IN THEIR POCKET, USUALLY ON THEIR SMARTPHONES.
INCLUDING TETRIS.
12:34
17458
87675

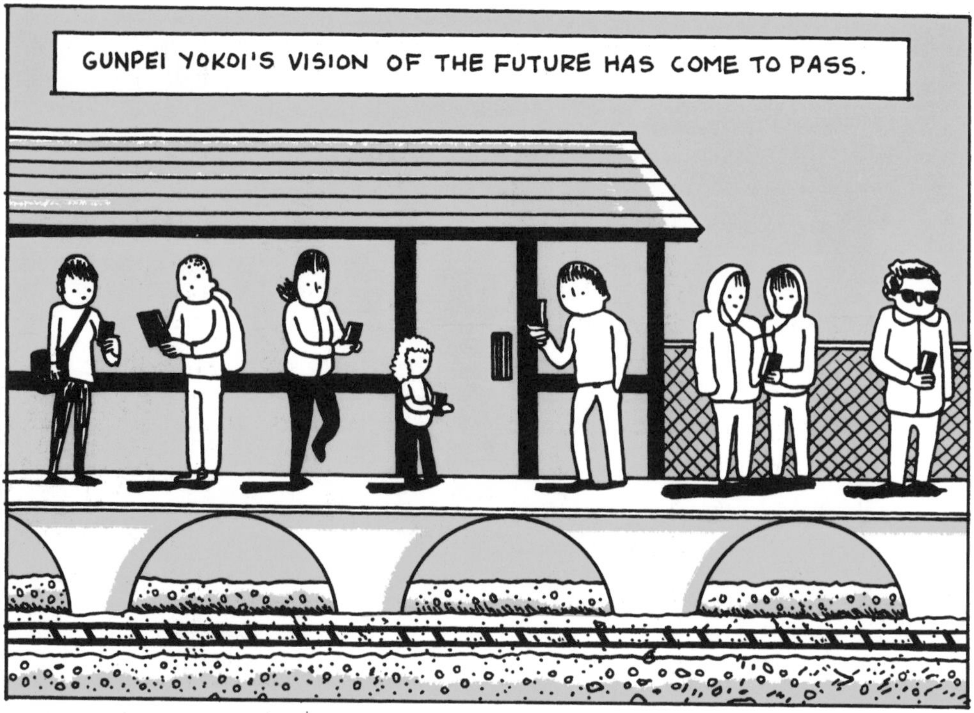
GUNPEI YOKOI'S VISION OF THE FUTURE HAS COME TO PASS.

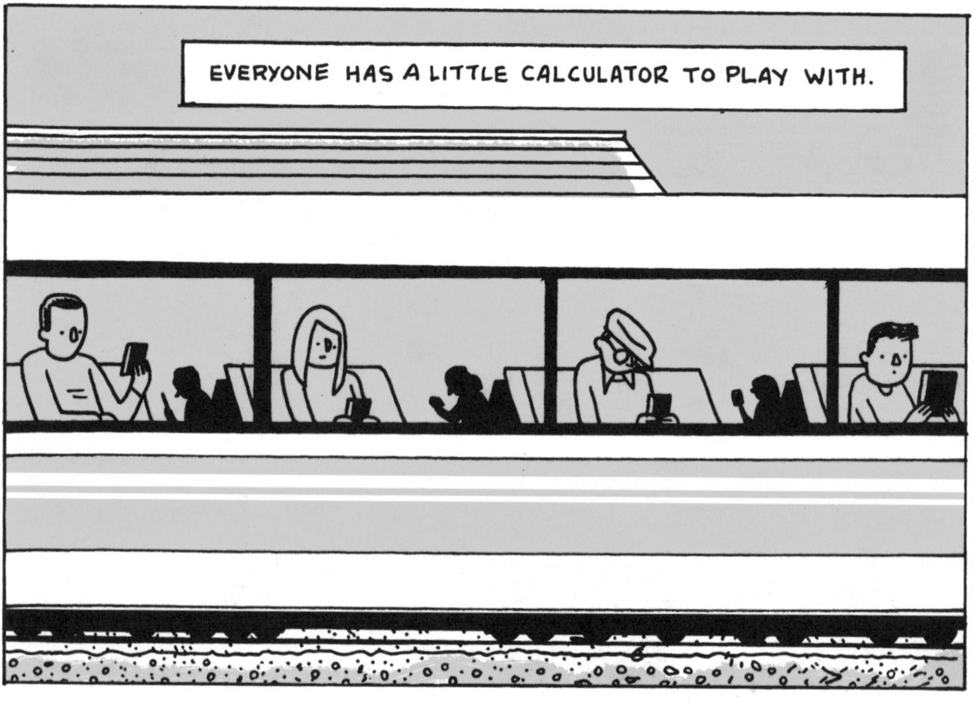
EVERYONE HAS A LITTLE CALCULATOR TO PLAY WITH.

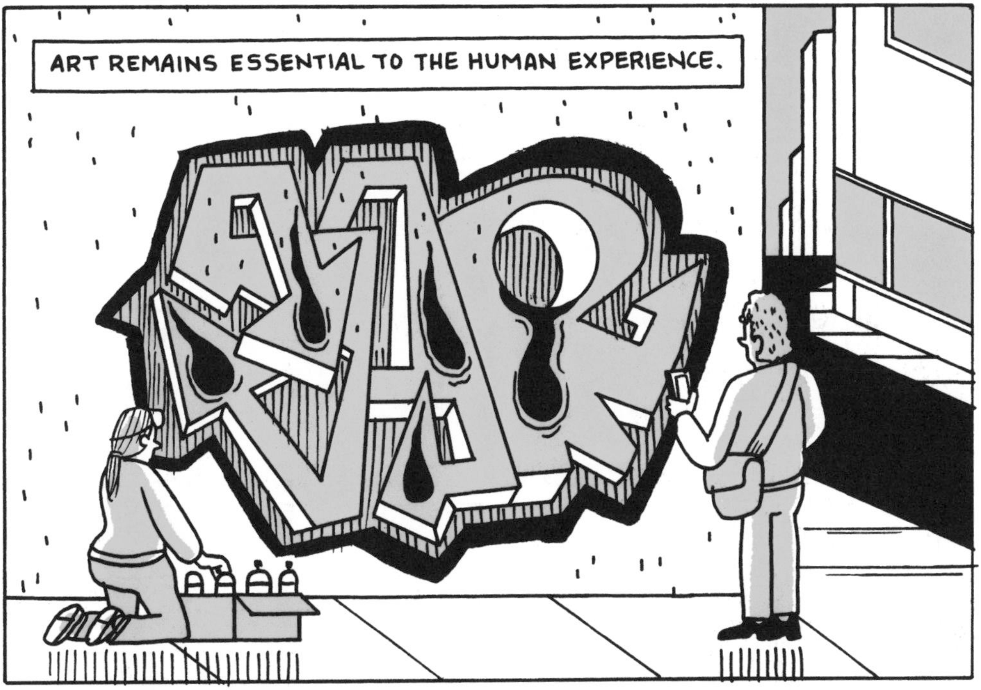
ART REMAINS ESSENTIAL TO THE HUMAN EXPERIENCE.

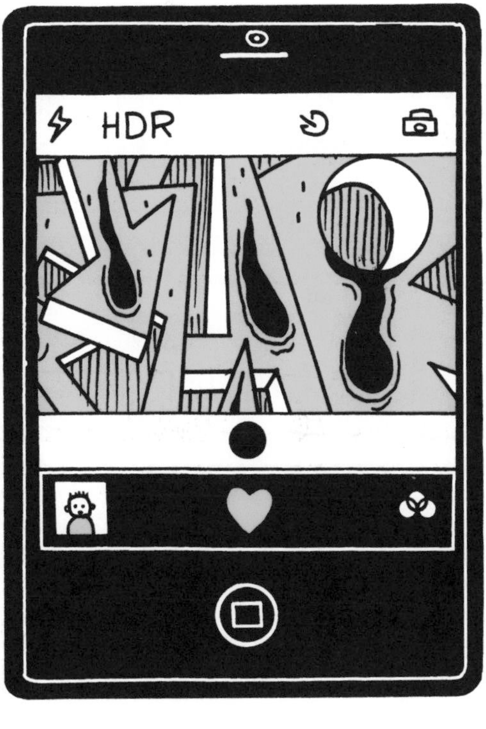
HDR

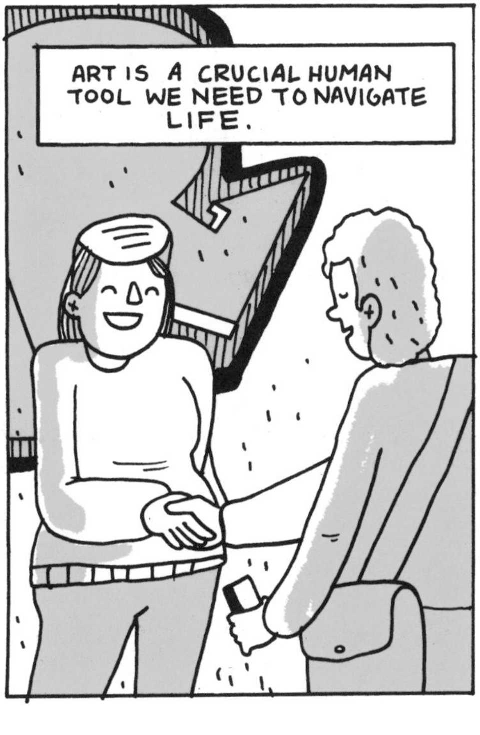
ART IS A CRUCIAL HUMAN TOOL WE NEED TO NAVIGATE LIFE.

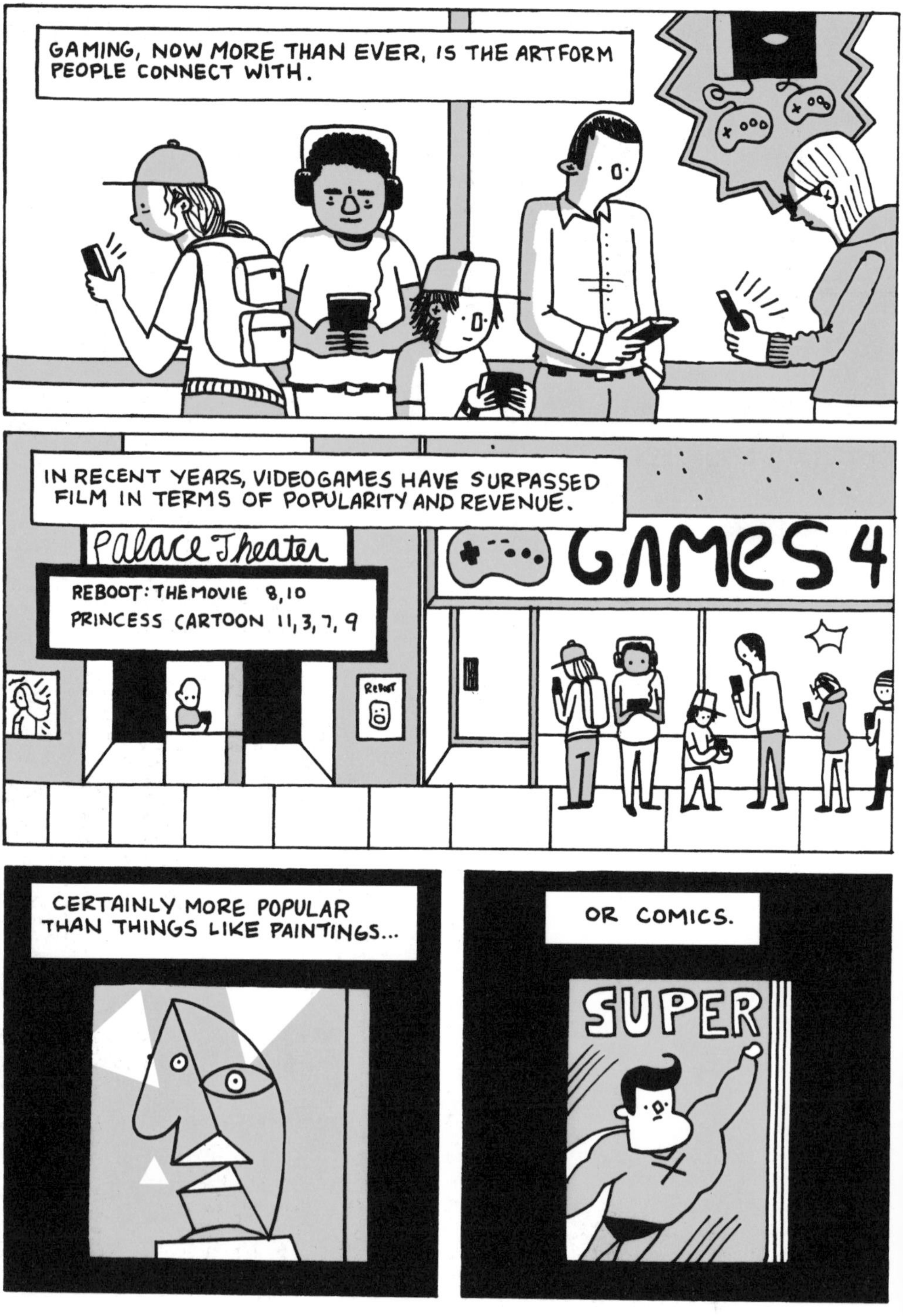
GAMING, NOW MORE THAN EVER, IS THE ARTFORM PEOPLE CONNECT WITH.
IN RECENT YEARS, VIDEOGAMES HAVE SURPASSED FILM IN TERMS OF POPULARITY AND REVENUE.
Palace Theater
REBOOT: THE MOVIE 8,10
PRINCESS CARTOON 11, 3, 7, 9
REBOOT
GAMES 4
CERTAINLY MORE POPULAR THAN THINGS LIKE PAINTINGS...
OR COMICS.
SUPER

TETRIS WAS ESSENTIAL TO
THE DEVELOPMENT OF THE
ARTFORM.

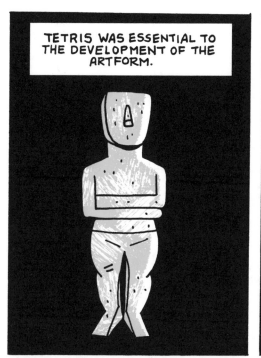

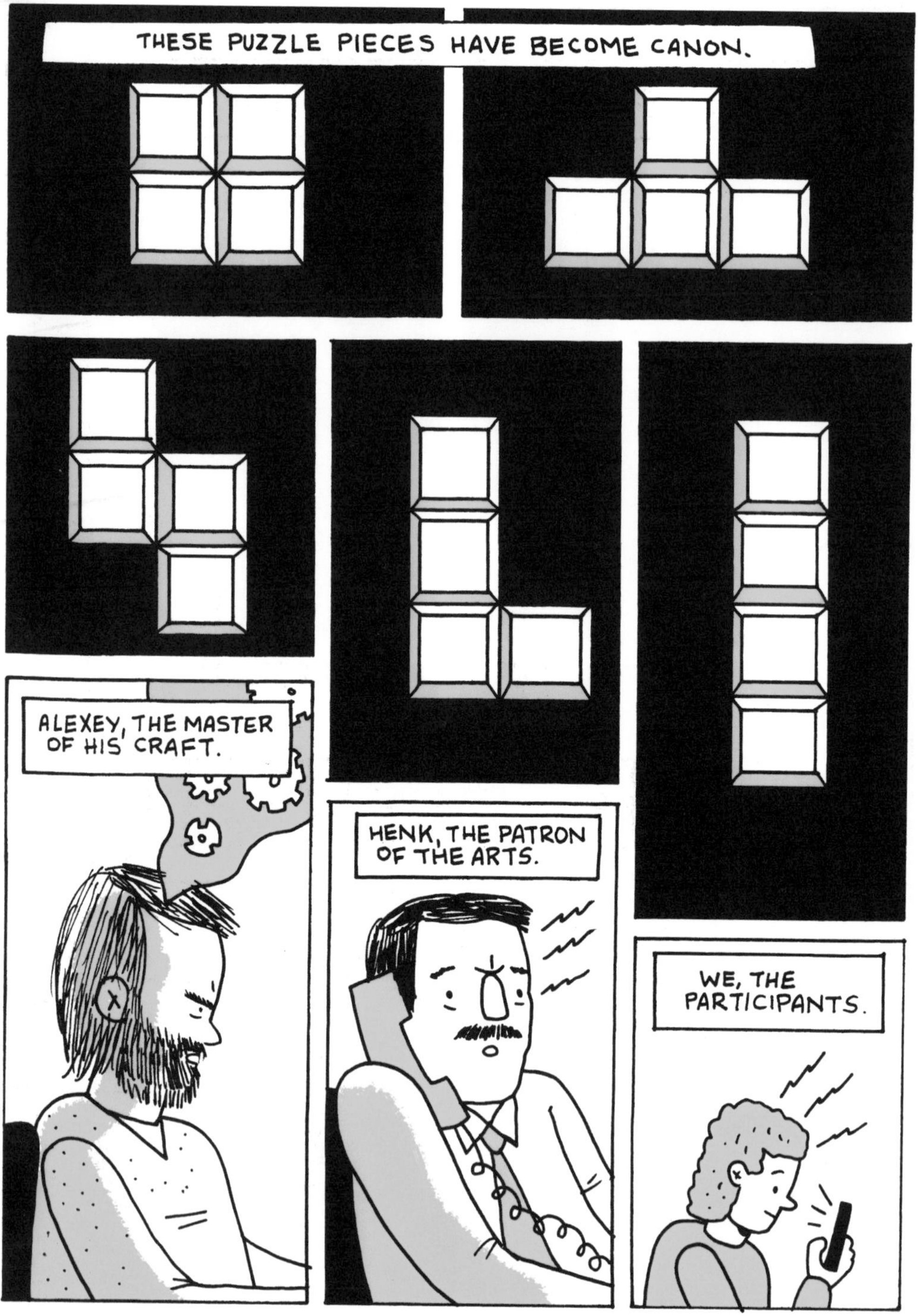

THESE PUZZLE PIECES HAVE BECOME CANON.
ALEXEY, THE MASTER OF HIS CRAFT.
HENK, THE PATRON OF THE ARTS.
WE, THE PARTICIPANTS.

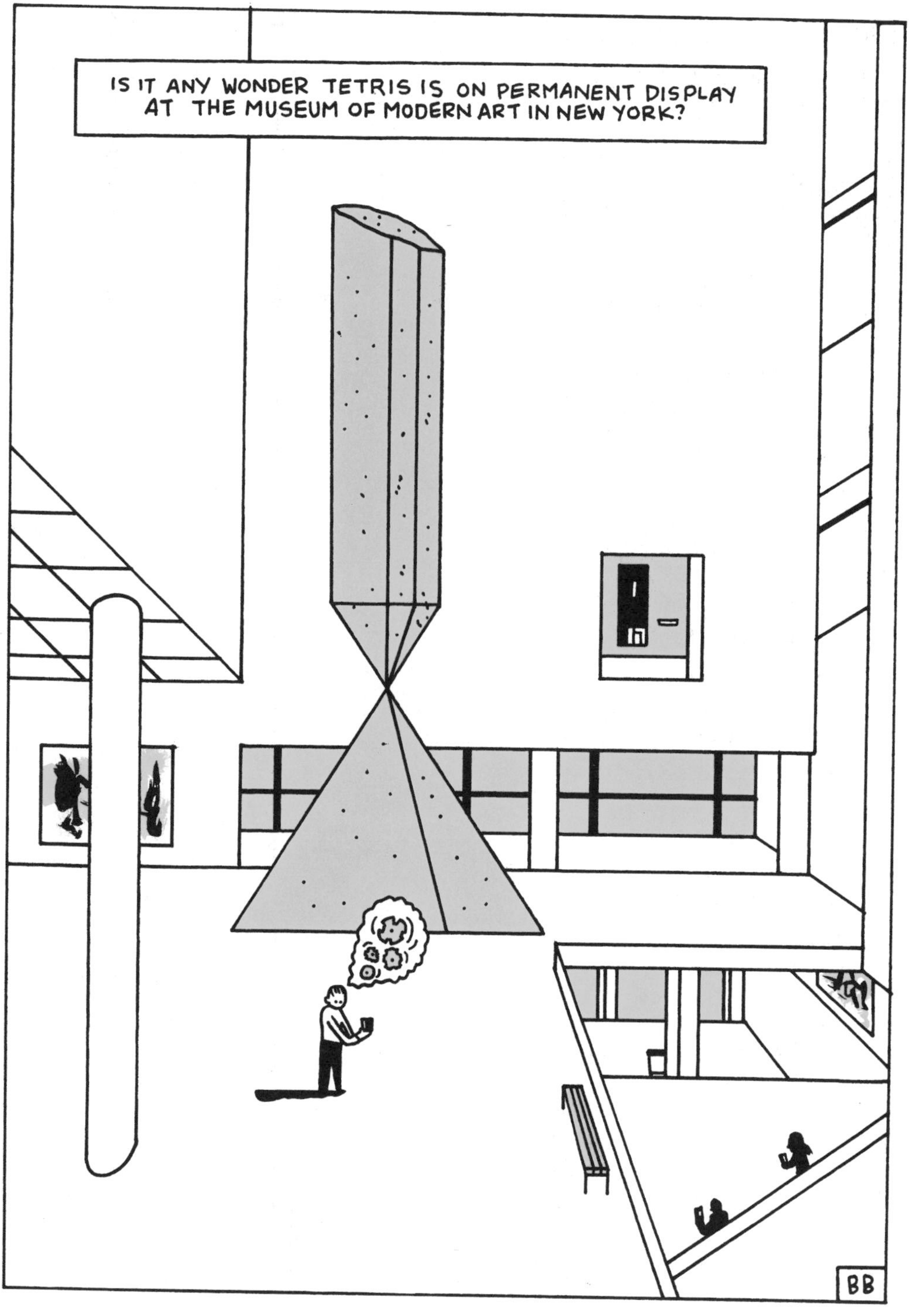
IS IT ANY WONDER TETRIS IS ON PERMANENT DISPLAY AT THE MUSEUM OF MODERN ART IN NEW YORK?
BB

First Second

New York

The author wishes to thank the following people who helped in the creation of this book: My dad who bought me an NES in 1985 and taught me to play. My nana whom we had to buy her own Gameboy in 1989 so she could play Tetris even when we weren't visiting. My mom who always supported the gaming habits of my youth. My wife who supports the gaming habits of my adulthood.

Also: James, Josh, Pat, Ian, Jared, Faith Erin Hicks, and everyone at :01.

Copyright © 2016 by Brian Brown
Published by First Second
First Second is an imprint of Roaring Brook Press, a division of Holtzbrinck Publishing Holdings Limited Partnership
175 Fifth Avenue, New York, New York 10010

Library of Congress Control Number: 2015951864

ISBN: 978-1-62672-315-3

Our books may be purchased in bulk for promotional, educational, or business use. Please contact your local bookseller or the Macmillan Corporate and Premium Sales Department at (800) 221-7945 ext. 5442 or by e-mail at MacmillanSpecialMarkets@macmillan.com.

First edition 2016
Book design by Danielle Ceccolini and Rob Steen
Printed in China by Toppan Leefung Printing Ltd., Dongguan City, Guangdong Province

Drawn with a Staedtler Mars Lumograph 3H and Eagle Chemi-Sealed Turquoise Drawing Pencils 3H and 4H. Inked with a Pigma Micron Size 08 and a Pentel Pocket Brush. Circles made with a No. T105 Timely Circle Template, straight lines made with a Staples steel ruler and a Westcott C-Thru plastic T-square. Lettered using an AMES Lettering Guide, and colored in Photoshop CS5 with a Monoprice tablet.

10 9 8 7 6 5 4 3 2 1